How the Other Half Banks

MEHRSA BARADARAN

How the Other Half Banks

Exclusion, Exploitation, and the Threat to Democracy

Harvard University Press
Cambridge, Massachusetts, and London, England
2015

Printed in the United States of America

First printing

Library of Congress Cataloging-in-Publication Data

Baradaran, Mehrsa. 1978–
How the other half banks : exclusion, exploitation, and the threat to democracy / Mehrsa Baradaran.
pages cm
ISBN 978-0-674-28606-1
1. Banks and banking—Social aspects—United States. 2. Financial services industry—United States. 3. Check cashing services—United States. 4. Postal savings banks—United States. I. —Title.
HG2491.B269 2015
332.10973—dc23 2015008022

Contents

Long ago it was said that "one half of the world does not know how the other half lives." That was true then. It did not know because it did not care. The half that was on top cared little for the struggles, and less for the fate of those who were underneath, so long as it was able to hold them there and keep its own seat. There came a time when the discomfort and crowding below were so great, and the consequent upheavals so violent, that it was no longer an easy thing to do, and then the upper half fell to inquiring what was the matter.

—JACOB RIIS, *How the Other Half Lives: Studies among the Tenements of New York,* 1890

Introduction

One of the great ironies in modern America is that the less money you have, the more you pay to use it. The American banking industry has stopped serving those who are too poor to bank. Those who are "unbanked" must pay high fees to "fringe banks" just to turn their paychecks into cash, pay their monthly bills, or send money to a spouse or a child. The unbanked pay much of their income—up to 10 percent—just to use their money. For these families, the total price of simple financial services each month is more than they spend on food. Indeed, it is very expensive to be poor.

This problem, however, reaches well beyond those traditionally considered poor. Ninety percent of Americans consider themselves "middle class," yet anywhere from 20 to 40 percent of the population must rely on alternative financial instruments.[1] And the tragedy of money being siphoned from the paychecks of ordinary Americans is the least egregious part of a much larger problem. Sometimes, those who live paycheck to paycheck face an unexpected emergency. Over half the people in the United States are so cash-strapped that they would not be able to access four hundred dollars without selling something or borrowing money.[2] The need to borrow to deal with emergencies—often at the very highest interest rates—adds another layer of financial strain on those least able to bear it.[3]

Tanya Burke is a single mother of two from North Carolina. She fell $500 behind on her rent and utilities when her eight-month-old son required emergency intestinal surgery. Tanya was insured, and the cost of this medical care was covered, but she had to take time off work to care for her son. When she went back to work as a secretary, earning eleven dollars an hour, her paychecks could not cover her day-to-day bills and her new debts. She was not in a position to ask friends or family for help, so Tanya went to the payday lending office across the street from her office. She took out a $600 loan, hoping to pay it back by the next payday. She could not, so she took out another loan to pay that one off and then another to pay that one off—and so on. After one year, Tanya had taken out a total of eight loans, and she now owed more than $2,000 in fees and interest.[4]

Thelma Fleming, a mother of three children and a grandmother of ten, lost one of her two jobs. To survive, she emptied her bank accounts, gave up her car, and pawned some of her possessions, including gifts from her grandchildren. When she still needed an extra $300 to cover monthly expenses, she went to a payday lender, who lent her the money at 300 percent interest. She would eventually take out five loans to buy the time she needed to pay off the original $300. When all was said and done, she had paid $2,500 in interest over the course of ten months in order to borrow just $300. She lost her bank account and ruined her credit in the process.[5]

These stories of being trapped in debt are awful but also quite common. Most payday loans are followed by at least another loan but usually another *ten* payday loans.[6] This life-ruining cycle of debt caused by high interest is an obvious problem, but it is just the tip of a much more pernicious iceberg. The very existence of the fringe banking sector is a symptom of a deep-rooted problem at the core of our financial system.

Consider another story. Steven earned great money before the financial crisis, but he had made some investments that all started to go bad during the crisis. From one day to the next, Steven couldn't pay his daily expenses. Despite all his best efforts, Steven was headed for financial ruin. He was confident he could get back on his feet if someone would just throw him a lifeline to survive this short-term financial emergency. Luckily, Steven found a miracle lender who would make generous loans and charge him interest at a rate well below market. The lender felt like it was in the lender's best interest that Steven avoid bankruptcy, so it was willing to ignore the obvious credit risk Steven posed.

This is a true story, but Steven is not a real person. "Steven" represents the largest American banks. That miracle lender is the federal government. This book will take a hard look at banking history to show why Tanya and Steven are treated so differently, why this striking inequality was not inevitable, and how it can be fixed.

Before discussing how we got here, a pervasive myth must be dispelled: this inequality is not caused by the basic economic laws of supply and demand, which require a higher cost of credit for the average person than for the average bank. For payday lending to be an appropriate market response or even a menacing market failure, basic economic rules and market consequences must govern our credit markets. They do not. Both Tanya and Steven should have failed, according to market rules, but the government intervened on Steven's behalf. In the United States, the banking market does not operate according to standard market rules.

The truth is that the source of Tanya's and Thelma's loans is the same as "Steven's" loan—only Steven got it for practically nothing, and Tanya and Thelma got it bundled with life-crushing interest. Put simply, payday lenders, which consist of a handful of large corporations, get their loans from the largest commercial banks at low interest.[7] These banks, of course, get most of their credit through customer deposits and the federal government. Even their use of our deposits, for which they pay virtually nothing, is made possible by an insurance scheme backed by the full faith and credit of the federal government.[8] Banks also receive direct Federal Reserve money at a cool 1 percent interest, not to mention "discount window" loans, which help banks survive a credit crunch.[9] When a bank, just like an individual, cannot pay its bills when they are due,[10] the Federal Reserve gives the bank a short-term loan, so it can survive without having to sell off valuable assets. All this federal government support makes the banking sector unlike other businesses that must create their own wealth, without the use of other people's money or cheap loans, when they fall short.

But that's just the beginning. None of this takes Steven's loan, the government bailout, into account. These loans went on full display after the 2008 financial crisis. When the government directly pumps money into insolvent banks whose failure is deemed catastrophic, this is known as a bailout. In the aftermath of the financial crisis, the federal government bailed out a failing banking industry with over a trillion dollars of equity infusions, loans, guarantees, asset purchases, and other forms of financial support.[11] The help came on very favorable terms with interest rates not available to the market. The arrangement was so good, the CEO of one of the largest bailed-out banks saw the terms of the deal and remarked, "This is very cheap credit!"[12]

The two presidents who administered the bailouts made it clear that the state must support the banking system, for if the banks failed, so too would the American public. President George W. Bush said in 2008 that he supported giving banks this "urgently needed money" so that they could "avoid collapse and resume lending." "This rescue effort," he emphasized, "is aimed at preserving America's overall economy . . . [and helping] American consumers and businesses get credit to meet their daily needs and create jobs."[13]

Two weeks later, then-presidential candidate Barack Obama sounded the same theme: "All of us—all of us—have a responsibility to solve this crisis because it affects the financial well-being of every single American. . . . In other words, this is not just a Wall Street crisis, *it is an American crisis*. . . . I understand completely why people would be skeptical when this President asked for a blank check to solve this problem. . . . *We are all in this together*. . . . We will rise or fall on that journey *as one Nation and as one people*."[14]

In other words, the banks and the people were one—if the banks fell, so too, would we. We must lend to banks so that they can lend to us. This codependency of the government-banking system is not always clear, but the justifications given for the bailouts brought this crucial relationship into sharp focus: we need them and they need us. Many describe modern banks as private enterprises, but this is illusory—half-revealing and half-concealing their true nature. To be sure, individual banks are private companies, but each of these private banks sits atop a foundation of state support. In discussing the bailout of 2008, Bank of America CEO Ken Lewis made this key point well: "We are so intertwined with the U.S. that it's hard to separate what's good for the United States and what's good for Bank of America . . . they're almost one and the same."[15]

Yet this depiction of unity between the banks and the people could not be further from the truth. If "we're all in this together," why must such a large segment of the public be left to modern-day loan sharks? The Wall Street Crisis cannot be "an American crisis" if its remedy means that unprecedented federal support goes to a banking system that has effectively shut out much of the population. We do not "rise and fall as one people" if two banking systems exist in America: government-supported banks that serve the well off, and a Wild West of fringe lenders and check-cashing joints that answer the needs of everyone else—at a hefty price.

This blatant inequality is not merely an economic problem; it is a threat to our democracy. When our presidents and our bankers explicitly acknowledge their unity amidst such drastic disparities, public, political, and social problems loom. A we're-all-in-this-together state-banking relationship cannot mean that the state must rescue banks and then let banks do what they want. A banking system supported by the people must serve all the people and not merely a subset.

Today, there is more reason than ever to embrace this principle, but the principle itself is not new. Most of the pivotal events in our nation's history—its founding, the Civil War, the New Deal—involved or centered around a struggle over how public needs would shape banking policy. For example, even before the U.S. Constitution was signed, debate raged over how to create a thriving banking system that would meet the needs of the budding economy and the populace. Many disagreed about what sort of system would best serve the country. Alexander Hamilton pushed for a national, centralized, and government-coordinated banking system. He argued that only this system of banking would produce a world-class economy and a unified, prosperous nation. Thomas Jefferson feared that powerful, centralized banking would threaten democracy and suffocate credit for the nonelite small farmers who would be the lifeblood of this nation. He proposed that these inequalities should be remedied by forcing banks to serve only local markets. Jefferson won in the short-term, but Hamilton was more prescient about the country's eventual needs and the central role the federal government would eventually play in the banking sector. The small-and-local versus big-and-national banking models represented ideological differences that were at the heart of the negotiations that formed our country. But *all* the founders absolutely agreed that banking policy should be dominated by the goal of serving the public.

To many of our nation's leaders, crafting banking policy meant protecting the people from too much bank power, which would inevitably lead to inequalities in access. But during this long struggle, mistakes were made. For example, Jefferson's vision of localized banking was embraced for over a century, even as it became clear that the United States would not persist as an agrarian society but was destined to grow into a complex economic machine. As the nation industrialized and urbanized, banks were forbidden to join other industries in forming nationwide conglomerates to pursue high profits in money centers.[16] Because it was so important that rural regions have sufficient access to credit, these laws were zealously protected even though they resulted in chronic panics, runs, and crises. For better or for worse, equality of access trumped bank profitability and stability. For two centuries, the democratic political process decided it would rather have less efficient banks that were available to all than more powerful and profitable banks that were only available to some. The same principle was iterated when Andrew Jackson vigorously fought a "bank war" to defeat the charter of a national bank; he viewed the defeat as a victory of the common man against the powerful banking industry. In reality, the absence of a central bank may have caused the unfettered Wall Street excess and widespread banking panic that led to the Great Depression.

Forcing local banking and opposing the central bank were not economic ideals but rather policy principles that had to counter market forces that naturally favored growth and concentration. Although Jefferson and Jackson may have been wrong in their solutions, they were prophetic in their fears. They worried that money tended to flow where there was more money and banks that became too large and powerful would only lend where profits were highest and thus create inequalities. But they miscalculated that keeping banks geographically dispersed could preclude centralized banking power. The modern world has made that solution insufficient. There is no doubt Thomas Jefferson would have been just as uncomfortable with our current bifurcated nationwide banking systems (one for the rich and one for the poor) as he was with a big-city banking monopoly that left out poor rural farms. The point was that the rich and poor should operate in credit markets governed by the same rules; banks must not have the power to anoint winners and losers.

The fight for equality in banking, which started before the ink dried on the Constitution, ended sometime in the last few decades as deregulation did away with most meaningful attempts to restrict bank power. What eventually happened was predictable: banks became large and powerful and stopped serving a large sector of the population. Instead of bank wars or even bank skirmishes, politicians pushed laws favoring bank profitability and efficiency over public needs. Any suggestion that banks should be forced to lend to less profitable borrowers was seen as a government intrusion into a private market. And because our politicians have gone from fighting the centripetal force of bank power to helping it along, the accumulated power of banks has become harder to dislodge.

Banks disowned their "state institution" past and clothed themselves in the language of the market. This was the whole point of three decades of deregulation—to free banks from state-imposed restrictions and separate them from the state so that they could compete in the market like other businesses. But in the banking business, deregulation turned out to be a one-sided deal. Banks enjoyed significant profits in the deregulated banking market for decades, but when the market turned on them, the federal government swooped in to save them. And so it is that we are now, once again, "all in this together." This uncomfortable realization may have been what prompted President George W. Bush to say: "I'm a strong believer in free enterprise, so my natural instinct is to oppose government intervention. I believe companies that make bad decisions should be allowed to go out of business. Under normal circumstances, I would have followed this course. But these are not normal circumstances." And when it comes to these large banks, they rarely are "normal circumstances."[17] The truth is that even while the banking industry was rejecting any public duties, they were being supported by public funds.

When commentators discuss this era of bank transformation, or deregulation, they tend to focus on the creation of Too-Big-to-Fail financial giants and their size, power, and riskiness. No less consequential, however, was the loss of banking services for average people. For much of U.S. history, the answer to banking for the poor—whether the rural farmer or the working-class city dweller—has been through local and community-controlled credit. Local banking institutions were supported by the government and enlisted to meet a clear-cut mission. Initiatives like the credit unions and savings and loans developed with the objective of lending to the poor by mutual ownership and reduced profits. The history of these institutions' successes reveals the roots of their eventual failures at the hands of both deregulation and economic evolution. That story is a rich one, but the bottom line is clear: these institutions, along with local and community banks, fell victim to the transformation of banking brought about by modern deregulation and cannot fulfill the banking needs of the poor in today's economy.

Once community banks left the scene, fringe lenders filled the void. So long as half the population needs to borrow money to deal with emergencies, and the banks won't or can't lend to them, the payday industry is here to stay. The payday industry has made policymakers, the media, and the public deeply uncomfortable since it began despite the industry's assertion that its rates are "justified" by "market prices." In fact, they are not charging market prices but the highest interest rate allowable by law. And so it is that federal and state governments have engaged in a frustrating game of whack-a-mole to ban the unscrupulous practices of payday lenders and the like. These lenders skillfully avert new rules by creating new products, crossing state lines, or escaping to do business from Native American reservations. They cannot be regulated away because the payday lending industry is doing what any successful business does: filling a market need.

One solution to our present-day banking crisis is to reinvigorate or replicate local banks and cooperatives so that they can again do what they did successfully for many years—overcome the costs of lending to the poor through a tight-knit membership with mutual ownership. Over the past several decades, nearly all of the government and industry initiatives aimed at financial inclusion have focused on community efforts to bank the poor—Jefferson's localism still runs deep in banking politics. However, the problem of access is fundamentally different today than it was historically. Disparities in access are not regional but based almost purely on income. Banks, local or otherwise, do not lend to the poor due to one straightforward economic reason: they can make more profits elsewhere.

Any effort to bank the poor must recognize that centralized, national, and large banks won a decisive victory over small community banks. Alexander Hamilton rightly believed that government-controlled central banking was essential to coordinating a modern economy. But Thomas Jefferson was also right that permitting banking power to accumulate in the hands of the few does so at the expense of the many. The dilemma of living in a Hamiltonian banking world without addressing the Jeffersonian nightmare of inequality has led to the current crisis of the unbanked.

But there is a Hamiltonian solution to Jeffersonian fears: a public option in banking—a central bank for the poor. The core function of the central bank, or Federal Reserve, is to infuse liquidity into troubled banks so that they can withstand a temporary credit crunch and get back on their feet. A public option would provide the same short-term credit help to individuals so that they, too, can withstand a personal credit crunch and get back on their feet. Indeed, in the modern banking landscape, only a large, liquid lender is able to lower the costs of lending to the poor.

Economies of scale and government backing can be used to bring down the costs of lending to the poor. The federal government is in a unique position to lend to the poor and cover its costs without having to answer to shareholder pressure to maximize profits. One way the federal government might do so is through the existing U.S. Postal Service structure. In fact, using the post office to achieve financial inclusion has deep historical roots. From its creation, the U.S. Post Office has been the practical means giving effect to our founders' democratic ideals. Postal banking was also the largest and most successful experiment in financial inclusion in U.S. history and remains the primary tool for financial inclusion across the world. A public option in banking balances the scales of government support for the banking industry and could potentially drive out the usurious fringe-lending sector, which profits from Americans down on their luck.

The high cost of credit exacerbates the already-strained lives of the poor and makes it even more difficult for them to escape poverty. Low-cost credit alone, however, is not a cure for poverty, nor does credit adequately substitute for better employment or higher wages. Still, access to reasonably priced credit can help a large portion of the population improve their financial lives. There are millions of individuals whose otherwise stable financial lives can be upended by one unexpected event. These people, like Tanya and Thelma, are creditworthy—often as creditworthy as "Steven"—but get snagged in an otherwise temporary liquidity crunch. For these people, paying several thousands of dollars in accrued interest can turn a temporary cash-flow problem into a full-blown financial disaster.

Reasonable credit not only serves as a bridge over financial trouble, but for millions of Americans, credit provides the only means to build assets, start a business, or get an education. Most Americans' lives are enhanced by loans, usually enabled by the federal government (virtually all mortgage and student loans are made possible by federal-government-created, supported, and bailed-out credit markets). Without this access to credit, most of us cannot take advantage of the American dream made possible by our robust market-based economy. So although inexpensive credit allows half the American public to improve their economic prospects, very costly credit is crushing the other half. A hard look into the history of banking and the role of banks in our society can help us find solutions to reach this other half.

1

Governments and Banks

[Government] support cannot go on forever, which underlines why the Social Contract for banks must be redrawn.

—SIR PAUL TUCKER, FORMER DEPUTY GOVERNOR OF THE BANK OF ENGLAND

One of the most important and oft-forgotten truths about any banking system is that it simply cannot exist without the government. Lending and borrowing have taken place for as long as recorded history. Before the nation-state, borrowing and lending were connected to religious temples, the nucleus of each society.[1] But the banking system we know today, which allows for the development of modern economies by issuing bank notes, lending, and accepting deposits, started with an original transaction between a government and private bankers. The Bank of England was formed in 1694 because King William III needed a loan of 1.2 million pounds to finance a war against France. Forty London merchants joined forces to issue the loan. In return, the crown gave them a monopoly on issuing bank notes—the genesis of state-sponsored paper money. The notes were, in fact, the king's promise to pay back the loan. He never paid it back and those notes and their successors have been circulating and multiplying ever since. The Bank of England and the network of banks it created became the model for the world's current banking system—a model where the bank initially existed to meet the needs of the state. Italy, Spain, and France, too, created the first banks to help the monarchy fund a war. The United States came late to the game, but it, too, formed a banking system whose existence depended on the state.[2]

Today, every stable (and even unstable) economy in the world is rooted in a state-supported banking system. The only exception, Somalia, had no state-supported banks from 1990 to 2011. Coincidentally, it did not have a functioning state during that time. In fact, Somalia's first act of statehood was to create a central bank. Even Costa Rica, which has no army, and Kuwait, which has no taxes whatsoever, still have a state-supported banking system.[3]

The essential relationship between banks and the governments that enable them has largely been forgotten, yet it makes banks completely unlike any other corporation or commercial enterprise. Banks need government support. In turn, governments need banks. Banks often serve as an appendage to the state and carry out its economic policies. In other words, banks do not operate in markets guided by an "invisible hand" but *are* the hands that move markets—often at the behest of the state.

Many people express discomfort with government "subsidies" to the banking sector. And there are subsidies, to be sure. To name just a few, take the billions of dollars of bailouts that flowed to the largest banks and prevented market corrections and lowered their costs of doing business.[4] Underpriced deposit insurance is the reason the deposit insurance fund had a $9 billion shortfall during the recent financial crisis.[5] Banks also pay less money for credit, as explained by the leading banking-law textbook: "On balance, we can conclude that banks receive a benefit not available to other firms—a subsidy notably evident in lower borrowing costs."[6]

Although these subsidies may be a cause for concern, to characterize state support of the banking system as solely a subsidy mischaracterizes the nature of the bank-government relationship. The federal government has created a structural framework without which banks could not exist. To call government involvement in banking just a "subsidy" would be like calling the wheels on your car a "bonus feature." The government does not just subsidize the banking system. The government allows it to exist. In order to discuss some of the inequalities in the banking system, this obvious point bears emphasis and explanation. To fully grasp how banks operate, we must first understand their basic functions.

HOW BANKS WORK

To oversimplify a complex system, we can say that banks are financial intermediaries that allow individuals to readily exchange money for goods. They also enable individual savers to grow wealth by lending their excess money to others at interest. To borrow from *Mary Poppins*'s "Fidelity Fiduciary Bank":

> When you deposit tuppence in a bank account
> Soon you'll see
> That it blooms into credit of a generous amount
> Semiannually
> And you'll achieve that sense of stature
> As your influence expands
> To the high financial strata
> That established credit now commands[7]

By lending, banks actually create money and multiply the money supply in the economy through leverage. For example, when you deposit $100 into the Fidelity Fiduciary Bank, the bank may keep $10 in reserve and lend the other $90 to a business or individual. That business or individual then uses that $90 to purchase real estate, a good, or a service, and the person on the other end of that transaction deposits the $90 into another bank. That bank keeps a similar reserve of, say, $9, and lends out the remaining $81, and on and on. If your initial $100 is lent out ten times and each bank keeps 10 percent of that as reserve, your $100 has turned into almost $600. The banks have created $500 by repeatedly lending your initial investment.[8]

Although the Fidelity Fiduciary Bank relied just on deposits from its customers (or little boys' pigeon-food money) to lend, modern banking is much more complex. Put simply, bank lending is not constrained by deposits or reserves. If that were the case, the economy would have halted in its tracks a century ago. Customer deposits are a major source of bank assets, but the relationship between deposits "in" and loans "out" is not direct. In fact, deposits are *created* by bank loans. To repeat, commercial banks create money, or bank deposits, by making new loans. For example, when a bank makes a mortgage loan, it does not just give someone $100,000 in cash to go purchase a house. Instead, it creates a credit—a deposit—in the borrower's bank account for the size of the mortgage. "At that moment, new money is created," explain Bank of England economists; this is "referred to as 'fountain pen money,' created at the stroke of bankers' pens when they approve loans."[9] It works the same in the United States. "Banks lend by simultaneously creating a loan asset and a deposit liability on their balance sheet. That is why it is called credit 'creation'—created literally out of thin air (or with the stroke of a keyboard)."[10]

The bank balance sheet now shows a new loan and a new deposit. The new deposit may mean that the bank needs to hold more "reserves" at the central bank in order to meet customer deposit demands. The central bank just provides the reserve in exchange for bank assets. But "[in] no way does the aggregate quantity of reserves directly constrain the amount of bank lending or deposit creation."[11] A Standard and Poor's economist explains: "The loan is not created out of reserves. And the loan is not created out of deposits: Loans create deposits, not the other way around. Then the deposits need a certain amount of reserves to be held against them, and the central bank supplies them."[12] The credit coursing through economic channels is propelled by the central bank.[13]

* * *

Bank lending is not just a balance-sheet decision made by individual banks; it is also a policy decision made by the government. The government uses bank credit to sway economic forces. Governments use banks to pump currency into and out of the economy, which affects how much money is available to lend at any given time and influences the cost of a loan. The government lowers interest rates across the country by pumping more money into the economy and increases rates by taking money out. The credit market, therefore, is not governed by typical economic rules of pricing through supply and demand. Because the central bank controls the supply of currency, the cost of credit circulating through the economy at any given moment is largely a policy decision made by the government's central bank.

Our central bank in the United States, the Federal Reserve, uses four levers to shape the economy and control monetary supply: (1) the federal fund rate, (2) the discount rate, (3) reserve requirements, and

(4) "quantitative easing." The central bank uses all of these measures, which are only possible with the help of the banking system, to influence the economy.[14]

The *federal fund rate* is the rate at which banks lend to each other, which influences the interest rate for all lending. Given the state of the economy and the Fed's policy goals, it sets a target interest rate that it believes will be optimal. To reach this rate, the Federal Open Market Committee (FOMC) buys or sells government securities from or to banks depending on whether it wants to increase or decrease the economy's money supply. The Federal Reserve holds government securities and so do banks. If the Federal Reserve wants to stimulate the economy, it tries to increase lending by lowering interest rates. If the Fed wants to push the gas pedal on a slow economy, it creates more money in the banking system by buying government treasuries from banks and giving them cash. The banks lend this cash to others, creating more money and more lending. If the Fed decides to rein in the economy to prevent inflation, it tries to increase interest rates and decrease lending. It takes money out of the economy by selling treasuries to banks, so they hold the government treasuries instead of all that cash.

The second lever, the *discount rate,* or the "discount window," is used to allow banks to survive a "run," or a large number of depositors demanding their money all at once. This liquidity, or cheap loans, from the federal government allows banks to remain in business amid a short-term credit crunch or a panic. The third lever permitting the Fed to affect the availability of credit is the *reserve requirement* it imposes on banks. Banks are required to keep a certain amount of money in reserve that they do not lend out. Banks use this reserve to operate and meet the withdrawal needs of their customers, while the Federal Reserve uses this reserve to achieve its own policy goals of either expanding or contracting the money supply. Increasing the reserve requirement (forcing banks to hold on to more money) contracts the money available to lend and decreasing the reserve requirement increases it.

Finally, the Federal Reserve has recently engaged in a controversial strategy called *quantitative easing* (QE) to get a slow economy moving when the above measures have failed to increase lending. Quantitative easing entails the Fed's purchase of a large *quantity* of securities in the open market to pump even more money into the banks—hence "quantitative easing." Under QE, the Fed purchases U.S. Treasury notes and mortgage-backed securities using newly created electronic cash, which increases bank reserves. In theory, this provides banks with more money to lend so they will lower interest rates and make more loans. In 2008, the Federal Reserve bought over $1.25 trillion in mortgage-backed securities from banks on the theory that the banks would use this money to lend. Instead, the banks used most of the money to triple their stock prices through issuing dividends and buying back stocks.[15]

The relationship between the U.S. government, its central bank, and the nation's private banks is complex and evolving. Borrowing from the Federal Reserve provides a significant source of bank assets. Some of this borrowing, especially during a crisis, is hard to measure. For example, in 2008 the Federal Reserve made trillions of dollars of overnight loans, the scale and nature of which were not disclosed for years.[16] What is clear, however, is the government's reliance on the banking system to advance its economic policies and the bank's reliance on a steady supply of government lending.

It is easy to see why individuals and governments need banks, but why do banks need governments? It all comes down to trust. Put simply, government support is the only reason depositors trust banks, and without trust from depositors, banks don't exist. Banks need us to entrust them with our money long enough for them to lend it out to our neighbor to buy a house or start a business. But we would not give them our money and leave it there if we did not trust that it would still be there when we wanted it back. Trust is the currency of banks—without it, they cease to exist. How can banks assure us that they are keeping our money safe? Banks have accomplished this in the past by erecting grand buildings made of marble to give the impression of stability, stature, and that plenty of money is stored there. Some banks would even display bars of gold in the window for all to see and feel confident the bank had money to spare. It is no wonder the bank in *Mary Poppins* is called the "Fidelity Fiduciary Bank": it is meant to convey trustworthiness, integrity, and soundness. But if customers smelled a hint of weakness, even the gold in the window could not prevent a show-stopping "run." In *Mary Poppins,* the run on the grand marbled Fidelity Fiduciary Bank is caused by a little boy, Michael, shouting when he can't get his coins back. Once a line forms to collect deposits, it is understood that the bank will not open for business the following day or ever again. This is the risk banks take when they lend out customer deposits to grow money. In order for your $100 to grow into $600, not everyone can ask for their money at the same time—it is not there. A bank only keeps a small reserve to pay out the occasional depositor. This is how banking works but only when people trust banks and allow them to hold on to their money.

The only historically proven antidote to fear-induced runs is a government willing to insure bank deposits. Since the inception of deposit insurance, bank runs have been a rare historical phenomenon—so rare that you and I are willing to put all our money in a bank and forget about it. We don't worry about who manages the bank or what they do with our money. Even if we hear on the news that our bank has started to lend large sums of money to piano-playing cats, which we think is a bad idea, we would not feel the need to show up at the bank the next morning to ask for all of our money back. If you had lent your money to an individual and they in turn lent your money to piano-playing cats, you would demand your money back immediately. But because you deposit your money into a bank account insured by the federal government, you feel no need to keep a watchful eye on what your bank does with the money. Insurance removes the incentive for customers to police a bank. It can also remove the incentive for banks to police themselves because they do not bear the full or even the most serious consequences of their actions. Removing the natural tendencies of the market to notice and punish bad choices creates a moral hazard that may result in well-funded cats and other undetected market risks.

In the United States, only federal deposit insurance has been effective at stabilizing banks. State and private insurance funds have been attempted and have failed because to be effective at deterring runs, an insurance system must be basically unlimited. If you suspected that because of a limited insurance pool, only ninety of a bank's one hundred customers would get their deposits back in the event of a bank failure, you would run to the bank to make sure you were among the ninety. You would refuse to take even a 10 percent chance of not getting your money back. The effect of a run is the same: the bank fails. State and private funds eventually run out. Federal funds do not. Even when the federal deposit insurance fund goes in the "red"—as the FDIC fund did in 2010—it can get a loan from the United States Treasury, which essentially has the power to insure all depositors.[17]

Therefore, banks need to be backed by the full faith and credit of the federal government in order to attract customer deposits. However, lending out customer deposits represents just a small portion of their lending business. The federal government also enables the major lending markets through the government sponsored-enterprises (GSEs) Fannie Mae, Freddie Mac, Ginnie Mae, and Sallie Mae.[18] These entities purchase almost every mortgage and student loan in the country and resell them to investors.[19] Because homeownership and higher education have been deemed important policy goals, these entities were created solely to generate credit markets where none existed and make loans available to the public. These GSEs enable banks to lend exponentially more money than what their customer deposits would allow. At the crux of our free market economy, then, is a state-enabled credit system.

Banks and the government have a mutually beneficial arrangement that consists of the government providing market-enabling structures and trust-inducing deposit insurance and banks, in return, play an essential role by financing the expansion of the economy and serving the needs of their customers and local communities. The relationship can be described as a social contract or an implicit promise or exchange made by the government and the banks.[20] This government support leads to a boon in profits for banks that benefit from loans they could not make otherwise. In exchange, the banking system must serve the people.

SHADOW BANKING

The above description of banking is accurate but too simplistic. Modern banking is much more complex than just lending and deposit-taking and so is the government's entanglement in the banking sector. The 2008 financial crisis revealed that government support goes well beyond FDIC insurance and that all financial institutions that operate with high leverage, not just traditional banks, can experience a run. The recent crisis resulted from many complex factors, but at its most basic, it was a run on the "shadow banking system"—financial institutions that operate with leverage similar to a bank, like investment banks, such as Lehman Brothers and Bear Stearns, and insurance companies, such as AIG.[21] Although Wall Street investment banks are not banks, "shadow banks" are still susceptible to the same economic realities as deposit banks. They are highly leveraged, and they lend long and borrow short. Like banks with their liquid deposits that can be withdrawn at any time, investment banks also have liquid assets (commercial paper or other lines of credit from other banks) and illiquid loans. Wall Street firms can and did experience a run, such as when investors lost confidence after the failure of Lehman Brothers.

Creditors lost trust in these banks and demanded their loans back, but these institutions could not pay. Because they were not banks and their creditors were not depositors, there was no established system of insurance. Once the run started, it rapidly spread and threatened to take down all of the uninsured shadow banks. This time, the federal government stepped in and stopped the hemorrhaging through bailouts. Thus began the era of "Too Big to Fail" institutions and a recognition that certain institutions are so large and powerful that the federal government cannot let them fail, lest trust in the entire financial system be undermined. This handful of banks controls the majority of the country's banking assets. Trillions of dollars in federal bailouts flowed to these banks.[22]

It is important to understand why the federal government bailed out these banks. A range of explanations exist. The cynical view, voiced by both the left (Occupy Wall Street) and the right (the Tea Party) is that the oversized political power of these firms made their desires a political reality. Elected bodies were powerless to resist them because of their outsized lobbying power. There is some truth to this view. Money's influence on political decision making has been documented in every sector, especially in banking.[23] It is not hard to imagine that policymakers would want to appease their large Wall Street donors. There are countless stories of bankers lobbying for loopholes and exemptions in banking laws and even accusations that bankers' lobbies have "captured" banking agencies.[24] Moreover, most of the policymakers who engineered the bailout were either former Wall Street bankers or part of former administrations responsible for regulating (or more accurately, *de*regulating) the banking industry.

This "revolving door" effect creates an environment where bank supervisors and bankers are often the same people. Henry Paulson, for example, the secretary of the Treasury who orchestrated the Troubled Asset Relief Program (TARP), was a former Goldman Sachs CEO, as was his predecessor in the Clinton Treasury, Robert Rubin. "In short," observes one commentator, "Paulson, CEO of Goldman Sachs, was pushing free money to his former colleagues."[25] It is hard to imagine a scenario in which Paulson would let Wall Street fail, even if the sector's economic contribution at the time was proven to be less than that of piano-playing cats. There is no doubt that these policymakers were at least influenced by their time inside the industries they eventually supervised, and a belief system partial to Wall Street interests may have affected their actions. The insider mentality can at least explain why the terms of the bailout were so favorable—instead of breaking up the banks or nationalizing them or requiring reduced profits or compensation, policymakers focused on returning banks to business-as-usual as soon as possible.

But even this is not the full picture. Putting aside the effects of campaign funds, the revolving door, and agency capture, it is still likely the federal government would have bailed these financial institutions out in order to maintain that *trust* so essential for the entire system to work. When the Obama administration met with the major bankers and they each emerged from the meeting saying, "We're in this together," they didn't just mean that they were in cahoots and that one had bought the other. Letting the banks fail would have eradicated trust in the financial markets, causing enormous damage to the entire United States economy. Treasury secretary Timothy Geithner explains that the bailout was akin to "putting money in the window," an effort to restore the public's confidence in a damaged system.[26] The failure of Lehman Brothers and the threatened failure of other large financial players caused a panic that likely would have destroyed the financial system, possibly taking years for the economy to recover. When President Bush asked Congress to approve the TARP bailout, he said, "There has been a widespread loss of *confidence,* and major sectors of America's financial system are at risk of shutting down."[27] When President Obama asked for even more bailout money, he quoted President Franklin D. Roosevelt on the Senate floor, saying, "There is an element in the readjustment of our financial system more important than currency, more important than gold, and that is the *confidence* of the people themselves. *Confidence* and courage are the essentials of success in carrying out our plan. Let us unite in *banishing fear.*"[28]

It appeared that even the Wall Street shadow banks needed the public and the markets to trust them in order to survive. Without something like deposit insurance, federal government bailouts are essentially an after-the-fact infusion of stability into the financial system. They are an attempt by the only entity with enough liquidity to stop the hemorrhaging of investments and trust from the financial system to show its strength and send a message that it will stand behind these banks with almost unlimited financial support. And despite the many valid criticisms of the bailouts, they achieved their aim. They kept the U.S. financial system intact by calming market participants and convincing them that their investment funds would be protected. The bailouts certainly introduced moral hazards and created unfair subsidies to banks, but the alternative could have been a lot worse.[29] Secretary Geithner asserts that "there would have been Shantytowns again" or "another Great Depression."[30] If the largest firms at the center of the financial system had been allowed to fail as spectacularly as predicted, it is possible that it would have taken years, perhaps decades, for investors to trust the financial markets again. It certainly could have been a blow to the entire economy—and not just the largest banks.

The purpose of restoring confidence, of course, is to assure the availability of *credit.* If the system works properly, banks can lend.[31] Therefore, saving them from collapse became necessary so that we as a society may benefit from the increased credit flow that they would enable—allowing individuals and businesses to put the economy back in motion. Consider how the two presidents and their officials explained the purpose of the bailout:

> *George W. Bush:* "This rescue effort is not aimed at preserving any individual company or industry. It is aimed at preserving America's overall economy. It will help American consumers and businesses get *credit* to meet their daily needs and create jobs."[32]

> *Henry Paulson (secretary of the Treasury for the Bush administration):* "I determined that the most timely, effective step to improve *credit*

market conditions was to strengthen bank balance sheets quickly through direct purchases of equity in banks . . . ensuring the financial system has sufficient capital is essential to get *credit* flowing to consumers and businesses and that is where the bulk of the remaining TARP funds should be deployed."[33]

Barack Obama: "We are in a very dangerous situation where financial institutions across this country are afraid to *lend* money. If all that meant was the failure of a few banks in New York, that would be one thing. But that is not what it means. What it means is if we don't act, it will be harder for Americans to get a mortgage for their home or the *loans* they need to buy a car or send their children to college."[34]

Timothy Geithner (secretary of the Treasury for the Obama administration): "The *credit* markets that are essential for small businesses and consumers are not working. *Borrowing* costs have risen sharply for state and local governments, for students trying to pay for college, and for businesses large and small. Many banks are reducing *lending,* and across the country they are tightening the terms of *loans.* . . . Our plan will help restart the flow of *credit.*"[35]

If the government supports banks because they provide credit to individuals, shouldn't the government also make sure the banks are providing that credit? The logic of the bailout is simple. People need credit. Banks are credit intermediaries. Banks will not lend when confidence is low. Government bailouts will increase confidence in banks. Therefore, banks will lend. But what if banks will not lend? Or will not lend to the entire population? The immediate aftermath of the financial crisis clearly illustrated this problem. For example, one banker who received a $300 million bailout discussed his bank's intended use of the funds: "Make more loans?" he asked. "We're not going to change our business model or our credit policies to accommodate the needs of the public sector as they see it to have us make more loans."[36] Most banks were not so explicit, but it was clear they planned to use this bailout money to build up their reserves instead of releasing those funds to grow the economy through credit.

Not only did banks fail to lend *more* because of bailout funds, they actually decreased lending. Even after banks recovered from the crisis with the help of the government, they decreased lending to small businesses. According to one study, "Capital injections from the TARP failed to increase their small-business lending; instead, they decreased their small-business lending by even more than other banks. This evidence shows that the TARP's Capital Purchase Program was largely a failure in this respect."[37] These banks also decreased lending to consumers—even while they were paying shareholder dividends. In effect, the bailout saved the banks, but not the public.

Why didn't the government make it clear that the bailout was *conditional* on banks actually lending the money? In fact, in Secretary Geithner's first speech as head of the Treasury, he did exactly that. Explaining the bailout to the public, Geithner said: "We believe that access to public support is a privilege, not a right. When our government provides support to banks, it is not for the benefit of banks, it is for the businesses and families who depend on banks . . . and for the benefit of the country. Government support must come with *strong conditions* to protect the tax payer and with transparency that allows the American people to see the impact of those investments."[38] The Treasury secretary did not mince words when he said: "The capital will come with *conditions* to help ensure that every dollar of assistance is used to generate a level of lending greater than what would have been possible in the absence of government support."[39]

His speech nearly brought down the U.S. economy. Not his actions, just the words. The stock market fell five hundred points, or 5 percent, as Secretary Geithner was talking. In his book, Geithner admits that the speech "did not go well." President Obama was "not happy" and called Geithner to ask, "How the hell did this happen?"[40] Many blamed the market reaction on the speech's lack of detail about the bailout plan and Geithner's lack of gravitas—he looked young and shifty and unsure. The old saying is "Treasury for confidence, Fed for liquidity," and he failed to induce confidence—one report called the speech "shock and Uh."[41] It is just as likely, however, that the market did not like what it did hear. In any case, the *conditions* were mentioned much less in subsequent discussions of the government's support of banks and not enforced at all.[42]

In the end, the government relied on the banks to disseminate the bailout funds to the public without actually making sure they would do so. The very banks that had caused the crisis through their recklessness were entrusted with taxpayer funds and just a mere hope that they would act in the public interest. Of course, the federal government could have opted to avoid the bloated bank middlemen and use the funds to help the public directly. It considered that option, if only briefly. The debate centered on mortgage relief, and although both administrations decided to help the people *through* the banks, they ended up helping the banks *instead* of the people. They were not always clear about their intentions, however. In 2008, Treasury secretary Henry Paulson sold the TARP to Congress and the public as an undertaking that would help relieve average Americans' mortgage debts through modifications and other direct relief. Paulson promised Congress that he would find ways to stem the tide of impending mortgage foreclosures. But after examining direct-relief plans, including a mortgage modification protocol developed by FDIC chairman Sheila Bair, Paulson concluded that these programs would "require substantial government subsidies" and "direct spending"[43] that he ultimately felt were unjustified.[44] This led one congressman to call the TARP "the second largest bait and switch scheme that history has ever seen, second only to the reasons given to us to vote for the invasion of Iraq."[45] Barney Frank also angrily cut off Henry Paulson during congressional testimony, saying that "the bill couldn't have been clearer" in being aimed at reducing foreclosures.[46]

When President Obama took office, his administration also promised, but failed, to achieve meaningful mortgage relief. In Geithner's stock-market tanking speech, he promised to launch "a comprehensive housing program," stating, "Our focus will be on using the full resources of the government to help bring down mortgage payments and to reduce mortgage interest rates."[47] In fact, the same bailout-fund-receiving banks increased foreclosures after the TARP.[48]

After many promises that bailouts were meant to help the struggling public and rhetoric linking bailouts to lending, only one program was geared at direct relief. In March 2009, the Treasury proposed and Congress passed the Home Affordable Modification Program (HAMP), a $50 million TARP carve-out (out of the almost trillion dollars in total funds) intended to create guidelines for banks to modify mortgages and, in turn, decrease foreclosures. The funds were intended to go through the banks to provide direct relief to struggling homeowners, thereby fulfilling the TARP's original purpose. Incredibly, these funds also ended up going directly to banks. In fact, the HAMP's faulty design caused many problems for mortgage borrowers across the country. When Treasury secretary Timothy Geithner was asked about the HAMP's failure to help mortgage borrowers, his response, as reported by Elizabeth Warren and TARP Inspector General Neil Barofsky, provided one of the most telling exchanges of the financial crisis: "We estimate that [the banks] can handle ten million foreclosures, over time. . . . This program will help foam the runway for them."[49] In other words, when asked about the one program specifically targeted to help the public, the Treasury secretary responded that it would return banks to profitability quickly.

This comment reveals the nature of the modern relationship between banks and the state. The Treasury secretary assumed that the government's paramount objective in a crisis is to assure bank profitability.[50] And to be fair, if banks are the central engine of the economy, their profitability is necessary for a thriving economy. Foaming the runway makes sense when we are talking about an engine that we want to move fast and often. But the engine analogy only works if the engine actually moves the machine.

Although banks emerged from the recent financial crisis with astonishing ease and profitability, it is important to stop and consider the terms of the social contract and whether the people benefited in parity with the banks. Indeed, it is clear that the social contract has become lopsided.

The recent financial crisis was not, historically speaking, the first government-bank tango. Throughout history, the relationship between the U.S. government and its banks has involved a quid pro quo bargain, and different eras have required different bargains. In order to assess the nature of the current bargain between the people and the banks, it is important to briefly consider the evolving bank-government relationships through different eras in our nation's history.

2

History of the Social Contract

I sincerely believe, with you, that banking establishments are more dangerous than standing armies.

—THOMAS JEFFERSON, IN A LETTER TO JOHN TAYLOR, MAY 28, 1816

Throughout U.S. history, the people, through their representative government, have had a social contract with the banks. This point is related to the observation that banking policy has always been deeply intertwined with politics.[1] The best way to understand bank structure at any given point in time is to view it through the lens of the dominant political ideologies and bargains of a given era. Many scholars have articulated this point through historical and political analysis, and it is an important and generally uncontested observation; every country's banking system is a reflection of that country's dominant political structure. If banks and governments are engaged in a partnership, it follows that different regimes will want banks to accomplish different political goals. Economists Charles Calomiris and Stephen Haber dispel the notion that banking design has evolved throughout U.S. history based purely on economic forces, calling it a "Libertarian fairytale."[2] Therefore, the banking system is not just a product of economic forces but also of social and political forces. Politics are, and have always, motivated banking change. But what, historically, have been the terms of the social contract in the United States?

For as long as there have been states and banks, the link has been "umbilical."[3] In the thirteenth century, Italian banks financed the sovereign.[4] As already mentioned, the Bank of England was established in the seventeenth century just to finance King William III's war debts. So linked were the state and its banks that "through the ages sovereign default has been the single biggest cause of banking collapse."[5] Even though this state-bank relationship has often been rocky, it has continued through the ages. Yet in the last century, the relationship shifted somewhat dramatically. Although states relied on bank financing for several centuries, the tables turned during the recent crisis. Whereas in the Middle Ages the key threat to banks was sovereign failure, today, as Andrew Haldane, director at the Bank of England, explains, "Perhaps the biggest risk to the sovereign comes from the banks. Causality is reversed."[6] One lesson of the recent global crisis is that fragility in a large and complex banking sector has the potential to sink nations. The implications of that shift affect how we should think about banking policy.

The nature of the bank/government relationship changed significantly throughout various phases of U.S. history, but the general contours of the social contract remained roughly the same. Banks were supported as long as they enabled the strength of the democracy and would be restricted if they came to present a threat to democracy. For hundreds of years, this country's leaders were afraid of excessive bank power and the inequalities of access it would inevitably produce. Many presidents and lawmakers fought and resisted the natural tendency of banks to grow large and powerful and favor the profitable few over the many. Then they stopped fighting. And what was always feared came to pass.

BUILDING A NATION

Banking started in the American colonies just as it had elsewhere in history, to help the new "country" fund its War of Independence. The New World, unlike the more established Old World, lacked a financial system and large pools of money to borrow or lend. The first bank in the New World, the Bank of Pennsylvania, was a public bank created to help the cash-strapped colonies feed the troops during the Revolutionary War.[7] Alexander Hamilton, then a twenty-four-year-old soldier, saw the bank as much more than a way to fund the war but wrote, "'Tis by introducing order into our finances by restoring public credit not by gaining battles that we are finally to gain our object."[8] His time in the army had convinced him that "military operations could not be made more effective without more money and more money could not be procured without new means."[9] And the bank would provide these means because "a bank has a direct relation to the power of borrowing money, because it is an usual, and in sudden emergencies an essential, instrument in the obtaining of loans to government."[10] The Bank of Pennsylvania was a public enterprise, but it was slowly absorbed into private business and never became the "national bank" Hamilton envisioned. Hamilton argued that the colonies' banks "within reasonable limits, ought to consider it as a principle object to promote beneficial public purposes."[11] When Alexander Hamilton responded to President Washington's inquiry about the advisability of a national bank, he wrote that "such a Bank is not a mere matter of private property, but a political machine of the greatest importance to the State."[12]

By 1790, four banks were in business in four cities—Philadelphia, New York, Boston, and Baltimore[13]—and "each bank was a public bank; that is, it was distinctly more than a private institution. Though its active management was private, it was bound as well as enfranchised by governmental authority, and the state was as often as not a shareholder."[14] The first few banks of the New World were started as public entities that would meet the credit demands of the public and the new government. Bray Hammond, the leading expert on early U.S. banking, describes the arrangement as such: "The community, whether shrewdly or not, had adapted private initiative and wealth to public purposes, granting privileges and exacting duties in return. . . . There persisted a strong conviction that a charter was a *covenant*."[15]

Though Hamilton thought a well organized banking system was the answer to a number of the early nation's problems, many viewed banks with suspicion and distaste. The divide generally existed between the elites, like Hamilton, and the Populist agrarian leaders, like Thomas Jefferson. In order to defeat the British, the colonial elites needed the support of America's population, which consisted of rural farmers.[16] Hamilton was the early bank advocate and Jefferson, the champion of rural farmers and an opponent of centralized power, its early opponent.

But Hamilton's support and Jefferson's opposition sprang from a similar understanding of the banking system's potential to shape the economy. Hamilton recognized that banks would be pivotal in turning an agrarian and rural economy into a national, interconnected economy with central planning and development.[17] Thomas Paine, another early supporter of a large national bank, believed that such a bank would help advance the nation beyond small farming by facilitating commerce. The public would benefit and the economy would prosper, Paine argued, by the increased efficiency in trade facilitated by banking.[18] Others in burgeoning colonial cities, inspired by the mercantilist spirit of capitalism, hailed banks for playing a central role in the "wondrous growth" of the American trade-based economy.

It was this same growth and the banks' central role in it that Thomas Jefferson opposed. Jefferson and the rural farmers of the American colonies feared that a robust centralized banking system would amass wealth and power in cities, away from farmers. He also feared that banks would provide too much credit, which would destroy the agrarian principles of hard work and thrift.[19] Jefferson, who derided banks as being "more dangerous than standing armies," was not alone in his disdain.[20] Banks and bankers were cast as villains flaunting easy money and debt; farmers were the protagonists whose work made the economy possible. In 1811, former president John Adams wrote: "Our whole banking system I ever abhorred, I continue to abhor, and shall die abhorring."[21] Similarly, in 1833, William Gouge, a Treasury official and economic advisor to Andrew Jackson, described banks and their outsized power as "the *principal* cause of social evil in the United States."[22]

These sentiments were rooted in the traditional Protestant and agrarian principles of thrift and self-reliance, as well as a distrust of artificial power derived from the concentrated control of money. The American republic was a distinct break from the Old World social order, and one of its central premises was that every person, regardless of social rank or accumulated wealth, would enjoy "equality of opportunity." One historian explains that as long as the "channels of ascent and descent were kept open it would be impossible for artificial aristocrats or overgrown rich men to maintain themselves for long."[23] This principle of equality of access was the "life and soul" of republicanism.[24] It did not mean that there would be no social or class differences—the Founding Fathers were clear that property rights must be respected and class distinctions must be tolerated in order for the economy to function. But they would strive for an "equality, which is adverse to every species of subordination besides that which arises from differences in capacity, disposition, and virtue."[25] This meant that access to opportunity would need to be available to all because "all men are created equal, that they are endowed by their Creator with certain unalienable Rights, that among these are Life, Liberty and the pursuit of Happiness."

Many saw excessive bank power through accumulated capital as a formidable threat and expressed fears that banks would amass political power and influence and wield it to thwart the budding democracy. William Findley described banks as "artificial creature[s] endowed with powers not possessed by human beings and incompatible with the principles of a democratic social order. . . . 'This institution, having no principle but that of avarice, which dries and shrivels up all the manly, all the generous feelings of the human soul, will never be varied in its object and if continued will accomplish its end, viz., to engross all the wealth, power and influence of the state.' "[26]

The growing economy needed those with money, which had been accumulated in the Old World, to lend in order to support new ventures. This formative tension between protecting the principles of democracy and enabling a burgeoning *laissez-faire* spirit of limitless prosperity shaped the evolution of the social contract. The fear of too much bank power led the government to keep banks under strict supervision. Banks were given state charters and allowed to lend with heavy restrictions as well as charters requiring them to honor a distinctively public mission.[27]

Thus, the policy goal of growing a prosperous nation of small farmers and landowners was achieved by limiting bank growth—the latter seen as a threat to the former. Though Jefferson turned out to be wrong in his judgment that the nation's economy would be agrarian and rural, he was remarkably prescient in his intuitive suspicions of the banking industry. He understood that money tends to flow toward more money, and the innate trajectory of any unregulated banking system is toward growth and concentration, which in turn breeds power.

These fears of centralized banking would continue for generations. They would erupt in full force during the debates over the First Bank and the Second Bank of the United States. The national dialogue involved in the chartering of these two banks became deeply charged and highly consequential for both their friends and foes and caused so much anxiety and debate that a national bank was twice created and twice defeated. The First Bank of the United States, championed by Alexander Hamilton, approved by President George Washington, and opposed by Thomas Jefferson and James Madison, was given a twenty-year charter in 1791.[28] When the charter expired in 1811, the Populist proagrarian opponents won over the commercial class's advocacy by a single vote, and the bank was dead.[29]

Increasingly, fears of bank power clashed with economic efficiency. The national government needed credit, and a uniform currency aided by a national bank was the only way to achieve it. This caused one early opponent, James Madison, to change his mind about banking once he became president. After the War of 1812, the fiscal state of the nation was in disarray, and President Madison pushed for a second national bank. The Second Bank of the United States was chartered in 1816. Madison used the bank to fund the government after the war and restore fiscal order, but the bank never became popular or widely accepted, in part thanks to President Andrew Jackson leading a vehement opposition to the bank, referred to as a "bank war." Jackson used his executive power to remove the bank's funds, and the bank fought back by calling in its loans and bankrupting many banks in the country.[30] The dispute was best described by Jackson himself: "The bank is trying to kill me, but I will kill it."

Jackson shared Jefferson's agrarian disdain for banks and was concerned that the national bank would concentrate financial power and influence to the detriment of the "common man."[31] Jackson believed that the bank was about "the advancement of the few at the expense of the many."[32] To Jackson, the bank embodied inequality. He wrote, "It is to be regretted that the rich and powerful too often bend the acts of government to their selfish purposes . . . many of our rich men have not been content with equal protection and equal benefits but have besought us to make them richer by act of Congress." He also opposed the "powers, privileges, and favors bestowed" by the government to the banks.[33] Others joined Jackson's opposition. Senator Thomas Hart Benton of Missouri stated in 1831, "I object to the renewal of the charter of the Bank of the United States because I look upon the bank as an institution too great and powerful to be tolerated in a Government of free and equal laws. Its power is that of a purse; a power more potent than the sword."[34] A strong coalition of small bankers and farmers and their strong ally in the White House led the charge, and in 1836, the second bank's twenty-year charter was allowed to expire.[35]

Jackson's fears were naïve and misguided. He thought that by killing the central bank, he was diminishing private bank power and elevating "the people." In fact, without a central bank to provide liquidity and stability, the nation would enter an era of repeated banking crises. Historian Charles Geisst explained: "By curtailing the development of a central bank, the commercial banking institutions of the day were given more de facto power over their own states' banking systems than otherwise might have been the case."[36] Investment firms took advantage of the federal government's absence from the banking sphere to enter unregulated securities and bonds markets, creating unstable and panic-ridden financial markets that otherwise could have been supervised and overseen by a strong central bank that had the nation's financial health as its first priority. Still, Jackson felt empowered to get rid of the bank, based on his fears. Government policies, no matter how erroneous, trumped bank profitability.

It is important to point out the stakes in these early debates. Both advocates and opponents of the early banks recognized that national and centralized banking could solve formidable financial problems and increase credit to both the government and the populace. The debates surrounding these banks did *not* focus on the profitability or success of the bank itself, but about what a national bank meant for the country. It was a debate about the nature of the democracy. Proponents argued that the banks would increase credit and spur growth in cities and financial centers. Opponents countered that the banks would impede rural farmers, who comprised the core of the economy before the Industrial Revolution, in competition with aristocrats from major money centers. Both sides viewed the central bank as either advancing or hindering their goals; a banking system was a means to an end. The debate concerned which ends were preferable and how banking could best help achieve those ends. Again, the issue was not what the banks wanted.[37]

As the ideological battles fought over the national bank raged during the nineteenth century, most of the business of banking was accomplished through state charters. Predictably, the relationship between a state and the banks it chartered was just as consequential as the national bank's. Charters were given and certain banking activities were restricted based on what the state government needed.[38] In particular, early state laws attempted to keep banks small and short-lived, in keeping with widely held fears of concentrated economic power. The state of New York, for example, issued all of its banks charters with an expiration date. Legislatures renewed the charters subject to conditions or more commonly, denied requests for charter extensions to keep banks from amassing too much power or market share. In addition, state law imposed participation requirements to prevent privately controlled banks from being dominated by a few individuals or economic interests. One historian asserts: "In practice state legislatures viewed banking corporations as instrumentalities of the state, established to serve various public purposes as well as the private interests of stockholders and borrowers."[39]

In *Schaake v. Dolley,* the Kansas Supreme Court explained that banking is not "a matter of private concern only, like the business of the merchant, and for all purposes of legislative regulation and control it may be said to be '*affected with a public interest.*' " The court made it clear that banking needs to be distinguished from "ordinary private business" because of its "public nature." Because banks received "public patronage," a state bank was "a *trustee* of the fiscal affairs of the people and of the state."[40]

The most important charter impositions, and the most long-lasting, were prohibitions on bank size and location. Unit banking, wherein a single bank operates in a single region, was the norm in U.S. banking for almost two centuries. Most banks did not open branches outside a state, or even within a state in many cases, for much of U.S. banking history.[41] The agrarians and Populists that controlled most state legislatures wanted to keep banking assets within the state. By restricting bank branching, they could prevent any banks from growing too large. The restriction was also meant to force banks to stay tied to one community and serve just that community's credit needs. For example, if a bank were permitted to take deposits from a rural town in Pennsylvania and lend them out in a growing city, like Philadelphia, the rural town would have to pay more for loans to compete with the profits the bank could earn in Philadelphia. Or if Pennsylvania state banks were able to take deposits from Pennsylvania farmers and make loans to New York City merchants for a higher profit, Pennsylvania farmers would be credit-starved. A coalition of community bankers warned against national bank branching, stating: "[Such branching would] create a brood of two hundred or three hundred great central banks, with 10,000 to 15,000 branches in large cities as well as small, and as such branches would have no capital and only figure-head management, individualism in management would cease, local taxes [would] be evaded, [there would be] no home distribution of profits, local progress [would be] retarded, in short, the great central banks would skim the cream from the whole country to enrich [their own] exchequers."[42]

These rules were anticompetitive and held banks hostage to a single region's credit markets. The situation was not only inefficient but also unstable. If the region in which a bank was forced to concentrate its resources suffered bad weather or a local disaster, the bank would sink. And many did. Banking crises and failures were chronic during this era. Nonetheless, these restrictions remained because rural farmers needed and wanted the lower rates for credit that unit banking uniquely enabled.[43] And the state, through chartering laws and restrictions, made it so.

During the era of state-chartered banking, some states experimented with unregulated banking. This phase, called "free banking" or "wildcat banking," lasted from 1837 to 1862 and is considered a disaster by most scholars.[44] This short experiment with free banking stands as the only example since the 1600s of any banking system worldwide operating without government support.[45] Not every state allowed free banking, but those that did saw bank charters explode because anyone could charter a bank.[46] But no one trusted these banks. Many of them would pop up in desolate areas for the sole purpose of not having to redeem the bank notes they had issued, thus earning the name "wildcat" banks.[47] The banks that existed during free banking lasted an average of five years, and half of them failed. The turbulence and constant bank failures were unsustainable, and the period ended relatively quickly.[48]

THE CIVIL WAR AND THE CREATION OF NATIONAL BANKING

The Union's financial emergency during the Civil War was the impetus that finally begat national banking. The Union needed credit to fund an expensive and protracted war, and because of the magnitude of the crisis, President Lincoln and Treasury secretary Salmon Chase were finally able to overcome agrarian opposition. But Congress had written Jacksonian opposition to national banking into laws prohibiting the Treasury from participating in nationwide monetary policy, and so to finance the war, the federal government had to depend entirely on private state bankers in New York, Boston, and Philadelphia.[49] This dependence on private loans significantly restrained federal spending. President Lincoln and Secretary Chase needed much more than what they could borrow from these banks. The way to loosen credit would be to establish a national paper currency so that the federal government could fund itself, allowing the federal government to print and sell "greenbacks" to banks and raise the money it needed.[50]

Up until this time, currency was backed by gold "specie," and money was exchanged via either gold itself or private "bank notes" backed up by a store of gold somewhere. Specie-backed currency restrained the amount of money available because banks could not lend more than the amount of specie they actually held in reserves. The White House suspended specie currency in favor of the newly minted greenbacks.[51] The use of paper "fiat" currency, or legal tender, untethered the monetary supply. But it also heightened the need for trust. The fiat currency Lincoln adopted, which we still use today, only works insofar as the public trusts the government's ability to make good on the claim. At that time and even today, each unit of paper money represents a promise from the government that it will stand behind it—it is a debt from the government to the holder of the paper money. Merchants and banks will only operate in paper currency if they have faith that the federal government, the issuer of the currency, is solvent and can pay its debts. But paper currency is unrestrained and incredibly flexible, and it was this quality that made it so appealing during the Civil War. The federal government needed to pay for an expensive war to defeat the South. President Lincoln and the U.S. Congress made unprecedented assertions of federal power through the Legal Tender and National Currency Acts of 1862 and 1863.[52] The idea of paper money was sold to the Union as the only way to advance the national economy.[53]

President Lincoln, in an 1862 address to Congress, explained that moving from specie to paper currency was a necessary, but temporary, action: "The suspension of specie payments by the banks. . . . [was] unavoidable. In no other way could the payment of the troops and the satisfaction of other just demands be so economically or so well provided for. . . . A return to specie payments, however, at the earliest period compatible with due regard to all interests concerned should ever be kept in view."[54]

Lincoln was a reluctant adopter of paper currency and was eager to return to the safer and more stable specie currency, which Secretary of State Hugh McCulloch eventually did in 1866 after Lincoln's assassination.[55] It would not be until 1971 and President Nixon's need to fund the Vietnam War that the United States would go back to fiat currency for good and fully abandon specie-backed currency.[56] President Lincoln was, however, an advocate of national banking, which provided a more permanent solution to the nation's funding problems:[57] "Is there, then, any other mode in which the necessary provision for the public wants can be made and the great advantages of a safe and uniform currency secured? I know of none which promises so certain results and is at the same time so unobjectionable as the organization of banking associations, under a general act of Congress, well guarded in its provisions. . . . The public credit, moreover, would be greatly improved and the negotiation of new loans greatly facilitated by the steady market demand for Government bonds which the adoption of the proposed system would create."[58]

The currency debate, which eventually merged into a debate about national banking, was not just a debate about how best to fund a war. It was a debate about the future of the Republic. Banking policy was, in many respects, as politically controversial, consequential, and enduring as the issue of Southern secession. The national bank came to represent the tension between state and federal power, with the Union pushing for national currency and national banking and the Confederacy vigorously opposing it. Arguments against a national currency and a national banking system paralleled those used in defense of secession. For example, those who opposed a national currency viewed it as a subordination of state rights. They believed that national banking/currency would make wealthy men wealthier and would press states into federal servitude.[59] But the nationalism brought on by the war led many Northerners to believe that a national currency and a national banking system would advance the public welfare.[60]

Issuing currency and creating a national bank were framed as being for the "general good of the whole" and had nothing at all to do with increasing banking efficiency or profitability. The national banking system would be "relied upon to carry the nation through its financial difficulties."[61] And this had nothing at all to do with what the banks wanted. In 1896, in *A History of Banking in All the Leading Nations,* William Graham Sumner describes the creation of the national banking system as a political act: "In short, the motives of the legislation which established the national bank system were political. It was desired to change the currency in a way to make it more useful in the financial exigencies of the government, and to borrow all the banking capital of the country as a further financial resource. There was no consideration of favoritism to the banks and they, almost without exception, opposed the change. The arrangement might also be regarded as a compromise by which the government, instead of depriving the banks of the privilege of circulation, shared it with them."[62]

Lincoln created national banking despite banks' vehement opposition because it is what the nation needed. These national banks, although privately owned and operated, would be tasked with circulating the new national currency. Lincoln overcame industry opposition in part because the nation's small banks, though a large and relatively influential group, had not yet amassed sufficient political power.

Legislation called the National Bank Acts of 1863 and 1864 governed the new national banking system. In accordance with existing state charter restrictions, and to allay fears of excess bank power, these acts formalized explicit activity and geographic restrictions.[63] National banks could not branch within any state that did not allow such nor could any bank branch outside of its state. The banks were also only to engage in traditional banking activities, such as lending and deposit-taking, and were to steer clear of the territory covered by Wall Street investment banks, such as underwriting, trading in stocks or private bonds, or merchant banking. These acts served as the template for later restrictions on state banks' activities as well.

Even after the national banks were created, the currency debate raged on and came to represent much more than just precious metal versus paper. William Jennings Bryan took up Jefferson and Jackson's torch and railed against the eastern and western banking powers that were enslaving the agrarian masses. Bryan contended that the United States should move from gold to silver specie, mainly to put more money into circulation and therefore, provide more credit to debt-burdened farmers.

Bryan gave his famous "Cross of Gold" speech in 1896 at the Democratic National Convention in Chicago, igniting considerable pent-up rage in the crowd "like one great burst of artillery." The next day, Bryan was nominated to run for president.[64] His speech illustrates how central the issues of currency and banking were to the time. He starts with what is perhaps an overstatement: "Never before in the history of American politics has a great issue been fought out as this issue has been by the voters themselves." The speech quickly sets farmer against banker in inflammatory terms: "You come to us and tell us that the great cities are in favor of the gold standard. I tell you that the great cities rest upon these broad and fertile prairies. Burn down your cities and leave our farms, and your cities will spring up again as if by magic. But destroy our farms and the grass will grow in the streets of every city in the country."[65] Like his Populist predecessors, he focused on the struggle of the agrarian against the banker:

> Ah, my friends, we say not one word against those who live upon the Atlantic Coast; but those hardy pioneers who braved all the dangers of the wilderness, who have made the desert to blossom as the rose—those pioneers away out there, rearing their children near to nature's heart, where they can mingle their voices with the voices of the birds—out there where they have erected schoolhouses for the education of their children and churches where they praise their Creator, and the cemeteries where sleep the ashes of their dead—are as deserving of the consideration of this party as any people in this country.
>
> It is for these that we speak. We do not come as aggressors. Our war is not a war of conquest. We are fighting in the defense of our homes, our families, and posterity.[66]

Bryan voiced the discontent of many during this era, which he framed as a "struggle between the idle holders of idle capital and the struggling masses who produce the wealth and pay the taxes of this country." In taking this position, he did not miss the parallel to Thomas Jefferson: "Those who are opposed to this proposition tell us that the issue of paper money is a function of the bank and that the government ought to go out of the banking business. I stand with Jefferson rather than with them, and tell them, as he did, that the issue of money is a function of the government and that the banks should go out of the governing business."[67]

The issue of whether the country should operate on gold or silver currency came to represent the farmer versus the banker. The farmer, indebted to the East Coast banks, needed a looser flow of currency, and the bankers preferred the gold standard because a change to silver would devalue their holdings. Bryan and the Populists would lose this fight. Most people today forget that it occurred even though the argument was memorialized in a classic American book, *The Wonderful Wizard of Oz*.

L. Frank Baum published *The Wonderful Wizard of Oz* in 1900, four years after Bryan's famous Cross of Gold speech, and many claimed that the book was an allegory of this very debate. According to historians Henry Littlefield and Quentin Taylor, each part of the story symbolizes either an actual political figure or subparts of the population. The yellow brick road represents the gold standard, and Dorothy's silver slippers, which were changed to ruby for the 1939 film, stand, of course, for Baum and Bryan's preferred monetary standard. Dorothy represents the American people, specifically, the nation's farmers. Following the road of gold leads her to the Emerald City, a place of pretend value, like the greenback paper money. The Wicked Witches of the East and West signify the banking and money centers in the East and West. The Scarecrow depicts the farmers who lack the brains to challenge the gold standard, while the Tin Man represents the industrial workers and specifically, steel workers, who do not have the heart to stand with the farmers against the moneyed centers. The Cowardly Lion depicts the political classes who lack the courage to intervene. Even the winged monkeys represent the dangers the Native Americans posed to the western expansionists. The cyclone itself portends revolution, and of course Oz symbolizes the standard measurement for gold, the ounce (oz).[68]

CREATION OF THE FEDERAL RESERVE

The era between the end of the Civil War and the Great Depression was as volatile as any point in the country's history.[69] Although the Great Depression was the culminating crisis of that period, it was by no means unexpected. Six major banking panics occurred in the thirty years from 1873 to 1907, each involving a run on the banking system.[70] The most severe of them all, the Panic of 1907, started on Wall Street and spread quickly across the country. The famous J. P. Morgan helped to subdue the panic by using his formidable holdings to buoy up failing banks, but everyone agreed that the banking system needed a permanent solution to its chronic instability. In 1908, Congress created a committee, the National Monetary Commission, to find a long-term solution to the problem. Led by Republican senator Nelson Aldrich, the commission studied the issue for years, even traveling to Europe to gather information. Bankers and financiers also organized a secret meeting in Jekyll Island, Georgia, that has been fodder for conspiracy theorists ever since.[71]

Eventually, the committee proposed the "Federal Reserve Association," which would be owned and run by bankers. The bankers would control the money supply and serve as the lenders of last resort—infusing liquidity into the market during a credit crisis. Progressives, including William Jennings Bryan, fiercely opposed it because they wanted central banking under public, not private, control. Democrat Woodrow Wilson agreed that the plan was unacceptable in a democracy and killed it during the 1912 election. He articulated his position on centralized banking power on the campaign trail: "The great monopoly in this country is the monopoly of big credits. So long as that exists, our old variety and freedom and individual energy of development are out of the question. A great industrial nation is controlled by its system of credit. Our system of credit is privately concentrated. The growth of the nation, therefore, and all our activities are in the hands of a few men, who, even if their actions be honest and intended for the public interest, are necessarily concentrated upon the great undertakings in which their own money is involved and who, necessarily, by every reason of their own limitations, chill and check and destroy genuine economic freedom . . . and the true liberties of men."[72]

Once in office, the Wilson administration set out to form a central bank to meet the needs of private bankers but allay Populist fears. The

1913 Federal Reserve Act reflected such a compromise. The act created twelve regional Federal Reserve banks across the country with the ability to offer transaction services and make emergency loans. These banks' shares would be owned by "member banks," individual banks within the geographic district that joined the system. They could also elect a majority of its directors. But a centralized Federal Reserve Board, appointed by the president and confirmed by the Senate, would have the final say about policy and make national monetary policy. The system was a blend of private and public, regional and central, Progressive and capitalist, Hamiltonian and Jeffersonian. It was a nod to big banks, small banks, and Populists, merging a desire for order and efficient banking on one hand with a fear of concentrated banking power and the control of money in the hands of a few on the other.

The central bank was up and running by 1914, but it had yet to gain the tools required to stem the panic of the Great Depression. The bank would grow much more powerful and centralized over time—in parallel with the general trends in banking.

It is clear, but bears repeating, that during the era from the founding until the Great Depression, banks were tied to their chartering governments and used to accomplish specific policy goals. The impetus behind bank policy and restrictions had more to do with fulfilling state or national policies than ensuring the most efficient and profitable banking industry. Although there was little in the way of an explicit social contract during the early colonial and post–Civil War era, banks were clearly used to serve the needs of the state. In addition, many pressing debates about the country's future were fought on the turf of banking policy. Although the government did not yet provide a safety net during this time, the granting of bank charters and the use of banks for monetary policy were ways in which the banks and the government relied on each other. This idea of unity carried with it, in its nature, a recognition that banks were subject to governmental control. And in fact, many controls were imposed, especially restrictions on bank size. There existed, however, a deep problem with this form of the banking social contract: it left banks open to failures that resulted from financial mismanagement and bank runs.

The Great Depression spread like a wildfire, engulfing the already fragile U.S. banking industry, and on that scorched earth, the New Deal–era banking laws built a brand new edifice that would define banking for the next century. Any skepticism about banks before the 1930s turned to outright hostility as the American people faced unprecedented suffering due to bank failures. The public anger and distrust of banks that peaked during the Great Depression led to an even stronger bank-state relationship. It was a high mark of explicit government involvement in banking, drawing from a rise in public anger and Populist fervor. However, the Great Depression banking reforms were a continuation rather than a change in the ongoing bank-state relationship.

Although Jeffersonian fears of centralized banking power had never been realized, many now saw the calamity of the Great Depression as Jefferson's and Jackson's worst fears coming to pass. It was Louis Brandeis who picked up where they left off, and he would be the most forceful reminder that banks were different than other institutions—that their growth and amassed power posed a threat against which the public and policymakers should constantly be vigilant. Brandeis ably articulated Jefferson's point and applied it to the modern landscape; he argued that these banks were injuring the very people whose deposits were used to secure the banks' dominant positions. The control of "other people's money" allowed financial oligarchies to turn high profits into outsized political influence. "If the banker's power were commensurate only with their wealth," Brandeis said, "they would have relatively little influence on American business."[73]

Instead, Brandeis noted that the large investment banks controlled, either directly or indirectly, a staggering $22 billion dollars, more than three times the value of all property, real and personal, in New England. With large investments in American business, including railroads, industrial corporations, and life insurance companies, banks and investment bankers requested directorships on company boards. J. P. Morgan himself held seventy-two directorships in forty-seven of the largest corporations in the country. According to Brandeis, this situation was ripe with conflict and self-dealing. Even though the era preceding the Great Depression saw increased concentrations of wealth in the hands of the few, Brandeis was not concerned about wealth inequality. What worried Brandeis was the increased influence of those who used other people's wealth. He explained the difference using J. P. Morgan's bank as an example: "They control the people through the people's own money. . . . [Personal wealth] does not endanger political or industrial liberty. It is insignificant in amount as compared with the aggregate wealth of America, or even of New York City. It lacks significance largely because its owners have only the income from their own wealth. [This wealth] is static. The wealth of the Morgan associates is dynamic. The power and the growth of power of our financial oligarchs comes from wielding the savings and quick capital of others. . . . The fetters which bind the people are forged from the people's own gold."[74]

The main problem with this control over the people was that the provision of *credit* was in the bankers' hands, and any self-dealing on their part created unequal access to credit and favored those affiliated with the money trusts. He explained that "the granting of credit involves the exercise of judgment" and that "however honestly the bank officials may wish to exercise their discretion, experience shows that their judgment is warped by the existence of the all-pervading power of the Money Trust."[75]

In addition to recommending conflict-of-interest legislation that would deter banker directorships, Brandeis suggested a more fundamental solution—turning banks into public utilities. Comparing them to the country's railways, then an essential utility of commerce, he argued that banks should be treated not as private business but as a public service: "The dependence of commerce and industry upon bank deposits, as the common reservoir of quick capital is so complete, that deposit banking should be recognized as one of the businesses 'affected with a public interest.' "[76] Brandeis was drawing not only from a century of American history that supported his proposition but on like-minded policymakers like Senator Robert Owen, chairman of the Committee on Banking and Currency, who Brandeis quoted in his treatise: "My own judgment is that a bank is a public-utility institution and cannot be treated as a private affair, for the simple reason that the public is invited, under the safeguards of the government, to deposit its money with the bank, and the public has a right to have its interests safeguarded through organized authorities. The logic of this is beyond escape. All banks in the United States, public and private, should be treated as public-utility institutions, where they receive deposits."[77]

Brandeis also quoted his colleague Justice Holmes, who, on deciding an Oklahoma bank case, said, "We cannot say that the public interests to which we have adverted, and others, are not sufficient to warrant the State in taking the whole business of banking under its control."[78]

Brandeis proposed a clear and formal solution to the evolving bank-state contract: treating banks as public utilities. The proposal to treat banks like national utilities may seem like a radical change today, but it was not perceived as such during that era. In fact, it just extended the bank-state relationship that had begun with the First and Second Banks of the United States, the national banking network initiated by President Lincoln, and the creation of the Federal Reserve. Banks were, for the most part, heavily controlled by the state. It was not a huge leap to nationalize the industry. Still, the idea did not gain enough political support. Even Brandeis himself seemed to recognize that quasi-nationalization would not become a political reality and proposed a practical alternative, stating that the banks should focus on people rather than profits, which he called "democratic banking."[79]

THE NEW DEAL SOCIAL CONTRACT

Drawing in part on Brandeis's vision of banks as public utilities, President Franklin D. Roosevelt seized on the calamity of the Great Depression to make explicit the existing social contract with banks. Roosevelt, much like his predecessors Thomas Jefferson and Andrew Jackson, viewed a large and powerful banking industry as a threat to the democracy. He also believed that it was the government's role to limit the excesses of the banking sector, and he crafted banking policy, as other presidents had before him, to achieve his political objectives. He fought effectively to limit the power of "a small minority of business men and financiers" by enacting wide-reaching activity restrictions and antitrust rules. Roosevelt and key legislators like Carter Glass and Henry Steagall (of the Glass-Steagall Act) also passed reforms to prevent destructive bank runs and to separate riskier investment banking activity from deposit-taking and lending. The federal government would provide a banking safety net, or deposit insurance, contingent on federal oversight and certain restrictions.

The bargain that was struck allowed unit banks to survive, even though most of the bank failures of the time were due to their concentrated investments and general instability. Unit banks across the country whose assets and liabilities were linked to local economies were unable to survive when crop failures devastated those communities. Branch banking could have prevented some of those economic problems, but the rural farmers and unit-banking advocates still enjoyed political popularity. Unfazed by the largest banks' opposition to his proposed reforms, Roosevelt used the public's anger at the banks and the unit bankers' support to catalyze the legislature to pass these measures.[80]

In President Roosevelt's famous inauguration speech, he justified this broad-reaching legislation. When he told the public that "the only thing we have to fear is fear itself," he was addressing the irrational bank runs that turned the tough economic times into an unprecedented banking crisis. He acknowledged the people's suffering and placed blame directly at the foot of the bankers:

> The rulers of the exchange of mankind's goods have failed, through their own stubbornness and their own incompetence, have admitted their failure, and abdicated. Practices of the unscrupulous money changers stand indicted in the court of public opinion, rejected by the hearts and minds of men. . . . Stripped of the lure of profit by which to induce our people to follow their false leadership, they have resorted to exhortations, pleading tearfully for restored confidence. They know only the rules of a generation of self-seekers. They have no vision, and when there is no vision the people perish. The money changers have fled from their high seats in the temple of our civilization. We may now restore that temple to the ancient truths. The measure of the restoration lies in the extent to which we apply *social values more noble than mere monetary profit.*[81]

Roosevelt continued by proposing the "supervision of all banking and credits and investments." He insisted that the "future of *essential democracy*" depended on getting these reforms right. "The people of the United States," he said, have a "mandate," and they require "direct, vigorous action." In fighting the banks, Roosevelt claimed he was acting as an "instrument of [the people's] wishes." The purpose of the New Deal–era reforms was not to achieve efficient banking; it was to protect the democracy.

The long-lasting and comprehensive reforms of the era included deposit insurance, a continuation of unit banking, and federal laws on activity restrictions. These rules imposed a separation of traditional banking activities, such as lending and deposit-taking, from commercial activities, such as securities underwriting and brokering. The Glass-Steagall Act, the pillar of the New Deal banking reforms, thus entrenched the doctrine of "separation of banking and commerce" in U.S. banking regulation.[82] The act also contained interest rate limits—the amount a bank could offer for deposits—intended to deter competition among banks. Reduced competition, it was believed, would lead to a more dispersed banking sector and more credit availability.

These reforms were a response to the recent banking crisis, but they also revealed a Jeffersonian and Brandeisian disdain for concentrated bank power. Although they were intended to make banks safer, they were also meant to limit banks' market reach and power. A few policymakers were convinced that too much bank power and concentration caused the Great Depression, although the conclusion has since been contested.[83] Brandeis, Roosevelt, and Carter Glass—much like their Populist predecessors—saw bank power as one of the great social problems of the day. These forces, they said, would create inequalities anathema to vibrant democracies and would amass too much political power in powerful factions—or "fat cat" bankers. A decade later, Frank Capra's *It's a Wonderful Life* captured the disdain and fear many felt toward the powerful Potters of the banking world.

George Bailey's fictional bank represents the second part of the New Deal for banks that is often overlooked. In his inauguration speech, Roosevelt alluded to "social values more noble than merely monetary profit." He took up the charge by aggressively enlisting specific banking charters and public programs. Roosevelt's primary goal was homeownership, which he supported through various federal programs and subsidies.[84] Congress established the Federal Home Loan Bank System in 1932 to "maintain and promote homeownership in the United States."[85] The National Housing Act was also created to provide federal funds to support savings and loan associations specifically charged with financing home purchases.[86] In addition, the Federal National Mortgage Association (Fannie Mae) was chartered as a government organization to aid in the underwriting of home mortgages to enable more of the public to own homes.[87]

Roosevelt's secondary goal was to increase access to consumer credit. He brought the people-over-profit models of the building and loan and the credit union into the banking fold. Although these institutions predated Roosevelt's reforms, the New Deal solidified their place in the national economy and gave them a formal charge backed by governmental support—both fiscal and legislative. Support without which they would not have thrived as they did.

The goal of homeownership, at least for the middle class, was a resounding success. The mortgage innovations and government programs introduced during the 1930s enabled the majority of the population to own homes, which led to economic stability and increased personal wealth. However, these progressive reforms also initiated a century of devastating race inequality. The federal mortgage subsidies and the agencies created to facilitate mortgage lending practiced racially discriminatory redlining. The Federal Home Loan Bank Board commissioned the creation of "residential security maps" for over two hundred cities, intended to determine which areas were safe enough to provide mortgage lending. Most minority neighborhoods were deemed ineligible for mortgage financing.[88]

These artificial borders created an impervious red line around the minority-populated neighborhoods and blocked the new, cheap credit from passing through to help those within build wealth. Most suburban homes had racial covenants that prohibited their sale to nonwhites, leaving nonwhites completely cut off from the federal subsidies. Both the private and public sectors used these maps for years and prevented minorities from benefiting from the subsidized mortgage loans used to grow the capital and wealth of the lower and middle classes. Redlining not only blocked the flow of beneficial credit to nonwhites, but it also led to the deterioration of many inner-city neighborhoods. The eventual downturn that "white flight" created in these urban areas also resulted in "bank flight" as private business followed the white customers out.

The social contract forged during the Great Depression stabilized U.S. banking for several decades. For fifty years, the banking sector experienced measured growth and success while the rest of the economy generally thrived. This growth and stability coincided with exceptional international economic growth. As Thomas Piketty explains in *Capital in the Twenty-First Century,* the time between the Great Depression and the 1970s marked a unique period in world history of relative equalities of wealth and remarkable economic growth.[89] Surely, sustained economic growth contributed to a stable and successful banking system. And so did the federal deposit insurance fund, which succeeded in finally ending the confidence-destroying runs that had historically wreaked havoc on banks. Ironically, deposit insurance and some of the other banking reforms, which were meant to control and limit bank power, actually sowed the seeds that would lead to increased government support of a large banking sector and a lopsided bank-government contract. At the time, deposit insurance represented just one side of the social contract in which the federal government imposed a framework of controls intended to minimize the moral hazard effects of such insurance and to protect the insurance fund from losses. Banks operated conservatively and bank regulators, unchallenged, enforced the Glass-Steagall Act and other New Deal regulatory mandates.

During this time, the regulatory goal of bank stability and the policy goal of reducing bank size and influence motivated banking regulation. Accordingly, the Bank Holding Company Act (BHCA) of 1956 would be added to the New Deal measures to limit bank size and power. The BHCA was created in response to a commercial company's (Transamerica) purchase of Bank of America, which would have resulted in the largest bank/business combination at the time. Although the proposed merger did not cause bank safety concerns, it posed a threat to small community banks across the country. Having a large company own a large bank made the policymakers of the day uncomfortable. As such, Congress responded forcefully. The BHCA prohibited any commercial nonbank company from controlling a bank. The act, although anticompetitive and even inefficient, was a follow-through of Brandeis and Roosevelt's desire to keep banks from getting too powerful. The act reinforced the long-held policy of the government stepping in to halt the natural movement of banks toward conglomeration. These hard-line rules stifled financial innovation and banking efficiency, but that was a tradeoff policymakers were willing to make to protect community banks and the public from too much bank power. Because the economy was booming, neither the government nor the banking industry agitated for a change of policy. That is, until the banking world was transformed in the 1970s.

CIVIL RIGHTS AND THE SOCIAL CONTRACT FOR EQUALITY

The social contract initiated during the Great Depression, whereby the federal government enlisted banks to further policy goals, was amended during the civil rights era to achieve the state's goals of racial equality. The civil-rights-era reforms added to this public-protecting conception of the government/banking relationship by specifying that the social contract must protect *all* members of the public, not just some. In keeping with the goal of ensuring benefits to *the public*—as opposed to only some of its favored members—a new set of laws emerged, which increased access to credit by eliminating discrimination in lending and banking services. In fact, Martin Luther King Jr. referred to these demands in the language of credit and banking in his "I Have a Dream" speech: "In a sense we've come to our nation's capital to cash a check. When the architects of our republic wrote the magnificent words of the Constitution and the Declaration of Independence, they were signing a promissory note to which every American was to fall heir. This note was a promise that all men, yes, black men as well as white men, would be guaranteed the 'unalienable Rights' of 'Life, Liberty and the pursuit of Happiness.' It is obvious today that America has defaulted on this promissory note, insofar as her citizens of color are concerned. Instead of honoring this sacred obligation, America has given the Negro people a bad check, a check which has come back marked 'insufficient funds.'"[90]

Though Dr. King spoke figuratively, there was an ugly reality of credit discrimination that had lasted for years. The government responded in part, passing over twenty civil rights reforms between 1968 and 1988 that declared and implemented citizens' "right" to bank without discrimination.[91] The largest and most important were the Fair Housing Act of 1968, the Equal Credit Opportunity Act of 1974, the Home Mortgage Disclosure Act of 1975, and the Community Reinvestment Act of 1977 (CRA). The civil rights reforms addressed the wrongs, such as redlining, that federal programs had started in the 1930s by prohibiting banks from discriminating against customers or neighborhoods. These reforms focused on removing barriers and expanding access to credit for people of color as well as for low-income communities. The imposition of normative values on banks was premised on the importance of banking services to all communities.

These reforms reflected both an extension of the civil rights legislation of the era and a reaction to market conditions. As the banking sector suffered competition from the capital markets in the 1970s and 1980s, banks increasingly shed lower-income and minority customers and closed branches in low-income neighborhoods in order to cut costs—a rebirth of redlining, but this time, not as obviously discriminatory. The "white flight" started in the 1930s increased in the 1970s and 1980s as many more banks abandoned these areas for those more profitable.[92] Businesses left, people lost jobs, banks continued to close, and crime increased, accelerating the downward spiral. Many of these communities have yet to recover from the exodus of businesses caused by the bank departures during that era.

If access to credit enables people to escape poverty, discriminatory barriers to credit were cutting off a portion of the population from upward mobility. The CRA, for example, explicitly mandated banks to increase lending in these communities. When introducing the Senate bill that would become the CRA, Senator William Proxmire, chairman of the Senate Committee on Banking, Housing, and Urban Affairs, commented that the bill was based on a few "widely shared assumptions," including that "a public charter conveys numerous economic benefits and in return it is legitimate for public policy and regulatory practice to require some public purpose."[93] Later, the chairman "compared a bank charter to a franchise to serve local convenience and needs and suggested that it is fair for the public to ask something in return." Like the early founders and the New Deal reformers, Proxmire recognized that government support of banks meant that they had public-serving duties and that banking legislation could be used to achieve important policy goals.[94]

The specific mandate that banking should be free of discrimination persists today. The Department of Justice (DOJ) recently brought charges and eventually, settled several cases against banks for discriminating against minority borrowers.[95] The DOJ used the controversial theory of "disparate impact," which can establish a violation of a law even without evidence of intentional discrimination. The DOJ only needed to show that minorities were statistically worse off: for example, that banks sold blacks mortgages that were inferior to those of whites with similar economic backgrounds. The Consumer Financial Protection

Bureau has also embraced the theory: "We cannot afford to tolerate practices, intentional or not, that unlawfully price out or cut off segments of the population from the credit markets."[96] The use of disparate impact analysis in the lending context sent shockwaves through the banking world. Many claim that disparate impact theory allows the government to punish banks without showing that they were, in fact, discriminating. The government defends its use by saying that discrimination in lending is hard to prove without a smoking gun. Lending decisions are subjective, the process is opaque, and discrimination is usually subtle and sometimes subconscious.[97]

Both the laws and the enforcement actions make clear a central point about banking. Just as Hamilton, Madison, Jefferson, Jackson, Brandeis, and Roosevelt understood, bank credit is not like any other market. Access to credit means economic advancement, just as limits on credit mean economic stagnation.

Although no recognized "right to credit" exists, as some would propose,[98] there is a right to credit without illegal discrimination. The state, as a guarantor of other rights, protects the right to credit without discrimination by imposing certain rules on banks and punishments if discrimination is found. This is at the core of the civil rights social contract between states and banks. A democratic state interested in preserving its citizens' rights cannot tolerate inequality of credit in a banking system that the state enables. Thus, Jefferson's fears that concentrated banking power would exclude farmers is based on the same principle that led the civil rights movement to impose a slew of laws to stop discrimination against minorities and inner-city residents.

THE BANKING TRANSFORMATION AND DEREGULATION

Beginning in the late 1970s and 1980s, the banking sector started facing an identity crisis. After years of operating a safe and boring model dictated by the regulations imposed during the New Deal, the model began to fall apart. Unit banking and the restrictions and prohibitions of the fifty years following the Great Depression had allowed banks to profit modestly by keeping their balance sheets focused on deposits and loans. But suddenly, technological advances, financial innovation, capital markets, and commercial paper markets started to offer safe and enticing alternatives to banks. Banks started hemorrhaging customers, a process called *disintermediation*, which means cutting out the middleman. Deposits went directly to high-yield markets and sidestepped highly regulated banks.[99] Concerns about banks' waning profitability led to growing pressure on the government to deregulate banks and allow them to compete more freely with other institutions. For example, Glass-Steagall's Regulation Q prohibited banks from paying interest on deposits in order to limit competition between banks for deposit funds—and so banks started offering toasters and umbrellas instead. The creation of interest-paying money-market accounts, which by the 1980s were just as liquid and safe as a demand deposit, threatened to put an end to traditional banks. Banks wanted Regulation Q abolished and it was—along with many other activity restrictions that were increasingly mismatched to modern banking.

The New Deal social contract proved to be outdated for the demands, speed, size, and complexity of modern finance. Slowly, banks and policymakers chipped away at the walls erected during the New Deal. The banking world had changed and the old rules were suffocating banks in new markets—the social contract needed to be revised. Instead of a holistic revision of the social contract, however, a patchwork of reactionary legislation ensued that chipped away at the New Deal–era rules without replacing them with modernized rules that stayed true to their aim. Congress passed seven acts over a span of two decades, which together, effectively deregulated the banking industry so that banks could compete with other credit and investment options. Among other things, these acts deregulated deposit interest rates, dismantled geographic restraints on bank expansion, repealed Glass-Steagall barriers between banking and securities activities, and allowed the formation of large financial institutions. The slow demise of the Glass-Steagall Act brought with it more powerful and more profitable banks. But that was the point. Regulators were admittedly trying to do anything in their power to make banks profitable again, even if it meant allowing concentrations of power or conglomeration.

To be clear, the government's deregulation of banking was a response to and not the cause of the banking transformation. Technology and market changes came first, and banks could not survive without a significant alteration of the New Deal rules and barriers. Something had to change, but deregulation was by no means the only option. The era also coincided with a conservative political revival in America and Europe and a deregulatory philosophy in other sectors. Ronald Reagan wanted to get the government off the people's backs, and the banking sector needed exactly that. But deregulation was not just about Ronald Reagan. A decade later, Bill Clinton finished what Reagan had started. Additionally, other changes occurred in the United States that explain the ideological transformations of the time, such as a historic rise of income and wealth disparity and an economic boom.

In the banking sector, deregulation concentrated not just on removing restrictions but was coupled with an underlying shift in thinking. The government's focus changed from the paramount objective of keeping banks small, powerless, and safe to ensuring that banks stayed profitable and efficient. Banks, in turn, claimed that they were just like other corporations and should be treated as such—meaning, of course, that the government should make little to no demands of them. During this adjustment, the government-bank philosophy changed fundamentally. In addition to lifting onerous and outdated restrictions, the government also abandoned previous banking policy goals, such as avoiding concentrations of power and favoring localism. Shifting the focus to the short-term maximization of revenues and profits allowed banks to engage in risky behavior that was immediately profitable but systemically destabilizing in the long run. The risky products and large banks that are endemic to our current financial system were initiated during this important transformation. To be clear, deregulation was not viewed as supplanting or abrogating safety and soundness concerns. Quite the opposite—regulators felt that in order to protect bank safety, they needed to assure their profitability. In fact, profitability became of such paramount concern that many regulators today view safety and soundness as synonymous with profitability.[100] Indeed, profitability is necessary to a safe banking system, but it is not sufficient.[101] Regulators saved banks by allowing them to become profitable and compete with nonbanks, but the focus on profitability did not shift once it became apparent that profitability is not always synonymous with safety.

Perhaps most importantly, banks fought the idea that they had any responsibilities to the public—or at least any that would threaten their bottom line. They sought to become purely "market" entities instead of extensions of the government. The revision of the social contract did not come about unintentionally. This was not a back-room lobbying deal—the shift happened in broad daylight. Government officials promised fewer rules, fewer duties, and more freedom. Regulators from the Office of Thrift Supervision (OTS) even took a photograph in which they held large scissors next to a stack of papers and red tape—one legislator brought out a chainsaw to show he was serious about letting banks loose.

There was ongoing debate among banks, politicians, and scholars about what it meant to be a bank in the modern world. Many continued to advocate that banks were distinct from other corporate entities because of their dependence on the government. Amidst the debate, Gerald Corrigan, president of the Federal Reserve Bank of New York, addressed this question head-on in a 1982 essay titled "Are Banks Special?" The fact that the question needed to be asked reveals how significantly the world of banking had changed in the prior decade. Corrigan answered the question in the affirmative and stated that:

> Banks and bank regulators have long since recognized the importance of banks acting in ways that preserve public confidence. . . . Deposit insurance and direct access to the lender of last resort are uniquely available to banks to reinforce that public confidence. Indeed, deposit insurance and access to the lender of last resort constitute a public safety net under the deposit taking function of banks. The presence of this public safety net reflects a long-standing consensus that banking functions are essential to a healthy economy. However the presence of the public safety net uniquely available to a particular class of institutions also implies that those institutions have *unique public responsibilities* and may therefore be subject to implicit codes of conduct or explicit regulations that do not fall on other institutions.[102]

Corrigan's view was in line with the history of banking, but it was out of sync in the 1980s, and he lost this ideological battle. A study released by the Federal Deposit Insurance Corporation (FDIC) titled "Mandate for Change: Restructuring the Banking Industry" illustrates the logic of the winning argument. The FDIC proposed that the Glass-Steagall restrictions and the BHCA "be abolished" in order to allow banks the "freedom to operate in the marketplace without undue regulatory influence."[103] And the FDIC responded to the "specialness" of banks due to government support by indicating that FDIC insurance would be priced more "efficiently" as banks became "subjected to greater market discipline through the refining of failure-resolution policies." In other words, FDIC insurance was only a "subsidy" if it was underpriced, and therefore, it was possible to find an accurate market price for this government support. The philosophy also relied on "market discipline" to supplant regulatory controls. The argument was that banks would not be incentivized to take risks because if they did, the market would punish them, and the FDIC would facilitate their failure, thus eliminating any concerns about moral hazard. Obviously, this was not the case twenty years later when government bailouts abruptly cut off market discipline. In fact, market discipline for banks, if it exists at all, is not robust because of the moral hazard introduced by deposit insurance.

And what of the fears of concentrated power that so consumed Jefferson, Brandeis, and Roosevelt? The FDIC was not too worried: "There will [not] be fewer banks or less competition in any given market. . . . While concentrations of political power may be undesirable, it is not clear that large organizations or highly concentrated industries are able to wield too much influence over government. In any case, the degree of concentration in banking is presently far below that of many other industries in which there is no apparent excess of political influence."

We could look back on these naïve pronouncements with amusement if the results of this logic had not ended so painfully—an era of outsized private profits ended abruptly with enormous public costs. The FDIC compared concentrated banks to other equally concentrated industries and claimed that because excessive political influence did not pose a problem in those industries, it should not cause worry in the banking industry.[104] Such was the general consensus of the time: banks should operate like other industries.

But this new theory flew in the face of history and reality. Jefferson and Brandeis were not worried about any and all concentrated industries. They were concerned about banks because a monopoly or an oligarchy is uniquely problematic when it controls the nation's money and credit supply. The idea that banks would be able to operate with market discipline just like any other industry also turned out to be a fantasy. As we saw, the government would not, or could not, allow banks to suffer market discipline or failure because banks, indeed, are special.

In the process of deregulation, several bedrock principles of banking policy were sidelined. First, the idea that banks had unique public responsibilities was rejected. Banks were relieved not only of public-*serving* functions, but even laws *protecting* consumers from harmful bank products were weakened by the regulators tasked with their enforcement. Any regulations deemed expensive or hindering bank competition were rolled back. For example, the two regulators of the national banks, the Office of the Comptroller of the Currency (OCC) and the OTS, announced that national banks did not have to follow state consumer-protection laws—or state laws designed to protect their citizens from predatory financial practices. This doctrine, "federal preemption of state law," appears in other sectors as well, but it usually means that a federal rule or point takes precedent over, or *preempts,* the state laws. Here, the state laws were "preempted" by exactly zero consumer-protecting federal laws.[105] These regulators, the agencies responsible for protecting the public from bank excess, made it clear that their primary objective was to make sure their banks were profitable.[106] This was exactly the sort of regulatory misconduct the new consumer-protection agency was meant to eliminate.[107]

In fact, a sort of double-speak entered into interpreting banking legislation, which had for years required regulators to consider the "public benefit" in their decisions. Reflecting the historical understanding that banks serve the public, most laws affecting banks had a requirement written into them that bank supervisors deciding on bank-related issues should only allow an action if it benefits the public. However, the question of whether a certain bank action would *benefit the public* morphed into an inquiry about *bank profitability.* For example, the Federal Reserve approved another case because of the public benefit of "[providing] Applicant greater resources for expansion and greater flexibility for diversification of business activities . . . [which would] allow Applicant to *continue to compete effectively* with other large Rhode Island financial organizations."[108] Bank "efficiency" and "profits" slowly became the proxy for "public benefit."

Additionally, the banks themselves underwent a coinciding cultural shift from acting as caretakers or fiduciaries for their customers to exploiting them. A former Goldman Sachs executive director explained this new culture that was rewarded, not by protecting customers, but by making money off of their ignorance. Bankers referred to clients as "muppets" and talked openly about "ripping the face off" clients or "hunting elephants."[109] Jim Wells, who had worked for Citibank and Hongkong Bank USA, wrote in *American Banker,* the trade magazine for the country's banks, about the misbehavior of the industry that was permitted by regulators: "As a former banker, I watched in amazement and disgust as the country's largest banks morphed from trusted fiduciaries of consumer financial assets to unrepentant predators of consumer financial assets in just a few decades . . . [and] as federal regulatory agencies morphed from policing the condition and conduct of the nation's financial institutions to defending abusive bank practices from state consumer protection laws."[110]

Even after the bailouts, the financial sector returned to its precrisis disregard for serving the public interest.[111] Taxpayer bailouts in hand, tone-deaf Wall Street firms turned around and paid hefty bonuses to the very same employees who had led the country off a cliff and spent decades abusing their clients, the taxpayers. The public outcry over bonuses was met with policymakers claiming that their hands were tied and bankers unable to comprehend the public reaction. Defending the huge bonuses while at St. Paul's Cathedral in London in October 2009, a Goldman Sachs executive said: "The injunction of Jesus to love others as ourselves is a recognition of self-interest . . . . We have to tolerate the inequality as a way of achieving greater prosperity and opportunity for all."[112] The statement accurately summed up the state of public-mindedness on Wall Street: "If it's good for us, it must be good for everyone."

Fears of concentrated bank power evaporated. Regulators encouraged bank mergers and nationwide branching to make banks more efficient and competitive. "Between 1980 and 2000, the assets held by commercial banks, securities firms, and the securitization they created grew from 55 percent of GDP to 95 percent."[113] The result of a series of mergers and expansions was predictable—today, a handful of behemoth banks control most of the country's assets. For example, Bank of

America makes one-third of all business loans, Wells Fargo provides one-fourth of all mortgages, and Chase holds 12 percent of all of our collective cash.[114] The six largest banks hold 67 percent of all the assets in the financial system, up from 37 percent just five years ago. Just four of the largest banks (Bank of America, Citigroup, JPMorgan Chase, and Wells Fargo) control almost *50 percent of all bank assets.*[115] JPMorgan holds $2.4 trillion in assets—the size of England's economy. And they are just getting bigger. Five years after the crisis, the top banks were bigger and more profitable by every measure.[116] This expansion and growth changed not only the size but the nature of the industry. These megabanks became more profitable, took on more risks, and expanded into more markets.

Wall Street's economic dominance quickly spilled over into the political realm. The deregulatory ideology of the new financial oligarchy infiltrated the "Wall Street-Washington corridor" by means of campaign money and ideological capture. In the last two decades, no industry has contributed more to campaigns than the financial industry. Its campaign contributions went from 73 million in 1990 to 332 million in 2006.[117] This money flowed into the campaign coffers of those who would be influential in deregulating the industry. Phil Gramm, for example, of the Gramm-Leach-Bliley Act, raised more than twice his entire campaign budget from the securities industry.[118]

Banks were arguing on the one hand that they were too big to fail while simultaneously leveraging their size and political power to fight off any government regulations aimed at lowering their chances of failure. As Barney Frank put it: "All these years of deregulation . . . as these new financial instruments have grown have allowed them to take a large chunk of the economy hostage. And we have to pay ransom, like it or not."[119] The government paid ransom, and Wall Street was up and running in no time, returning to precrisis profits.[120]

This is not a new or surprising development. This is exactly the scenario that most worried the early leaders of the Republic and the framers of the Constitution, specifically, James Madison and Thomas Jefferson—a powerful political oligarchy with outsized influence in politics, to the detriment of the population. In 2009, Senator Richard Durbin said, "The banks—hard to believe in a time when we're facing a banking crisis that many of the banks created—are still the most powerful lobby on Capitol Hill. And they frankly own the place."[121] Senator Elizabeth Warren has also repeatedly voiced outrage at the coziness between Washington and Wall Street, repeating the phrase, "The game is rigged."[122] Demands are rising across the political spectrum, including from Joseph Stiglitz, Simon Johnson, Paul Krugman, Richard Fisher, and even the king of deregulation, Alan Greenspan, for breaking up the banks.[123] We cannot have a banking system that is so large and powerful that it relies on government bailouts. Their size leads to bailouts, and the promise of bailouts in turn leads to more risk-taking, a cycle some have called a "doom loop."[124]

If the deep-seated fears of concentrated bank power had not been pacified over the last several decades, they would surely have intensified during the recent government bailout of the banking industry. As it turned out, the banks and bankers had become so powerful that many efforts to regulate the industry after the bailouts were thwarted. When President Obama proposed a bill in Congress that allowed judges to modify home mortgages so borrowers could avoid foreclosure, the banks swiftly killed the bill and refused to even negotiate with senators over some of its provisions.[125] The banking sector hired more lobbyists and gained unprecedented access to Washington insiders, leading a senior Obama advisor to remark, "You would hope after American taxpayers stepped in to save these companies from a disaster of their own making they would be deploying their army of lobbyists to strengthen and not thwart financial reform."[126] According to a congressional staffer, the path to reform looked like "an orchestrated, well-funded effort by banks to manipulate our legislation and leave no fingerprints."[127] Banks fought most attempts at major banking reform, arguing that any reforms that lowered bank profits would lead to a longer crisis and recovery period.

The political influence was not gained just through donations. An ideological capture of key policymakers—Larry Summers, Robert Rubin, Alan Greenspan, Timothy Geithner, Henry Paulson, and others—who had spent their careers marinating in the industry, working in "captured" regulatory agencies, or captivated by extreme *laissez-faire* ideology, also took place during this era. Agencies also went along with or even pushed deregulation. The OCC and the OTS, agencies funded by their regulated entities (their customers), courted them through lax regulations.

The executive branch was also sold on the vision of finance free from state control. Each president, from Reagan to Obama, operated with a similar view about the dangers of overregulation. Each also received significant funds from Wall Street.

Agency capture is perhaps one of the most significant aspects of this political story. Because of the increased power and size of these firms, government regulators have become impotent against them—that is, those who have continued to fight. The Federal Reserve Bank of New York (FRBNY), one of the most sophisticated of all the banking regulators and the one tasked with overseeing the largest Wall Street firms, illustrates how capture works. After the financial crisis, Columbia Business School professor David Beim conducted a report of the FRBNY's process of regulation. The report aimed to identify the faulty processes and practices that may have resulted in regulators missing the growing problems in the financial sector. What he found surprised him. The regulators knew of the situation, but because of the culture of the firms, they did not feel comfortable raising issues about the firms without their superiors' blessings.[128] Senior regulators even admitted to having witnessed "the capture set in."[129] This culture resulted in inaction in the face of mounting risks. In September 2014, a former employee of the FRBNY who was one of Goldman Sachs' designated regulators released secret recordings of her time regulating the large firm. The tapes revealed what most banking experts suspected for years—Goldman Sachs, not its regulator, called the shots. The FRBNY regulators stationed at Goldman Sachs, many of whom would end up working at the investment bank, cowered at meetings with bankers where it should have been their role to press. When former employee Carmen Segarra did push, she was fired for having "sharp elbows" and "breaking eggs." Segarra explained that "they were all sort of afraid of Goldman, and I think they were a little bit confused as to who they were working for. What I was sort of seeing and experiencing was this level of deference to the banks—this level of fear, and just not really showing a lot of interest in putting two and two together."

Finally, the government started to allow banks to regulate their own risks with unquestioning faith in market discipline. Instead of telling banks where they could operate and what they could do, they trusted in the market to appropriately punish harmful behavior. The separation of banking and commerce gave way to more "competitive" and "efficient" structures that increased the size and power of banks. Federal Reserve governor Daniel Tarullo summarized the change in his 2009 speech: "The regulatory system accommodated the growth of capital market alternatives to traditional financing by relaxing many restrictions on the type and geographic scope of bank activities, and virtually all restrictions on affiliations between banks and non-bank financial firms. The result was a financial services industry dominated by one set of very large financial holding companies centered on a large commercial bank and another set of very large financial institutions not subject to prudential regulation."[130]

As the "Thou Shalt Nots" of Glass-Steagall were replaced with a more fluid system that depended on firms' internal models of risk weighing, risks also increased.[131] For several decades, banks became very profitable, and the financial world grew exponentially as barriers disappeared. Even so, bank failures started to occur much more often during the deregulatory era. Empirical researchers have found that "the probability of a banking crisis occurring was similar during 1880–1913 and 1973–97 . . . and essentially zero during 1945–71."[132] The deregulatory era culminated in the financial crisis of 2008, proving most of the deregulatory era's assumptions wrong.

It was inevitable that in an era of deregulated banks, large failures would occur. What was surprising was that the market rules would only be applied when banks were making profits and not when they ultimately failed. Instead of allowing the market to enforce its discipline and allow banks to fail, as the repudiation of the social contract dictated, the government stepped in and bailed out the banking industry.[133] As the 2008 financial crisis deepened, policymakers faced a choice: they could let free markets take their course and allow a wide-scale failure of the financial sector (which was what was envisioned by the preceding era of deregulation), or they could intervene in the private markets. They chose to intervene in a way that revealed "the lasting influence and power of the Wall Street ideology—that big, private, lightly regulated financial institutions are good for America."[134] In other words, instead of using the crisis to effect real reform in banking like Roosevelt did, these policymakers focused myopically on maintaining bank profitability without requiring anything in return—"the government bent over backward to make the deal attractive for the banks, charging *below-market interest* and eschewing any significant ownership—so shareholders, not taxpayers, would benefit when the banks recovered."[135] Simon Johnson and James Kwak articulated the incongruity of it all: "Never before had so much taxpayer money been dedicated to save an industry from the consequences of its own mistakes. In the ultimate irony, it went to an industry that had insisted for decades that it had no use for the government and would be better off regulating itself—and it was overseen by a group of policymakers who *agreed* that governments should play little role in the financial sector."[136]

Ultimately, this period of transition resulted in an asymmetrical erosion of the social contract with banks. The revisions abrogated many of the safety and soundness regulations and the public-serving obligations imposed on banks but did not take away the government safety nets, such as FDIC insurance and access to the Federal Reserve discount window. To be fair, some bankers and supporters of deregulation advocated for a complete free market model and an imposition of market discipline without any government support. However, policymakers, wary of the bank failures so common prior to FDIC insurance, continued to support government insurance. Thus, the banks and the state forged a lopsided arrangement that continued until it was fully tested in 2008.

The pivotal transition in U.S. banking that occurred over the last several decades was, in effect, an abandonment of both the conceptual vision of banks as inextricably bound to the state and the practical emphasis on safe and public-protecting approaches to banking regulation that took hold after the Great Depression. Rather, it reflected a foundational shift from both the practical and political understanding of banking that has run through our nation's history. The bank deregulation that took hold in the 1980s was not just an experiment in the government's ongoing effort to decide what kind of banking system best meets the people's needs. During this era, bankers agitated to be relieved of rigid rules and restrictions. They sought to be treated more like ordinary corporations and less like public utilities. They got what they wanted, for the most part, as many century-old restrictions on operations were lifted. To be sure, this program of deregulation might have been driven by a public-regarding effort to help society as a whole by increasing bank competitiveness, fostering the development of new bank products, generating expanded capital formation, and increasing economic efficiency. But in the end, it wasn't. Policymakers lost their way because they lost sight of the special social contract that must exist with banks.

3

Banks with a Soul

Just remember this, Mr. Potter, that this rabble you're talking about . . . they do most of the working and paying and living and dying in this community. Well, is it too much to have them work and pay and live and die in a couple of decent rooms and a bath?

—GEORGE BAILEY, IN DIRECTOR FRANK CAPRA'S 1946 FILM, *IT'S A WONDERFUL LIFE*

Until the 1900s, most commercial banks serviced the wealthy. The poor and middle class (before such terms even existed) put their savings under their mattresses and, should they need credit, were left to the mercy of loan sharks. Eventually, alternative movements began to fill the void, and in time, the state blessed each. Banks with specific missions to help the poor overcame economic obstacles to challenge and ultimately reject the profit-motivated culture of mainstream banks.[1] They were movements aimed at wage-workers, small farmers, and the unbanked—and their innovative structures would revolutionize the banking sector. But over time, and largely because of deregulation, these missions changed. Today, those banks once established for the purpose of helping the lower classes are practically indistinguishable from mainstream banks. It is one of the biggest losses of deregulation, and one that is universally ignored—the United States has lost its banks with souls.

CREDIT UNIONS

The credit union was based on the principle of cooperative credit: a group of people would pool their funds and lend them to group members on a rotation or based on need. This is essentially how traditional banks operated—pooling a community's deposits and lending them out to the same community—but the traditional bank had an owner or shareholders making a profit from the interest paid on loans. Credit unions cut out the owners and the profits in order to serve the poor. Their motto was "Banks of the people, by the people, and for the people."[2]

These cooperative credit unions started as a way to help European farmers purchase land after the breakdown of feudalism. In 1864, Friedrich Wilhelm Raiffeisen created the first one in Germany. As mayor of several agricultural towns, Raiffeisen wanted to help the farmers in his region. At the time, the only mortgage credit available to farmers came from high-rate moneylenders who foreclosed on properties after one missed payment and loan sharks who lent at very high rates.[3] Raiffeisen first started a philanthropic banking organization to aid farmers, but after several donors demanded larger profits, he decided that a self-help cooperative would be the ideal structure to provide fair credit. The distinguishing feature of the "Raiffeisen banks," or "credit unions," included being mutually owned, managed by volunteers, and distributing minimal profits. The credit union caught hold. By 1913, over twenty-five thousand cooperative societies existed in Germany. The idea began to spread across Europe and eventually crossed the Atlantic.

The buzz about credit unions started to appear in northeastern newspapers and public dialogue in the late 1800s. In 1869, Henry Villard, writing for the *New York Times,* reported: "Nothing in the various trials of cooperation for the working classes throughout the world has been so successful." Villard claimed that the credit union could solve "the great struggle which is agitating the civilized world between labor and capital" and the concentration of capital in the hands of large capitalists.[4] Though the United States never had a feudal system like Europe, the poor could only access credit through loan sharks and pawnshops that offered interest rates at up to 50 percent of the value of the loan. Many decried the injustices of the system as "legalized robbery."[5] Early credit union advocates thus aimed to bring "banking facilities to all classes—to the poor man as well as the rich man, to the workingman and the farmer as well as the manufacturer and capitalist."[6]

In 1900, Alphonse Desjardins organized the first credit union in North America in Levis, Canada. Desjardins was frustrated by the lack of banking options for wage-earners in Canada and the high-rate lenders that dominated the market. As a journalist, he had been particularly moved by testimony he had heard while reporting on parliamentary hearings of a low-income worker who had been charged 1200 percent interest on a small loan.[7] Desjardins began studying possible remedies to this growing problem and ran across a mention of the European credit union movement. He decided to start a cooperative, modeled after the German Raiffeisen credit unions, from his own home. He handled all the transactions himself and did not pay himself a salary. Membership was open to anyone in the community who was determined to be in "good standing," and a committee of members decided which loans to make based on a person's character and record of financial stability.[8] Desjardins focused on small loans, which came from members' deposits. During its first six years, the credit union made $200,000 in loans, with zero defaults, and actually earned modest profits, which it distributed to members as dividends. The close group dynamic was the reason behind the low default rate. With such a low default rate, the credit union didn't need to charge high interest and thus, could successfully lend to the poor.[9]

The credit union movement migrated to the United States a few years later. And its father would be Edward Albert Filene, the son of a Jewish immigrant and the owner of Filene's department store. Filene was a fair and conscientious employer as well as a wealthy and curious philanthropist. In 1907, he traveled around the world and was shocked by the poverty he witnessed in India and the Philippines. His travels convinced him that these poor villagers needed adequate credit and the ability to own land. He was appalled that they had to borrow money at very high interest just to pay for special occasions, such as weddings.[10] He admired the agricultural cooperative banks developed by the British as the villagers' one true hope, and upon his return to the United States, discussed his experience with President Theodore Roosevelt.[11]

Nothing came of it until Filene crossed paths with Pierce Jay, the bank commissioner for Massachusetts. Jay, the son of the first Supreme Court chief justice, John Jay, had already started to study the credit union movement in Europe and even invited Desjardins to Boston. Jay began advocating credit unions and convincing the legislature that they were necessary despite the fact that building and loan organizations already existed in the state. He argued that there were many people "who have neither real estate nor shares as security [who] undoubtedly have legitimate need for loans." He saw a "demand for loans which [was] not being supplied by existing banking institutions." He recognized that borrowing was sometimes "improvident," but said that "there can be but little doubt that much of it is the borrowing that comes of necessity."[12] The legislature approved his bill, and Filene immediately jumped behind it. Testifying in support of the bill, Filene said: "As a large employer I have long felt that some provision should be made by which people of small means can, in case of necessity or distress, borrow at reasonable rates of interest and under thoroughly honest and fair conditions."[13]

The Massachusetts Credit Union Act of 1909, which would be the model for the subsequent Federal Credit Union Act, defined a credit union as "a cooperative association formed for the purpose of promoting thrift among its members."[14] The charter required that the credit unions be run democratically with one vote per member—regardless of how many shares that person owned. Volunteers would run the credit union with no compensation provided—not even for board members. Jay, wary of reputation-damaging failures, proceeded cautiously and conservatively.[15]

But eventually, the movement spread across the Northeast, starting in New York, where it gained the attention of two high-profile philanthropic organizations: the Russell Sage Foundation and the Provident Loan Society of New York. After meeting with Jay and Desjardins, the Russell Sage Foundation proposed that the New York legislature pass a credit union bill. Senator Franklin D. Roosevelt was responsive but wanted the credit unions to specialize in lending to farmers. Jay and the other philanthropists opposed limits that would have created purely agricultural credit unions and passed a general credit union bill. This question would resurface again.

The movement didn't have a robust start, but with state recognition and specialized charters, applications began to roll in.[16] During this time of expansion, credit unions' most important challenge was staying true to their mission of serving the poor by rejecting high profits while also staying viable enough to protect the savings of their members and retain state support. And because of political opposition from bankers and existing moneylenders, state support was not easily won.[17]

Credit unions were awkward institutions operating in the space between categories, but their leaders took advantage of this in-betweenness to gain broad support and overcome opposition by banks. They were philanthropic organizations but adamantly not charities. This fit nicely into the post–World War I ideology of self-reliance and "welfare capitalism" that appealed to the industrialists. Credit unions were also often linked with business for the benefit of employees. Their leaders framed them as being a boon for both labor and capital. "It is for the employer's interest as well as the employee's," said Filene, "because instead of having his workmen harassed by loan agents, he gets workmen, who if they have to borrow in some emergency, borrow among the men with whom they are working and who will help them get on their feet and keep steady."[18] Carving out this space allowed the credit union to gain the support of the wealthy industrialists—support that was needed to defeat the movement's political opponents.

Before 1920, the credit union movement had stalled, with only sixty-four branches nationwide. But now Filene had joined forces with Roy Bergengren, an evangelical believer in the mission of the credit union, and the new director of the Massachusetts credit union organization. Filene and Bergengren set off on a nationwide campaign to convince more states to pass credit union legislation, organize individual credit unions, and form a national association to promote the industry. Their message was that credit unions would promote self-help and teach "the principles of banking to a class of people in whose lives, heretofore, banking has meant less than nothing."[19] For its early advocates, the movement was bigger than just providing banking services to the poor. The credit unions were "valuable projects for the prevention of the business, economic and social evils that threaten our democracy."[20]

Credit unions were an ideological rejection of mainstream banking—a purposeful system of credit that favored the common good above profits, communities over institutions, and mutual control over hierarchy. The movement was a practical Populist response to the deep-seated antipathy toward concentrated power and control in banking that, by the 1900s, was one of the defining features of the United States. Bergengren built on the Populist rhetoric of the time when he described the credit union as "the schools for the masses" that would beget "financial democracy" or freedom from "the absolute control of those who . . . are using money solely for their own profit, without the requisite understanding that they have no right to use money except for the common good and social interest of all the people, and that the wholly selfish use of it will bring with it radical movements, revolution and war."[21] Bergengren was convinced that cooperatives were the way of the future and that "in the long run we cannot develop economic democracy on the principle of dog eat dog and the theory that the shrewdest, the most unscrupulous, the smartest of our number, should survive at the expense of all the rest of us." He denounced Fascism and Communism, claiming that a truly democratic economy could only be achieved through cooperatives and the "principle of human brotherhood."[22]

Bergengren and Filene disagreed about where the credit unions were most needed, with Bergengren advocating for the small farmers of the South who were "the foundation of our whole social and economic structure" and in "a desperate plight," but Filene favoring a broader focus.[23] The industry grew quickly during the 1920s because of its inclusivity. Credit unions also fit nicely into the booming 1920s economy. Growing prosperity meant that an increasing population of wage earners had more money to save and no place to put it because existing banks did not cater to small savers. Workers also needed small loans to buy cars, refrigerators, radios, and the other life-enhancing products that were suddenly accessible to them. The Great Depression also acted as a boon for the movement. The credit union was seen as a more stable institution because it failed at a much lower rate than banks.[24] Paralyzed by the risks of failure, the banks that survived the Great Depression had stopped lending, thereby halting the engines of the economy. Credit unions, their advocates claimed, could provide more credit faster. Credit unions also lowered the risks inherent in lending because they knew their borrowers. By providing an infusion of consumer credit, advocates claimed, credit unions would lead to a speedy economic recovery.[25]

Filene and Bergengren knew that for the movement to have any chance at spreading, it needed to be seen as legitimate and trustworthy. And they agreed that federal government support was the best way for any financial institution to achieve trust. Filene and Bergengren sought and eventually achieved that support, enabling the movement to survive and proliferate. The first federal government boost occurred when the U.S. Postal Service asked Bergengren to organize a credit union for its employees in 1923.[26] Also proposed, but ultimately rejected, was linking the postal savings system with the credit union movement—as many post office branches already operated credit unions.

(The relationship did solidify over time, leading to legislation that allowed federal post office buildings to house credit unions.)[27]

The second round of federal support came in 1932 when President Hoover signed a house bill, referred to as "the poor man's bill," to authorize credit unions in the District of Columbia. Filene and Bergengren sold the bill to President Hoover as a remedy to the problem of loan sharks. The suffering endured during the Great Depression had contributed to a Populist fervor that made cooperative banking a preferred alternative to profit-motivated commercial banks.[28]

But the major animating force legitimizing the credit union came when President Franklin D. Roosevelt, already familiar with the movement, included credit unions in his expansive New Deal reforms. Roosevelt said of the credit union: "I have sort of a hunch that we owe a duty to our fellow citizens not to violate the biblical injunction against usury."[29] He urged Congress to pass the Federal Credit Union Act (FCUA) in 1934 to address the "great national problem" of addressing the credit needs of the "poorer and working classes."[30] The FCUA facilitated the establishment of credit unions in all states to "make more available to people of small means credit for provident purposes through a national system of cooperative credit, thereby helping to stabilize the credit structure of the United States." Legislators emphasized the ability of credit unions to "enable the general public, which had been largely ignored by banks, to obtain credit at reasonable rates." Much like early state charters, the FCUA required that credit union members elect management, again with each member having only one vote. Furthermore, membership in a credit union was "limited to groups having a common bond of occupation, or association, or to groups within a well-defined neighborhood, community, or rural district."[31]

The credit union movement stood apart from the general banking industry in several important ways. First, as neither a bank nor a charity, confusion existed as to what government agency should oversee it. Its initial administering agency was to be the Farm Credit Administration, as opposed to a financial regulator, a reflection of the problem credit unions were anticipated to remedy. However, it became clear during the 1930s and the 1940s that credit unions flourished in urban, not rural, areas. In 1936, only about 5 percent of the 5,100 credit unions served farmers. Credit unions' mutual structures worked best with a stable stream of deposits and small loans, which is one reason why they were not the answer to farmers' problems. Farmers needed large loans, and their income came in all at once. By contrast, the credit union was perfectly suited to help low-income wage-earners, who would invest their paychecks and borrow when needed as an advance against future income.[32] In fact, the charter would become most popular for employees of large companies. Reflecting this reality, the industry was moved from the Farm Credit Administration to the Federal Deposit Insurance Corporation (FDIC); then to the Federal Security Agency; and then to the Department of Health, Education and Welfare. Eventually, the credit union movement grew large enough to warrant its own administrative agency, the National Credit Union Administration, in 1970.

Second, credit unions were not included in the federal insurance scheme created for banks through the FDIC insurance fund. But credit unions knew that a federally backed insurance fund was essential to their survival, and so the industry created its own mutually supported private fund, the Credit Union National Association Mutual Insurance Society, in 1935. Credit unions across the country paid premiums into the fund, with much discussion and care given to preventing the fund from retaining any profits at the expense of credit union members.[33] In 1970, the formation of their new governing agency, the National Credit Union Share Insurance Fund, created a federal insurance scheme much like the FDIC, with the full faith and credit of the U.S. government.[34] To the public's mind, this insurance fund and the new agency legitimized the credit unions as safe alternatives to banks.

Third, the credit union enjoyed some relief from the activity restrictions placed on banks as a part of the New Deal–era legislation. For example, they were allowed to borrow and lend from other credit unions and were able to sell insurance to their members. Most importantly, they received federal government tax relief. Although initially subject to taxation just like other banking institutions, concern arose that subjecting credit unions to the same taxation as commercial banks would place "a disproportionate and excessive burden on the credit unions."[35] Responding to this concern, three years after initially passing the FCUA, Congress amended the statute by extending significant tax exemptions to credit unions—a government subsidy aimed at helping them fulfill their socially useful mission.[36]

This preferential tax treatment became a sticking point for banks when credit unions began competing with them for customers during the post–WWII era. Banks waged many battles to convince Congress to level the playing field by eliminating the tax preference. A 1956 *American Banker* article noting the growth of the industry warned: "It's better to be swallowed by a whale than nibbled to death by minnows. . . . This frame of mind is increasingly shared by bankers, who have watched with mounting concern the spawning of quasi-public-welfare units that have invaded financial feeding grounds hitherto allotted to chartered banks." The author warned that credit unions seem "so innocuous when evidenced in small, purely localized units" but exhibit a "vastly different character when they appear in town as major-sized competition with chartered bank services."[37] However, the Credit Union National Association (CUNA), the industry's trade group, enjoyed strong legislative support in Congress and was able to retain their favorable tax status.

Finally, the movement was designed differently than banks in order to fulfill a different mission. By design, loan repayment was limited to two years, and the maximum interest rate chargeable was 1 percent per month.[38] A law required there to be a "common bond" among credit union members, which was the movement's most important feature and the reason it could fulfill its mission.[39] Instead of charging high interest to offset the risk of default, the credit union used personal knowledge of an applicant and group supervision of a loan. Congress wrote this innovation into law to create "a cohesive association in which the members are known by the officers and by each other in order to 'ensure both that those making lending decisions would know more about applicants and that borrowers would be more reluctant to default.' "[40] This structure enabled "credit unions, unlike banks, [to] 'loan on character.' "[41]

These founding principles allowed the credit union industry to thrive and help its members for many years. In 1935, only 3,372 credit unions existed across the country, with approximately 640,000 members. After the FCUA, the industry grew rapidly, with one hundred new credit unions and 6,000 new members joining each month. After World War II, from 1945 to 1955, the number of credit unions in the United States doubled (from 8,683 to 16,201), and membership tripled (from 2.8 million to 8.1 million).[42] Credit unions met the credit needs of the postwar economic boom—a population hungry for consumer goods and buoyed by increased wages.

* * *

The philanthropic and Populist mission of the credit union movement did not match postwar prosperity as members moved from dire financial need to relative comfort. Thus, members and industry advocates turned their evangelical zeal outward and sought to spread the democratic mission of the movement abroad. In 1954, at the height of the Cold War, credit union president H. B. Yates advocated that credit unions be used around the world to prevent the spread of Communism, which was strengthened by usury. Aided by other nonprofits as well as the United Nations, the spirit of the original movement motivated the development of credit unions in other countries to propagate their original mission. Yates explained the new role of the credit union: "One of the greatest dangers of democracy is the unequal distribution of wealth. The greatest chasm between rich and poor among individuals, as well as nations, causes distrust, dissatisfaction and trouble. The credit union movement helps permanently solve this problem of unequal distribution by enabling man to help himself permanently improve his condition. When man is able to help himself, character is strengthened and improvement is permanent. When man is aided only by gifts and subsidies, character is weakened, self respect is lost and no problem is solved, since relief is only temporary aid and giving must be continued. The credit union movement is a foundation stone of democracy today."[43]

During the 1960s, credit unions also began to launch philanthropic credit unions to address growing poverty in urban areas. The need became so great that it forced the industry to subsidize these credit unions. Delinquencies ran high because members used the loans to pay for basic needs, such as food and rent. CUNA developed an Equal Opportunity Department that partnered with the federal government's Office of Economic Opportunity to support credit unions serving the low-income population. However, the federal government stopped funding the sector in the 1970s due to inflationary pressures and changing political interests.[44]

Slowly and then quickly, credit unions went from being a "movement" to being an "industry." They were becoming more successful and getting larger,[45] and by the 1970s, the credit union industry had its own federal regulator and strong support in Washington. This rapid growth and power came with a price. As is often the case, success led to profitability, which began to threaten the original mission of the movement. Two leading credit union scholars have conceded this:

> Credit union leaders had to confront the fact that the nature of the movement had changed greatly and that they were serving members with different patterns of employment and needs. Adequate savings could not be derived from the lower income groups and the very poor were not good credit risks. The ultimate effect was that the credit union movement developed more of a middle income orientation than one devoted to lower-income groups. Thus, the main thrust of management became one of establishing sound management practices designed to stabilize the individual units while permitting steady growth.[46]

Caught up in the banking transformation that started in the 1970s, credit unions faced both internal and external pressure to compete with banks and seek higher profits. Small credit unions began to merge and carry out a wider range of investment activities. Soon, the movement that began with small mutually owned and managed units was, by the end of the 1980s, full of large and profitable credit unions under professional management.

Furthermore, in order to compete for the savings of the middle class, the credit union industry's now-sizable lobby sought to completely overhaul its charter. The credit unions specifically asked for relief from the common-bond requirement—their defining characteristic.[47] The National Credit Union Administration (NCUA), the industry's regulator, responded by interpreting the common-bond requirement to include multiple occupational groups, as long as each group shared a common bond.[48] This dilution of the common-bond requirement naturally led to increased credit union size and competition with banks.[49]

The banking industry challenged the NCUA interpretation, and in 1998, the Supreme Court sided with the banks in *First National Bank and Trust Co. v. National Credit Union Administration* and held that the industry could not change its defining trait unilaterally.[50] The court said that only Congress could change the charter, and in swift response, the NCUA and the credit union industry began lobbying Congress.[51] The now-formidable credit union lobby argued that its customers should have the freedom to choose credit unions over traditional banks.[52]

It worked. Six months after the Supreme Court's decision, Congress passed the Credit Union Membership Access Act (CUMAA)—with near unanimous support—to "ratify the longstanding policy of the [NCUA] with regard to [the] field of membership [in] Federal credit unions" by "specifically authoriz[ing] multiple common bond federal credit unions."[53] Most significantly, the act exempted credit unions from the Community Reinvestment Act, an act aimed at providing banking access to low-income individuals.[54] The exemption resulted directly from credit union lobbying. To repeat, the credit union industry, created to serve the poor, now fought against a law requiring it to serve the poor.

Moreover, Congress ignored the blatant contradiction initially raised by the courts regarding how an expansive and unrelated membership group can adequately determine and evaluate the creditworthiness of additional members. The seemingly rushed nature of the CUMAA made it inconsistent. Specifically, although Congress imposed numeric membership requirements that sought to limit the growth of multiple common-bond credit unions, these limits were easily subverted, which led to an increase in credit union membership. The act also did nothing to assuage the banking industry's fears that credit unions were acting essentially like banks without having to pay taxes or comport with Community Reinvestment Act requirements.

Today, credit unions are much like mainstream banks. The American Bankers Association argues that credit unions are not fulfilling their mission to serve the underserved.[55] Of course, the banks are biased, but the assertion is not unfair. A 2006 Government Accountability Office study concluded that compared to banks, credit unions are more likely to serve middle- and upper-income people than lower-income people.[56] Notably, some even claim that credit unions "come in and cherry-pick the most profitable [banking] business and then give nothing back to the community," a practice far from the original mission of the cooperatives that Filene and then Roosevelt embraced.[57]

The lore of the credit union has outlived its reality. For many, the credit union still stands as the answer to everything that is wrong with banking. To be sure, credit unions do differ from banks. Though they are now quite large, none are as large as the Too-Big-to-Fail banks. In addition, their structure limits their appetite for risk. Credit union boards still consist of community members. Even though their mission is to make a profit, they are not willing to make profits at all costs. However, most credit unions do not see banking for the poor as a part of their mission.

The credit union was a twentieth-century response to a twentieth-century problem. Insisting that this once-revolutionary institution continue to solve twenty-first-century problems of access misunderstands not only the modern credit union industry but also the modern problems of credit.

Specifically, many place the onus of helping the poor on a small subset of credit unions called Community Development Credit Unions (CDCUs). As the credit union industry abandoned its initial mission, some held their ground. An umbrella organization, the National Federation of Community Development Credit Unions, was organized in the 1970s "to strengthen [CDCUs'] financial position and expand their impact on the low-income communities they serve."[58] However, these credit unions have struggled to remain viable.[59] Some estimates even place the CDCU failure rate during the 1990s at near 90 percent.[60] Yet, time and again, when people discuss the problems affecting the poor and the payday lending trap, they turn to CDCUs as the answer.[61] For example, many studies end with essentially this sentiment: "Fringe banks do not meet the short-term credit needs of a population that has not been well-served by traditional banks. Nonprofit credit unions are a promising alternative being more receptive (than most banks) to offering low-cost financial services and credit to low- and moderate-income customers." Today, about two hundred CDCUs remain in the country after many recent failures and mergers because of the financial crisis.[62] In other words, the 40 percent of the population who must rely on payday loans can be saved by fewer than two hundred nonprofit credit unions.

However, their financial struggles should not be allowed to diminish the CDCUs' good work. One study of New York City's Lower East Side People's Federal Credit Union showed that the vast majority of its borrowers were low-income minorities with little or no credit and no relationship with mainstream financial institutions.[63] Moreover, loans were small—$1,700 on average—and for shorter terms, thus tailored specifically to meet the needs of the individuals it served.[64] The CDCUs demonstrate that it is possible, though financially very difficult, for credit unions to fulfill the mission that they were initially equipped to serve.

If credit unions are the answer to providing credit to the poor, that mission will once again have to be of central concern. Profits will have to be secondary, and government support will be essential. However, credit unions remained successful for so long in offering low-cost credit because of their innovative use of relationships as a proxy for high interest. The common-bond requirement was essential for such a transaction. Today, credit union membership is no longer limited to groups with any meaningful common bond that can be used to lower the costs of credit. This is not to say that the model cannot be replicated on a small scale in communities across the country through the CDCU movement. This small subsector, however, is no match for the pervasive modern problem of credit inequality.

SAVINGS AND LOANS

In the 1800s, "saving" was more than a wise financial investment; it represented a social policy, a moral and a religious good, and a way of maintaining social order. Policymakers believed that a "small saver," a word used frequently at the time, "would be less likely to depend on public assistance, turn to crime, or engage in revolution."[65] A wave of savings institutions proliferated in Europe and in America. Leading historian Sheldon Garon described these banks as "nonmarket institutions" and nonprofit banks designed specifically for a social mission.[66] He stated that "during the first half of the nineteenth century, contemporaries regarded the savings bank as one of the grand social experiments of the time—on par with public schools, public health measures, orphanages, prisons, and citizen-armies. . . . The savings bank, in short, was far more than a financial institution. It was where the authorities and public-spirited individuals endeavored to mold the humbler classes into self-disciplined members of the community and nation."[67]

A variety of forms of savings banks proliferated during the 1800s, with distinct variations—some lent money, others just guarded savings, many were linked with the state, and others were nonprofits run by wealthy philanthropists. All of them were designed to help the poor and explicitly and legally rejected profits; for example, there was no capital stock or dividends—no return on investment at all in savings banks.[68] A contemporary historian defined a savings bank as an institution that is "managed entirely in the interest of the depositors."[69]

The philosophy of the savings bank was didactic—to teach the poor self-discipline and middle-class morality, or "thrift" and "patience." And the venture was primarily taken on by wealthy philanthropists with heavy paternalistic tones.[70] Some early savings banks came to be mistakenly known as "mutual savings banks," but they were nothing like the mutually owned credit unions or buildings and loans that would arise later. Depositors were just the poor pupils of the rich who were being taught how best to conduct their lives.[71] In his 1876 history of the savings bank movement, Emerson W. Keyes, the former deputy superintendent of the banking department of the state of New York, described these banks as the "vital organs" of society adapted "to accomplish a great purpose" and an "expression and embodiment of public sentiment." As to the "purpose for which it was designed," he said: "And what is the great underlying fact in human experience, this all-pervading, ever-present condition or need in the social state, to minister unto which, Savings Banks were conceived and ordained, and in behalf of which they have successfully and triumphantly wrought during the last sixty years? In one word, it is POVERTY!"[72]

The "poor" were not the destitute or the paupers but those "who with steady, patient industry can from day to day, earn barely the necessaries [*sic*] of life for himself and family" and who "gain their living by their own labor of hand or brain, with no accumulated capital yielding an assured income." These people, Keyes explained, yearned for opportunities beyond what their wages could offer and would be "insulted" by charity.[73] Another Boston savings banker described his customers as "humble journeymen, coachmen, chamber-maids, and all kinds of domestic servants and inferior artisans, who constitute two thirds of our population."[74] During the nineteenth century, half of the new account holders at the largest savings banks were women. And in the early savings banks in both the United States and Europe, female domestic workers comprised the largest constituent of depositors. Wives were specifically tasked with keeping their households and their profligate husbands thrifty and sober.[75]

The savings banks started with the mission and rhetoric of promoting *saving,* but they also gave loans to their customers.[76] In 1876, one industry report boasted that they had helped seven million people with more than $4 billion in loans during a span of sixty years (1816 to 1876).[77] These banks provided modest business and consumer loans but were restricted in mortgage lending. Only about 5 percent of the total deposits was used to loan on mortgages (legislation allowed up to 10 percent),[78] and when they did loan mortgages, they required the borrower to provide up to 60 percent of the purchase price.

The savings bank would not cure poverty, but it would give the poor a place to build capital. At the time, commercial banks actively repelled the poor. With typical hours of operation between 9:00 a.m. and 2:00 p.m. (when everyone but the aristocrats was working), their doors were literally closed to the working poor. But it was more explicit than that. One Chicago banker described his disinterest in small deposits: "The bank with which I am connected not only does not invite savings deposits but imposes a prohibitory charge upon all accounts which average less than $300 for the express purpose of *driving them away.*"[79]

Massachusetts was the first state to pass legislation, creating the Provident Institution for Savings in Boston in 1814.[80] The legislation was specifically designed to ensure that these banks stayed focused on their mission of helping the poor. The articles of incorporation for these early savings bank charters clearly stated that all profits from the bank "shall be divided among depositors . . . in just proportion." These banks were prohibited from making certain investments because "it is to be borne in mind, in the first place, that *safety* and not *profit* is the consideration mainly to be regarded in the investment of trust funds. There must be no ambition to make large dividends; no alluring of depositors by promise of extraordinary interest; no trenching on the ground reserved for banks." The savings banks also pled for and received tax exemption because, they argued, "The depositors should be dealt with, protected, encouraged and vigilantly watched, as a means by which a great public good is conferred upon the community."[81] Several other states even imposed maximum savings amounts from $1000 to $3000 dollars to reinforce that the mission was not to accumulate capital, but to teach thrift. These banks were geographically concentrated, with 98 percent of the deposits in a few New England states and a few banks in California.[82]

The industry would not grow substantially because it was based on a top-down philanthropic model and was never quite able to meet the credit demands of the poor. After the Great Depression, the surviving banks would be renamed "savings and loans," with an emphasis on the *loan*.

FREEDMAN'S SAVINGS BANK

The Freedman's Savings Bank, the only savings bank chartered by the federal government, was also created for the purpose of helping the poor—in this case, the newly freed blacks. This bank, like other savings banks, was a paternalistic endeavor by wealthy white philanthropists to teach thrift and civic responsibility. It actually, as a contemporary observed, "not only ruine[d] thousands of colored men, but taught to thousands more a lesson of distrust which it will take them years to unlearn."[83] The story of the Freedman's Savings Bank serves as a warning about a bank-state partnership gone awry and illustrates the problems inherent in banking to the poor and marginalized.

The Civil War was not just a military or even political victory of the North over the South or abolitionists over slaveholders. It also marked the triumph of capitalism and industry instead of agrarianism and the plantation economy as the economic future.[84] And no group struggled more to adapt to the forces of capitalism than the newly freed slaves. President Lincoln's party, the Republicans, demanded equal citizenship for blacks for moral reasons, but also because capitalism required political liberty, universal suffrage, and equality. The Republicans were divided on how to integrate blacks into the economy. Radical Republicans, led by Thaddeus Stevens, advocated a liberal democratic and middle-class ethic of complete economic inclusion, which entailed the right to vote, hold office, buy property, and "attain economic independence within the framework of the existing business economy."[85] The more moderate conservative Republicans viewed equal citizenship as a goal to be gradually attained through "education, business and the accumulation of property."[86]

But for a decade after the Civil War, the conservatives and the radicals agreed on one thing: in order to attain political equality, blacks needed to acquire education and wealth. Howard, Fisk, and Virginia Union universities and some trade schools were created to educate the freed slaves. And the Freedman's Savings and Trust Company was intended to help blacks build wealth. Frederick Douglass observed: "While it is impossible that every individual of any race shall be rich—and no man may be despised for merely being poor—yet no people can be respected which does not produce a wealthy class. The mission of the Freedman's Bank is to show our people the road to a share of the wealth and well being of the world."[87] The road to wealth would not be easy because slavery had set the race so far behind. Douglass said of the freed slave, "He had neither money, property nor friends—he was turned loose naked, hungry and destitute."[88]

President Lincoln created the Freedman's Savings Bank on March 3, 1865, with the federal government's benevolent desire to aid in the financial inclusion of blacks. During the Civil War, many black soldiers deposited substantial sums of money in military banks, but when the war ended, much of this money went unclaimed.[89] Pamphlets promoted the bank as "Abraham Lincoln's Gift to the Colored People. . . . He gave *Emancipation,* and then this Savings Bank."[90] The bank would be run by "white friends of the Negro ostensibly for his benefit." And blacks were "induced to believe that the bank was a government institution or that at least the government was responsible for their funds."[91] A U.S. Senate hearing described the federal imprimatur as follows: "The pass book issued to the depositors in the Freedman's Bank bore on its cover the likeness of President Lincoln, General Grant, also General Howard and others whom the freedmen had learned to revere as the special benefactors of their race. The flag of the United States was draped over the buildings, and designed to assure them that the United States would protect their interest."[92] How else could a bank run by whites convince newly freed blacks to trust it with their long- and hard-earned savings?

The bank was built on a philanthropic foundation with the goal "to instill into the minds of the untutored Africans lessons of sobriety, wisdom, and economy,"[93] elements integral to "the economic and industrial development of a people."[94] The bank was not to be operated as a profit-making business but was created to "safeguard the interests of the nation's 'wards.'"[95] The bank's charter and Articles of Incorporation clearly stated this mission by limiting the bank's investments and the types of financial arrangements bank managers could make.[96]

John W. Alvord, the superintendent of the Freedman's Bureau Department of Education, was a driving force behind the bank's creation and became an original trustee. Alvord convinced Congress to create a board of trustees with fifty prominent citizens, including William A. Booth, Peter Cooper, John Murray Forbes, George Whipple, Thomas Webster, and John Jay. Many of these trustees, however, never got involved with managing the bank. Instead, "they were thrust in for appearance' sake and to make the delusion attractive and complete."[97] Most who accepted their nominations immediately distanced themselves from the bank's management, leaving "a small minority of the acting trustees" in control.[98]

Perhaps because of its benevolent mission, the trustees were vested with broad discretionary powers over many aspects of the bank's management.[99] Notably absent from the charter was any requirement that trustees invest in the bank themselves. Moreover, the charter did not provide for federal government oversight of the bank's operations. Still, the freed slaves trusted the bank and the federal government, and they deposited their money. Within ten years of its inception, it handled more than $75 million in deposits made by more than seventy-five thousand depositors, an amount that would equal approximately $1.5 billion today. In 1865, during its first year in operation, the bank opened eleven branches across the Southeast. By 1870, this figure grew to thirty-two branches, spanning the entire Southeast, New York City, Philadelphia, and Washington, DC.[100]

Motivated by the bank's success, the trustees decided to move its headquarters from New York City to an affluent neighborhood in Washington, DC. The magnificence of the newly constructed headquarters convinced even the most cautious depositors of the bank's stability and its managers' acumen. When Frederick Douglass saw the building for the first time after accepting his appointment as a trustee, he described "its magnificent brown store front, its towering height . . . the whole thing was beautiful." He said he "felt like the Queen of Sheba when she saw the riches of Solomon."[101] In fact, Douglass placed so much confidence in the institution that he deposited $12,000 of his own money into the bank, believing that doing so would reflect his trust and the legitimacy of the bank.[102]

However, as Douglass would soon discover, the bank's projected image of success and stability masked its true vulnerabilities. Instead of being the key to African American economic success, the bank was "full of dead men's bones, rottenness, and corruption."[103] Originally, the bank's charter circumscribed the types of investment activities in which trustees could engage. After all, the bank was established for benevolent ends: to help freed African Americans achieve economic empowerment.

But at the urging of the bank's managers, Congress amended and deregulated the charter on May 6, 1870. This amendment lifted the original restrictions on permissible investments and authorized the trustees to invest deposits "to the extent of one-half in bonds or notes, secured by mortgage[s] on real estate in double the value of the loan."[104] The bank managers pushed for the deregulation, and because the depositors did not oppose the measure, the request was granted. To be sure, the 1870 amendment did not give trustees unfettered discretion to issue loans, but now, half the "available fund" could be invested in property or other secured investments. Even with the expanded charter, no one enforced this rule, and bank cashiers did a notoriously poor job of organizing and maintaining the bank's books. Thus, the amendment "paved the way for all sorts of speculative loans and investments."[105]

Some loans were secured by real estate without the bank first assessing the value of the underlying property. Often, the collateral proved to be encumbered or falsely or fraudulently valued. Other loans were simply categorized as "miscellaneous," deviating substantially from acceptable lending practices.[106] These loans were not made to advance the purpose of the bank and were certainly not issued to safely guard the hard-earned funds of its depositors but instead to benefit the managers and their cohorts. And because no mechanism existed to resolve such conflicts of interest, these transactions went unnoticed.[107]

These vulnerabilities evaded detection by bank inspectors because they were either truly ignorant of the bank's actual condition or they simply did not care about its fate. However, the scheme began to unravel following the financial Panic of 1873, when investments failed and depositors demanded their money. Freedman's, like many other financial institutions, experienced several runs at the height of the Panic. In a last-ditch effort to save the bank, the trustees appointed Douglass—who was unaware of the bank's balance sheets—as its president in March 1874. Once in office, Douglass set out to determine the bank's true condition.[108]

The bank's perceived stability motivated Douglass to lend the bank $10,000 of his own money to aid the bank to reach profitability.[109] Rather than validating his confidence, however, this loan tipped Douglass off that something was awry. The multiple runs following the Panic had exhausted the bank's reserves so that it was unable to meet its obligations. Upon learning its true condition, Douglass imposed drastic spending cuts to limit depositors' losses. He then relayed this information to Congress, underscoring the bank's insolvency and declaring that he "could no longer ask [his] people to deposit their money in it."[110] Despite the other trustees' attempts to convince Congress otherwise, Congress sided with Douglass. And on June 20, 1874, Congress amended the charter to authorize the trustees to end operations. The bank's doors were shut for good on June 29, 1874, leaving 61,131 depositors without access to nearly $3 million in deposits.[111] Most depositors lost all of their money and some were able to recover only a portion of their hard-earned savings.

W. E. B. Du Bois said of the bank failure that "not even ten additional years of slavery could have done so much to throttle the thrift of the freedmen as the mismanagement and bankruptcy of the series of savings banks chartered by the Nation for their special aid."[112] If the government and the philanthropists purported to teach the freed slaves thrift and responsibility, the lesson they actually learned was to distrust the government and philanthropists.

The Freedman's Savings Bank serves as a cautionary tale for government support of banking for the poor when that support is just a façade. Draping a flag over a building and then installing private profit-motivated management inside is the most dangerous sort of government support. It induces trust in a vulnerable customer base that not only suffers from financial loss, but also loses all faith in public institutions. It poisons true government efforts to help. A similar phenomenon was at the heart of the failure of the government-sponsored enterprises Fannie Mae and Freddie Mac during the recent financial crisis.

BUILDING AND LOAN

In the eighteenth century, land was cheap and raw materials abundant, so there was little demand for home financing. But after the first Industrial Revolution, many people moved to cities, and land prices, and thus the need for financing, began to rise. Only those with accumulated capital could afford to buy land, and only those with connections to individuals with excess capital could borrow the necessary funds. Some commercial banks started offering these loans, but because of the instability of the banking model (highly liquid bank deposits and illiquid real estate), banks required a down payment of up to 60 percent.[113]

The building and loan (B&L), also known as a "thrift bank," worked alongside the savings bank, but each had a different structure and mission—if the savings bank was a philanthropic mission to reach down to teach the poor, the B&L represented the poor helping themselves. These banks, which were owned and operated by their own members, did not require any philanthropic capital at all and were more concerned with capital accumulation than ideology. These banks were also designed primarily for the poor, but the poor funded and managed them as well.[114] The B&L, similar to the credit union in its cooperative structure, had the express purpose of financing homeownership.

A group of men in a suburb of Philadelphia created the first B&L, called the Oxford Provident Building Association, in 1831. The first building and loan societies aimed "to enable persons in the humbler ranks of life to become *owners* of real property, instead of continuing mere *renters* of it."[115] The wrong to be corrected was that "the *many* pay rents for the benefit of the few," and these groups would allow "the *many* [to] combine together so as to put the rents into their own pockets."[116] The B&L was established by mutual stock ownership; each member contributed a small amount each month with profits shared equally among members. They would lend based on the need and "character" of the borrower and each member had input on loans. Investments as well as the profits from interest on loans, which could be considerable, would stay in the association, multiplying the pool in order to help more members obtain financing.[117]

By pooling resources in this way, the B&L was able to lend up to the full purchase price of a property so people with very little capital could buy homes and pay back the loan incrementally. The majority of B&Ls were small, local, and focused, with assets consisting 90 percent of real estate loans.[118] The B&Ls were lauded as conferring significant benefits on society—"an unlimited amount of good, by the encouragement of careful habits" as well as "self-reliance and the true spirit of independence" in the working classes.[119] In 1874, Edmund Wrigley titled his prominent national treatise on building associations *The Working Man's Way to Wealth*. He saw these institutions as a way to give "the working classes" control and knowledge over how their money was invested instead of deferring to aristocracies. He described the institutions as "perfectly Democratic" because there would be "no separate class." The working man "becomes his own capitalist, combining the small means of many men into one large sum, which, by rapid, profitable, and safe investment, returns a gain that under other plans goes into the hands of capitalists." The B&L was about "the principle of co-operation applied to money," a "People's Banking System."[120]

Frank Capra's classic film *It's a Wonderful Life* exemplifies the mission of the B&L as well as its enemies: purely profit-oriented banks. Mr. Potter, a heartless banker, tries to persuade George Bailey's building and loan association to stop providing unprofitable home loans to the poor. But George Bailey believes in the community-building mission of his bank and is dedicated to building Bailey Park, an affordable-housing community. As displayed in the movie, the thrift movement was accompanied by a missionary zeal. The leaders described themselves as "apostles of thrift and homeownership" and urged local thrifts to "send out men to preach the gospel you profess to believe."[121] The B&L was a "brotherhood," a "society of friends," a soft financial institution that protected its members from harsh capitalistic forces—"should misfortune overtake a borrower, his interests are in the hands of friends, from whom he will receive more lenient treatment and more well-directed help than from private capitalists or industrialists."[122]

Based on these Populist and Progressive ideals, the B&L was best characterized as a "movement," and the movement spread from the Northeast to the South and the Midwest as it joined with other Populist groups like the Knights of Labor and the Farmers' Alliance, which focused on providing rural farmers access to credit amidst the forces of industrialization.[123] The need for these alternative sources of credit resulted from the collapse of the banking system in the South following the Civil War and the lack of banking services in the still-undeveloped West. Most functioning banks were in the Northeast and the Midwest. This lack of credit forced farmers in the South to turn to tenant farming, "borrowing from their landlord against their next year's crop at exorbitant prices, . . . [while in] the West, they often managed without credit by living as subsistence farmers."[124]

The building and loan industry had spread from coast to coast by the end of the nineteenth century and formed a national organization in order to promote thrift formation. David Mason, a historian of the thrift movement, explains that the B&L movement mobilized because its principles coincided with a rising Progressive spirit.[125] Several natural harmonies existed between the Progressive Movement and the thrift movement. First, B&Ls would help alleviate some of the problems with inner-city living standards, a Progressive-era preoccupation, by providing an opportunity for homeownership.[126] Second, the Progressives wanted to induct recent immigrants into the mainstream economy, and the B&L movement provided a way. The movement's leaders advocated homeownership in order to reduce labor unrest and Socialism—"every time you make a home, you make a citizen."[127] The third Progressive-era goal, of "thrift" as a virtue, was aided by WWI efforts to turn household savings into investments in the government. Policymakers encouraged personal savings and even hosted national events supporting thrifts, which the B&L national organization used to promote its institutions and gain more members.

And finally, Progressives saw homeownership as an important policy goal in itself. Homeownership not only advanced personal wealth but also strengthened democracy and morality. The push also coincided with a post–WWI housing boom. President Hoover believed that homeownership was intrinsically good for individuals and for society and evangelized the cause throughout his tenure.[128] Hoover claimed that the "large proportion of families that own their own homes is both the foundation of a sound economic and social system and a guarantee that our society will continue to develop rationally as changing conditions demand."[129] Hoover's sentiment was not unique at the time. In 1925, the California Supreme Court stated: "With ownership comes stability, the welding together of family ties, and better attention to the rearing of children. With ownership comes increased interest in the promotion of public agencies, such as church and school, which have for their purpose a desired development of the moral and mental make-up of the citizenry of the country. With ownership of one's home comes recognition of the individual's responsibility for his share in the safeguarding of the welfare of the community and increased pride in personal achievement which must come from personal participation in projects looking toward community betterment."[130]

Federal backing of the thrift industry, which helped the industry thrive, would be swift and strong both because it aligned with Progressive principles and because it was already an organized and stable movement. Thrifts that did not fail during the Great Depression consolidated with other thrifts or joined the national league in order to modernize their practices, leading to national organization of the industry. The national director Morton Bodfish sought to streamline business practices in order to help the industry survive. He said that in order for the thrift to withstand modernizing forces, it must follow "a business procedure with the same demands for skill and managerial ability, which characterize any business enterprise" while remaining "essentially cooperative and quasi-public."[131] Thrifts still maintained their mission to provide home financing for the low-income and sacrificed profits to do so, but their cooperative structure became diluted after the Great Depression. They remained local, community thrifts, but their pure cooperative structure, though alive in theory and in their corporate charters, was no longer the heart of the movement.[132]

B&Ls survived the Great Depression remarkably well. Only 2 percent of thrifts failed, compared to 20 percent of banks. This success, combined with President Hoover's continued interest in promoting homeownership, led to the passage of the Federal Home Loan Bank Act in 1932.[133] The act would involve the federal government in subsidizing mortgage loans by providing liquidity and central banking services for the building and loan industry. The act created twelve home loan banks across the country, which would be cooperatively owned but funded by an initial federal government investment of $125 million to support the work already begun by the B&L sector. President Hoover, in passing the act, stated: "The purpose of the system is both to meet the present emergency and to build up homeownership on more favorable terms than exist today. The immediate credit situation has for the time being in many parts of the country restricted the activities of building and loan associations, savings banks, and other institutions making loans for home purposes. . . . In the long view we need at all times to encourage homeownership and for such encouragement it must be possible for homeowners to obtain long-term loans payable in installments. These institutions should provide the method for bringing into continuous and steady action the great home loaning associations which is so greatly restricted due to present pressures."[134]

Despite the B&Ls being described as "Hoover's Banks," Roosevelt made the thrift industry a key part of his New Deal package. President Roosevelt, who wanted to make mortgage lending easier and available to all, threw the support of the federal government behind the B&L and created a long-lasting and stable institution. The Home Owners' Loan Act of 1933 provided a federal charter to thrifts, which combined the savings banks and the B&Ls and called both "Savings and Loans" and imposed federal control over them. Savings and loan (S&L) members initially resisted federal help and control because they wanted to preserve the "local" nature of the S&L. Eventually, realizing that their survival depended on federal government support, they accepted it but made certain that their special mission was written into the charter: S&Ls were to loan to customers within fifty miles of their office to build homes valued at $20,000 or less.[135]

Roosevelt combined the various thrift efforts and backed them through federal recognition, insurance, and other measures to increase their lending ability. For example, the creation of the Federal Deposit Insurance Corporation (FDIC) fund in 1933 caused deposits to flow out of S&Ls and into banks. Roosevelt immediately responded by creating the Federal Savings and Loan Insurance Corporation (FSLIC) to preserve thrifts and help them compete with mainstream banks. S&Ls also got their own federal supervisor, the Federal Home Loan Bank Board (FHLBB), with recognition that the industry operated distinctly from mainstream banks. Thrifts were also exempt from many of the restrictions placed on commercial banks at the time. For example, thrifts were allowed to branch interstate, or in other words, they could merge or affiliate with other thrifts across state lines.[136]

Roosevelt ensured the continued existence of the thrift by mooring the benevolent outsider to the federal government. He also boosted the industry through several federal programs and subsidies. For example, the Federal Housing Administration (FHA) was created to aid the thrifts and administer federal housing initiatives, and the Home Owners Loan Corporation (HOLC) was formed to provide quick relief to homeowners with defaulting mortgages.[137] The HOLC, acting with the thrifts, created the fifteen-year mortgage, allowing more people to own homes. (It was also, by the way, the agency that created the problem of redlining through their neighborhood maps and labeling some urban minority neighborhoods "undesirable" lending areas.)[138]

The clear purpose of this comprehensive federal backing was to help the S&L industry channel resources into homeownership. The savings and loan industry, bolstered by federal government support, "democratized" the home loan and effectively made the United States the nation with the highest percentage of private homeownership in the world.[139] Homeownership, enabled in part by thrifts, created wealth for millions of middle-class Americans. And that was the point of all that government support. Before the S&L, home financing remained out of reach for most Americans—banks only provided home financing for 40 to 60 percent of the home's value, meaning that the borrower would have to come up with the rest, and the loan had to be paid back within one to five years. No loans were available for older or low-value homes. Many people needed to get a second mortgage—through an unregulated lender at very high interest rates—in order to finance their home. The S&L created the modern home loan, which allows the borrower to pay it back over a long term and to put down a relatively small down payment.[140]

The S&Ls were distinctively not profit-making entities—they were self-help institutions for the poor, made possible by government subsidies and regulation. Even after the New Deal changes, the thrift industry's model remained "neighbors helping neighbors" and emphasized mutual ownership; it focused on building homes for neighbors, not making profits. Members also participated heavily in governance and elected the institution's officers, who were often community leaders.[141]

THE INDUSTRY CHANGES

The post–WWII housing boom not only made thrifts the predominant mortgage lenders in the country but also led to unprecedented industry growth. Their mission focused on residential housing, and their business plan was simple: collect deposits, make mortgage loans. Because of high demand, it was easy to lend and become profitable, illustrated by the famous "3-6-3 Rule"—pay 3 percent on deposits, charge 6 percent on loans, and be on the golf course by 3:00 p.m. The thrift industry just sat back and watched its loan volume grow. It had a significant advantage against banks in collecting deposits—that first "3" in interest, though modest, was more than commercial banks could pay for consumer savings.[142]

As we saw with credit unions, these large profits changed the industry. By the 1960s, the industry bore little resemblance to the charitable and mission-oriented industry of the 1800s or even the 1930s. S&Ls possessed over $100 billion in assets and competed vigorously with banks for consumer deposits.[143] Having graduated their customers into the middle class through affordable homeownership, they had abandoned their mutual ownership and no longer rejected profits. They looked nothing like the Bailey's Building and Loan, and soon the industry's growth naturally led to increased political influence.

Not only had the industry stopped pursuing its mission, it appeared to be actively fighting it. The industry forcefully opposed the first federal legislative attempt, the Housing Act of 1949, to provide public housing for the low-income. It labeled the attempt "Socialism" and a threat to private business. Apparently, the S&Ls had already forgotten that they owed their very existence to heavy federal government support. They believed that if the government started building housing for the poor, they would lose their prime spot atop the mortgage-finance industry. Senator John Bricker, cozy with the S&L industry, revealed this fear to Congress: "Where do we stop? . . . With government threatening to encompass between one-third to one-half of the home-financial field, [the thrift industry's] very existence is at stake."[144]

By the 1970s, market competition hampered the 3-6-3 gravy train, and thrifts joined banks in pushing for deregulation so that they could remain profitable. Congress and the thrift regulators famously responded with several deregulatory actions that would allow the weakened thrift industry to survive in a hypercompetitive financial sector.[145] The "reforms" removed their interest rate caps, broadened their permissive activities beyond home mortgages, and removed geographic restrictions. S&Ls could now offer credit cards and traditional interest-bearing checking accounts as well as engage in commercial and general consumer lending.[146] They could also invest in commercial paper and corporate bonds before commercial banks were able to invest in any type of securities.[147] Mutual ownership was also abandoned. Previously, an S&L was required to have at least four hundred shareholders, with no one shareholder owning more than 25 percent of the stock. Now, a single shareholder could own an S&L. At the same time, Congress increased their insurance from $40,000 per account to $100,000 per account and placed the full faith and credit of the United States behind the FSLIC insurance fund.[148]

The moral hazard introduced by increased FSLIC insurance, combined with deregulation and increasing competition, led to a toxic mix. Thrift owners could deal fast and loose with deposits that were fully insured and backed by the government. The industry immediately became an attractive target for many unscrupulous investors and organizations. The loosened regulations attracted the interest of anyone, including people with ties to the Mafia and other organized crime, who wanted access to millions of FSLIC-insured dollars without much fear of close scrutiny from regulators. In reference to the S&L industry in the 1980s, Representative Jim Leach said, "What has developed . . . is a giveaway system where the potential profit has been privatized while the potential loss has been socialized."[149]

One of the ironies of deregulation is that it bred problems that could only be remedied through more deregulation. Without an orienting mission, the thrift was just like any other bank—but with a more compliant regulator. For example, the repeal of the interest rate cap posed a problem for S&Ls, whose assets were primarily composed of long-term home loans that continued to pay interest at low rates. S&Ls had to pay a sudden jump in rates to attract deposits, but their existing long-term borrowers were not paying the corresponding jump in rates, meaning that much more money flowed out than in. S&Ls were caught in an interest rate squeeze. The Garn-St. Germain Act addressed this by allowing S&Ls to lend to short-term and higher profit products like securities or commercial paper—products that had nothing to do with the S&Ls' core mission. The act, in an attempt to allow the industry to bring in more loans, dropped the down payment requirement for home loans and allowed S&Ls to offer variable-rate mortgages to shift some of the interest rate risk onto their customers.[150] These products included the exotic Adjustable Rate Mortgages that were among the highest defaulting loans during the 2008 financial crisis.[151]

The point of deregulation was to help the S&L help itself in an unregulated free market. The strategy, called "gambling for resurrection," indicated the general banking philosophy of the time. Many blamed the industry's lack of profitability on onerous regulation and advocated deregulation so that S&Ls could compete with other market entities on an even playing field. But these institutions had been playing a different game; they were distinctly not pure profit organizations. All of their restrictions, such as mutual ownership, a singular focus on home loans, and interest rate caps, served a purpose. But once they became profit-oriented banks with any public purpose set aside, they suffered not only an interest rate squeeze, but a mission squeeze. Trying to serve two masters—profits and the public good—proved impossible, so they chose to chase profits, rather unsuccessfully. Disaster eventually struck, and the thrift industry famously imploded.[152] The federal government bailout cost somewhere between $87 billion and $130 billion.[153]

Some claim that deregulation caused the collapse by allowing risks to enter the previously sound industry. One expert notes that the thrift industry "captured its regulatory process more thoroughly than any other regulated industry in the country."[154] Responding to this charge, the thrift regulator was changed from the FHLBB to the Office of Thrift Supervision (OTS), a slap on the wrist to a defunct agency. In reality, in 1989 President George H. W. Bush gave a speech promising regulatory reforms and said that "never again will America allow any insured institution [to] operate without enough money." Meanwhile, the FHLBB employees walked outside their agency to a hotel to watch the speech and walked right back to work—the sign on the door was soon changed to reflect the name of the new agency.[155] Predictably, the OTS would be in trouble again in 2008, regarded as the most irresponsible of federal regulators for failing to meaningfully oversee the large and powerful thrifts, like WaMu, AIG, and IndyMac, under its charge.[156] Dodd-Frank finally abolished the OTS in October 2011.

Others claim that it was not deregulation that caused the industry's collapse but that the industry failed because it was forced to focus on home loans even when it was not economically feasible to do so. In this telling, deregulation came too late to save an already doomed industry. By the 1980s, homeownership was no longer the main financial obstacle of the poor because home financing was more accessible than at any other time. Moreover, as mutual ownership was abandoned, and the industry became larger and more national, the neighbor-helping-neighbor appeal lost its significance. Former S&L "members" knew their deposits would quickly move out of their communities and felt no obligation to "buy local." The S&L industry's new profit-focused mission certainly was at odds with the heavy-handed government restrictions and protective apparatus that insulated the industry from competition. The framework had to be revised, and it was through deregulation.

The S&L's core mission could not survive the changes in the industry, at least not without significant federal government and industry support, neither of which existed. That support might have included a refocused mission on the current needs of the poor, made possible through federal support coupled with industry leaders' refusing to compete with banks and focusing on the low-income at low profits. Neither of these things happened because the S&Ls had already changed their focus from helping the poor to helping themselves.

MORRIS BANKS AND INDUSTRIAL LOAN COMPANIES

While the credit unions and the S&Ls were booming, situated atop a substantial government-created structure, other ambitious banks attempted to meet the needs of the poor without federal government support. Rather, they relied on market innovation. Most were very short-lived and quickly forgotten, but one had a longer lifespan than the others due to unanticipated allies and favorable market forces. Morris Banks, also referred to as industrial banks or industrial loan companies (ILCs), were created in the 1900s to fill the gap in consumer lending. Salaried workers needed small, short-term credit. Banks were not interested in this market, leaving only loan sharks and other high-interest lenders.[157] In 1910, Arthur Morris, a Virginia lawyer who first coined the phrase "democratization of credit," felt a personal motivation to meet the credit needs of the poor. Many of his legal clients were low-wage workers who often relied on loan sharks to meet their daily expenses. Morris, bothered by the high interest charged by these unscrupulous lenders, would often lend to these men himself. The story goes that Morris was approached by a railroad clerk, employed for fourteen years with a solid salary of $2500 a year, who needed $500 to pay for an operation for his wife. He could not get a loan from any banks in Norfolk, Virginia. The state had capped the interest rate banks could charge at 6 percent, which made it difficult for any bank to profit from such a small loan.[158]

Morris saw a market gap and wanted to fix it. The credit union was then just getting started, and philanthropic societies such as Russell Sage and the Provident Loan Society also provided a form of charitable lending, but Morris wanted to approach this problem as a capitalist problem-solver. Morris wanted to correct this "weak spot" in the banking system and combed the existing laws in search of a solution "that would correct the existing evils and supply credit to the needy."[159] Morris, in his own words, described his motivation for pursuing the Morris Bank: "I began the first Morris Plan bank . . . for the sole purpose of making a start in the democratization of credit. . . . I was not long in discovering the fact that more than 80 percent of the American public had no access to credit of any kind except as they resorted to loan sharks or charitable institutions. . . . The Morris plan is intended to correct . . . the loan-shark evil in the cities, and the present existing misapprehension that prevails in the minds of the laboring classes with respect to capital . . . [and it] was intended to be to the wage earner what the national banks are to the men of commerce. . . . [However,] [t]he patron of the Morris Plan company is not a recipient of charity. . . . The Morris Plan helps people help themselves."[160]

Morris, convinced that the large majority of Americans were "being denied adequate banking services,"[161] designed a system whereby loans were made to the poor based on three governing principles: (1) "character, plus earning power, is a proper basis of credit"; (2) "loans made on this basis of credit must carry the privilege of repayment over a period long enough to match the [borrower's earning power]"; and (3) "money so borrowed should always be for some constructive and useful purpose."[162] But he needed to overcome the high costs of lending to those with low income. The credit unions and the S&Ls were able to drive down lending risk and therefore, lending costs by relying on close relationships between lenders and borrowers. Morris banks took a different route to lowering credit costs. Morris developed a system that replaced collateral with the signatures of two cosigners, both of whom agreed to pay the loan should the borrower default,[163] an innovation in lending that is still used today.

By requiring cosigners to the loan, the "Morris Plan" mitigated some of the risks with lending to the poor. However, by itself, the cosigner innovation would not have been sufficient. The loans also had to carry a higher interest than average bank loans to make up for the risk of default. The legal hurdle of state usury laws also needed to be overcome; otherwise, the lender could not make any profit. Morris, playing the lawyer, solved this problem through a "dual plan" that skirted the laws by using two separate transactions.[164] The loans stayed within the letter of the usury law but still recouped the full cost of making relatively small, unsecured personal loans to unfamiliar borrowers.[165] In order to make a minimal profit, the interest rate on the loan was about 20 percent—much less than what the loan sharks were offering.

Although the idea proved workable, and the demand for loans remained high, Morris Plan Banks encountered some difficulty in obtaining charters because of the confusion about their exact nature. In response to Morris's original application for incorporation of his charter bank in Virginia, a member of the Virginia Corporation Commission responded by letter: "I have carefully considered your application for a charter for your hybrid and mongrel institution. Frankly, I don't know what it is. It isn't a savings bank; it isn't a state or national bank; it isn't a charity. It isn't anything I ever heard of before. Its principles seem sound however, and its purpose admirable. But the real reason that I am going to grant a charter is because I believe in you."[166]

The first of these "mongrel" Morris Plan banks—the Fidelity Savings & Trust Company—was opened in Norfolk in 1910 with a state charter.[167] In 1914, Morris banks were making 49,500 loans aggregating $6 million, with an average loan size of $123.[168]

Morris became a salesman not only for his bank, but for credit in general. He told a group of Wall Street bankers in 1914: "The industrial supremacy of this country depends on mass production. Mass consumption must be in order that mass production may be. Where there is mass production and mass consumption properly coordinated, it follows as the night follows day that mass employment and the continuity of employment are assured." Further, he saw credit as the antidote to Communism. To Morris, the political significance of credit could not be underestimated. Credit was a "remarkable lever in the realization of human hope." Credit and the Bill of Rights (on equal footing to Morris) were "two of the great elements that have justified my coinage of the expression: Democratization of Credit."[169]

Morris's innovations went beyond the loan structure. He also created the first bank holding company to connect several branches of the Morris banks as well as credit life insurance so that cosigners would not have to pay the debt of a borrower who died.[170] Morris organized a national organization called the Industrial Finance Corporation that helped expand the charter across the country. He set out on a zealous campaign to encourage the enactment of laws that would enable the Morris banks to accomplish their mission of lending to low-income workers.

By 1928, there were 106 Morris banks in various cities. By 1938, there were over 150, with outstanding loans of over $250 million and a total number of borrowers of about 1.5 million that year. By 1940, Morris Plan banks were operating in thirty-one states that had special statutory provisions. Some of these states enacted specially tailored legislation to support the Morris banks; in other states, Morris banks operated under state banking or even general corporation laws. Some states would not allow these institutions to call themselves "banks," so many started to use the name "Industrial Loan Company" (ILC).[171] In other states, they were called Morris banks or industrial banks.

The Morris bank movement stood apart from the S&L and the credit union movement because the federal government never supported the industry, and the states did so erratically. As a result, the mission was quickly dissolved and the institutions were rapidly absorbed into commercial banking. In 1940, a National Bureau of Economic Research study written by Raymond Saulnier struggled to find a defining feature of the industry. Saulnier described the ILCs as "institutions which extend consumer loans, repayable on an instalment [*sic*] basis, and obtain at least part of their working funds from the acceptance of deposits or the sale of investment certificates."[172] Increasingly, the industry became divided in operations and in customer markets. By the 1940 study, it served proportionally more higher-income clients compared to other personal finance companies.[173]

By the 1940s, the industrial banks no longer specialized in cosigned loans but extended a range of consumer credit. As such, they faced competition "not only with firms in their own field but also with personal finance companies, credit unions, sales finance companies, and the personal loan and time-sales departments of commercial banks."[174] Further, the industry was small compared to the other sectors. And because it no longer focused on a mission apart from commercial banks and personal finance companies, the industry kept shrinking.[175]

When Morris banks originally started, banks offered no consumer loans, but soon the market for consumer loans became competitive. Commercial banks' expansion into consumer credit affected industrial banks acutely "since commercial banks competed directly for Morris Plan clients, and could draw on much cheaper money."[176] Commercial banks moved into the personal loan market to meet the high demand after the Great Depression; an observer noted in 1961 that the ILCs had "departed widely from the original ideal which was to limit such an institution's facilities to the individual with modest credit requirements. They now serve business and professional people as well. They have come more and more to resemble commercial banks and to employ conventional bank lending techniques and types of loans."[177] It was not much of a stretch for these institutions to go from operating like a commercial bank to converting into one, which is what happened with more and more regularity as the ILC grew further distant from its founding mission.

Although it may have been Arthur Morris's wish to make the low-income wage earner the perpetual focus of Morris bank loans, the drift away from this original mission was accelerated by the simple fact that, even from the very beginning, Morris Plan institutions were locally owned and operated and would respond to the demands of local owners.[178] A statement by H. B. Jackson, secretary of the Morris Plan Company of New York, was illustrative: "While the remedial loan was the entering wedge of the Morris Plan and must always remain an important part of our work, it is to the constructive loan that we look with the greatest expectation of results."[179]

As the industry lost its mission-based focus on lending to the poor, the innovation Arthur Morris had created, the installment loan, morphed into an occasionally harmful and predatory product against the poor. Mission drift can happen in two ways: either toward a more profitable customer base or toward more profitable (i.e., predatory) contracts with the same customer base. Several corporations, such as World Acceptance, have taken the installment loan created to help the poor and turned it into a weapon against them. These corporations, primarily in the South, are registered as industrial banks and lend small loans through legislative loopholes that shield them from banking regulatory oversight. Consumers complain about their exorbitant interest rates, fraudulent and predatory practices, hidden fees, and brutish collection practices.[180]

Morris banks were never fully supported by the federal government and never formed a cohesive movement with a clear, defined mission. This rapid shift demonstrates that profit-seeking ownership will always search out the most efficient use of capital for the desired appetite for risk. Morris banks quickly abandoned their mission, and the legal and regulatory environment increasingly made the commercial bank an attractive model for the ill-defined industrial bank.

Today, no ILCs operate as Arthur Morris intended. Their early mission remains just a curious historical note. You might expect, then, that this small nonmovement would eventually fade quietly into commercial banking—which did occur for several decades. But in one of the most interesting twists in modern banking history, this "mongrel" charter experienced a dramatic rebirth and was unexpectedly thrust into the national limelight. Indeed, in 2005, the ILC became the most controversial and hotly contested banking form in the country. The story of its rebirth begins in the 1980s amid the already discussed banking transformation. During this era, when firms blurred boundaries between securities, commercial, and investment banking and created behemoths like Citibank that were involved in all of them, there was also a movement to allow commercial firms to buy banks.

This form of separation between banking and commerce, however, was more firmly entrenched in the law and more guarded by the banking industry protecting its turf. The Bank Holding Company Act (BHCA) strictly prohibited any commercial firm from "controlling" a bank. Therefore, a market developed for "nonbank banks," or banks that were exempt from the BHCA.[181] Lawmakers quickly responded, at the behest of banks, by closing most of these loopholes but specifically exempted

ILCs for no other reason than political maneuvering.[182] Senator Bennett from the state of Utah, one of a handful of states where the ILC charter was still alive, was serving as the head of the Senate Banking Committee. Bennett created a loophole that made the ILC one of only a few banks that a commercial firm could purchase.[183] As soon as the loophole originated and the ILC received FDIC insurance, the industry took off. The FDIC summarized it this way: "In 1988, the first commercially owned ILC applied for FDIC insurance. Once the precedent had been set, more applications followed."[184] Quickly, large commercial firms, such as General Electric, General Motors, and American Express, started operating ILCs that they used to finance their own products.[185] The ILC sector grew exponentially—between 1995 and 2006, industrial bank total assets grew from $12 million to over $213 billion.[186] By far, Utah saw the largest increase in ILC assets, from 11 to 82 percent, during this period.[187]

Still, the entire ILC industry, even at its peak, comprised only about 1.8 percent of the banking industry, and it operated in banking backwaters outside of public or regulatory attention.[188] That suddenly changed when Wal-Mart Stores, Inc. applied for an ILC charter in 2005.[189] To say that Wal-Mart's application was "controversial" would be a significant understatement. What ensued was a media firestorm over the Wal-Mart bank and a fierce and coordinated bank lobbying attack against both Wal-Mart and the ILC charter, neither of which stood a chance against the opposition. Congress imposed a moratorium on new ILC charters, which has yet to be lifted.[190] Finally, Wal-Mart conceded to the massive opposition and withdrew its application.

Many worried that despite their stated intention, which was to eliminate the 2 to 3 percent they were paying to outside banks for credit card servicing, Wal-Mart planned to open a national bank offering competitive pricing that could drive traditional retail banks out of business.[191] The fears appeared to be somewhat justified, despite the company's denial. Wal-Mart already operated a full-service bank in Mexico, and many feared that it would do the same in the United States because of its repeated attempts to enter the banking industry.[192] Eventually, Wal-Mart did enter banking services by partnering with a bank and offering financial services to its customers, making Wal-Mart the only competitor to the high-cost check cashers and the money transfer operations (though it does not lend money). Today, many suggest that large nonbank companies can provide credit to the unbanked. This story shows the magnitude of bank opposition they can face when they try.

* * *

The point of retelling stories of past trailblazing movements is not to provide a detailed instruction manual for treating today's banking problems. When local banking was the law of the land, community control of credit was the utopia that promised to open credit channels to the disenfranchised. Today, money crosses community borders faster than people, goods, and even drugs and guns; local banking is almost dead. Many want to resurrect the cures of the past to deal with modern problems. We can honor and applaud these banks with a soul that did so much good for so long, but we need to move on while heeding the rich lessons of this history. The movements that succeeded in serving the poor received heavy support from the federal government. And they only succeeded in achieving their mission insofar as they remained committed to a public purpose and explicitly rejected a purely profit-oriented model.

4

How the Other Half Borrows

If one of your brethren becomes poor, and falls into poverty among you, then you shall help him. . . . You shall not lend him your money for usury.

—LEVITICUS 25:35–37

I am just a banker "doing God's work."

—LLOYD C. BLANKFEIN, CHAIRMAN AND CEO OF GOLDMAN SACHS, IN A MAY 2010 INTERVIEW WITH *THE TIMES* OF LONDON

Just as banking is not and has never been a system governed by pure market principles, the transaction at the heart of banking—the loan—has always been as much about morality as market exchange. One of the foundational concepts of contract law, called *consideration,* is that the law does not concern itself with how much parties are willing to pay in an agreed-upon exchange. As long as there is a "bargained for exchange" and a "meeting of the minds," courts will enforce a legal contractual exchange.[1] However, the law treats money very differently. In the exchange of money now for payment in the future, the law has always set a maximum price—even if that price has recently risen dramatically. Each state in the United States, and most countries, has a legal maximum one can charge in interest, or a limit on excessive interest, called *usury.* How much is too much depends on the moral and social mores of a given community at a given point in time.

The conversation about debt and usury, then, is a discussion about the commonly agreed-upon principles of what is right and wrong. Some even claim that morality is the whole of it. In fact, every major religion has spoken directly about usury or interest and has expressly prohibited it at one point or another.[2] Most of these ancient cultures considered any interest collected on a loan to be forbidden usury, and the word *usury* was synonymous with interest.[3] Today, nearly all societies allow a lender to charge reasonable interest and consider usury to be "too much interest," or above what their laws allow. Laws on usury, then, are just how much a society deems is too much to charge on a loan.

In the years 2000 BC to 1400 BC, the Vedic texts of ancient India mentioned usury; in the years 700 BC to 100 BC the sutra texts, as well as the Buddhist Jatakas of 600 BC to 400 BC, prohibited usury. Vasishtha, a well-known Hindu lawmaker of that time, forbade usury and disparaged the practice, saying that only "hypocritical ascetics are accused of practicing it."[4]

The Torah and the Talmud contain various passages prohibiting the Jews from charging any interest on loans—it was all prohibited usury. Ezekiel 18:13 states: "He [who] hath given forth upon usury, and hath taken increase: shall he then live? He shall not live: he hath done all these abominations; he shall surely die; his blood shall be upon him." There were, however, loopholes in the blanket prohibition. Specifically: "Unto a stranger thou mayest lend upon usury; but unto thy brother thou shalt not lend upon usury, that the Lord thy God may bless thee in all that thou settest thine hand to in the land whither thou goest to possess it" (Deut. 23:19). Jewish leaders interpreted this to mean that although Jews could not lend with interest to other Jews, they could lend freely to Gentiles. Ignoring these prohibitions led to painful debt stories. Nehemiah, a Jew living under Persian rule in 445 BC, gives a vivid account of the people's outcry over their mounting debts and mortgaged fields and their growing sense of powerlessness as they sold their daughters into slavery to pay their debts. He responded with indignation: "When I heard their outcry and these charges, I was very angry. I pondered them in my mind and then accused the nobles and officials. I told them, 'You are charging your own people interest!' . . . 'You are selling your own people. . . . What you are doing is not right. . . . let us stop charging interest! Give back to them immediately their fields, vineyards, olive groves and houses, and also the interest you are charging them—one percent of the money, grain, new wine and olive oil.' 'We will give it back,' they said. 'And we will not demand anything more from them. We will do as you say.' "[5]

Nehemiah's account is interesting not only because of his moral qualm with usury but because when he presents the situation to the nobles and officials, they too acknowledge the unfairness. And even though it meant smaller financial gains on their part, they promised to—and did—stop the practice. For these Jews, the practice's immorality was enough to end it. It was not dissimilar to the custom in ancient Persia where rulers issued periodic amnesty for all debts every few years. The slates would be wiped clean and all debts forgiven.[6] This ceremony had not only religious significance but also political and practical utility. Canceling the debts subdued unrest that might threaten political power.

In many early European societies where usury prohibitions were common, Jews were the only sources of loans. Laws prohibited Jews from entering many other professions, but Jewish scriptures expressly permitted lending to non-Jews. Jews operated as the primary moneylenders during much of the Middle Ages. Jewish lenders would sit on benches near the market, or *bancas* in Italian (from which the word *bank* originates), and lend to others with interest. Cultural disdain for all moneylenders, combined with or perhaps leading to rampant anti-Semitism, resulted in horrible violence and appalling injustices toward the Jews. Even though their borrowers knew the terms of the bargains they so willingly made when they needed money, they nonetheless vilified their lenders. In 1190, after destroying their lenders' account books, the nobility of Europe massacred the Jews of York to whom they were in debt. European historian Joseph Patrick Byrne reported: "Money was the reason the Jews were killed, for had they been poor, and had not the lords of the land been indebted to them, they would not have been killed."[7] King Edward I later expelled the Jews from England in 1290 based on a similar antagonism.[8] And then there are the accounts of Christian rulers imprisoning their Jewish lenders and extracting teeth and other body parts when their debts became due. Perhaps this cultural guilt led Shakespeare's fictitious Jewish lender, Shylock, to famously demand "a pound of flesh."

For centuries, Christians were also forbidden to lend with interest. Gospel writer Luke proclaimed: "Lend, hoping for nothing again" (Luke 6:5). Amid his message of peace and love, in an uncharacteristic display of anger, Jesus Christ expelled the "moneychangers," or lenders, from the temple grounds. The temple was, at the time, a place of considerable commerce, but Christ acted in "righteous anger" and purged those who profited from loans because he regarded lending on interest not as common business but rather a moral perversion. He drove the point home with his parable of the unforgiving servant, in which a certain man owing a large amount of money to his master or king is forgiven his debt and then turns around and imprisons his servant for failing to pay him a debt much smaller than what he himself owed.[9] "Forgive us our debts as we forgive our debtors," Christ prayed.

Early Christian codes reinforced this message and made it explicit. In 325 AD, the Council of Nicaea banned the practice of usury—charging any interest—among clerics. In 789 AD, Charlemagne forbid usury among all people, perpetuating St. Ambrose's characterization of usury as a transaction in which "more is asked than is given."[10]

Things escalated from there. In 1139, the second Lateran Council in Rome called usury "theft" and forced those who had demanded interest to pay it back. The church was strict about this prohibition and even punished transactions that tried to hide usury. The Council of Vienne in 1311 declared heretics of anyone who said usury was not a sin.[11] The sixteenth-century reformers continued the prohibition. Martin Luther was rather vociferous in his disdain: "Therefore is there on earth no greater enemy of man, after the Devil, than a gripe-money and usurer, for he wants to be God over all men. . . . And since we break on the wheel and behead highwaymen, murderers and housebreakers, how much more ought we to break on the wheel and kill . . . hunt down, curse and behead all usurers!"[12] But the historian Roger Ruston claimed that around the 1620s, persuaded by the forces of capitalism that became harder to ignore, "usury passed from being an offence against public morality which a Christian government was expected to suppress to being a matter of private conscience [and] a new generation of Christian moralists redefined usury as excessive interest."[13]

And yet even as recently as 2014, the pope spoke out against usury, calling it a "social ill." He explained, "When a family has nothing to eat, because it has to make payments to usurers, this is not Christian, it is not human!" and stated that "this dramatic scourge in our society harms the inviolable dignity of the human person."[14]

Muslims are also forbidden to require any interest of borrowers. They are the only religion that still abides by this rule, although creative adherents of Sharia law have found loopholes that permit something equivalent to modern loans. An entire field of law called *Islamic banking* helps businesses involved in trade with Muslim institutions find ways to engage in credit transactions that do not run afoul of usury laws. The Qur'an (2:275) states: "Those who charge usury are in the same position as those controlled by the devil's influence. This is because they claim that usury is the same as commerce. However, God permits commerce, and prohibits usury. Thus, whoever heeds this commandment from his Lord, and refrains from usury, he may keep his past earnings, and his judgment rests with God. As for those who persist in usury, they incur Hell, wherein they abide forever."

One prominent Protestant theory behind the prohibition of usury was that it was a sin to make money without doing any work. English theologian Thomas of Chobham wrote: "The usurer sells nothing to the borrower that belongs to him. He sells only time which belongs to God. He can therefore not make a profit from selling someone else's property."[15] In Islam, economist Ahmad explained that God "permits trade yet forbids usury . . . the difference is that profits are the result of initiative, enterprise and efficiency. They result after a definite value-creating process. Not so with interest."[16] These prohibitions also contained clear social justice elements—those who had money could not extract "rents" from those who did not because it would magnify existing inequalities. The Indian tradition holds that "it is Usury—the rankest, most extortionate, most merciless Usury—which eats the marrow out of the bones of the [cultivators] and condemns him to a life of penury and slavery."[17] Islamic thinkers claim that "interest in any amount acts in transferring wealth from the assetless section of the population to the wealthy."[18]

Religion has also used the language of financial transactions to describe the "debt" man owes to God.[19] Some Christian texts portray the devil as a greedy moneylender—holding humanity in his debt. Christians often portray Jesus Christ as a redeemer, implying a balance sheet shortfall. Christ "paid the price" for sins—both Adam's original sin and those committed by repentant individuals, depending on the theology—and humanity is in his debt. Sin is therefore synonymous with debt.[20] And the Redeemer stands between the debtor (all of us) and the creditor—either God, who demands justice, or the devil, who owns the sinners' souls—if the debt is not paid. It is, of course, sometimes helpful to use a commonly understood framework, like financial transactions, to describe hard-to-grasp religious principles, but in the process, financial concepts and religious ones may have become muddled together. In fact, the word *debt* is associated with "guilt," "fault," and "transgression" in most languages.[21]

The disdain for the usurer was not restricted to the religious. Even the "Father of the Free-market Capitalism," Adam Smith, supported legal restrictions on usury.[22] John Maynard Keynes agreed: "The disquisitions of the schoolmen [on usury] were directed towards the elucidation of a formula which should allow the schedule of the marginal efficiency of capital to be high, whilst using rule and custom and the moral law to keep down the rate of interest, so that a wise Government is concerned to curb it by statute and custom and even by invoking the sanctions of the Moral Law."[23] Many philosophers, including Plato, Aristotle, and Thomas Aquinas, to name a few, considered moneylending a vice. In 300 BC, Aristotle wrote in *Politics:* "The most hated sort [of moneymaking], and with the greatest reason, is usury, which makes a gain out of money itself, and not from the natural use of it. For money was intended to be used in exchange, but not to increase at interest. And this term usury, which means the birth of money from money, is applied to the breeding of money because the offspring resembles the parent. Wherefore of all modes of making money this is the most unnatural."[24]

Folklore and literature also often vilify usurers. Dante, Shakespeare, Dickens, Dostoyevsky, and many others cast moneylenders as their villains. Dante placed usurers in the seventh rung of hell: "From each neck there hung an enormous purse, each marked with its own beast and its own colors like a coat of arms. On these their streaming eyes appeared to feast." In Dickens's *A Christmas Carol,* Ebenezer Scrooge is a greedy moneylender. In Dostoyevsky's *Crime and Punishment,* the disgusting old lady whom Raskolnikov murders is a usurer. And in *The Brothers Karamazov,* Dostoyevsky writes: "It was known too that the young person had . . . been given to what is called 'speculation,' and that she had shown marked abilities in the direction, so that many people began to say that she was no better than a Jew. It was not that she lent money on interest, but it was known, for instance, that she had for some time past, in partnership with old Karamazov, actually invested in the purchase of bad debts for a trifle, a tenth of their nominal value, and afterwards had made out of them ten times their value."[25] Shylock the Jew, in *The Merchant of Venice,* provides a most complicated villain, who offers a soliloquy against racism ("If you prick us, do we not bleed?"). But he is also a greedy and unforgiving lender who demands a pound of flesh for his loan.

In some part, modern society still holds a degree of contempt for both the foolish debtor and the greedy moneylender. For example, as the financial crisis unfolded, some economists and policymakers proposed the remedy of providing direct mortgage relief to underwater borrowers. Mortgage defaults were the eye of the storm, and tackling them seemed to make sense. But the idea was dead on arrival as many clamored about the "moral hazard" of rewarding foolish speculators by relieving their debts.[26] In 2013, *Forbes* writer John Tamny illustrated the feelings some of the public felt toward the "victims" of the crisis:[27] "The notion that those who borrowed to buy houses they couldn't afford were the ones victimized is laughable. . . . Far from deserving our sympathy, these people deserve our disgusted scorn." Tamny called underwater mortgage holders "the irresponsible, imprudent, revolting victimizers of their prudent fellow citizens who have been, and will continue to be forced to pay for their egregious errors committed with money not their own."

Rick Santelli's famous rant that some say was the genesis of the 2008 Tea Party movement illustrates this scorn toward borrowers:

> You know, the government is promoting bad behavior. . . . I'll tell you what, I have an idea. [Mr. President], Why don't you put up a web site to have people vote on the Internet as a referendum to see if we really want to subsidize the losers' mortgages, or would we like to, at least, buy cars and buy houses in foreclosure and give them to people who might have a chance to actually prosper down the road, and reward people that could carry the water, instead of drink[ing] the water. (Trading floor clapping and cheering.) This is America! (Turns around to address pit traders.) How many of you people want to pay for your neighbors' mortgage that has an extra bathroom and can't pay their bills? Raise their hand. (Traders boo; Santelli turns around to face CNBC camera.) President Obama, are you listening? How about we all stop paying our mortgage? It's a moral hazard. . . . We're thinking of having a Chicago Tea Party in July. All you capitalists that want to show up to Lake Michigan, I'm going to start organizing. . . . I'll tell you what, if you read our Founding Fathers, people like Benjamin Franklin and Jefferson, what we're doing in this country now is making them roll over in their graves.[28]

Plenty of scorn was also directed at the modern moneylenders. Journalist Matt Taibbi called Goldman Sachs "a great vampire squid wrapped around the face of humanity, relentlessly jamming its blood funnel into anything that smells like money." The Occupy Wall Street movement embodied this disdain for reckless moneylending with demands that bankers be sent to jail. Their signs could have been written by a modern-day Nehemiah or Andrew Jackson: "Tax Wall Street Leeches," "Turn Wall Street into Tahrir Square," "JP Morgan is a Kleptomaniac," "Jail the Bankers," "Tear Down this Wall Street," "Jesus was the 99%," and "Kick 'M in the Junk Bonds."[29] (Timothy Geithner dismissed those who were uncomfortable with bailing out banks as demanding "Old Testament Justice,"[30] which seems accurate given the admonitions against usury in the book, but the modern state is no longer persuaded by Nehemiah's arguments.)

And so, perhaps having inherited some of these long-standing prejudices and moral pronouncements, we find ourselves today in a society that disparages some mortgage holders, payday borrowers, and the bankrupt as irresponsible or even immoral. At the same time, our collective disdain for usury and moneylending leads to the vilification of moneylenders, including banks.

Still, the American legal system has come to accept usury over time, most dramatically during the 1980s, when many state limits were lifted or significantly increased.[31] Usury limits, which had hovered around 6 to 12 percent for most of U.S. history, were allowed to reach 300 to 700 percent. Inflationary pressures caused the initial deregulation of interest rates by the states, but it was a Supreme Court decision that ultimately eradicated real interest rate caps in the country. In *Marquette National Bank v. First Omaha Service Corporation,* the Supreme Court said that a credit card lender could export the interest rates of one state to any other. Banks immediately lobbied for and were granted the same privilege. Predictably, lenders began to charter in states with the highest rates, which they then exported nationwide. This in turn caused a "race to the bottom" as states competed for lending businesses by lowering borrower protections and increasing usury limits.[32]

The U.S. Supreme Court case allowing rates to be exported did not apply to payday lenders because the industry was not prevalent at the time. However, payday lenders were able to quickly take advantage by "borrowing" bank charters, a practice dubbed "rent-a-bank," in order to "benefit" from high interest rates. After banking laws prohibited this arrangement, payday lenders fled to charter on Native American reservations, which are exempt from state usury laws, in order to charge high rates. These lenders have been known to charge effective interest rates of up to 2000 percent.[33] The result? As explained by one scholar, "The problem of loan-sharking was brushed aside by making [high interest rates], once typical only of organized crime, perfectly legal—and therefore, enforceable no longer by just hired goons and the sort of people who place mutilated animals on their victims' doorsteps, but by judges, lawyers, bailiffs, and police."[34]

* * *

Today, American society not only accepts credit as a way of life, we embrace it. The average American has $15,000 in credit card debt, $33,000 in student loan debt, and $156,000 in mortgage debt.[35] Not only do the majority of the American public borrow their way up the income ladder, but federal mortgage and student loan markets and loose credit policies led to the creation of the American middle class. We, the people, have decided (through laws and policies enacted by our elected representatives) that as a society, we want access to affordable credit for both big wealth-building items like homes, education, and businesses and day-to-day smooth-out-the-bumps sorts of things via credit cards and car loans that would have even higher interest rates if not for government policies. However, in a society built on credit as a means to wealth, a large proportion of people at the bottom are currently left out. If the state enables the banking system (and therefore, the credit markets), the provision of credit certainly becomes a matter of political and social concern, and we, as a society, must determine what we will and will not accept.[36] We cannot tolerate such heavy state involvement in providing credit to the banks while leaving the less well-to-do at the mercy of the modern day sharks.

This is a weighty and consequential issue because equality in the credit market leads to a more fair and just society. Leveling the credit playing field extends to the poor the possibility of improving their lives, as well. But inexpensive credit will not cure or even reduce poverty. The causes of poverty are varied and complex and its cures, elusive. Even so, insofar as policy initiatives can provide ladders out of poverty, we need to understand the chutes that affect the poor—financial setbacks from which it takes years (or lifetimes) to recover: job loss, unexpected healthcare costs, and other minor and major pitfalls that are a part of life. Fringe banks are the market response that fill this void. We must understand them to see how wide the divide is to bridge; how deep the wound is to dress. Only after fully appreciating the moral perversion of such lending can we find the urgency to act.

THE SHARKS

When banks sloughed off their low and moderate income customers and opted out of lending to the poor, a new "fringe lending" industry popped up to meet their needs and has grown ever since. There are a variety of fringe loans across the country. The most common are payday loans, which are currently permitted in thirty-eight states.[37] A payday loan is so-called because the borrower must have a regular paycheck against which she borrows, usually up to $500, with a typical term of anywhere from a week to a month. The borrower gives the lender access to her bank account in the form of either a postdated check or permission for direct withdrawal. The lender then deducts the outstanding payment when it becomes due, typically, the next payday. Consider these staggering statistics about the payday lending sector:

The average payday lending customer is indebted for 199 days, "or roughly 55% of the year. A quarter of consumers were indebted for 92 days or less over the 12-month study period, while another quarter was indebted for more than 300 days."[38]

Over 80 percent of payday loans are rolled over or followed by another loan within fourteen days (i.e., renewed).[39]

Of the loans that are rolled over, *half* are made in a sequence of *at least ten loans*, and the majority, 62 percent, are in sequences of seven or more loans.[40] The payday industry relies on the constant renewal of these loans. One large payday lender even instructs its employees on how to perpetuate the loans with a circle diagram that reflects the need for constant renewal.

A staggering 90 percent of payday lending business is generated by borrowers with five or more loans per year, and over 60 percent of business is generated by borrowers with twelve or more loans per year. Fees on these loans quickly add up. If a typical payday loan of $325 is flipped eight times—this usually takes just four months—the borrower will have paid $468 in interest. In order to fully repay the loan and principal, the borrower will need to pay $793 for the original $325. Most borrowers pay even more than that.[41]

Few borrowers amortize, or have reductions in principal, between the first and last loan of a sequence. For more than 80 percent of the loan sequences longer than one loan, the final loan in the sequence is the same size or larger than the first. Loan size is likely to go up in larger loan sequences, and principal increases are associated with higher default rates.

The average borrower pays an average of between $500 to $600 in interest.[42] One quarter of borrowers pay $781 or more in fees.

A Pew report also found that a payday loan takes 36 percent of a borrower's pretax paycheck.[43] That is, once a loan is made, a person uses more than one-third of their income just to pay it off.

Crushing debt is, after all, the business model for the industry. The Consumer Financial Protection Bureau (CFPB) director has stated that "the payday lending industry depends on people becoming stuck in these loans for the long term, since almost half their business comes from people who are basically paying high-cost rent on the amount of the original loan."[44]

Payday lending requires no credit report. In most cases, a borrower only needs a bank account (which they allow their lender to access) and a paystub to verify income. Over half of payday borrowers end up overdrawing their bank accounts (and incurring bank fees), usually a direct result of payday lenders taking money from their accounts. The fees and interest generally range between $10 to $30 for every $100 borrowed.[45] A typical two-week payday loan with a $15 per $100 fee equates to an annual percentage rate (APR) of about 400 percent. By comparison, APRs on credit cards can range from about 12 percent to 30 percent.[46] But APR vastly underestimates the costs of these loans because they are short-term, and the interest compounds quickly and exponentially if they are held for a year. Because most of these loans are rolled over, the interest is much higher than what the APR reflects. For example, say a borrower takes out a $300 loan. When she is unable to pay the loan at the end of the payday cycle, she pays $50 to extend the loan term, a "rollover," for another two weeks. The borrower still owes the original amount of the loan, the principal. Until she can come up with that amount, she continues to make a $50 payment every two weeks to avoid default. As demonstrated above, this can and usually does go on for months and years, with the borrower paying $50 in fees every two weeks just for the original loan amount. If continued for a year, the borrower will have paid $1,300 in interest in exchange for the use of $300 in cash.

In those states where payday lending is prohibited, title loans take their place. Title loans emerged in the 1990s and are essentially payday loans secured by collateral—the title to the borrower's car. (The loans are often configured this way in order to avoid prohibitions on payday lending.) With title loans, not only do borrowers pay extremely high interest rates, but they also stand to lose what is perhaps their most valuable asset: their car. In other words, despite being a "secured" loan that fully protects the lender, the cost is still exorbitant. A typical borrower receives a cash loan equal to about 26 percent of a car's value and pays 300 percent APR.[47] This means that borrowers are paying very high interest for loans that are carrying significant excess collateral. One in six borrowers also faces repossession, and repossession fees average half of the outstanding loan balance. Title loans have grown into a massive industry. Approximately 8,138 car title lenders operate in twenty-one states and generate nearly $2 billion in loans annually, with borrowers paying more than $4 billion in fees.[48] In states where they are not expressly authorized, lenders are able to operate through loopholes in the law.[49]

Because title lenders can rely on the threat of repossession, the majority of borrowers repeatedly renew their loans, turning what is described as a short-term loan into long-term, high-cost debt requiring borrowers to pay more than twice in interest than what they received in credit. The average amount of a title loan is $1,000, much higher than what can be borrowed from payday lenders.[50] Much like a payday loan borrower, the average car title borrower renews a loan eight times, paying $2,142 in interest for $951 of credit.[51] Title lenders have recently taken a more high-tech approach to ensuring repayment. Rather than having to undergo the costs associated with finding and repossessing a car, many lenders, at the time of borrowing, now install chips in borrowers' vehicles that will remotely disable them.[52] This happened to one borrower whose car was disabled while she was at a shelter hiding from her abusive husband, as well as others whose cars have shut down in dangerous neighborhoods or even on the way to pick up their children from school.

Even pawn loans, the oldest and perhaps least financially ruinous form of fringe loans, exact a high price. The Catholic Church created the first pawnshops in the 1300s in Italy and Spain as a philanthropic venture to lend to the poor. They were motivated to eradicate usury but also had the more sinister goal of eradicating Jewish moneylenders. As such, they extracted involuntary "contributions" from the Jewish lenders to fund the pawn lenders.[53] Today, the borrower takes something of value to the pawnshop and gets a loan worth much less than the value of the item, usually around 20 percent of the value. There is a flat interest on the loan, around 30 percent, which the borrower must pay to retrieve the item within a predetermined period of time—typically, two weeks to one month. The borrower can pay another 30 percent to take out another loan if he or she cannot pay at the end of the term. If a borrower chooses not to pay back the loan principal, the borrower loses the pawned item. Although these loans have very high interest rates, they are not as punishing as other fringe loans because the loss to the borrower is capped at the interest paid each time and the value of the collateral offered. Pawn lenders do not require any credit check or bank account information, as all loans are secured by an item that can be seized.

Many also rely on their future tax returns as a source of credit. These loans, called Refund Anticipation Loans, are high-cost loans secured by a taxpayer's expected refund. The usual term is two weeks, and the average loan is for a few hundred dollars. The borrower pays about 300 percent APR for the ability to receive the tax refund a few weeks early.[54] The tax preparer files the return and collects the refund when it is issued. The borrower walks away with a tax refund reduced by a hefty interest payment, preparation, filing, and finance fees. These fees can be quite high, anywhere from $150 to $500 per transaction, depending on the lender. Banks provided many of these loans for years, but new laws prohibit them from offering these loans. They are now primarily offered by a few fringe lenders and are unregulated in most states.

THE BORROWERS

Just who borrows these usurious loans? Studies conducted by the Consumer Financial Protection Bureau, the Federal Deposit Insurance Corporation, the Federal Reserve, and the Pew Charitable Trusts reveal the characteristics of the population that must rely on the fringe-banking industry.[55] To take out a loan, consumers generally provide a paystub, deposit account statement, or other information to document income as part of the application process. Payday borrowers usually have a steady job and must have a bank account. The average payday borrower profile is a white woman who is divorced or separated, does not have a college degree, and is between twenty-five and forty-four years old. Single parents, blacks, Hispanics, and recent immigrants were more likely to use payday loans than other groups. Payday advance customers are also relatively educated, according to one survey (74.4 percent had a high school diploma or some college), with incomes that most would describe as middle class (over half had incomes between $25,000 and $49,999, with an average income of $40,000).[56] The studies clearly indicate that the customer base is not the destitute but those households with low to moderate income.[57] The average loan this borrower needs is only $350, but because none of the high-interest payments on these loans goes toward the principal, the debt can quickly compound.[58]

Payday borrowers are not, as is often assumed, financially illiterate or casual about borrowing under such demanding terms. The reality is that for many of the poor, these loans represent their only access to credit, and they go to them reluctantly. A Pew study found that desperation often influenced the choice to borrow, as 37 percent of borrowers said they have been in such a difficult financial situation that they have taken out a payday loan on any terms offered. To pay off their loans, many of these borrowers (40 percent) turned to friends or family, sold or pawned personal possessions, or took out another type of loan. One in six has used a tax refund to eliminate payday loan debt.[59]

Nor is the borrowing frivolous. Surveys reveal that loans are used to pay for food or rent, but the budget shortfalls are likely due to a variety of setbacks, such as medical emergencies, car repairs, or other unexpected life expenses.[60] Most Americans do not have savings large enough to cover unplanned expenses. Government studies show that over half the households in the United States could not come up with just $400 to cover a medical emergency without having to borrow, and 60 percent lacked enough money to get by for three months.[61] People just do not have a financial buffer large enough to deal with even small emergencies, as shown by the fact that unexpected medical expenses are the number one cause of bankruptcy in the United States.[62]

And for many, incomes have gotten less predictable, as well. Since the 1970s, household incomes have become much more volatile and yet household bills have remained constant. "More than 30 percent of Americans reported spikes and dips in their incomes. Among that group, 42 percent cited an irregular work schedule; an additional 27 percent blamed a span of joblessness or seasonal work."[63]

Financial education has been embraced by policymakers as a way of turning the poor into "responsible" and "empowered" consumers who can use these tools to increase their own welfare. The thinking goes that if consumers would only learn to avoid financial land mines, the poor could ably maneuver through various credit options and avoid harmful products. If they only knew how to manage their money, they would not be so poor!

It is not stupidity but rather necessity that drives people to borrow. If lower-cost credit options were available to the poor, wouldn't they use them? A study of payday borrowing showed that payday loan customers searched extensively for preferred credit before deciding on a payday loan. Loan applicants had an average of over five credit inquiries during the twelve months leading up to their initial payday loan application.[64] Research shows that the poor understand debt and the costs of the loans they take out—they weigh options when in need and they choose these loans.[65] In a 2007 California survey, 92 percent of respondents said that they were aware of the fees on their loans before taking them out.[66]

According to the research, financial education simply does not work to discourage this borrowing.[67] This seems obvious. Educating the poor to choose better options must mean that better options exist. Although more education and financial savvy would certainly help all of us make the most of our money, financial education is not what separates the poor and the middle class. Contrast, for example, the financial literacy required by an average middle- to high-income family who puts money into the local bank and perhaps invests any extra money in a 401(k) provided by an employer with someone who is poor and must manage several loans at a time while making small payments on each. Factor in the costs and fees on this person's simple financial transactions, such as cashing a paycheck. Managing multiple loans and fees shows a level of financial literacy that many in the middle class don't have and frankly, don't need. The middle class juggles too—transferring credit card debt from one card to a new one that offers 0 percent APR for six months in the hopes of paying less than 16 percent interest for a while.[68] But in comparison, the middle class seems to be juggling with beanbags, and the poor are juggling with knives. Dipped in poison.

If anything, the pervasive usage of payday lending does not show irresponsibility or ignorance. It just shows that many people need small loans. Consider the following comments that the CFBP and the Pew Charitable Trusts gathered from payday lending customers in support of payday loans:[69]

> "Well I can say I normally get a payday loan only for emergency like [*sic*] if I need to pay a bill. I feel I get great service and the money I need." —*J. B. from Birmingham, AL*
>
> "I have unfortunately had to use the services of the Payday loans. Again, unfortunately it is easier to get these loans than to apply for and receive a loan from the bank that is using your money to supply others with loans and other functions." —*D. M. from Alliance, OH*
>
> "Payday loans have helped several times when bills and unexpected circumstances arise. The limits are great, not too high so an individual can keep it under control. It's less hassle than going to a bank for those without the best credit." —*Craig from Wellington, AL*
>
> "Payday loans have helped me pay medical bills and buy medicine for me and my mom, bought me gas and helped me get my car fixed when money was tight. I was between checks and this was the only option I

had as I do not have any credit to speak of. Much easier than going and being rejected by the banks." —*Lance from Birmingham, AL*

"Although many are predatory and charge way too much, it is the only type of loan I can get right now, so Payday Loans are something I need access to. Regulation to these could prove troublesome." —*Thomas from Dana Point, CA*

"I am a commission based employee for the automotive industry and some weeks my pay is less than expected. I use the payday advance services to make up for the weeks wher [*sic*] I am short cash. I do not use credit and this gives the additional cash when needed." —*D. B. from Bessemer, AL*

"It seems like you never catch up and it, it's just check-to-check, and something breaks down, and the house needs work, kids have school, just never catch up." [And how long have you felt that way?] "Twenty years."[70] —*Storefront borrower, Chicago*

These are real people who live and work in cities and towns, poor neighborhoods and wealthy ones, both public servants and blue-collar workers. They borrow to pay for things that are widely considered essential. They borrow with forethought and with care. They are mainstream, ordinary people forced to borrow at the fringe. And fringe lenders are the only ones meeting this large market demand because banks, credit unions, and other mainstream lenders have chosen not to.

CREDIT AND MORAL OUTRAGE

Still, there is a stigma associated with those who must use fringe lenders. Pundits and radio hosts give paternalistic financial advice against debt, which is based on the assumption that if people only *realized* how bad debt was, they would not take out loans.

The dominant cultural narrative is that when people of lesser means than us borrow from payday lenders, it reveals their ignorance. The rich are also guilty of financial mismanagement, but financial mismanagement by the poor is seen as more morally reprehensible. Dave Ramsey, a talk radio financial guru and a vocal opponent of debt of any kind, regularly derides those who rely on payday loans as "idiots" or says that they are living above their means: "If you're taking out a payday loan to cover regular living costs, then your living costs are way too high." He also cites "research" that supposedly shows that "81% of people who used these ridiculous loans say they would've cut back on expenses if they didn't have access to the loans." He insists, "Instead of changing their behavior—which is what brought on the problem in the first place—they temporarily cover it up with a terrible 'solution' that only makes their problems worse."[71] Liz Weston, a financial advice columnist for *MSN Money,* states: "Payday lending doesn't solve the underlying problem, which is often poor money management."[72] Under "7 Brainless Borrowing Behaviors," Sheyna Steiner lists the first three as payday loans, car title loans, and tax refund anticipation loans.[73]

This moral outrage about credit, however, is usually only directed at the poor or middle class. The wealthy are advised by pundits and financial advisers to use "leverage" (a.k.a. debt) to grow wealth.[74] The hedge fund and private equity industry that provides its "qualified investors" the most return on capital relies on high levels of credit. One obvious example is the leveraged buyout (LBO), a common tactic used by these funds to increase returns. *Investopedia* defines the LBO as "the acquisition of another company using a significant amount of borrowed money (bonds or loans) to meet the cost of acquisition. Often, the assets of the company being acquired are used as collateral for the loans in addition to the assets of the acquiring company. The purpose of leveraged buyouts is to allow companies to make large acquisitions without having to commit a lot of capital."[75] But the LBO is just one simple example among a myriad of complex financial transaction products that are built on debt and that are the daily work of traders, money managers, and other investors.

The financial crisis was in part caused by all of this leverage, debt, and risk-taking. Many investment banks had leverage ratios of thirty to one.[76] In other words, for every one dollar of equity, they had thirty dollars of debt, which means that firms can make high returns with very little initial investment. High leverage can produce high profits, but it also means higher risks. Regulators have been in the process of mandating lower amounts of leverage since the financial crisis, but the world of finance has convinced the regulators, as well as the public, that the only way to do business properly is through large amounts of debt—in other words, to borrow Brandeis's terminology, by leveraging "other people's money."[77] However, through all of the debates between the government regulators and the banks over the right debt-to-equity ratios (or "capital"), no one has expressed moral outrage that these firms and wealthy investors should "live within their means" or "not buy things they cannot afford"—they talk in terms of "systemic risk" and "value-at-risk," not moral virtue or responsibility.

Even though the banks' high debts are what crippled the U.S. economy, our collective moral outrage is still reserved for the poor and the underwater mortgage owners. Many pundits, politicians, and even some well-respected academics made the completely unsupported claim that the financial crisis was caused by poor people borrowing money to buy homes they could not afford. These people, they claimed, were greedy and irresponsible, and their credit demands caused our financial system to fail.

In tandem with the moral censure, the legal system has responded with harsh punishments for debt, including the rebirth of debtor's prison. Our country decided two hundred years ago that people should not be imprisoned for failing to pay debts, but the 1983 case *Bearden v. Georgia* has revived the practice.[78] The case allows judges to detain and imprison debtors who the judge determines have "willfully" refused to pay their fines or debts. This loose standard of "willfulness" has been left to the discretion of judges—with some judges using the standard broadly. A May 2014 NPR study revealed that in one Washington prison, a quarter of people jailed for misdemeanors were there because they owed money. One judge in that district explained that he decided on ability to pay based on how the persons presented themselves in court. "They come in wearing expensive jackets . . . or maybe a thousand dollars' worth of tattoos on their arms. And they say, 'I'm just living on handouts.' "[79] In June 2014, a mother of seven children died in debtors' prison. She was sent to prison for failing to pay $2,000 in fines related to her children's school attendance, plus court fees for the ensuing legal actions.[80] Meanwhile, *not one* Wall Street banker has spent a single day in prison based on the massive debts accrued using our pension funds.[81]

For better or for worse, our entire financial sector runs on cheap credit. The average American household, too, runs on debt. Many Americans are living beyond their means, and some say that as a society, we "save too little, spend too much, and borrow excessively."[82] People will live above their means at *every* income level, and it is not the case that the poor live *more* above their means than the rich. It is also true that many people live responsibly and wisely invest in homes and businesses based on this very credit. Debt can be an effective way to grow a society and build individual wealth. Credit is the foundation of our economy—we even measure the economy's success based on consumer *spending,* not saving. Since the post–WWII era, government policies and rhetoric have encouraged people to spend to grow the economy. When asked how the American people could help the nation recover after the devastation of 9/11, President Bush urged everyone to go out and spend as if nothing had happened.[83]

Many of us get educated, buy a home, and even pay our bills through credit. Government programs exist that subsidize credit markets for the middle class, making it easier for the middle class to buy life-enhancing things. Government-created entities like Fannie Mae and Freddie Mac create a market for home mortgages, and Sallie Mae subsidizes student loans. Although it may be wise for all of us to save more and learn to live within our means, that standard is not the basis of our current economy. There is currently no outpouring of political or public support to reduce lending. In fact, policymakers worry about too little lending and borrowing. And it is not obvious that restricting lending will lead to better outcomes—that is just one issue debated by the Keynesian versus Austrian economists (American economists have been guided by Keynes since the Great Depression). Perhaps we Americans will renounce our easy credit culture, call for structural change, go back to the gold standard, eliminate the national debt, or force the financial world to take on less debt, but until we do, it is sanctimonious to direct our collective aversion to debt at just one portion of the population.

It is especially unfair to morally oppose the use of fringe lending when there are no meaningful options. The rise of fringe banking correlates directly with the decline of banks in poor communities. The result is a disparity in banking services today: government-funded large and small banks compete for the deposits of the wealthy and middle class while the other half is left to fringe institutions that are often usurious, sometimes predatory, and almost always much worse for low-income individuals than the services offered by traditional banks.

Chris Peterson's *Taming the Sharks* noted that since "low-to-moderate income consumers have lost access to banks and credit unions since the late seventies, [they] have naturally moved to [fringe lenders] for their financial needs."[84] Economist John Caskey and others have observed that it was only after the banks left that the fringe banking industry exploded. Payday lending emerged during the 1990s "to serve a void created by the withdrawal of traditional lenders from the very small loan market."[85] Fringe banking has grown exponentially since the 1980s and hasn't stopped. "There are more pawnshops today, both in absolute numbers and on a per capita basis, than at any time in United States history." Prior to the mid-1970s, check-cashing institutions existed in only a few urban areas, but throughout the 1980s, these institutions rapidly expanded across the country. "Virtually nonexistent in this country 20 years ago, [this sector] has grown into a $100 billion business. Since the mid-1990s, the number of payday lenders nationwide has grown over 10 percent annually."[86] With over twenty thousand stores, the payday lending industry makes $40 billion in loans annually.[87] There are more payday lender storefronts than Starbucks and McDonald's *combined.*[88]

An important aspect of fringe lending success has been the precision with which they reach their customers. When the poor have been asked about using fringe banks rather than mainstream banks, many claim that they are "not comfortable" dealing with banks.[89]

It is no surprise. Due to various regulatory measures, mainstream banks require extensive documentation, such as utility bills, a driver's license, and a social security number or alien documentation number, just to open an account. Providing an array of documentation can prove a significant barrier to banking for many, in contrast to the ease with which they can access funds from fringe banks. In addition, many of the American poor, who are immigrants or uneducated, often do not speak English, may be illiterate, or might confront complex barriers to traditional banking structures. Intangible barriers of class and culture also occur. Thus, mainstream banking has abandoned poor areas not only by shutting down branches but also by failing to speak the financial language of the poor. Even when banks are available geographically, they often remain out of reach.[90]

Conversely, payday lending businesses operate behind a façade of informality. These lenders operate in cash, at all hours, on a short-term basis, in the direct vicinity of their customers, and usually in their language. This business model seems to be in direct contrast to banks with their rigid hours, requirements, fees, and procedures. In addition, banks rarely make small consumer loans, and larger loans need a lot more paperwork, processing, and formalities. Surveys reveal that many low-income individuals feel "snubbed" by mainstream financial institutions and are "pride-conscious" more than "price-conscious"; therefore, they are "susceptible to the appeal of the secondary sector's 'merchandising of respect.' "[91] Banks do give credit in the form of credit cards and overdrafts, but relying on these products as loans can get expensive, and banks hide many of their fees and interest rates in small print and do not make them clear up front. Research has shown that payday borrowers who have "credit card liquidity," or the ability to borrow on a credit card, still opt for payday loans.[92]

And yet, despite the informal façade, fringe banks are highly profitable corporations whose rigid practices come into play as soon as debts become due. These businesses can resort to intimidation, harassment, and legal process in order to collect payments.[93] By mimicking informal markets, these fringe banks have convinced their customers that they operate in an informal, flexible realm, but their debt collection practices are anything but. As one commentator observed about a Washington, DC, check-cashing outlet: "The primitive hands-on processing and tawdry exterior of the outlets both exude welcome to poor customers and mask [the firm's] close ties to and substantial financing from large corporations and big banks."[94] This is another critical, and somewhat ironic, aspect of the alternative financial service industry's success: its ability to take advantage of the federally sponsored banking system, using its access to clearinghouses and even its banking charters to lend.

FIGHTING THE SHARKS

Fighting the payday industry has been a Sisyphean task. Consider an analogy: a person might begin to experience headaches and fatigue. She takes ibuprofen, gets some sleep, and cleans up her diet, hoping to stop the headaches. Then she starts getting nauseous. She takes some medicine, drinks some ginger ale, and eats some saltines. It turns out that none of these things work. Unfortunately, what she's experiencing are symptoms of cancer in her brain. The cancer must be treated now, and there may be hope because she has caught it early. By treating it, she may be able to resume her normal life. On the other hand, if she continues to treat the symptoms with pills and tonics, the cancer will continue to grow until it kills her.

Fringe lenders are creating problems in our society that are cause for alarm. We might approach them with temporary solutions and relief, but if we look deep enough, we will find a cancer eating away at our democracy. Centralized power amassed by a state-supported financial industry is creating vast inequalities of access. This is a disease foreseen and feared by our founding fathers and other leaders, who tried in era-specific ways to contain it. But just as treatments for cancer have evolved over time, so must our response to this current threat.

The extent of the problem is revealed by the fact that despite the incredible efforts of advocates and concerned policymakers, these lenders continue to flourish. They are exploiting a fundamental void in our financial system. So fighting the problem of *how* and *what* and *how much* fringe bankers are lending is an important task but one that is necessarily limited in its reach. A survey of the various strong and comprehensive measures deployed by our concerned policymakers will ultimately lead to the recognition that a more fundamental approach is needed.

There is a wide spectrum of state regulation of payday lending. States can regulate interest rates, terms, and various other dimensions of payday loans. Many states have chosen to not regulate payday loans or to set high maximum APRs. In fact, the maximum rates allowed by law have steadily increased over the last decade, with rates ranging from a 300 percent APR to a 1900 percent APR.[95] These APRs significantly exceed the rates allowed by credit card companies and banks.

The grievances against the industry have led some state and federal regulators to crack down on it, but this has proven to be difficult, both politically and practically. The fringe banking industry is a powerful lobbying group that has successfully fought attempts at regulation. And the regulations that have been enacted have been skirted just as quickly because the industry creates new products to replace the banned ones and implements new fee structures to avoid interest rate caps. Engaged in a frustrating game of whack-a-mole, state legislators have banned payday lenders or certain products only to see high-interest loans pop up in another form.

Those states that have banned payday lenders contain a proliferation of title lenders. Those that cap interest rates see a rise in "fees" on the same loans. States that set firm interest caps that cannot be skirted (so far, only Oregon) see a shift to customers paying overdraft fees and bank late payments, which often equal or surpass payday lending limits, to give themselves short-term loans.[96]

For many years, payday lenders skirted these rules by "renting bank charters" from banks in states with high usury rates and operating from another state. Payday loan companies partnered with banks in states with no usury laws or very high interest rate ceilings, like South Dakota or Delaware. When banking regulators put an end to this practice a decade ago, payday lenders seeking to avoid usury limits fled to Native American reservations or offshore regulatory havens like Malta.[97] Today, many payday lenders operate on the Internet and can charter in the states with the highest interest rate ceilings. These lenders are the most usurious (with average rates of 650 percent), the most complained about, and the hardest to regulate.[98] Research conducted by Pew has also shown higher instances of fraud and abuse by online lenders.

Because usury law is primarily a state matter, the enforcement of rules has also varied among the states. New York State has been particularly active and has even indicted payday lenders under state criminal laws that prohibit usury of over 25 percent.[99] Payday lenders chartered in other states and offshore islands were providing loans to New York residents at interest rates of over 500 percent.[100] The New York State attorney general charged these firms with criminal violations in 2014. However, this level of enforcement activity is incredibly rare and hits only the most brazen and egregious lenders who seem to willfully flout state laws.

Still, the industry is being restrained by several states. Leading expert John Caskey notes that "payday lending is a big business that would be even bigger if restrictive states were to liberalize their regulations."[101] And political forces have been overcome through public pressure or powerful allies. One recent example of such an ally is Holly Petraeus, General David Petraeus's wife, who championed exactly the problem described above after she witnessed its destructive effects on the rank and file of the U.S. military. Military bases are currently surrounded by alternative financial providers. In 2007, The Military Lending Act capped interest rates to military borrowers at 36 percent and required the written and oral disclosure of interest rates and payment obligations before loans were issued.[102] But the law was underenforced and easily skirted. Payday and title lenders simply changed the terms of the loan agreements to circumvent the regulations.[103] Holly Petraeus pushed for amendments to the law, and in 2012, she testified before the Senate, calling for reforms to the Military Lending Act structure to improve enforcement. After those amendments were passed, she called for further reforms to ensure that lenders could not again skirt the regulations by changing the terms of their loan agreements. She gave a few examples, including a story about the spouse of a wounded warrior in the Illinois National Guard who took out an auto title loan of $2,575 at an APR of 300 percent. The finance charges on the loan were $5,720.24, for a total amount of $8,295.24. The loan was not subject to the act's protections under the current rule because it had a term longer than 181 days.[104] Petraeus also told the story of an airman from California who borrowed $6,000 for thirty-six months at 102.47 percent APR, which, even though it was secured by the title of his car, ended up costing him $13,463.04. Again, because the loan was for longer than 181 days, it was not covered by the law. Holly Petraeus was appointed to the CFPB with Senator Elizabeth Warren's help and has stayed involved in addressing these problems.

The CFPB, created in 2010, is the first federal regulator with the direct mandate to protect consumers from harmful or abusive financial products. The agency has already gained a reputation as a tough and effective regulator and has placed payday lending reform near the top of its agenda. The federal agency cannot lower state interest rates, but it can curtail the abusive and predatory aspects of the industry. The agency has already proposed rules that would either require payday lenders to do underwriting for loans and show that the borrower can repay the loan or prohibit excessive renewals of the same loan. These rules have not yet been made final, but President Obama has voiced his support for the rules: "If you lend out money, you have to first make sure that the borrower can afford to pay it back. . . . We don't mind seeing folks make a profit. But if you're making that profit by trapping hard-working Americans into a vicious cycle of debt, then you got to find a new business model, you need to find a new way of doing business."[105]

Recently, the Department of Justice (DOJ) used creative means to try to stop the industry. Unable to directly attack the lenders, they went to the lenders' source of credit in an attempt to "choke off" their funding. Operation Choke Point, which was initiated in March 2013, aimed to sever ties between banks and payday lenders—the premise was to "combat mass-marketing consumer fraud by foreclosing fraudster's access to payment systems."[106] Only chartered banks are allowed access to the payments and clearing system, which is a network created and operated by the Federal Reserve.[107] The DOJ targeted banks that were "involved with or willfully blind" to consumer fraud schemes that require payment systems to debit funds from consumer accounts.[108] In August 2013, New York Financial Services Superintendent Benjamin Lawsky sent 117 financial institutions (including Bank of America, Wells Fargo, JPMorgan Chase, and Citigroup) a list of thirty-five payday lenders who violated New York usury laws. Lawsky instructed the banks to develop safeguards to "choke off" the offending lenders as well as the payday lending industry as a whole.[109] By December 2013, the DOJ had issued over fifty subpoenas to banks and payment processors.[110]

In January 2014, Four Oaks Bank was the first bank to settle with the DOJ for $1.2 million and agreed to restrictions on its ability to do business with Internet payday lenders.[111] Almost 100 percent of Four Oaks Bank's customers were Internet payday lenders, and the company was granting them access to the payment system only to be used by banks. Not only were these lenders charging between 400 percent and 1800 percent interest, in excess of state usury laws, but they were gaining unauthorized access to their borrower's accounts. According to the consent order, the lenders offered borrowers loans with an agreement that customers would pay their loan via a debit on a particular date, at which point their obligation would be discharged. However, the lenders did not deduct the amount on that date and instead manipulated customers into extending the loans and racking up multiple finance charges. In some cases, the lenders manipulated the amount and frequency of debits to obtain greater profits by keeping consumers constantly in debt. No other banks have been prosecuted under Operation Choke Point and no others likely will.

The reason is that the payday lending industry immediately sued the DOJ over unfairly targeting them, and Congress stepped in to stop the project. The initiative faced significant political blowback right away, with many arguing that payday lending is a legitimate business being unjustly accused. Chairman Darrell Issa of the House Committee on Oversight and Government Reform found: "Contrary to the Department's political statements, Operation Choke Point was primarily focused on the payday lending industry," which is made up of "entirely lawful and legitimate merchants."[112] There was nothing "fraudulent" about the industry, Issa argued. Chairman Issa also released a staff report in 2014 highlighting key failures of the initiative,[113] including (1) the operation was "choking out" companies the administration considered a "high risk" or otherwise objectionable, despite the fact that they were legal businesses, (2) the operation forced banks to terminate relationships with a wide variety of entirely lawful and legitimate merchants, and (3) the project primarily focused on the payday lending industry. Indeed, according to some state laws, it is legal for payday lenders to operate and charge the rates they do. However, roughly 40 percent of the industry's volume consists of organizations that do not have the legal right to originate loans. Nearly all of the online-only payday lenders are lending in states that prohibit lending outright or that prohibit loans by lenders without a state-issued license. Even though these loans are void or voidable as a matter of law, these companies collect on their loans while failing to disclose this crucial legal fact—an omission that is likely actionable under mail and wire fraud statutes.[114] The argument is that banks can lend to any legitimate business that they deem creditworthy, and payday lending is not illegal.

Issa's report was factually incorrect, as up to 40 percent of payday lenders' rates and activities are illegal. However, even if all payday lending operations were perfectly legal, one would have to be willfully deaf to the imbalance of services in the financial industry to bless the relationship between payday lenders and banks. Perhaps Operation Choke Point stemmed from a sense of injustice that an industry should be permitted to use credit from banks and turn around and lend it out at high interest. It may have occurred to the regulators that though not strictly illegal, there was something "immoral," perhaps *wrong,* with payday lenders partnering with federally supported banks and both making hefty profits at the expense of the poor. Not to mention that the reason the poor were left with payday lenders in the first place is because the banks stopped lending to the poor. If that was the impetus behind Operation Choke Point, no one quite verbalized it. We're still treating the symptoms without taking a hard look at the roots of the problem.

Regulating the industry, or "taming the sharks,"[115] is, in part, difficult because of the incredible market demand for what they offer. Of course, quipped comedian John Oliver, "the customer demand for heroin is also overwhelming, and that doesn't mean it's a product you'd *necessarily* recommend to your friends to get them out of a jam."[116] But where does your friend go in a financial jam? What if your friend needs to fix her car to get to work or falls short on her food budget and needs to feed her kids? Many community leaders and financial advocates to the poor give presentations to groups about the dangers of payday loans. Inevitably, they are faced with the question: What if I need to borrow money? Where should I go? They have expressed frustration that they usually do not have a satisfying answer. Comedian Sarah Silverman provided an answer in a satirical sketch that offered potential borrowers another alternative—she called it the "anything else" alternative. She said: "Literally, just do anything else."[117] Her ideas included giving blood, jumping in front of rich people's cars, and a few other off-color suggestions. It wasn't meant to be serious, of course. But the problem's serious suggestion, offered by the Pew Charitable Trusts and other serious institutions, is to go to family and friends. Borrowers with options do not become clients of fringe lenders. Those who turn to payday lenders have exhausted those resources or come from communities and families of people in similarly financially stressed situations.

State and federal actions may make existing loans less disastrous, which would be an excellent outcome, but increased regulation may also make it harder for the poor to borrow, relegating individuals that need credit to finding options on the unregulated and much more dangerous informal market. Fringe loans, like payday and title loans, exist because a large portion of the population needs them. The mole pops up to meet a massive consumer demand. So although these lenders may be rightly described as less "whackable" animals like vultures, predators, or sharks, their customers rely on them to get them out of a jam. Until the demand stops (that is, people are less poor) or fair credit becomes more widely available, variations on high-interest small loans will keep popping up.

Because those who need payday loans are already struggling financially, there is some evidence that prohibiting these loans may actually hurt consumers. Paige Skiba found that check bouncing, customer complaints, and Chapter 7 bankruptcies all *increased* significantly in Georgia after payday loans were prohibited in 2004.[118] Donald Morgan and Michael Strain also used data from Hawaii and found similar results. Pew found that if individuals were faced with a shortfall and payday loans were unavailable, 81 percent of borrowers said they would have to cut back on expenses such as food.[119]

For years, economists have tried to study the effects of payday loans on their borrowers. After a recent review of all the economic research attempting to answer the big question, "Do payday lenders, on net, exacerbate or relieve customers' financial difficulties?" John Caskey has concluded that there is no reliable answer.[120] Brian Melzer's research indicated that instead of alleviating economic hardship, payday loans contribute to or cause more hardship. His research has presented "robust evidence" that payday loans make it more difficult for households to pay their mortgage, rent, and utility bills, and it also causes them to delay medical and dental care and prescription purchases.[121] Paige Skiba and Jeremy Tobacman have shown that payday loans increase Chapter 13 bankruptcies even though other research found that prohibiting payday loans increases Chapter 7 bankruptcies.[122] Jonathan Zinman's research demonstrated that borrowers suffered as a result of Oregon's cap, which drove payday lenders from the state.[123] Caskey reviewed all the research and has ultimately concluded that "we cannot have substantial confidence in the results of any of these studies."[124]

The question of whether payday loans are categorically good or bad for borrowers is unanswerable, in part, because it is the wrong question. On the one hand, payday loans are the only credit option for many households. Cutting off access to a loan that can help a family make it from one paycheck to the next can result in severe financial distress. On the other hand, these loans are too costly and can lead to a debt trap.

The very loan that can help one person avoid a catastrophe can be the *cause* of that very catastrophe for another similarly situated individual. The more relevant question is whether there are better, less costly, alternatives.

LENDING MARKETS AND INTERMEDIATION

The question of whether the current high costs of payday loans are justified is another difficult and perhaps unanswerable question. The payday lending industry claims to be serving the needs of the poor and promoting "the democratization of credit."[125] The industry and its supporters argue that their profit margins are not high; that the fees they charge reflect the actual cost of lending to the middle- and low-income classes. Although it is certainly true that it costs more to lend to the poor, it is by no means the case that payday lenders price their loans based on the borrower or even the "market." In fact, across the board, these lenders are charging the maximum interest rates allowable by law.

The first comprehensive study of payday lending pricing, released in 2009, revealed a "strong relationship between actual payday loan prices and the payday loan price ceiling imposed by [the state legislature]." Even if some price competition existed between lenders when they first opened, "with the passage of time, the average finance charge on payday loans . . . gravitated upwards toward this ceiling." This pattern, suggest the researchers, is consistent with Nobel Prize winner Thomas Schelling's theory of implicit collusion around pricing focal points.[126] Although there is no smoking gun, the study reveals that there is not only little market competition among lenders, but possible price controls. The irony, they point out, is that these alleged "collusive focal points were provided by the state legislatures."[127] An earlier study had indeed revealed evidence of price collusion among credit card companies Visa and MasterCard in the 1980s to drive up interest rates.[128] Not only did the comprehensive payday pricing study show possible price collusion, it also showed discrimination: "The larger data contain stronger evidence of third-degree price discrimination: loan prices were higher in neighborhoods near military bases and in disproportionately minority neighborhoods, consistent with exploitation of price inelasticity among these demographic groups."[129] The study concluded that these prices could be reduced only if banks or other providers of credit could compete in this space. In other words, credit alternatives, not regulation, would drive down prices.

Even without the allegation of price fixing, fringe borrowers in the states with the highest caps pay the most. Lenders can charge the maximum allowable because, despite economic theory, market competition has not worked to lower interest rates. Payday loan customers come in desperation. Almost 40 percent of borrowers admit that when they need these loans, they are not "price-sensitive"; they would agree to the loan under *any terms* offered. As a result, there is no competition between lenders to lower prices.[130] Payday lenders do not compete on price (they charge as much as they are legally permitted) but on location.[131]

Data on payday lending profitability is hard to find because these firms are private companies. The industry trade organization, the Community Financial Services Association, claims that because of fixed store operating costs and loan default losses, they can only break even by charging fees of about $15 per hundred borrowed.[132] Alternatively, a presentation prepared by potential investors in a payday lending company found that "a store set up for $30,000 will generate more than $258,000 in operating cash flow over its first five years of operation, which implies an extraordinary average annual pretax rate of return—around 170 percent—on the initial investment."[133] Another study found that state laws limiting fees per loan did not reduce profitability but just increased loan volume. In other words, payday lenders were able to retain their profit margins by issuing more loans at lower costs.[134] Economic analysis of the rates of default on these loans are also mixed, with some saying that the high costs correlate with high default rates and others proving that the default rates are similar to other loans, with the costs linked to higher store operating expenses.[135] Reporting of default rates can be easily manipulated. If a customer takes out $300 and rolls the loan over several times, they will have paid the lender back in fees and interest much more than the loan amount, but if they fail to pay off the last loan in the series, it is considered a default. The lender has not lost any money and perhaps has made a healthy profit on this "defaulted" loan. The industry is clearly profitable. And yet lending to the poor is more costly, so higher-than-average rates are justified. Because there is little to no price competition, it is difficult to know what the right "market rate" should be.

Unlike most banks, fringe lenders make no effort to individualize the interest charged. All loans have the same fees, terms, and high interest. They do not differentiate the creditworthy from the risky or offer lower interest rates to more qualified borrowers. The extent of payday underwriting is basically to determine whether the borrower has a bank account, a paycheck, and a heartbeat. The assumption is that anyone who needs one of their loans must be highly risky, and so they charge all borrowers the same high rate of interest. This "sorting" function is one of the main reasons banks exist. Being able to distinguish "good" credit, the kind that helps a borrower reach a better financial outcome or avoid a financial pitfall, versus "bad" debt that adds water to a sinking ship and accelerates financial decline, is one of the principle values banks provide to society. Ben Bernanke, a scholar of the Great Depression before he was appointed chairman of the Federal Reserve, found through empirical analysis that the most devastating and long-lasting aspect of the Great Depression was that banks stopped their essential function of credit intermediation. He stated that "the real service performed by the banking system is the differentiation between good and bad borrowers."[136] This differentiation is the central question in lending and is the reason banks are bailed out. If they do not sort, credit is frozen and unable to go where it is most useful.

Bankers use objective and subjective factors, or soft data, to determine the good borrowers from the bad. This intermediary function has changed over time and has been advanced by numerical formulas. For example, although a bank may have used your "character" to lend in the past, today, they will use your "credit score," your income, and your assets and liabilities, which are likely to be more objective because they represent your historical track record as well as your financial cushion. Still, these numbers are supplemented by subjective factors or character traits. Using objective factors is a blunt tool in determining creditworthiness, both overinclusive and underinclusive. In other words, there are those who are more creditworthy than their "scores" indicate and there are those who are less. Still, these tools have revolutionized lending by streamlining decision-making and increasing accuracy.

And yet, the banking industry has determined that because it can make much higher margins on larger loans, it is not worthwhile for it to spend resources to differentiate borrowers for small loans. The result is that the poor are generally determined to be "bad borrowers." However, there is a difference between the poor who are creditworthy and those who are not. This is one of the reasons that credit unions, savings and loans, and Morris banks were able to lend to the poor. By differentiating a good credit risk from a bad one, a lender *can* effectively lend to the poor at low costs. An important distinction that must be understood first is the difference between illiquidity and insolvency.

To illustrate the difference, the example of central bank lending to banks proves useful. A bank is *illiquid* when it has a future income stream and enough assets to pay off its debts, but just not now. If a bank creditor (a depositor) demands his or her money immediately, the bank cannot pay it even though the bank expects to get paid itself within a short time (through a loan payment by a borrower). This bank is creditworthy because it has enough total money coming in to cover its total debts. It is just illiquid at the moment—it doesn't have enough money *right now* to cover its debts. The central bank can provide it with a fast loan to pay off its debtor without having to sell assets or call in loans, which would be incredibly disruptive to business. On the other hand, a bank that is *insolvent* is not just short on cash today. Its balance sheet doesn't add up. If you total all of its assets and liabilities, they come up short—the bank is in the "red." If the Federal Reserve gives this bank a loan, it isn't just helping the bank cover a temporary shortage but delaying its eventual and necessary failure. This bank is not creditworthy. It is important for the central bank to distinguish between these two banks because an insolvent bank needs to be liquidated, or shut down, and a solvent one does not.

However, the line between insolvency and illiquidity is not so clear. For example, if the illiquid bank doesn't get that credit, it quickly becomes insolvent. It will have to sell its assets at too low of a price (called a "fire sale") to pay off its creditors, or it may simply default on its debts and be unable to borrow again—spelling certain disaster for the bank. Similarly, if an insolvent bank is given enough credit at a good price, it can make solid investments and climb its way back into the "black." This is what the bailouts did for the banks during the financial crisis. In 2008 and 2009, most of the nation's largest banks were, in fact, insolvent. They did not have enough assets to pay off their debts because their assets had quickly turned to junk. The credit that flowed into these insolvent banks helped them recover their losses, saving them. Ideally, the central bank would only lend to illiquid banks because otherwise, it is interfering with market discipline by "picking winners and losers." However, during the recent crisis, the government decided that it would strong-arm the market's "invisible hand" and bail out the banks because their failure was more detrimental than the long-term effects of moral hazard. Instead of letting the market punish the foolish debtors so that they would learn their lesson, the government smoothed their transition and let them live another day.

Generally, we do not categorize individuals as insolvent or illiquid. The reality is that the poor, or those without a financial cushion, teeter on the ledge of insolvency and illiquidity, making it somewhat difficult to distinguish the illiquid from the insolvent. Many people are easily pushed into insolvency by very common life events. Some people, just like many banks, need every dollar of their paycheck (their assets) to pay their bills. These people may become illiquid when a new debt arises, like a car accident or an unexpected medical emergency. They cannot wait until the next paycheck to pay off a debt, so they must obtain a loan to bridge the gap between future income and present need. A low-cost loan can help these people avoid insolvency while they slowly work their way back to financial health. These people are creditworthy. Others, however, have debts that are bigger than their income—future and present. These people are insolvent, and any loan to these borrowers will sink them further into debt and likely go unpaid. The best hope for those whose assets will never cover their liabilities is to declare bankruptcy and start over. These people are not creditworthy.

The current market for lending to the low and middle income does not distinguish between the two. And often, the losses from those who are insolvent raise the prices for those who are merely illiquid. If the two types of borrowers could be adequately sorted, those who are illiquid could get lower cost loans that would help them stay solvent. But here's the irony: the only loans available to the merely illiquid are high-cost loans that make it much more likely they will become insolvent.

This is where the contrast between the credit markets for the average people-as-borrowers and the credit markets for the banks-as-borrowers becomes stark. The government provides banks low-cost loans when they are illiquid and also when they are insolvent. The reverse is true in the credit market for the poor. Fringe lenders lend at oppressively high interest rates to the illiquid as well as the insolvent, with the result that often, those who were merely illiquid become insolvent. Whereas the government, through the central bank, is in the business of resurrecting dead banks through credit, the fringe lenders are in the market of suffocating the illiquid until they are insolvent.

Some might argue that we should not compare banks with people. Bank failure is much more consequential than individual failure. Banks serve a much more important social function and thus, providing them with low-cost credit benefits us all. Bailing out the banks is not a problem, per se, because they do have the capacity to help people. But we must not lose sight of the reason we support and even save banks. The purpose of bank bailouts is *not* to enhance bank profits, it is to enhance credit markets to the *people.* Government support enables bank customers to benefit from this socially useful credit. But banks can choose their customers, and those they reject do not get to take part in this abundance. When banks categorically exclude half the population from the credit they are entrusted to provide, leaving that unprotected group to the wolves, it creates a glaring disparity and a grotesque irony.

It is important, at this point, to revisit the reason the government is so invested in the banking system. As the history of U.S. banking makes clear, and as both the Bush and Obama administrations' bailouts have underscored, the state relies on the banking system to efficiently allocate credit and capital in the economy. The banking system is supported, protected, and even saved from its own malfeasance because the state needs it—both to effect the state's own monetary policy as well as to lend to the people. If banks fail, it is reasoned, so will the American people.

But many people *are* failing. They are failing even as the banks are succeeding, and they are failing because the banks are no longer involved in providing them credit. The government has outsourced the provision of credit to the banking system, and it provides this system with state support and cheap credit—cheap credit that is not flowing out to reach those who need it most. In fact, while the government has provided interest rates to banks at 0 percent, it has allowed interest rates to the poor to skyrocket to triple digits. If the intended result is to help the public with credit, why continue to use banks as a medium when they are clearly leaving out a significant portion of the population? Why not provide credit directly to those who need it in order to be certain they get it?

5

Unbanked and Unwanted

You're either growing or dying.

—HUGH L. MCCOLL JR., FORMER CHAIRMAN AND CEO, BANK OF AMERICA

A lawyer once wrote that "poverty creates an abrasive interface with society; the poor are always bumping into sharp legal things."[1] They are also constantly bumping into sharp financial things. Without a financial cushion, every mistake, unexpected problem, or minor life change can quickly turn into a financial disaster. This is why those who live paycheck to paycheck often rely on fringe lenders. But the high cost of borrowing money to avoid small or large disasters is just one dimension of what it means to live without access to banking.

Michael Barr noted that not having a bank account reduces take-home pay and makes it difficult for families to save and establish a credit history.[2] When an unbanked person gets her paycheck, she must go to a check casher; in the process, she loses up to 10 percent of her paycheck.[3] She must then pay her bills, and because most institutions will not take cash for bill payments, she must purchase money orders, which can cost anywhere from five to twenty dollars. To be clear, that is one payment in order to convert an article of commercial paper (a paycheck) into cash and then several payments in order to turn that cash back into commercial paper (money orders) in order to pay bills. Some institutions will accept cash for bill payments but never by mail, and so paying by cash requires possibly missing work, which is stressful, to show up at their office during business hours and wait in line every time the bill is due.

Most Americans and nearly all U.S. businesses operate in an electronic currency economy. Only those left out of the banking sector must operate in a cash economy—at a great cost. These people do not have access to credit and debit cards, which are the primary payment methods most of the population uses. For everyday purchases, the unbanked use either cash or a fee-based prepaid card. (Cash is much easier to lose and more likely to be stolen than an electronic transfer.) In addition to these expenses, if the unbanked need to send money to anyone, they must pay a significant fee—anywhere from ten dollars to eighty dollars—depending on the size of the transfer. These charges, which are only borne by the poor, pile additional expenses and stresses on top of their already strained lives.

In fact, the average unbanked family with an annual income of around $25,000 spends about $2,400 per year, *almost 10 percent of its income,* on financial transactions. This is more money than these families spend on food.[4] In 2012, the unbanked spent a total of $89 billion on financial transactions alone.[5] And these expenses can mean the difference between a family's financial survival and its failure. For example, on average, families who filed for bankruptcy in 2012 were just $26 short per month on meeting their expenses.[6] Saving $2,400 per year, or $200 per month, could save many families from the devastation of bankruptcy. The fact that so much money is being spent by the poor to pay for simple financial services that the nonpoor get for free is a tragedy.

Nor are we talking about a small group of people. Approximately 70 million Americans do not have a bank account or access to traditional financial services. That is more people than live in California, New York, and Maryland combined. It is more than the total number of people who voted for Barack Obama (or Mitt Romney) in the 2012 election.[7] The term "unbanked" or "underbanked" describes a group of people who rely on fringe lenders, but these terms underestimate the problem. An even larger and less quantifiable number of people do have bank accounts but rely primarily on alternative banking services for a variety of reasons.[8] In fact, recall that you must have a bank account in order to use a payday lender. We are talking about anywhere from 30 to 50 percent of the population—the 30 to 50 percent at the bottom of the income ladder.[9]

* * *

What are the simple economic realities of banking for the poor? Several barriers keep mainstream banks from serving the poor—the most important is simple math. Banks can make much higher profits elsewhere. The poor may need banks, but banks most definitely do not need the poor. Banks' transaction and overhead costs are much the same whether they lend $500 or $500,000, but of course, the larger loan yields a much higher profit. The American poet Ogden Nash put it this way: "One rule which woe betides the banker who fails to heed it; Never lend any money to anybody unless they don't need it."

Maintaining simple checking or savings accounts costs banks money. They must hire staff, pay for buildings, update technology, build automated teller machines (ATMs), send monthly statements, and more. Different estimates say that each deposit account costs a bank between $48 and $200 every year.[10] They can make up these costs by lending customer deposits. To a bank, customer deposits are microloans from the customer to the bank (notably, relatively interest-free loans) that the institution can use to make profit and create income-paying assets: customer loans. And of course, the more deposits invested, the more loan volume and the higher the profits. Thus, when a bank is considering whether or not to open a new account, it must determine whether the profits made from the new customer's deposits will outweigh the costs associated with providing that customer services.

If an account contains too little money, the profits will be low or nonexistent. Simple business math suggests that if a product (like a small account) is not profitable, it should be avoided—which is exactly what banks do. But the logic is not so straightforward when applied to banks. Although it is true that these accounts do not yield profits, it is also true that banks do not necessarily lose money by providing these services; the infrastructure is already in place. Sophisticated technology has made it easy and virtually risk-free to cash most checks, create money orders, or transfer funds. If banks were to offer these products to small-account holders, their wealthier clients would essentially be subsidizing the services, which is how community banks were able to serve the poor for much of the nation's history. And importantly, because government support and protection guaranteed banks healthy profits, they did so willingly.

Although the state support is still there, the onus of serving the public has been lifted from banks. Most banks, especially the financial giants, no longer see their role as serving a community at large but view each customer as a potential source of profit. And those deemed unprofitable are either rejected outright or repelled by punishing fees. The most prevalent fee on small accounts are overdraft fees, which make up 75 percent of all bank fees.[11] These costs are borne primarily by the poor—90 percent of the fees are paid by 10 percent of the customers. A 2014 report studied the annual costs of checking accounts at large banks among five categories of spenders and found that by far, the people in the lowest category, the "cash-strapped," paid the most to use a checking account.[12] Comedian Louis C. K. quipped: "You ever get so broke that the bank starts charging you money . . . for not having enough money? The bank called me up, they said, 'Hi, we're calling you because you don't have enough money.' I said, I know! They said, 'You have insufficient funds,' and I said, well, I agree with that. I find my funds to be grossly insufficient! So they charged me $15, that's how much it costs to only have $20. But here is the f***ed-up part, now I only have $5! What am I paying the $15 for if I don't get to have the $20 . . . that I paid to have!"[13]

These fees are used both as a way to repel and punish low balances and as a significant source of revenue.[14] When a bank customer writes a check and there isn't enough money in the account to fulfill the check, the bank can still clear it. This would effectively be a loan to the customer who has overdrawn her account. Or the bank could just freeze the account without allowing the transaction to go through. The bank risks no loss at all by not covering the transaction for the customer. Instead, the bank issues a fee right away. These fees can be quite high; up to thirty-five dollars for the first overdraw and repeated every day—or every few days if the account remains overdrawn.[15] If you consider the fee as a payment the customer makes for the extension of credit for the overdrawn amount, a 2008 Federal Deposit Insurance Corporation (FDIC) study showed that these fees carry an effective APR in excess of 3,500 percent![16]

These draconian fees haven't gone unnoticed, and in recent years bank regulators, perhaps spurred by lawsuits, have tried to rein in some of the large banks' most egregious practices.[17] For example, Bank of America entered a settlement in Florida for its "unfair and unconscionable assessment and collection of excessive overdraft fees." The civil court settlement explained the problem and its roots succinctly: "For years, banks covered customers who occasionally bounced checks and even did so for a time for customers using debit cards without charging their customers. Since the early 1990's, however, banks have devised methods to provide overdraft 'protection' for customers and charge them in each instance."[18] In this particular case, Bank of America charged a twenty-five-dollar fee for each transaction on the first day and a thirty-five-dollar fee for the second day and all subsequent days the account had an "occurrence," defined as "a day with at least one overdraft item or one returned item."[19]

Another case brought against Bank of America showed that "on December 4, 2007, the Bank sent their customer Mr. Yourke a notice that, as of December 3, 2007, the Bank had received notice of five transactions, for $32.83, $4.35, $4.35, $6.05 and $39.46, that his account had become overdrawn for each of those transactions and that the Bank had charged $35 fee for each such transaction, for a total of $175." These charges were legal and disclosed, but the suit was about the bank's "bad faith" reordering of the transactions so that the highest withdrawal was taken from his account first.[20] Of course, this meant that the bank could charge maximum fees for each of the transactions. In the end, Mr. Yourke incurred five overdraft fees—if the bank hadn't manipulated the transactions, he would have only incurred two during the twenty-two days it took to pay for the overdraft. The five fees, corresponding to the amount his account was overdrawn, yield an equivalent interest rate of 3,335 percent.[21] This is 3000 percentage points higher than a payday loan, and the payday lender would likely have had better hours, given him the option to roll over the loan, and been easier to reach than Bank of America's customer service. Bank of America eventually settled both these cases.[22]

Banks rarely charge customers with large accounts these fees. In fact, if you are willing to put enough money in a bank, you are often afforded free overdraft protection. In other words: no fees for the small loans a bank might have to make when you overdraw your account.[23] Billboard offers of "free checking" often only apply to those willing to deposit enough money. A 2014 study showed that only 28 percent of accounts are actually free—the majority charge about $150 per year—costs that have risen sharply in recent years and are likely to increase in the future.[24]

The average minimum balance requirement for free checking is around $400. The cumulative effect drives the poor away. The FDIC has noted that overdraft fees, service charges, and minimum balance requirements are among the top reasons people do not open bank accounts.[25] Those with small means are hearing the banks' message loud and clear.

Banks simply deny bank accounts to those who may have a history of overdrawing. The majority of banks, credit unions, and thrifts use a database called ChexSystems, which allows them to screen potential account holders.[26] A blemished ChexSystems screening is the number one reason banks give for declining account applications.[27] Banks that use the database, and the company itself, claim that the system's primary purpose is to weed out fraud, but only 2 percent of the accounts in the system are placed there because of fraudulent activity.[28] Of the activities used to permanently block people from the banking system, 97.5 percent were overdraft, or "account mishandling," activities.[29] But unlike a credit score, ChexSystems information is not available to customers (even though they stay in the database for five years).[30]

The *New York Times* reported the story of one would-be credit union customer, Tiffany Murrell of Brooklyn, who despite holding down a steady job as a secretary, was denied an account because of a ChexSystems report. Two years earlier, Tiffany had an overdraft of roughly forty dollars. Even though she had already repaid the amount plus interest and fees, she was "barred from opening an account at nearly every bank she has tried, an experience she called 'insulting and frustrating.' "[31] Tiffany lamented that "the sting of being rejected . . . can make lower-income individuals feel like second-class citizens." Twenty-three-year-old David Korzeniowski, blocked out of the banking system for seven years, acknowledged that "he made a mistake" but that "the fees he pays for cashing checks, paying bills and wiring money cannibalize the paycheck he gets from part-time construction work . . . 'Everything is more expensive,' he said."[32]

Banks have no need for small accounts because they do not yield high profits. Therefore, they have employed a variety of tactics to slough off their low-yield customers. High fees and barriers to entry have accomplished their desired result: those with small savings have weighed the costs and have decided to leave the banking system entirely.

BANKING MARKETS

But we can't necessarily blame the banks. Everything *is* more expensive for those outside the banking system, but the business of banking has also become more costly. If the effect of fees, account minimums, and account denials is to disenfranchise the poor, the cause of these fees is the changed atmosphere in which banks now operate. Bank competition has increased significantly in the last several decades. In order to survive, banks must be as efficient as possible—getting the most profits possible for the minimum amount of resources expended. This, of course, makes the costs of bearing low-income clients even riskier.

Gone are the days of boring banking, when a highly regulated industry monopolized the nation's deposits and loans. For much of the nation's history, banks were geographically restricted, and nationwide competition was discouraged, if not prohibited. In fact, many bank charters were essentially a monopoly in a given region. States could and often did deny charters if there were too many banks in one region, which sometimes meant *more than one bank*.

The clash between community and behemoth-banking is a recent phenomenon. In fact, community banking was just *banking* until the 1990s. For nearly two hundred years, banks were effectively prohibited from competing based on size and were restricted to just one region. (These geographic restrictions lasted longer than any other form of banking regulation.) All of the nation's banks operated within their respective single communities with local control and local investment. This was purposefully so. Throughout history, the central tension and debate in banking had been between the forces of efficiency and localism, with localism holding ground for two centuries. Before the creation of national banking during the Civil War, state charters prohibited bank branching or affiliations across states, and almost all prohibited branching within a state. A few Southern states made an exception and allowed banks to have affiliates within a state to support the complex system of cotton harvesting, distribution, and export. In 1927, the McFadden Act made it official and prohibited any bank from branching outside of its chartering state.[33]

The downside of this system was inefficiency—banks could not achieve maximum profits because their assets and loans had to stay within one geographic region. They could not seek high returns in booming markets or lower costs through mergers. This also left banks vulnerable to regional declines. The upside, and the reason this inefficient framework remained the law of the land for so long, was that most communities had banks and access to credit.

Thus, during the era of mandated community banking, and once FDIC insurance made banking less risky, the large majority of communities had banks. The numbers and locations of banks increased steadily after the Great Depression, reaching their peak in the 1970s.[34] Most Americans could afford a bank account because banks were prohibited from charging fees.[35] In fact, Reg Q prohibited banks from paying interest on checking accounts and had caps on interest for other accounts, which is why they gave out free toasters and umbrellas to attract new accounts.[36] And remember, this golden era of banking also coincided with a general rising tide of prosperity in the United States. Between the Great Depression and the 1970s, the American public would experience significant wage growth and historically low rates of inequality.[37]

Of course, profitable banks kept trying to expand to make more profits but were stopped each time by state and federal laws. The ever-present forces of market efficiency favoring large and efficient banking conglomerates were persistently met with laws that compelled small and local banking. For example, large banks eventually found loopholes around the McFadden Act by creating a holding company with subsidiaries in different states. The Douglas Amendment to the Bank Holding Company Act of 1956 effectively ended this violation of the McFadden Act by giving states the power to determine which out-of-state banks could operate within their borders. According to Senator Paul Douglas, the purpose of the amendment was "to prevent an undue concentration of banking and financial power, and instead keep the private control of credit diffused as much as possible."[38]

Little by little, however, barriers to bank expansion began to fall as states and banks pushed the limits of the laws.[39] The official repeal of both the geographic restrictions and the Douglas Amendment came in 1994 through the passage of the Riegle-Neal Interstate Banking and Branching Efficiency Act, which allowed banks to open branches across state lines. The purpose of the act was baked right into the title: to increase bank "efficiency."

Another felled barrier included interstate branching, which means that a single bank can operate branches in more than one state without having to comply with the corporate and banking forms of that state. The state of New York repealed this provision for its banks in 1992 and demanded reciprocity. Once this door was opened, other states followed suit. Federal law lifted the restrictions in 1997, but the federal law allowed banks to branch only through acquisitions or mergers.

And merge and acquire, they did. And to anyone paying attention, the number of mergers was alarming. (Or at least, it would have alarmed Thomas Jefferson!) These mergers resulted in the actualization of Jefferson's worst fears about the banking sector. As Senator Douglas had hinted, the restrictions had been based on fears that if banks were allowed to merge, cross borders, and send funds where they wanted, banks would conglomerate in cities, grow large and powerful, and threaten community banks across the country. Which is exactly what happened when the restrictions were lifted. Between 1984 and 2014, the amount of bank charters fell by over 60 percent, from 18,000 to 6,500. But counting banks doesn't begin to show the radical changes in banking concentration. Noncommunity banks are much more profitable than community banks and overwhelmingly dominate the banking market.[40] In 1984, the disparity in asset sizes between community banks (those with less than $1 billion in assets) and noncommunity banks was twelve to one; in 2011, it was seventy-four to one. Today, only 6 percent of bank charters are noncommunity banks, but these banks account for 63 percent of all bank branches and *85 percent of total assets*. In fact, just the top four banks control *over half* of all bank deposits.[41]

This trend has led to an increased rate of closures, even amidst high profits, by the largest banks.[42] A recent study showed that from 2008 to 2013, banks shut down two thousand branches—*93 percent* of which were located in postal codes where the household income is below the national median.[43] A market analysis of acquisitions by Bank of America and JPMorgan predicted that branch totals could fall by 40 percent in the next decade.[44] Meanwhile, the percentage of bank branches in neighborhoods with incomes higher than the national median rises.[45] As the largest banks merge with each other, they cut down branches in less profitable areas and replace them with online services or ATM machines, increasingly shifting their income from small-time deposit-taking and loan-making to more profitable markets.

To be absolutely clear, it was not the Riegle-Neal Act or the states' liberalization of the banking laws that *caused* the mergers, though lifting prohibitions certainly sped them up. The mergers had already begun in the 1980s as enterprising banks, with the help of their lawyers and lobbyists, found ways around the merger prohibitions. And regulators allowed them to do it. Market forces coupled with regulatory inaction resulted in heightened competition and the creation of large banking conglomerates led by the new mantra "go big or go home." Hugh McColl, the CEO of Bank of America from 1983 to 2001, embodied this principle. His bank grew exponentially during this time by acquiring hundreds of banks and merging itself with competitors—even the name *Bank of America* was acquired through a merger. McColl explained the ethos of the era: "It was a function of getting large enough to be . . . both efficient and effective. . . . As I see it, you're either growing or dying. There's no middle ground. You can't hold what you have. That doesn't work in business. So we grew."[46]

COMMUNITY BANKS STRUGGLE TO COMPETE

As Bank of America was growing, the community banks of America were dying. When most people discuss this trend of mergers and consolidations in the banking industry, they focus on the resulting Too-Big-to-Fail banks that have come to dominate the industry. But these banks were built using an already existing checkerboard of community banks across the country. Each bank that Bank of America purchased originally started as a small community bank before being turned into a megabank branch or closed in the name of efficiency and replaced by an ATM machine.

Market forces have always applied to banks, but the tight-margin, high-stakes nationwide banking market is new. The full range of intensely competitive market forces have applied to banks to a much greater degree during the last thirty years—with the clear exception of the largest banks, which are too big to fail. Community banks' struggles to stay profitable, however, emanate not only from market principles, but also, more recently, from regulatory pressure. The Dodd-Frank Wall Street Reform and Consumer Protection Act (Dodd-Frank) regulatory regime, a response to the 2008 financial crisis, primarily purported to address the risks in the large-bank sector. Most scholars and industry observers claim that the act falls short of true reform for the large banks. But when applied to small banks, Dodd-Frank is overkill. Dodd-Frank has placed added rules on community banks, which claim that they are "too small to comply." Community banks claim that its onerous regulatory demands create compliance costs that are reducing their already small margins. Large banks can absorb these costs and have large compliance departments to deal with the regulatory mandates. Small banks are spending limited resources to comply with these laws, which are mismatched to the risks their industry faces.[47]

Though Dodd-Frank may have added to the struggles of the small banks, it did not create them. Increased market competition and natural economic forces have threatened small banking for decades. First, community banks still operate on a simple banking model of deposit-taking and lending, so their primary revenue comes from interest income. Their only source of noninterest earnings comes from fees charged on deposit accounts. On the other hand, large banks have a variety of other sources of noninterest income, for example, through their various securities, brokerage, and insurance subsidiaries that operate a full range of financial products for their customers. The large banks benefit from "economies of scope": by selling a variety of products to their customers, they can reduce the average cost per product, sell more of each product, and increase their revenue. As a result, in communities hosting both large banks and community banks, the larger bank can offer cheaper financial services and therefore, control a greater market share. The second and related competitive force is "economies of scale." Large banks can lower costs and increase efficiency for each product across the board, which means they can reduce the price of a single product by selling more of it.

Larger and more diversified institutions can lower costs, offer more services, streamline marketing and products, and undersell small competitors. This holds true for fast food, grocery stores, and retail stores—and for banks. The large banks can modernize their infrastructure and offer more products and services for less. They can also house a variety of financial services under one roof in a one-stop-shopping model that has benefited many other industries. Chris Duhigg, of the

New York Times, explained the "bank supermarket" model of the last two decades:

> Every single type of financial need that you, my customer, has, I'll be able to satisfy it for you. . . . What happened was that there came about this idea that I make a little bit of money from you when I hold your checking account; I make a little bit of money from you when I hold your mortgage; I make a little bit of money from you when you use one of my credit cards. But I'll bet you I could make a ton of money from you if I did all three of those things for you, because I could figure out how to get you to actually do more of each one. . . . This is what the supermarket of banking allows. I can use information from one part of the bank to drive profitability in other parts of the bank. And the bigger and bigger I get, the more and more information I have. And the more information I have, the more profitable I can make every single customer that I have.[48]

Economies of scale and scope are not a new phenomenon. Even Thomas Jefferson intuited that banks would naturally conglomerate and that banking markets would always prefer large banks to small ones. It was just state legislation that fought this natural pull for so long. Once the state stopped fighting it, consolidation was inevitable. A Federal Reserve study on why banks consolidated from 1982 to 2000 concluded that they did so because the resulting large banks were more efficient than the smaller ones. The efficiency hypothesis predicts that technological progress improves the performance of large firms, and this increased competition results in decreased revenues and/or increased expenses for smaller firms.[49]

The final large-scale economic shift that favors large banking over small banking is the widespread use of loan "securitization," or pooling individual loans to sell them in secondary markets, and the accompanying loan "standardization," or approving loans based on a set of boilerplate criteria. The standardization of loans has made the loan approval process formulaic, which favors large banks. Community banks have historically been better suited to deal with "relationship lending" or "soft data," such as a person's character, network, and job stability. In other words, community banks could profit from their ability to lend to those who are short on data but strong on potential—people or businesses who are creditworthy despite having no record to prove it.

However, the use of "soft data" is increasingly becoming irrelevant in lending decisions because loan products, specifically mortgage loans, have become completely standardized. In the 1950s, if you wanted to purchase a home, you might meet with your local banker to convince him that your job was stable and that you could support the mortgage interest. You and your banker would discuss the rate of interest, the length of the loan, and the price of the home. Then, once you got the loan, you would continue to pay it off to the bank that originated it for the life of the loan. Today, you need not meet with a banker, or even a person. You can get a mortgage loan from a nonbank loan originator, an online bank, or your local bank. The mortgage broker or banker will put your information, including income, assets, liabilities, and credit score, into a formula, and your loan will be approved at a designated interest rate and term.

Once you are approved for a loan, you give the bank a "note," a promise to pay interest in the future on the loan, and a "mortgage," which is a property interest in your home. The note and mortgage are first sold to Fannie Mae and Freddie Mac, government-sponsored mortgage purchasers. Fannie Mae and Freddie Mac tell the banks what kind of loan products they will buy and at what price, which in turn becomes a baseline formula for bank underwriting. After Fannie Mae and Freddie Mac buy the note and mortgage from the bank, they pool the loan with other loans, repackage these loans into bonds secured by the underlying mortgages, and sell the bonds to investors. This process happens quickly. It will be out of the hands of the bank that originated your mortgage by the end of the week. Thus, the soft data is irrelevant. Banks and other originators aren't very concerned with a borrower's reputation, or even a borrower's potential to pay, because they do not hold the liabilities. As long as the loan fits the formula provided by its eventual purchasers, they will make the loan. Wall Street banks and their clients, such as institutional investors like pension funds and mutual funds that hold the savings of average Americans, eventually purchase the loans. Large and small banks also hold mortgage loans on their books, either because they originated them and kept them or because they purchased the loan from another bank.[50]

Loan standardization took away the competitive advantage, if not the whole point, of community banking: differentiating between "good" and "bad" borrowers. There is still some room for that expertise when it comes to business loans or large commercial loans, but these loans are based more on hard data than on the character of a borrower. The bulk of the consumer lending market (mortgages, credit cards, auto loans, student loans) has been securitized and standardized, and community banks no longer have a market advantage. A bank competes with other banks not by making more good loans but just by making more loans, period. The more loans they originate, the more they can sell off into the secondary markets for a profit. This was, after all, the point of the government policies that enabled the securitization and standardization of these loans. The government-sponsored enterprises (GSEs) were created to make lending easier and to produce more loans, so long as the loan "conformed" to predetermined guidelines. (This also meant, by the way, that borrowers with loans that did not "conform" had a harder time getting a loan.) Community banks cannot possibly compete with larger banks based on how many loans they can originate because of their limited customer base and geographical footprint.

Predictably, the trend of bank mergers and consolidations had the most devastating effects on the middle to low income. As mentioned above, community banking has historically been the average person's only access to banking because of small banks' focus on relationship lending as opposed to standardization. In the past, community bankers overcame the risk of lending to someone of small means through relationships and extending credit to those they "believed in." In fact, *credit* derives from the Latin *credere,* or "to believe." As community banks have struggled for profitability, they have focused on higher-profit-margin products. Products offered to small savers and small borrowers were the first to be cut.[51]

The economic struggles of community banks met with the rising poverty of the 1970s, which meant that many impoverished communities lost access to their banks altogether. This was aided along by a banking sector that had shrouded itself in the ideology of free markets as well as deregulation that allowed it to jettison any duty it might have to serve anyone who did not help its bottom line. Banks began to leave low-income areas, and if they stayed, many dropped these less profitable customers by increasing fees and charges on small accounts. The Government Accountability Office, the Federal Reserve, and various scholars studied these trends and found that these increased prices led to a wide-scale shedding of low-income bank accounts.[52] John Caskey reported that those families further down on the income spectrum were much more likely to lose their bank accounts.[53] This trend has persisted, and the number of the unbanked has risen yearly since the 1980s and will likely continue to increase as banking becomes more competitive and conglomerated and as income inequality and wealth inequality continue to grow.[54]

This trend was especially acute in the inner cities. If community banking nationwide is an endangered banking species, it is extinct in urban areas. Today, large banks dominate urban areas and control 90 percent of their bank assets. And because these banks do not offer small loans to the poor, there are very few banking options for the inner-city poor. The banks' abandonment of the cities left the financial needs of the poor unmet; fringe banks moved in to fill the void.

* * *

Most policymakers and scholars have given up trying to force banks to meet the needs of the poor, claiming that cost considerations simply prevent banks from operating in this market.[55] Frustrated, one observer even said that "banks' potential for service improvement [to the poor] is modest even were they run by God's angels."[56] But banks don't have to be run by "God's angels" to properly serve the poor—although they must be run differently than they are today. Profit-oriented banks in a hypercompetitive banking environment will not provide the kinds of services that are beneficial to the poor.

Banking regulators have tried numerous times to induce mainstream banks to provide small loans to the poor, but perhaps because the current gods of banking have not been willing participants, these attempts have failed.[57] By way of illustration, consider a 2008 attempt, the FDIC's "Small-Dollar Loan Pilot Program." Recognizing the growing problem of access to banking services, the two-year campaign enlisted a group of thirty-one volunteer banks to provide small loans and check-cashing services to the poor.[58] The project sought to prove that banks could earn profits while they served the poor and was promoted as "a case study designed to illustrate how banks can profitably offer affordable small-dollar loans as an alternative to high-cost credit products, such as payday loans and fee-based overdraft protection."[59] Unfortunately, the program ended up illustrating something else entirely. The Subcommittee on Financial Institutions and Consumer Credit of the House Committee on Financial Services met in September 2011 to review the program, and there was bipartisan agreement that the program had failed.[60]

The program's failure was inevitable. The "volunteer" banks, it seemed, begrudgingly participated after being promised by regulators that they would be rewarded by a good Community Reinvestment Act (CRA) rating.[61] Once signed on, the banks charged their low-income clients the maximum interest and fees allowed: 36 percent APR and 20 percent charges on cashed checks.[62] Observers noted that these products were much like payday loans and check cashers. Spelling further doom, several congressmen expressed outrage that mainstream banks should have to take on the risk of lending to the poor, and in the end, the banks and the policymakers made it clear that the banks would stop providing these services after the program ended because they were simply not profitable.[63] The enlisted banks could have forged new relationships with the unbanked; aggressively marketed desirable, market-tested products in high demand; or even designed new procedures or products that might prove attractive to the poor. None of them did.

The banks' half-hearted response to yet another regulatory mandate is instructive. Banks simply do not have the incentive, even at the behest of their regulators, to sacrifice profits in order to meet the needs of the poor. The reason that the credit unions, savings and loans, and Morris banks were able to successfully reach the poor was because they were motivated to do so; in fact, that was their primary goal. Policymakers misunderstand the nature of mainstream banks if they are relying on them to adequately meet the needs of the poor. At best, they can be incentivized to do a half-baked job in order to appease regulators. The products they offer are not innovations resulting from market research about what the poor really need—instead, the banks offer the bare minimum so that they can maintain profitability while fulfilling a regulatory mandate. Forcing banks, whose purpose is maximum profit, to make loans to the poor will inevitably lead to inadequate loans and disgruntled bankers.

THE COMMUNITY REINVESTMENT ACT

Because the FDIC program was only limited to "volunteers," the banking industry did not meet it with intense opposition. To really see bankers' vitriol over onerous regulatory mandates, we must look to one that asks *all* banks to consider the needs of the poor. The most expansive and controversial of all such efforts is the Community Reinvestment Act (CRA).[64] The CRA was created to respond to banks fleeing from low-income neighborhoods, a process labeled "redlining," or drawing a literal or figurative line around geographic areas and refusing to lend there either because of profitability concerns or racial discrimination.[65] The CRA responds to this phenomenon much the same way that affirmative action laws respond to discrimination: it imposes duties on banks to lend to underserved communities even while recognizing the economic barriers involved.[66]

This law is the very embodiment of the tension at the heart of the banking industry. The CRA's genesis, application, and vilification are where banking past meets banking present—where the public nature of banks is asserted and then rejected. When the bill was passed in 1977, Senator Proxmire, chairman of the Senate Committee on Banking, Housing, and Urban Affairs commented that the bill was based on a "widely shared assumption" that "a public charter conveys numerous economic benefits and in return it is legitimate for public policy and regulatory practice to require some public purpose." The senator claimed that banks are "a franchise to serve local convenience and needs" and therefore "it is fair for the public to ask something in return."[67] Although this law may have been entirely consistent with the banking norms of the last century, it is very much out of sync in today's deregulated sector. The law has also come to represent the paradox of banking regulation—the act is one of the most vilified of banking laws, while at the same time, community groups criticize it for being ineffectual and "toothless."[68]

"It's unbelievable," fumed one anonymous southeastern banker. "These people are trying to enforce a change in social policy over the back of the banking industry."[69] What modern bankers have forgotten is that many bankers before them had social policy goals imposed on their backs too. Most opponents to the CRA complain that the act is economically inefficient. Leading banking law scholars Jonathan Macey and Geoffrey Miller claim that the CRA "promotes the concentration of assets in geographically non-diversified locations, encourages banks to make unprofitable and risky investment and product line decisions, and penalizes banks that seek to reduce costs by consolidating services or closing or relocating branches." Policymakers have made several attempts to roll back or to eliminate the bill since its passage.

Although derided as too onerous, the CRA is also discounted as gutless.[70] The CRA does not force banks to lend or even open branches. It gives banks a rating—from "Outstanding" to "Substantial Noncompliance"—depending on how effectively a bank is "meeting the credit needs of its assessment area."[71] The CRA rating is used when a bank applies for a merger or some other significant change. The regulator has the option to reject the request for a merger if the rating is too low. Because the CRA rating and much of the examination report is public, the press and community groups can publicize that information to pressure an institution to improve its practices. Opponents of the CRA claim that community activists have used the CRA rating as "blackmail" to extract unprofitable and risky lending in inner cities.[72] For example, when a bank applies for a merger application, activist groups can convince a regulator that the bank has failed to meet the credit needs of a neighborhood, holding out the threat of a merger denial. However, this effect grossly overstates the power of community activists in altering both bank and regulatory behavior. In fact, the studies that have attempted to measure what effect, if any, community groups exert over bank lending have concluded that it is minimal to none. Banks do not change lending behavior to appease activists or even regulators in order to get merger approval.[73] Still, even if it is largely untrue, the narrative of community groups forcing banks to lend at a loss has been pervasive.

This simmering three-decade-long debate over the CRA erupted after the financial crisis. As the guise of private, market-based banking began to lift, many of its devoted disciples made final efforts to keep the ideology intact by blaming the CRA for the financial crisis. When the Financial Crisis Inquiry Commission released its report on the causes of the financial crisis, namely heightened risks and lack of oversight, Peter Wallison, a senior fellow at the conservative think tank the American Enterprise Institute, was the report's sole dissenter.[74] Wallison claimed that the financial crisis was caused by the CRA and other government policies that promoted lending to the low-income by lowering underwriting standards. Many politicians and academics also joined in.[75] In diagnosing the causes of the financial crisis, prominent scholars Charles Calomiris and Stephen Haber also blame the CRA and weakened underwriting. They said that because the CRA forced banks to lend in low-income areas, the banks took on too much risk in mortgage loans, causing failures. Calomiris and Haber point, as well, to inner-city activists, or "populists," who used the CRA as a threat to coerce the banks to lend subprime mortgages and overextend themselves. Economist Thomas DiLorenzo wrote that the financial crisis was "the direct result of thirty years of government policy that has forced banks to make bad loans to un-creditworthy borrowers."[76]

This story not only feeds the narrative that the poor are irresponsible while relieving banks of any responsibility, it is also a complete fiction. The theory that the CRA in any way led to the financial crisis has been debunked by all the scholars who have measured it as well as influential policymakers, including former Treasury secretary Timothy Geithner and former Federal Reserve chairman Ben Bernanke.[77] There are many reasons the CRA is not to blame for the financial crisis. For one, the act was passed in 1977, and the subprime mortgage market only started heating up in 2003—the causal link is weak. However, the main reason is that the majority of the crisis-causing subprime loans were not given out by lenders with any CRA obligations—only 6 percent of subprime loans were even CRA-compliant.[78] David Min explains that the CRA myth, which originated with Peter Wallison, stemmed solely from data from Wallison's colleague Edward Pinto—data based on "a series of faulty assumptions and serious methodological flaws that render his findings unusable." For example, in analyzing the CRA's influence on subprime loans, Pinto estimated the number of CRA-produced loans at a shockingly high 2.24 million "subprime" and "high-risk" loans, but almost every other scholar estimated the number of CRA-produced loans to be about 378,000. These drastic errors took on a life of their own, and instead of being quickly corrected, have been cited by every single scholar or policymaker who blamed the CRA for the financial crisis.

Although it may be absurd to implicate the CRA, is there any truth in blaming the weaker underwriting standards espoused by both the Clinton and the Bush administrations? The claim is that in an effort to increase home lending to low-income and middle-class borrowers, policymakers allowed the GSEs Fannie Mae and Freddie Mac to lower standards for mortgages and created a race to the bottom that other mortgage buyers were all too willing to join. This increased mortgage lending in general and exacerbated the bubble. However, these lowered standards *did not create* the subprime market, which was the main cause of the financial crisis. Again, policymakers started pushing these initiatives in the 1990s—well before the subprime market heated up. In fact, the GSEs' market share of mortgages went from 50 percent to 30 percent from 2002 to 2005. Meanwhile, non-GSE mortgage buyers, or private label securitization, increased their market share from 10 to 40 percent during those years. David Min explains, "this is, to state the obvious, a very radical shift in mortgage originations that overlapped neatly with the origination of the most toxic home loans."[79] The push toward homeownership may have led to more relaxed regulatory oversight of these loans, but these policies did not create the market demand for subprime loans. That market was created specifically to meet Wall Street's demand for those loans. The causes of the financial crisis are tangential to the main point of this book, but they are worth discussing briefly in order to debunk the theory that social policies to increase credit to the poor bred the subprime market.

DID LENDING TO THE POOR CAUSE THE FINANCIAL CRISIS?

In short, the crisis was not created by the poor demanding subprime loans. In fact, most respected analysts who have studied the mortgage crisis have concluded that Wall Street demand created the troubling subprime loans in the first place.[80] The subprime mortgage market was a private market creation, and the GSEs neither created nor contributed to its supply or demand. The data is clear on this: "More than 84 percent of the subprime mortgages in 2006 were issued by private lending institutions."[81] The *Turner Report,* the most comprehensive review of the financial crisis, as well as most other serious analyses of the causes of the crisis, start the economic story with the problem of a "savings glut." Put simply, the U.S. markets became flooded by foreign money seeking a high return on investment. While these funds would usually have bought up U.S. Treasury bonds, the large demand for them lowered Treasury yields and the pool of money flowed toward Wall Street, seeking a better return. The next safest asset class after U.S. treasuries was asset-backed securities, or home mortgages. Wall Street banks, trying to meet investor demand, sold and resold as many of these securities as they could through bundling and creating new "structured products," but the demand was practically insatiable. So they originated more mortgage loans. But the pool of qualified borrowers was limited, leading them to seek higher and higher risk borrowers and creating a massive subprime market. Mortgage brokers and free-standing originators went looking for borrowers, knowing that they could always find a bank willing to buy the loan without asking too many questions. The flow of new subprime mortgages were packaged, given a stamp of approval from credit agencies, insured by AIG, and sold to the line of hungry investors. To be sure, there were many other problems. The financial system had grown too large and too complex, the regulators had grown too hands-off, and the population had grown too consumed by the housing bubble. But at the heart of the bubble were investors willing to buy anything that looked like a mortgage-backed security and banks and financial institutions willing to put lipstick on any pig they could get their hands on.

Those who blame government policies want to start the narrative with the poor who sought out high-risk mortgages, which banks begrudgingly doled out to appease their powerful and high-minded regulators or to ward off robust coalitions of inner-city activists. However, this sort of dynamic has never actually played out in banking history. It not only overestimates regulators' and community activists' power over banks, but it also misconstrues modern banks. The banks wanted more subprime loans because they were making unprecedented profits from the massive industry they had built around these Mortgage Backed Securities. Wall Street was innovating and buying up subprime loans and lenders at record rates. Banks were aggressively marketing subprime loans that were not CRA-compliant because they could quickly sell them off to investors. For example, JPMorgan Chase marketed its "no doc" and "liar loans" (where the lender did not verify any of the information provided on the application) and used slogans such as "It's like money falling from the sky!" As Simon Johnson and James Kwak explain, even though "subprime lending was pioneered far from Wall Street, by the 2000s Wall Street couldn't get enough of it."[82]

Many consumer advocates tried to shield their customers from these loans, but regulators were not a sympathetic ear. The Office of the Comptroller of the Currency (OCC) and the Office of Thrift Supervision (OTS) had long since made clear that any consumer protection rule the state legislatures might pass would not be applied to national banks, and they themselves would not enforce any. Georgia and North Carolina both passed Fair Lending acts that constrained subprime lending, and the OCC and the OTS promptly responded that those laws were preempted, meaning they could not be enforced against banks chartered by OCC and OTS federal regulators. Federal courts sided with the regulators. This effectively "disarm[ed] state governments and [gave] the mortgage lenders (and the investment banks securitizing their loans) free reign throughout the fifty states." The regulators reasoned that so long as lending was "profitable" and access to mortgage credit ubiquitous, consumer protection was unimportant.[83]

Consumer groups did complain about predatory mortgages in the inner-city and asked the Federal Reserve to enforce the Truth in Lending Act, which states "A creditor shall not engage in a pattern or practice of extending credit to consumers under [high cost refinance mortgages] based on the consumer's collateral without regard to the consumer's repayment ability, including the consumers' current and expected income, current obligations and employment." But the Federal Reserve refused to do anything, falsely claiming that it lacked jurisdiction.[84]

Although the CRA did not lead to a meaningful increase in lending to the poor, the poor were getting more loans of a wholly different breed. These banks and mortgage lenders, while criticizing the CRA, willingly came back to the inner cities to peddle a variety of "exotic" loan products with rates that "adjusted" and "ballooned" and cryptic point systems and fees—mixed with even some outright fraud. Many of these "subprime" loans came with high premiums for brokers and unprecedented fees and interest for borrowers.[85] Indeed, banks were more than happy to lend to poor borrowers if it meant that they could earn a substantial profit. Spurred by the high interest, premiums, and fees linked to subprime loans, many banks started *seeking out* poor borrowers with limited options. The Department of Justice (DOJ) sued Wells Fargo in 2009 for intentionally and systematically targeting minority borrowers and pushing them toward subprime loans. The DOJ claimed that Wells Fargo and Bank of America, two of the largest mortgage lenders, had steered thousands of minority borrowers into costlier subprime loans while whites with similar credit scores received regular loans.[86] A New York City study also found that 33 percent of those borrowing subprime loans could have qualified for less costly prime loans. Instead, these customers were given loans that were ticking bombs. Bombs that not only blew up on the firms' balance sheets but shattered many lives.[87]

The CRA myth lays bare the problematic core of the modern market-based banking dogma. Banks have rejected the imposition of social norms on their bottom line, which made the CRA an easy target when things started to fall apart. Unfortunately, the poor are also an easy target, and the theory of too much credit for the irresponsible poor tends to be a much more digestible storyline than the complex Wall Street web of products. The CRA myth allows the proponents of continued banking deregulation to flip the narrative. Instead of admitting that the banks' high levels of debt were a central problem, they can claim that the irresponsible poor and middle-class—enabled by federal government largesse—brought down the banks with their mortgage debt. Subprime borrowers were certainly not always hapless victims, but they were also not the villains in this story.[88]

The debate over the CRA suggests two broader questions about providing banking for the poor: (1) whether mainstream commercial banks should be tasked with providing these services, and (2) whether they can do it in a way that benefits the poor. If it is even appropriate for regulators to impose social burdens on banks whose primary purpose is to maximize profits for their shareholders, will the products that result from this coerced exchange be of any use to the poor? Or might such an attempt lead to harmful products or the manipulation of regulatory loopholes? If the CRA or the FDIC experience is at all instructive, it seems to be the case that these banks are not equipped to meet the needs of the poor, and their motivation to maximize profits runs counter to the needs of the poor. Either their motives need to change, or they need to be relieved of these duties.

6

Changing the World without Changing the Rules

Part of a new American order ought to be a national network of community development banks in all the cities of this country modeled on those which have worked, like the South Shore Development Bank in Chicago, operating under what today has become a radical premise: that banks ought to loan money to people who are in their neighborhoods and who deposit in them.

—GOVERNOR BILL CLINTON, SPEECH AT THE RAINBOW COALITION NATIONAL CONVENTION, WASHINGTON, DC, JUNE 13, 1992

Although the Community Reinvestment Act (CRA) represents a top-down approach to lending to the poor, grassroots efforts have also taken place—perhaps none more famous than Chicago's ShoreBank. In the midst of redlining and bank flight from poor neighborhoods, a community solution emerged and quickly became the lodestar for banking the poor; ShoreBank was ground zero for the idea that communities can help themselves. In fact, before Nobel Peace Prize winner Muhammad Yunus launched Grameen Bank to provide credit to the world's poor, he visited ShoreBank in Chicago to ask for advice. Bill and Hillary Clinton used the ShoreBank model as an example of socially responsible microfinance lending in America. After visiting the bank in 1985, Bill called the bank "the most important bank in America."[1]

The bank was the most celebrated attempt to provide banking services to a poor community. Its motto—"Let's Change the World"—was not an empty marketing pitch. At its peak, the bank had $4.1 billion invested in its inner-city Chicago community, and it became the model for a new banking movement in the United States, the Community Development Financial Institution (CDFI).[2] It would also become one of the most controversial and scrutinized bank failures during the financial crisis, with some press circles dedicating more time to its ill-fated rescue than the rescue of AIG. The story of ShoreBank's rise and demise reveals both the idealism of community banks that can "do good while doing well" and the economic pressure that makes "doing good" often incompatible with "doing well."

A group of community activists and bankers in South Chicago founded the bank in 1973, but the conversations about the bank first started amidst the civil rights movement of the 1960s. Frustrated by the redlining and the discrimination that was threatening the economic advancement of urban Chicago, Ronald Grzywinski, Milton Davis, James Fletcher, and Mary Houghton set out to acquire a bank. Starting in the 1960s, the South Side of Chicago went from being a primarily white middle-class neighborhood to being predominantly black as whites fled to the suburbs. As they did in many other inner-city communities, the South Side banks followed their white customers out. In the end, three banks were left to serve 78,000 people. ShoreBank was one of those remaining but only because its request to move was denied by its regulators. The activists bought ShoreBank with the goal of making it an "agent of change" that would lend to businesses in the inner city to grow the community. Grzywinski, a banker from Hyde Park Bank, stated, "Community-based organizations appeared to be the only organizations in society that cared about the broad range of needs that exist in urban communities."[3] The bank looked to be the modern-day Bailey's Building and Loan from *It's a Wonderful Life:* "Like old-fashioned bankers, they could loan not just by the numbers, but also out of intimate knowledge of the character of the borrower and the neighborhood."[4]

Not only would it lend to the community, but it would help rebuild it—again, reminiscent of George Bailey's development "Bailey Park." Although most banks pursued a single bottom line of maximizing shareholder profits, ShoreBank "took pride in its triple bottom line: profitability, community development impact, and an environmental return."[5] The founders organized a bank holding company, which allowed them to conduct a variety of community development activities that were not strictly "banking." The theory was that "access to credit was only one of the keys to successful community development." And so they set out to form a full-service financial organization whose aim was to fight the decline of a major urban community.[6]

It was this ambitious mission that drew so many admirers. The bank would be the community's answer to market forces. Of course, the philosophy was nothing new at all. Community banking was rooted in the Jeffersonian theory present since the beginning of banking in the United States. The difference was that the bank would attempt this project alone, in the midst of a competitive market, without any state support.

Despite the bank's popularity with political stars and its intuitive appeal, the math of its mission always proved difficult. For the first ten years, the bank lost money because it had less-wealthy clients, which meant smaller loans, smaller account balances, and a smaller profit margin than other banks.[7] The problems facing ShoreBank were not unique—"ShoreBank's loan business had smaller average transaction sizes than traditional banks, which meant that fees collected as a percentage of administering the loan were less than larger loans typical in upper income markets, although they required the same administrative time."[8] In short, banking the poor is not highly profitable. But ShoreBank managed to do it with the help of private funders who "invested with the understanding that the primary purpose of their investment is to do development and not maximize return on capital."[9] Still, the amount of "socially inclined" capital was limited, and the profits were modest, which hindered its growth.

Still, during the 1980s, ShoreBank expanded on the wave of the decade's banking boom, including creating a bank in Arkansas to aid rural development with the support of Bill and Hillary Clinton. The bank's influence grew during the era as a beacon of community-building from the inside.[10] Over time, the bank became "modestly profitable" and was quickly becoming a blueprint on how to make profits and bank the poor. According to founder Grzywinski, the bank had figured out how to "use the nation's banking system to advance the cause of development. . . . More broadly, we have contributed . . . to democratizing the availability of *private nongovernment* credit to low income and otherwise disadvantaged people."[11] The banking community noticed and lauded ShoreBank as a model of profitability as well as community-mindedness.[12] Here was a bank that could serve the poor *and* make profits for its investors.

And then, even the modest profits screeched to a halt during the financial crisis, and the bank quickly ran out of capital. In 2010, ShoreBank was taken over after being declared insolvent.[13] ShoreBank's failure was just as publicized as its success—the press couldn't resist reporting on the demise of Clinton and Obama's favorite bank. A quick Internet search of ShoreBank would lead to the casual observation that the bank represents everything that is rotten about politics and banking. But its failure was simply a textbook bank failure—similar to thousands of others across the country. Inner-city Chicago was financially devastated after the 2008 financial crisis, with skyrocketing unemployment.[14] The bank had not made subprime loans,[15] but it still had a capital shortfall of at least $190 million.[16] The bank, with the help of Eugene Ludwig, former comptroller of the currency and then head of Promontory Financial Group, raised $150 million from banks, private equity funds, and nonprofits.[17]

When ShoreBank applied for $70 million in Troubled Asset Relief Program (TARP) funds to bridge the capital gap, all hell broke loose.[18] Rumors circulated that the bank had "friends in high places" and that Wall Street heavyweights, such as Goldman Sachs, were pledging millions to save a bank to curry favor with the White House. Glenn Beck used his infamous blackboard to put ShoreBank at the center of a conspiracy that linked the bank to all things destructive, dangerous, and liberal, including: "Senator Obama, the Service Employees International Union, Tony Rezko, the Community Reinvestment Act, Tim Geithner, Hillary Clinton's college roommate, the Ford Foundation, Bill Ayers, Van Jones, green energy, Fannie Mae, and the ability of the federal government to lock everyone's electrical outlets from outside their homes."[19] Even though Barack Obama had nothing to do with the failure of the bank, or even its founding (his only link to the bank seems to be that he lived in the vicinity), conservative conspiracy theories abounded about the president bailing out his favorite bank.[20] Representative Judy Biggert (R-IL) picked up where Beck left off, demanding information in a letter to the White House asking why ShoreBank bank was singled out and suggesting that "the government was rescuing a politically connected bank while letting hundreds of others fail."[21]

Many criticized the bank's overzealousness and wondered whether the bank failed because it was "too much into the social welfare thing."[22] When it became clear that the $70 million in TARP funds was a political bomb, the bank was allowed to fail with the Federal Deposit Insurance Corporation (FDIC) exposed to a $367.7 million loss. Somehow, letting the bank fail with the FDIC absorbing the loss was more politically palatable than using a tiny slice of TARP funds to save the bank. Eventually, a Wall Street consortium called Urban Partnership, funded by American Express, Bank of America, Citicorp, JPMorgan Chase, Goldman Sachs, Wells Fargo, and others, bought the insolvent bank after the FDIC took it over. So in the end, TARP funds did save the bank but only after being funneled through Wall Street, laundering them into something politically acceptable. David Roeder wrote that the "takeover essentially relaunched Urban Partnership as an outsourced social conscience for major banks that put up the equity."[23] It is worth noting that these banks' social consciousness was abetted by a taxpayer bailout, and the banks all received credit under the CRA for their purchase.

Robert Solomon, an advocate for the community banking model, summarized the story of ShoreBank's rescue as such: "If the lesson is that we will use taxpayer funds as a last resort for necessary interventions for those banks whose failure places an untenable risk on the financial system, i.e. those too big to fail, then we are privileging those institutions at the expense of smaller banks. Once we accept that, we can take for granted that small banks are inefficient, have no special purpose, and will inevitably be absorbed into larger, more efficient banks."[24] Perhaps ShoreBank failed because of toxic politics and the federal government's decision to favor Too-Big-to-Fail over "Too Good to Fail," but the bank also failed because of unavoidable financial realities: its loans were concentrated in a struggling geographic area, which probably exposed it to more significant risk during the economic downturn.[25]

REVIVAL OF BANKS WITH A SOUL?

Despite ShoreBank's politicized failure, the bank had already created a modern banking movement. In 1992, Bill Clinton made a campaign promise that he would establish one hundred banks modeled after ShoreBank across the country.[26] One hundred banks would hardly be enough to meet the needs of the many struggling communities, but Clinton did follow through with the modest promise. During legislative discussions about Clinton's promised community banks, both Republicans and

Democrats seemed to recognize the problems of credit disparities. Republican congressman Tom Ridge remarked that "communities without credit are very much like land without rain, nothing grows."[27] Republican representative Jim Leach (of the deregulatory Gramm-Leach-Bliley Act) agreed: "America has a problem. The economy is clearly improving on a very slow basis, yet pockets of America are truly islands of hopelessness that society ignores at its peril."[28] Democratic senator Ted Kennedy said that "whole segments of our people in this country are unfairly denied access to credit, [it is our job] to make certain that financial institutions make credit available to all of those people who can afford to pay it back."[29] Considerable debate took place about the level of government involvement, but not about community banking. One Democratic senator put it this way: "The issue at hand, as I see it, is not *whether* community development banks are a good idea . . . but rather how do we establish them."[30]

Bailey's bank would live again! The Riegle Community Development and Regulatory Improvement Act of 1994, commonly known as the Community Development Banking Act (CDBA),[31] promised to "promote economic revitalization and community development through investment in and assistance to community development financial institutions."[32] These banks, formed in the likeness of ShoreBank, would be given specific charters to provide financial services to poor communities. The banks were called Community Development Financial Institutions (CDFIs) and would be defined as institutions that (1) had "a primary mission of promoting community development," (2) "[served] an investment area or targeted population," and (3) "provide[d] development services in conjunction with equity investments or loans."[33]

However, ShoreBank's ambitious vision—"Let's Change the World"—was watered down into legislation, and even what made it into law was quietly gutted by subsequent legislatures. Congress never appropriated the full amount authorized by the CDBA for the CDFI fund, which would have enabled government investments in community banks.[34] The George W. Bush administration sharply reduced funds to the CDFIs.[35] The funds, never robust or popular, diminished even more significantly after the financial crisis. At their peak, there were one thousand CDFI's in the country, much more than President Clinton had promised. However, the majority of the funds went toward community development projects, as opposed to banking services for the poor. According to the fund's financial disclosures, the majority of investments were allotted first to real estate development in low-income communities and second, to businesses operating in those areas.[36] Although these are important community-building investments, they are usually undertaken by external firms and developers and do not increase financial services to community members.

The CDFI industry suffered many bank failures during the recent crisis that wrought havoc on small banks nationwide, but even earlier, these institutions struggled to remain profitable. Compared to their more conventional peers, CDFIs routinely showed weaker financial performance: "An analysis of regulated CDFI Fund awardees found that these CDFIs typically had fewer total assets, higher loan delinquency and charge-off rates, and lower returns on assets than their non-CDFI contemporaries."[37] CDFIs simply operate in a more costly way than their traditional bank counterparts, and it would thwart their objectives if they attempted to achieve comparable profitability with excessively high interest rates.

Still, ShoreBank's founders and many CDFI supporters claim that this model is "on the right side of history"[38] and that these banks are uniquely able to meet the needs of their communities. These banks have gone and can go a long way toward meeting the needs of the poor. However, if they are to continue and do so in a way that significantly addresses the entrenched poverty affecting so many communities, they must be able to function with minimal profits and more government support. Lending to the poor at reasonable rates is not a highly profitable business, and the government must not outsource this important social need to the mainstream-banking model.

Many CDBA supporters confidently assumed that these institutions would not only serve the poor but lend profitably and achieve returns on investments.[39] Former Treasury secretary Lawrence Summers envisioned "a successful CDFI [as] perhaps best compared to a niche venture capital firm that deploys its superior knowledge of an emerging market niche to invest and manage risk better than other investors."[40] Summers labeled these banks "market scouts" that would seek out profits in overlooked markets.[41] Donald Lash, an early CDBA advocate, claimed that competition in banking would open the way for CDFIs to expand in response to market needs. Lash gave examples of banks whose lending in underserved areas was "surprisingly profitable."[42] The CDFI fund envisioned that modest funds and incentives could induce profit-maximizing institutions to meet the needs of struggling communities without structurally changing the banking framework.

Although modeled after ShoreBank's bold change-the-world mission, the CDBA was not intended to change the business of banking to meet the needs of the poor but to fit the needs of the poor into the business of banking. Unlike the Progressive and the Populist movements that brought about the credit union and the savings and loan, the CDBA movement was rooted in the market ethos that defines modern banking. Both the CDBA and the CRA, the proverbial carrot and stick, attempt to coax or force the mainstream-banking equation to do something inherently inconsistent with its business model. They are part and parcel of the deregulatory mission—the flip side of the same coin. No wonder, then, that the CDBA had advocates in high places. It was simple: banks did not need to be treated as special or restricted from market competition. Niche "poverty banks" would simply pop up in the market and fill the void created by competitive forces.

MICROCREDIT: MARKET-BASED PHILANTHROPY

Microcredit, a market-based lending principle, has been the most heralded and controversial modern effort to lend to the poor. Though not a significant part of the financial landscape in the United States, it has swept over the developing world. Just as the credit union movement had evangelical leaders who saw it as the wave of the future and the cure to all sorts of social ills, microcredit was also seen as a potential cure to poverty. Microcredit's quixotic mission was to help the poor through profitable lending. Muhammad Yunus, the founder of Grameen Bank and the most vocal advocate for worldwide microcredit, won the Nobel Peace Prize in 2006. A true philanthropist and visionary, he has been described as a genius, has appeared on many lists of the most influential thinkers and entrepreneurs, and has even inspired "Muhammad Yunus Day" in Houston, Texas. Yunus has called credit a basic human right and claims that the Third-World banking industry is the prime cause of chronic poverty and welfare dependency: "I [am] proposing to put a right to credit. It's . . . a human right, so that people can create their self-employment with that money. If they can create income for themselves, they can take care of right to food, right to shelter much more easily than government can ever do it. . . . Money begets money. If you don't have that, you wait around to be hired by somebody at the mercy of others. If you have that money in your hand, you desperately try to make the best use of it and move ahead. And that's generating income for yourself. All human beings are very creative—full of potential, full of energy. . . . So, money kind of allows them to express it. . . . And if you're successful, you can take more money. You can expand your capacity, reach next level of capacity, and so on."[43]

The Grameen Bank model of lending is based on giving small groups of women a loan of between ten and fifty dollars with the goal of them using the funds to start a business and help their families escape poverty. These women form a "solidarity circle," which is meant to reduce defaults by "effectively leaving to the borrowers in the circle the task of determining whether each individual borrower is a good credit risk."[44] The successful returns on their business endeavors are then used to pay back the loan. Grameen also provides life training of sorts titled "sixteen decisions." According to law professor Rashmi Dyal-Chand, these decisions are akin to training in Western culture. The principles range from the broad ("Discipline, Unity, Courage, and Hard work") to the specific (promising to build and to use latrines, not to give or to receive dowries, and to keep families small). The women also pledge to socialize with members of the group and to discipline each other for any breach of the collective promises.[45] Grameen Bank boasted a 98 percent loan repayment when these principles were followed.[46]

Both the Left and the Right lauded and embraced Grameen Bank. The Left embraced Yunus's social-justice-through-economic-justice mission and praised him for focusing on women. In 2009, President Obama gave Yunus the Presidential Medal of Freedom and promised an investment of $100 million for microcredit in the Western Hemisphere.[47] The Right embraced the bank as a way to address poverty through market principles and self-help without involving governments.[48] And the loans would turn a profit to boot! Grameen Bank was another manifestation of capitalism's answer to poverty. The poor would help themselves without any handouts or subsidies. The loans would make entrepreneurs out of the world's poor, who would be trained in the art of capital accumulation.

Microcredit did not begin or end with Grameen—informal banking institutions have existed for centuries on practically every continent—but Grameen did give the concept new legs.[49] Today, thousands of institutions worldwide offer "microcredit," and the term, stretched by overuse, has become almost meaningless. Nonprofits like Kiva connect small-scale "entrepreneurs" in developing countries with small-scale financiers, usually from developed countries. Kiva lends small loans at or near 0 percent interest and only lends to verified borrowers with a business plan. Large "microcredit" corporations similar to formalized loan sharks also operate in the Third World.

It wasn't long before the honeymoon with microcredit gave way to widespread criticism. With such ambitious aims and universal hype, the metrics were never quite reachable. Microcredit would not, after all, be the cure to poverty. In fact, the data have been "mixed" as to whether microcredit has even reduced poverty.[50] Additionally, the collective group pressure to repay loans, a critical feature of the Grameen model, became oppressive, leading to duress and public shaming. In the span of a few months in 2010, eighty people in the Andhra Pradesh region of India committed suicide after defaulting on microloans, leading Indian officials to instruct the population to stop repaying the loans.[51] The model was built on social pressure to repay as a stand-in for contract enforcement in Third World areas where rule of law is not well established. Still, even the problematic social pressure system and nearly complete repayment rate were not enough to reap profits. That would come from the high interest on the loans. Even Grameen Bank has reported annual interest rates as high as 60 to 70 percent—technically usurious by U.S. standards but necessary to make a profit.[52]

Eventually, what was intended as a means to help the poor turned into a way for big corporations to make money. A 2010 *New York Times* report described the hand-wringing by microcredit supporters surprised at the direction it has taken: "Drawn by the prospect of hefty profits from even the smallest of loans, a raft of banks and financial institutions now dominate the field, with some charging interest rates of 100% or more."[53] Yunus himself expressed frustration and said: "We created microcredit to fight the loan sharks; we didn't create microcredit to encourage new loan sharks." The article went on to state that the microfinance industry, "with over $60 billion in assets, has unquestionably outgrown its charitable roots." Investor capital has aided some of these firms, and their success has even driven up interest rates in countries like Mexico where some of the biggest corporate lenders operate. "You can make money from the poorest people in the world—is that a bad thing, or is that just a business?" asked one industry observer. "At what point do we say we have gone too far?" This is an unfortunate, but predictable scenario. Microcredit certainly started with a mission to help the poor but refused to sacrifice its other bottom line: profit.

Formal microcredit institutions have not been successful in the United States for a variety of reasons, including our robust and formalized economy and the fact that U.S. poverty differs from poverty abroad. And the market for small loans in the United States is not composed of would-be entrepreneurs but rather people who have steady employment and need to respond to an emergency. The major microcredit institution in the United States is Accion USA, but other companies like Kabbage, Square Capital, and PayPal offer microloans.[54] Loan sizes in the United States are much larger than abroad—$7,000 compared to less than $100. These loans are meant to be used to start or aid a struggling small business and the terms are slightly higher than credit card loans.[55]

However, an informal microcredit market in the United States is operating in certain immigrant populations. These "lending circles," much like the cooperatives of the past, offer a way for those excluded from the banking sector to work together informally to meet certain limited credit needs. In the United States, groups of undocumented workers and other recent immigrants have organized informal lending circles in which individuals pool resources—sometimes fifty dollars a month—and pick a member of the group by lot to receive a loan of the entire accumulated amount. The communities that develop informal lending circles are usually tightly knit and share a cultural bond or language.[56] These groups do not rely on government enforcement or intrusion and are entirely self-funded.[57] Their only enforcement mechanism is mutual trust. Studies in New York's Chinatown and California's Japanese communities reveal that these institutions are the dominant form of banking among these groups. A staggering 80 percent of Koreans in the United States belong to at least one informal credit group.[58]

These groups operate in the shadows of mainstream banking. Still, they have been lauded as a "borrower's solution to market imperfections, a consumer-driven arrangement that is a solution to an inherent market deficiency soluble neither by state regulation nor by open market arrangements."[59] Because these groups operate on the fringes of the mainstream-banking model, they have several constraints. First, members of informal lending circles are not able to develop a credit history to eventually enter mainstream banking. Second, their deposits are not protected, and their investments are vulnerable to fraud or mismanagement by others. Third, credit is no less costly from these groups than from alternative lending sources. Members pay about 20 percent APR interest on loans, usually making these loans a last-resort alternative.[60] Fourth, these groups usually cannot help with emergency or everyday credit needs because borrowers must wait their turn for the funds. Last, although informal lending circles might help tightly knit groups of immigrants sharing a shared language and a culture, they do not arise among the large majority of American urban and rural poor who do not share common social norms.[61]

Despite the challenges and mixed results, many still cling to the idea that the answer to poverty must be found through microcredit. But microcredit and microinstitutions keep coming up short in meeting macro problems. Large multinational banks meet the needs of the well-off, and the poor are expected to fend for themselves by forming small groups and collecting their limited funds. But the fact that Wall Street now owns ShoreBank and a few large corporations control many of the world's microcredit organizations reveals the limits of the small and the powerless to help themselves while the government helps the banking industry.

MARKET INNOVATIONS

These market answers to the problem of banking the poor have involved pressing mainstream banks into lending small-dollar loans, targeting neglected communities through the CRA, or employing grassroots community solutions such as ShoreBank and microcredit. Today, many claim that the answer to banking the unbanked lies in yet-to-be-developed technology. These "disruptive innovators" can use new technology to underprice banks. As self-described "visionaries," these innovators view the issue of reaching the unbanked as a specific market problem.[62] A venture capitalist who funded companies trying to offer services to the unbanked explained to *Bloomberg News* that he saw the unbanked as a "tremendous market opportunity" for his firm to invest in and claimed that the answer to banking the unbanked lies in technology creating new products. He explained that because the underbanked consist of not only the poor but over a third of the public, this was a trillion-dollar "mass market" they hoped to enter. As such, there is a race between many nonbanks to create a product or service that will fill a market void. These companies are interested in meeting the needs of the unbanked, usually not for any social policy reason but because they want to make profits. These companies are hoping to use technological innovations to design products that can underprice banks or payday lenders. The major contenders so far are prepaid cards, retail banking, mobile banking, and peer-to-peer loans. Others, like virtual currencies, are still in their infancy.

PREPAID CARDS

One of the most recognizable products on the market, prepaid cards allow the user to load money onto a card and then use the card as if it were a debit card. This provides the unbanked an alternative to checking accounts, with the ability to avoid the threat of overdraft fees and to make cashless payments for goods and services, including online purchases. Unlike a bank account, the funds on the card are not FDIC insured.[63] Some banks, as well as companies like Target, Wal-Mart, Western Union, American Express, and H&R Block, offer prepaid cards. MasterCard even issues Suze Orman, Magic Johnson, and Russell Simmons prepaid cards. Fees can vary from $5 to $10 per month to up to $500 per year, with the celebrity-backed cards being the most expensive.[64] The average fees are $300 per year.[65] Most have an activation fee, and many have monthly maintenance fees, automated teller machine (ATM) fees, and reloading fees. Some even have a $1 to $2 "swipe" fee added on every time the card is used.[66] At one extreme, the MoneyGram prepaid card has eighteen different fees versus the American Express Bluebird, which only has two. Over the last few years, card fees have risen by over 20 percent and so has their popularity.[67] Still, prepaid cards have not been widely embraced by the underserved because of their high fees and their limited utility as just a makeshift debit card.

WAL-MART

Wal-Mart is the leader in providing services to the unbanked and is the most interested in doing so. Wal-Mart has built an empire using economies of scale and scope to lower costs. It hopes to do the same with banking services, even though its 2005 attempt to secure a bank charter failed. Wal-Mart currently offers prepaid cards, including the American Express Bluebird card, low-cost check cashing ($3 per check compared with up to $25),[68] and money transfers ($10 for over $900 as opposed to fees of up to $76 at Western Union).[69] In September 2014, Wal-Mart and its partner Green Dot Bank launched an FDIC-insured checking account. The account costs $8.95 a month for deposits of $500 or less and has a $3 start-up fee, a 3 percent foreign-transaction fee, and a $2.50 ATM fee. Customers can get a credit card, checks, and bill-pay services through this account.[70] The account has no overdraft fees—it will simply block transactions when there isn't enough money in the account. Green Dot also allows any customer to open an account and will not use Chex-Systems to blacklist potential customers.

Despite so many low-cost banking alternatives (or perhaps because of them), no company is as mistrusted and feared by the banking industry as Wal-Mart. The banking industry immediately, and predictably, opposed the move: "Wal-Mart should not offer financial services . . . Wal-Mart is a retailer, not a bank."[71]Many worry that Wal-Mart will quickly dominate this field and do to small banks what it has done to small stores around the country: underprice competitors and then raise prices when its products become the only option in a community.[72] In Massachusetts, Wal-Mart already holds 30 percent of all check-cashing licenses, easily eclipsing the long-established franchises. Still, profits from financial services accounted for less than 0.1 percent, or about $280 million, of Wal-Mart's $279.4 billion in U.S. sales last year. Their financial offerings clearly have the complementary benefit of customers going to the stores for financial services and spending some portion of their cashed checks on other products within the stores.

Wal-Mart has, in the past, partnered with banks across the country to provide traditional bank services to its customers.[73] What is interesting, as reported by the *Wall Street Journal*, is that these banks collected more in fees than in loan income, unlike all the other U.S. banks, in which the reverse is true. The majority of the fees came from *overdraft charges*. In fact, a *Wall Street Journal* analysis found that the "five banks with the most Wal-Mart branches . . . ranked among the top 10 U.S. banks in fee income as a percentage of deposits in 2013." These banks do not necessarily charge more for overdrafts, but rather, the Wal-Mart customers who use these banks overdraw their accounts more often than most bank customers. The reason, as recounted by one customer who willingly pays the fees, is because "it's cheaper than a payday loan." And what is the cost of using overdraft protection as a line of credit and overdraft fees as the cost of that credit? An APR of over 300 percent, which if charged on a loan would be considered usurious and illegal in many states.

Wal-Mart has been unable to obtain a banking charter or offer loans in the United States, but it does have a banking charter in Mexico, where it offers small-dollar loans.[74] If Wal-Mart could enter that market in the United States, the company could be the best potential market-based alternative to payday lending. Small-loan borrowers could certainly benefit if Wal-Mart's entry into the field drove down payday loan prices. However, there are some reasons to be skeptical. First, if Wal-Mart did engage in large-scale consumer lending, it would add another behemoth Too-Big-to-Fail firm to the already growing roster. A cautionary tale can be found in General Motors' experience with its bank, the General Motors Acceptance Corporation. The bank was established as a Utah industrial loan company to help General Motors finance auto purchases. Soon, the bank's revenues eclipsed the struggling automakers', and the bank took on a life of its own. It entered the subprime mortgage market, and the rest is sordid history. The bank and the company were bailed out during the aftermath of the financial crisis.

Second, Wal-Mart's current Green Dot MoneyPaks have become the payment device of choice for affinity fraudsters—those who target a group based on a shared feature like race or religion—because the payments are so difficult to track.[75] Wal-Mart has not demonstrated that its main incentive is to protect its customers. It is interested in making a profit, and small lending for the sole purpose of profit-making has not had an exemplary history. The main roadblock to a Wal-Mart bank will be the nation's large and small banks, who will certainly wage war on any proposed law that allows Wal-Mart to lend—just as they did in 2005 when Wal-Mart applied for a banking charter.[76]

MOBILE BANKING

Mobile banking, or conducting financial transactions using your mobile phone either through a bank or through an independent provider, has not taken off in the United States but is an international phenomenon. The M-Pesa program in Kenya is the most-cited example of mobile banking successfully leading to financial inclusion. In 2007, Kenya's leading mobile company, Safaricom, joined up with the Central Bank of Kenya to launch M-Pesa for Kenyans, who are 80 percent unbanked. As of January 2013 (in just under six years), 17 million adults (approximately 74 percent of Kenya's adult population) used M-Pesa, and over 25 percent of Kenya's gross domestic product was funneled through mobile money services.[77] With over forty thousand agents across the country, users can make deposits, transfer funds to anyone with a mobile phone, pay bills, distribute employee salaries, and even get loans.

Financial inclusion of the unbanked in Kenya has resulted in significant benefits. Not only do Kenyans waste less time waiting in lines at banks or paying bills, one study even found that in rural Kenya, households that used M-Pesa enjoyed increased incomes of 5 to 30 percent! In addition, the network's ease and reliability has led to a host of new startups, which are building their business models on M-Pesa. This success has influenced many countries, including the Philippines, Uganda, South Africa, India, Afghanistan, and Romania, to attempt similar programs. None of these programs have yet to enjoy the broad success of M-Pesa. In some ways, Kenya had the perfect political and economic environment to launch this product: a strong central bank, a powerful mobile provider with a monopoly, a weak coalition of national banks, and a large majority of the public with a mobile phone but no bank account.

The United States differs significantly from Kenya in its political and economic landscape, but could mobile banking offer similar benefits here? The FDIC and the Federal Reserve seem to think so. Both agencies issued reports in the years 2013 and 2014 with optimistic findings regarding the potential for mobile banking to offer a platform for financial inclusion.[78] The findings showed that the large majority of unbanked or underbanked households have access to mobile phones, and at least for those who cite "inconvenience" as a barrier to banking, mobile banking promises to take banking services to them. Both agency reports envision large banks administering mobile banking services but not eliminating the fees associated with account maintenance mentioned above.

Wide scale adoption of mobile banking will likely make simple banking much easier and more convenient for the entire public—including the poor. Mobile bill-pay, money transfers, and deposits could mean less wasted time for everyone. This is the story of South Africa's foray into mobile banking: In South Africa, where only half the population has bank accounts, but nearly everyone has a mobile phone, a company called WIZZIT set out to bank the unbanked with an aspiring worldwide mission to "change the world by providing banking opportunities to the 4 billion unbanked and under-banked [globally] through cell phone technology, leading to a reduction in poverty and the creation of economic citizens."[79] However, the company not only failed to reduce poverty worldwide, but as it turned out, the banked and higher-income population, who relied on the service to conduct more banking transactions at increased convenience, comprised most of its South African customer base. A 2011 Harvard Business School case study on WIZZIT criticized the plan as presumptuous; said one author: "The mistake a lot of us make is to look at the folks at the base of the pyramid and assume they must need the same types of services we need."[80]

There is reason to think mobile banking will not be the unbanked's answer in the United States. Because it is usually linked to a bank, it offers no immediate benefits to those who are not banking because of the expense instead of the inconvenience. For example, it is unlikely to meet the high demand for small loans (which isn't even its goal). On the other hand, if the services were linked to a mobile provider (as envisioned by a T-Mobile proposal to enter this field), they would be fee-based financial transactions without FDIC insurance protection or a route to a bank account.[81] In other words, mobile banking may make banking easier for the banked, but at least in the United States, it is unlikely to offer the low-cost products needed by the unbanked. Still, it is too soon to deliver a verdict.

PEER-TO-PEER LENDING

Taking advantage of Internet technology knocking some of the barriers between people down, peer-to-peer (P2P) lending cuts out the bank middleman and allows individuals to loan to others at an interest rate negotiated by the two parties. The difference is that the loans are provided with the lender's own capital as opposed to others' capital. Lending Club, one of the leading P2P lenders, hopes to help its investors earn a higher return and its borrowers get a lower rate on personal loans than through traditional financial institutions.[82] These companies match potential borrowers with willing lenders and facilitate the transaction. Most of the loans are relatively small and short term. One popular use of the loans is for credit card debt consolidation, although many startups with a P2P model, like Funding Circle, offer small-business loans. Other companies link not "peers" but big-time investors like hedge funds willing to take on small high-yield and short-term loans that earn profits. One P2P lender, QuarterSpot, pays banks an origination fee for referring bank customers who were denied loans.

P2P loans got off to a rocky start, with Prosper (one of the first companies to offer these services) seeing an almost 33 percent default rate. However, over time the business models have improved. Now these platforms are even getting multimillion-dollar investments from companies like Google and Sequoia Capital, and total lending for more established P2Ps is in the billions per year. Loan size varies by lender, with Lending Club averaging $13,625 and Prosper averaging $6,830. Most companies use borrower credit scores as a way to determine risk and price interest rates accordingly. As such, interest rates are varied and can sometimes be lower than payday lenders.'[83]

Philanthropic P2P lender Kiva has introduced "Zip," which offers zero interest loans based on fixed criteria to American entrepreneurs. Borrowers post worthy projects on an online platform, and volunteer lenders choose which one to lend a small amount of money. When enough money has been put in to cover the loan, the loan is disbursed directly thru PayPal. These loans are not designed to cover emergencies or living expenses but are geared toward entrepreneurs who cannot get traditional loans.[84] P2P lending is often confused with crowdfunding, but in P2P lending, the lender receives interest and eventual repayment of the loan. In a crowdfunding project, like Kickstarter, supporters of a particular project do not get their money back, but depending on the venture, receive some form of a prize, such as a CD or even a sample of potato salad.

In essence, a P2P lending company is a financial intermediary. It links a source of credit to a demand for credit. Some companies even screen or rate borrowers, offering true intermediary functions. Basically, they operate like a bank but without customer deposits. The other difference is that regulators have so far treated P2P lenders with a soft touch. However, once the industry becomes bigger and fraud inevitably sours some investors, it is likely that there will be calls for the sector to be regulated and required to comply with certain norms of borrowing and lending. Perhaps people will want some insurance to protect them against loan losses. Then, P2P companies begin to look much more like banks. In a way, P2P seems to be reinventing the wheel and substituting one financial intermediary for another. Perhaps the reinvention is necessary because the current wheel is broken, but P2P lending is just another form of financial intermediation for the Internet age. As such, it will likely face the same sorts of problems as banks face, such as profitability concerns for small loans and market pressure from other lenders.

P2P lending has been and will likely continue to be a boon to small businesses—especially to artists, musicians, designers, and makers of all sorts who are too small for banks to bother with. But if P2P lending is to help the poor, it will require many socially minded lenders to lend charitably. This is, of course, the principle of Kiva and others. There exists a good deal of inherent kindness in people and surely enough goodwill among the well-off in our population to offer this hand of support to the less well-off among us. Realistically, however, meeting the immensity of the demand will be a monumental logistical undertaking, requiring oversight, coordination, and meaningful consumer protections. Usually, this sort of endeavor is within the sphere of the government and not private entities. And interestingly enough, this is why the government got involved in the central coordination of credit allocation in the first place.

This was, of course, one of the principal lessons in the history of the credit unions, the savings and loans, and the Morris banks and one key takeaway from the market-based philanthropy models of ShoreBank and Grameen Bank. Philanthropic ventures that lack mission-reinforcing government support can fall victim to the simple economic principle that lending to the poor is unprofitable. Or alternatively, they can earn high profits through subsidies or high interest rates and become coopted by shareholders demanding higher returns.

* * *

All of these technologies will affect the banking industry and have the potential to make transacting in the modern world easier and less costly. As such, they should be encouraged and allowed to prove themselves in the consumer markets. However, it is not obvious that technological advances will necessarily lead to more equality in services. In fact, there is reason to suspect that they will not. For example, the revolutionizing technology of the ATM made banking services more convenient and accessible to those with bank accounts, but it also turned out to be a pivotal factor in the increased competition between banks that led to cost (and customer) cutting.

Today, small banks worry that the rise in digital technology will favor the largest banks and drive them out of business. Two recent industry reports confirm these fears. They found that "35 percent of banks' market share in North America could be in play by 2020 as traditional branch banking gives way to new digital players." The reports' findings for the survival of community banks are grim: "research indicates that 15 to 25 percent of today's roughly 7,000 North American financial institutions could be gone as a result of consolidation before 2020."[85] In other words, technological advances will make large firms larger and will squeeze small banks even more.

One of the key takeaways of modern finance is that the banking oligarchs are growing in size and power, controlling more of the market, and making it even harder for small and local institutions to compete. The other takeaway is that mainstream banks have no interest in serving the poor because it is inconsistent with pursuing high profits. If so inclined, commercial giants like Wal-Mart, Google, or Amazon can potentially use their market dominance to lend small amounts to the poor at a profit. But we must be cautious about outsourcing the credit needs of the most financially vulnerable portion of the population to unregulated corporations. Doing so is essentially admitting that the government-created and government-supported credit market and banking sector is only meant for one portion of the population. The other portion must get by through self-help or charity; or alternatively, unregulated, unsupported, and unprotected companies that might eventually, or so we hope, figure out how to make a buck from banking the poor.

7

Postal Banking

It is not a money-making adjunct to the Post Office Department. . . . Its aim is infinitely higher and more important. . . . It places savings facilities at the very doors of those living in remote sections, and it also affords opportunity for safeguarding the savings of thousands who have absolute confidence on the government and will trust no other institution.

—CARTER B. KEENE, CHIEF POST OFFICE INSPECTOR, 1913

The Postal System, with Benjamin Franklin as the first postmaster general, was created in the United States in 1775 to ease correspondences during the Revolutionary War. And for nearly two hundred years, it operated as a part of the federal government, with a mission to reach individuals and communities across the far-flung nation. In an 1832 encyclopedia article about the American post office, political theorist Francis Lieber ranked it with the printing press and the mariner's compass as "one of the most effective instruments of civilization."[1] Most nineteenth-century Americans agreed: the postal system was "one of the most notable features of American public life."[2] It erased community borders and connected the spacious country—leveling the information playing field by disseminating information and public discourse. One contemporary observed that it enabled a better democracy than that enjoyed by the Greeks, Romans, or any other celebrated civilization because it provided a medium for communication to spread to each corner of the land, "penetrating its darkened regions, and equalizing, elevating, and harmonizing . . . the social position and geographical distribution of the people."[3] And, said one historian, it was the "agent of change" that set in motion a democratic revolution that "transformed American public life." The U.S. Post Office Department was "quite literally without precedent in the history of the world."[4]

The rich history of the post office is worth reviewing because its crucial role in developing America's unparalleled democracy and market dominance cannot and should not be understated. Much of what Alexis de Tocqueville observed when he came to America and famously lauded the early development of the Republic in *Democracy in America* was made possible by the postal system. Tocqueville remarked that in America, unlike in European countries, an uneducated "backwoodsman" in far-flung Michigan knows just as much about the affairs of the government as those living in the capital: "There is an astonishing circulation of letters and newspapers among these savage woods. . . . I do not think that in the most enlightened rural districts of France there is intellectual movement either so rapid or on such a scale as in this wilderness."[5]

Before the telegraph, telephone, car, or railroad was a possibility, rural constituents in every corner of America knew what their congressional representatives were doing and were able to communicate with them. Before the financial giants of America made shipping canals, railroads, highways, and wires that created the most productive and efficient economy in the world, the United States had nationwide trading routes unparalleled in the contemporary world—all made possible by the United States' postal system.

The post office, the primary facilitator of commercial trade, "provided merchants with the only reliable means for transmitting information, bills of exchange, and money."[6] Historian Richard John explained that it was only after the post office *created* a national marketplace that private entrepreneurs could compete with each other outside local markets. The post office created a decentralized public sphere that made commerce and trade available to all—not just the elite clustered around the centers of political and market power. More importantly, "only the central government possessed the necessary resources to finance the establishment of such an extensive network." Only the central government had the capacity, the "moral authority," and the public "trust" to create this system.[7]

In fact, the post office required a formal pledge of public trust from postal employees and instilled a sense that it was invested with a high moral purpose.[8] Postal employees could not open mail or engage in market manipulations such as taking money, holding back mail, or speeding it up for financial incentives. The highly coveted, distinctive position of postmaster in each town was given to its most prominent and trusted citizen. The fact that women and blacks were explicitly excluded from being postmasters was a fighting cause for both groups for nearly a century. The exclusion instilled institutional racism and sexism that prohibited their full participation in public and political life. Frederick Douglass complained that the fact that blacks were "not trusted even to carry a mail bag twenty yards across the street" stigmatized the race and inculcated a sense of their inferiority.[9] The postal policies of racial and gender exclusion proved to be significant barriers for these groups precisely because the post office came to represent democratic equality.

The Post Office Act of 1792, supported by George Washington, James Madison, and Alexander Hamilton, has been called "one of the most important single pieces of legislation to have been enacted by Congress in the early republic."[10] The act made several crucial decisions that would shape our first-rate democracy and economy. First, it was decided that the federal government would financially support the post office without requiring it to produce a surplus like its counterparts in Europe.[11] It was to be self-sustaining but *not profitable* and when needed, supplemented by the Treasury. This made the post office department the largest government agency by far during this time. Second, the post office would serve *every* community without regard to profit. In other words, profitable routes (along the Eastern Seaboard) would subsidize the east-to-west routes. Other shippers could compete with the post office along these routes, but the post office could not discontinue any route without congressional approval. Third, Congress would *subsidize* the dissemination of newspapers through the post office. The subsidy, financed by merchants who paid handsomely to mail letters, reduced the price of newspapers by 700 percent. In other words, wealthy northeasterners were paying for information to be carried to the rural farmers of the South and West.[12] Information was critical to participating in the economy and in the political process, so the federal government enabled the flow of information to all regions without worrying about costs.[13]

The central rationale behind the act was that it was "absolutely necessary" that the government circulate "knowledge of every kind . . . through every part of the United States."[14] In 1782, James Madison asserted that the postal system was the "principal channel" through which the citizenry secured its "general knowledge" of public affairs.[15]

James Madison saw the post office as a way for the citizenry to check political power, whereas George Washington saw it as a way to secure the allegiance of a widespread population. As such, the federal government "established a national market for information sixty years before a comparable national market would emerge for goods."[16] The policy of expansive information dissemination reoriented the character of the country and transformed the "eighteenth-century Atlantic community of the Founding Fathers into the nineteenth-century national community that hundreds of thousands of Americans would fight and die for during the Civil War."[17] It was also postal policy that made the "orbit" of the government so small "as to embroil the country in civil war." The founders had not anticipated that ordinary Americans would be able "to actively participate in a truly open-ended national discussion on the leading events of the day, rather than merely to receive periodic broadcasts from the seat of power, as Washington had envisioned, or to engage in carefully structured two-way consultations with their elected representatives, as Madison had hoped."[18] And unfortunately, the same platform that eased informational exchange and enabled national trade routes also helped drive people apart as it forced those with political and cultural differences to deal—and often clash—with each other.

This broad public engagement was even beyond the imagination of the great proponents of local control, such as James Madison, whose *Federalist* essays of 1787 and 1788 only envisioned interactions with representatives during periodic home visits—not the regular contact that the post quickly enabled.[19] The continuous conversations between congressional representatives and their constituents augmented even Madison's vision of public participation in lawmaking.

The federal government was, in the modern words of Grover Norquist, "so small you could drown it in a bathtub" when it decided to financially support the post office. In effect, the postal service was one of the *only* services the federal government provided. Even fiscal conservatives like Alexander Hamilton endorsed its foundational principle: communities over profits.[20] (The federal government rejected this principle in 1970 when it decided that the post office should be cut off from the government and left to fend for itself.)

Many have forgotten that the post office made much of the budding American economy possible. Upon explaining successful retailer Montgomery Ward's ability to use free market competition to revolutionize sales in America, even Thomas Sowell, an unabashed proponent of *laissez-faire* free markets operating without government intervention, observed: "Montgomery Ward cut delivery costs by operating as a mail-order house, selling directly to consumers all over the country from its huge warehouse in Chicago, using the government's already existing mail delivery system to deliver its products to customers at lower cost."[21] The beauty of this organization is that because it focused on access to communities over profits, it was able to adapt and offer different services to accommodate the needs of the country. Its central mission being equality of access, it was not long after its creation before that encompassed financial inclusion.

POSTAL BANKING PROPOSED

Postal banking started in Great Britain in 1861. From the beginning, the goal of postal banking abroad was financial inclusion. Postal banks were such a success in England that one contemporary called them "the greatest boon ever conferred on the working classes of this country."[22] In England, postal banks were geared toward "the humbler classes" and offered a low interest rate of 2 percent on deposits, below those of existing banks.[23] Once the British system started, word spread internationally through the fastest means available at the time: the post office. The idea quickly spread across the British Empire to New Zealand in 1876, to Canada in 1868, and to New South Wales in 1871.[24] After two decades, almost every Western country—plus Japan—had adopted nationwide postal banking.[25] Germany was the only country that chose not to implement postal banking because it already had an extensive network of savings banks and credit unions. Germany's savings banks formed a national union to fight the creation of a postal-banking system, and it wasn't until 1939 that Hitler's Third Reich overcame this opposition and established postal banking.[26]

In 1871, President Ulysses S. Grant's postmaster general, John Creswell, proposed postal savings banks in the United States modeled after those in Great Britain. They would look much like the philanthropic banks prevalent in the Northeast in the 1800s.[27] The post office originally proposed the savings banks as a means to pay for a telegraph system, but because the mission of financial inclusion was inherent to the savings bank concept, the dual purposes were immediately fused.[28] Creswell's initial 1871 proposal intended to yield a modest profit for the post office and offer a 4 percent interest rate to attract deposits—which would compete with banks. This would obviously need to be changed in order to overcome bank opposition. And it was. After the banking Panic of 1873, Creswell's annual report reduced the competitive features—lowering interest paid from 4 to 2.5 percent and limiting deposits to $300 annually or a total of $1000.[29] He also repurposed postal savings banks as a tool of economic reform—a way to reintroduce hoarded money back into circulation to counteract the inevitable credit freeze that accompanies a crisis.

President Grant endorsed the postal banks as a method of financial inclusion for remote regions of the United States in his annual message to the country on December 1, 1873:

> The population of the country has largely increased. More than 25,000 miles of railroad have been built, requiring the active use of capital to operate them. Millions of acres of land have been opened to cultivation, requiring capital to move the products. Manufactories have multiplied beyond all precedent in the same period of time, requiring capital weekly for the payment of wages and for the purchase of material; and probably the largest of all comparative contraction arises from the organizing of free labor in the South. Now every laborer there receives his wages, and, for want of savings banks, the greater part of such wages is carried in the pocket or hoarded until required for use. . . . I urge favorable action by Congress on the important recommendations of the Postmaster-General for the establishment of United States postal savings depositories.[30]

The advocates of post office savings banks were not just trying to expand savings banks across the country; they were interested in providing a state-supported institution. In 1882, Congressman Edward Lacey said, "Private enterprise alone does not, and cannot, in this respect, meet the necessities of the industrious poor in any country, and least of all in the United States."[31] The point was that "the working poor . . . would be more inclined to deposit earnings in the Post Office, a *public* institution, than in the local savings bank run by sanctimonious clergymen and philanthropists."[32] The post office, with its rich history and public mission, proved the obvious choice for providing this service. With branches in communities where no bank and certainly, no savings bank, would go, the post office could potentially do with savings what it had with information—democratize banking.

The environment in America after the Civil War was reform-friendly, and postal banking appealed to a variety of different groups, each discontent with certain aspects of the financial sector. America's farmers, the strongest lobby for postal banks, saw postal banking as a means to save without having to rely on northeastern savings banks. Other groups, like the Knights of Labor, the Populists, and the Free-Silverites, also pushed for postal banking. And it appealed to those who had originally opposed government banking, such as the Jeffersonians and the Jacksonians, because despite being a strong government action, postal banking would serve to oppose business concentrations and that most feared of monopolies: bank monopolies.[33]

The Populist Party platform of 1892 stated: "We demand that postal savings banks be established by the government for the safe deposit of the earnings of the people and to facilitate exchange."[34] The Populist vision of the postal bank, however, differed from the system in England and that proposed by the postmaster general. The Populists wanted the postal banks not only to receive deposits but also to *lend* to rural farmers.[35] Lorenzo D. Lewelling, Populist governor of Kansas, explained how postal banks could increase credit: "One of the means of contraction of the currency is the holding of money in the bank's vaults. Why does the banker keep it in the bank vaults? Because he is afraid to loan it to you and me, because we may not pay it back. Why don't you put your money in the bank? You say you are afraid the bank will break. . . . You are both 'skeered.' What is the remedy? Take the Postal Savings Bank. You can put your money in there and the government is security for it. . . . The bank isn't afraid there will be a run and so the money is kept in circulation and business is stimulated."[36]

In early public discussions about postal banking, two distinct purposes were mentioned: providing banking services to those who didn't have them and stabilizing the turbulent banking sector. As to the first, Creswell's proposals endorsed financial inclusion using the same paternalistic language employed by early savings bank proponents: "[Postal banks] would . . . encourage economy and habits of saving on the part of all who might be in the way of earning small sums of money."[37] Many advocated the postal bank as an extension of the building and loan and savings banks: "Experience with building and loan associations have demonstrated the fact beyond all question of doubt that they are of inestimable value to the wage-workers of the country. . . . Well-conducted savings banks are also a boon to those who desire to make small weekly or monthly deposits."[38]

Not only would the postal banks build on an established foundation of savings banks and building and loans across the country, they could also overcome the class and comfort barriers many of the poor experienced with the formalized banks. "The mechanic or day laborer who would have a feeling of timidity about entering a big banking house to deposit a small share of his earnings, would gladly avail himself of an opportunity to make the deposit with the local post-master, for the reason that he feels that he has as much right to be there as any other man, for the post-office is a part of the Governmental structure he helps support, and he reckons justly that he is entitled to share in its benefits."[39]

The second purpose of general reform was also present from the beginning. Creswell reasoned that the postal banks would cure the bank runs that were endemic to the banking system in the nineteenth century: "The financial difficulties in which the country has been . . . involved . . . have demonstrated the necessity for some means of maintaining confidence in times of threatened disaster, and of gathering and wisely employing the immense wealth scattered among the people, to prevent panic and escape the ruin which inevitably follows in its track."[40] Indeed, many bank runs occurred between 1880 and 1910, afflicting both national and state banks and causing nationwide distrust.[41] A government-supported bank would go a long way toward infusing trust back into the system.

The postal banks would accomplish this, according to Creswell's first proposal, by essentially creating a central bank that could provide liquidity help to struggling banks. Forty years before the central bank's creation, the post office proposed that it could meet that need by pooling deposits into the Treasury, where they would be used "by judicious investments . . . to afford to monetary and banking institutions the very relief they now so eagerly seek."[42] In other words, the post office would pool the savings of the poor nationwide into a central location and then lend those savings to banks with liquidity problems.

As originally envisioned, postal banking would export and enlarge the savings banks geared for the poor to the rest of the country and also cure the distrust in the system. From the start the bankers, who might have stood to benefit greatly, opposed any direct government competition. Creswell responded to these critics in much the same way that Louis Brandeis would fifty years later:

> [National Banks] are organized to afford facilities to the community by lending money on personal security, dealing in exchange, issuing notes, and receiving deposits, not for permanent investment, but as *temporary custodians*. Bankers should own the capital they employ. When they attempt to do business on *borrowed capital* they are operating on a fictitious credit and become mere speculators. . . . With the Government it is totally different. . . . [Its] paramount consideration should be the best interests of the people, whose agent it is. . . . When the Government can arrest panic, restore confidence, call forth the hoarded treasure of the country, and revive the pursuits of industry, by a simple pledge of the people's credit for the people's security, who will say that the pledge should not be given?[43]

The post office continued to advocate for the establishment of savings banks, and bankers continued to oppose the proposal. Indeed, it would be debated in Congress and in public forums for forty years before its passage.[44]

Almost every postmaster general, from the time of Creswell's initial proposal until it passed, supported postal banking.[45] The only gap occurred during the two terms of Grover Cleveland (1885–1889, 1893–1897), the only Democrat to hold office during the forty years of debate. The bills introduced in Congress came from across the political spectrum; of the seventy-two bills from the Forty-Third to the Sixtieth Congress, forty-eight came from Republicans, fifteen from Democrats, six from Populists, and three from Independents. But although postal banking may not have been a partisan issue, it was certainly a regional one. Only two of the seventy-two bills introduced during that time originated from New England representatives, and only three were from mid-Atlantic states. Exactly half, thirty-six, came from representatives west of the Mississippi while sixteen came from the Midwest and thirteen hailed from the South. The majority came from agrarian states.[46] Interestingly, not *one* of these bills made it out of committee despite support from four presidents and nine postmaster generals.[47]

Though Creswell had first proposed it, the most enthusiastic champion of postal banking was John Wanamaker, President Harrison's postmaster general. Wanamaker proposed postal banking in his first three annual reports and had long been an advocate of banking for the poor.[48] He had worked to change the banking laws in Pennsylvania to allow churches to finance nonprofit savings banks, and he was the first president of one such bank, the First Penny Savings Bank of Philadelphia.[49] A former banker himself, he reinforced his advocacy of postal banking with a sophisticated market study that included cross-country data about postal savings banks abroad as well as detailed provisions for allocating the money from the U.S. system. He proposed that such funds be sent back to the savings banks of each state or used to purchase government and school bonds. He also added a new argument to the mix: that the post office had far more *locations* accessible to farmers and laborers than banks.[50] Wanamaker continued his advocacy into the 1890s, even after his term as postmaster general had ended. He remained convinced that the Panic of 1893 could have been avoided if the hoarded money of the nation had been gathered and redistributed by postal banks.[51]

DEALING WITH THE OPPOSITION

Throughout the long debate over postal banking, the major opposition came from two places: the bankers who did not want to compete with the federal government, and the Democrats who opposed too much federal government power. One of the most interesting aspects of the objections voiced over a hundred years ago is that the same objections will likely be raised in future discussions of postal banking: too much government, private enterprise should do it, the post office doesn't know how to bank, there isn't a need for it, and so on.

The first line of arguments came mostly from Democrats, *laissez-faire* capitalists, and bankers opposed to any federal intervention in business. Postal banks, they argued, would breed state paternalism that would lead to more government control. In 1891, the *Philadelphia Record* claimed that "the people of this country are shrewd enough to know where and how to deposit their money, without the kindly aid of a grandfatherly Government."[52] That same year, an editorial in the *New York Sun* stated that "the business of the Post-Office Department is to carry the mails. The business of the Government is to mind its own business. The citizens of the United States ought to have sense enough to take care of themselves."[53] The *Philadelphia Herald* repeated the then Democratic maxim "that government is best which governs least."[54] The *New York Sun* claimed, "We are against any extension of Federal power. To turn every post-office in the land into a savings bank would only tend to strengthen the authority of the Federal officeholders throughout the country."[55] Others went even further, claiming that postal banks would "render the Democratic party obsolete and the system of individual enterprise ultimately impossible," and even more worried that they would turn people to "communistic channel[s]"[56] or "Socialism."[57] Some warned of the slippery slope: if the government started operating banks, soon it would be operating other businesses as well.

The most comprehensive response to all of these arguments came from Marion Butler, president of the National Farmers' Alliance and a Populist Party senator from North Carolina. Incidentally, Butler became a Republican when he lost his Senate seat for opposing white supremacy as "un-Populist." Butler was an advocate of postal banks, like many Southerners who claimed that "the South will never attain the financial strength which it should have until it learns to concentrate and aggregate its money by means of well-managed savings banks."[58] In an 1897 speech, Butler gave an impassioned and thorough response to every single objection against the postal bank. His feelings were representative of Southerners and Westerners alike—groups largely deprived of access to the savings banks concentrated in the Northeast. Again, perhaps the most fascinating aspects of Butler's speech are the striking similarities between it and the banking debates of today.

Butler's response to those claiming that postal banks would lead to the government's involvement in other businesses as well was "that it

[was] an admission that postal savings banks would work successfully and be popular, and that their successful operation would be a strong argument for other reforms along those lines."[59] Butler also turned the tables on those who complained of state paternalism, claiming that they were the same people who wanted to control monopolies. "Any form of government is paternalism," he said. Butler drew upon the earlier greats who had also vigorously fought against the banking powers: "That none except those who want to control the nation's money and use this powerful instrument of commerce as a means to force the whole producing world to pay tribute to the money changers can consider this an objection. *With all who stand on the money question where Jefferson, Jackson, and Lincoln stood, it is a strong argument in favor of postal savings banks.*"[60]

The second line of objections to the postal banks came not from bankers or monopolists, but from Democrats or Populists who warned that "the money collected through the savings banks scattered over the country would be concentrated and hoarded at Washington, and thus cause a contraction and congestion of currency." But, Butler pointed out, this was exactly what was happening with the national banking system at the time. However, the federal government would redistribute any centralized capital and "put it to use" more efficiently and *for the benefit of the people.*[61]

Others argued about the necessity of the postal banks. There was no need for government intervention; private enterprise could meet the needs of all people. In fact, the American Bankers Association claimed that the banks were already "doing a savings business."[62] The *Minneapolis Journal* wrote in 1891: "The fact is, the saving bank system as operated throughout the country is perfectly satisfactory. . . . The Government can't conduct the business better than private concerns can. It is very seldom that a savings bank fails irremediably. Under our State laws they are perfectly safe."[63] (That last assertion was simply inaccurate; there were many savings bank failures at the time and there would be many more in the next decade.) Many opposed the banks because, they claimed, there was no money to put in them. "Postmaster-General Wanamaker," wrote the *Omaha Herald,* "believes that the reason there is a scarcity of money in circulation is due to the fact that millions of dollars are secreted under carpets and in stockings. He is laboring under a serious misapprehension."[64] The *Boston Globe* stated that "it is easy enough for anybody to find a savings bank; the trouble is to find the savings to put in it."[65] Others just stated that the reason rural dwellers were not saving in banks was because of the "ignorance of the common people" or that "the inhabitants of remote rural districts are not so well posted in the world's wicked ways as those who have the opportunity of perusing the daily papers."[66] In other words, rural dwellers were too poor and too stupid to bank.

But much like today's banks, the private banks of that time were out of reach to most of the working poor. These banks were "not open enough of the time, nor at the most convenient hours for working people, nor for long-continued periods; they are not situated at all the convenient points." These private institutions, Butler claimed, "do not care to deal with small sums" and were "not sufficiently adapted to the convenience of our population, nor have they either the incentive of philanthropy or of gain to induce them to become sufficiently so."[67]

Savings banks simply weren't reaching the lower strata of income. In 1898, Charles Burwell compared postal banks in England to savings banks in the United States and observed that "the vast majority of private banks have their depositors among persons of greater means, as is plainly shown by the fact that, while the seven million depositors in the English postal savings banks average $70 each, the five million in the savings banks in the United States average $370."[68] This was, of course, the void postal banks were to fill. Newspaper accounts wrote that the main purpose of the postal savings banks "is to afford the poor a convenient means of saving small sums"[69] and that "the strongest arguments in favor of this system is the fact that it will bring banking facilities within easy reach of all classes of the people and in every section of the nation."[70]

And the savings banks encompassed just too small a sector to meet the large demand. Nearly all of the country's savings banks were located in a few northeastern states and California. This was still true twenty years later in 1909, as was made clear in a *Law and Banker* article: "One-third of all the savings deposits of the United States are in the New York state savings banks, one fifth in Massachusetts, or more than one-half of all savings deposits in the United States is in these two states. The six New England states, with New York, Pennsylvania, Ohio,

Illinois, Iowa and California have 98.4 per cent, or $3,590,000,000 of the savings of the United States. . . . There are some states in the Union that have no savings banks. . . . There are but 1453 savings banks, while there are 62,000 Post Offices."[71]

Butler responded to the claim that private institutions would meet this large market with impatience: "Shall we wait fifty years, or one hundred years, or one thousand years, until countless generations are born and dead, until private capital will see fit to establish a sufficient number of savings banks conveniently located to the people?"[72] Postmaster General Gary's response was similar: "It is often urged that whatever can be as well done by private enterprise as by the Government should never be entered into by the latter, but a century of demonstration has shown that private enterprise can not supply even adequate means of exchange, let alone the great instrument for the collection and increase of the small savings of the people."[73]

Clearly, there was a market demand for banking institutions and not enough of them to meet it, leading to the creation of several alternative financial products that proved both confusing and burdensome. For instance, many people would buy money orders addressed to themselves from the post office and keep them as a form of savings, which was safer than holding paper money. "They buy them simply to secure a safe deposit for their money," Butler said. "They not only do not get any interest, but pay a fee for the privilege of using the Government as a custodian of their small earnings and savings. There is scarcely a money-order office in the United States that has not had this experience."[74] Furthermore, those people risked losing the savings because the money orders were only good for a few years. By 1909, the post office reported that "money orders aggregating more than $100,000 became invalid during the last fiscal year in the five western states of Colorado, Kansas, Nebraska, Oregon and Washington." All of these money orders were addressed to self.[75]

The idea that "hoarded money" existed was much debated in Congress. Those opposed to postal banks insisted that those with money to save were already investing it. But others relayed experiences of seeing money crumpled and molded because it had been out of circulation for so long.[76] A representative from Illinois, Martin Madden, offered a related story to Congress in 1910 about his district outside of Chicago.

He said there was a large Polish Catholic church in his district with a parochial school attached. The school burned down and the pastor needed $10,000 to build a new structure. Congressman Madden recommended the pastor announce to his congregation that he needed to borrow $10,000 at a small rate of interest. The following Sunday, the pastor told his congregation that he would prefer to borrow from the parishioners if any of them had money to lend. By Monday morning at 10:00 a.m., the pastor had $50,000 "wrapped up in rags and paper and stockings and things like that from his people, who were not supposed to have any money." Madden claimed that a bank in the town had $25,000, but "nobody had any confidence in it."[77] These immigrant parishioners, labeled too poor to save, were in fact sitting (or sleeping) atop a substantial hoard of money.

What was labeled as "the greatest objection to the bill" shows the stark differences between banking today and banking a century ago. The main opponents of postal banking argued that the federal government had no way to use the deposits collected by the savings banks—that the United States "has not enough of a national debt to absorb the hidden savings of the people."[78] Postmaster Mitchell responded that the United States would surely need a plan and must "have a certain prospective use for the money." He asserted, "Herein lies the whole problem of the post-office savings banks, and herein also lies the main obstacle which heretofore has successfully prevented their establishment."[79] Butler responded that the funds would go to the Treasury and be redistributed. This was not the right response, and the bills would continue to die until the proposals suggesting that the money be collected at the Treasury died as well.

THE CRISIS THAT WOULD PAVE THE WAY

As is often the case with banking, a crisis was necessary to initiate structural reform. The Panic of 1907, which reminded everyone of the vulnerabilities of U.S. banks, brought postal banking to the United States. President Theodore Roosevelt endorsed postal banking right away:

> I commend to the favorable consideration of the Congress a postal savings bank system, as recommended by the Postmaster-General. The

> primary object is to encourage among our people economy and thrift and by the use of postal savings banks to give them an opportunity to husband their resources, particularly those who have not the facilities at hand for depositing their money in savings banks. Viewed, however, from the experience of the past few weeks, it is evident that the advantages of such an institution are still more far-reaching. Timid depositors have withdrawn their savings for the time being from national banks, trust companies, and savings banks; individuals have hoarded their cash and the workingmen their earnings; all of which money has been withheld and kept in hiding or in safe deposit box to the detriment of prosperity. Through the agency of the postal savings banks such money would be restored to the channels of trade, to the mutual benefit of capital and labor.[80]

President Roosevelt repeated his support in his "Special Message to Congress on Labor" by saying that "these postal savings banks are imperatively needed for the benefit of the wageworkers and men of small means, and will be a valuable adjunct to our whole financial system."[81] Roosevelt's postmaster general, George V. L. Meyer, the most enthusiastic advocate of postal banking since Wanamaker, pressed the issue once again and this time, faced a much more responsive public. Meyer followed the postmasters before him in focusing his proposal for postal banking on the dual benefits of poverty alleviation and banking stability.

Even with Roosevelt's backing and broader public support, the postmaster needed to assure banks that postal banks were not a threat. Immediately after the crisis, the American Bankers Association carried out an extensive propaganda campaign against postal banking.[82] Meyer's annual report contained a clear message to bankers: *postal banks will not compete with you.* For one, he made clear that the people who would use postal savings banks were not currently bank customers: "The people to be reached are in the main those who, because of locality, have not had the opportunity to place their money in safe-keeping, or through prejudice or fear have kept it in hiding."[83] The congressional debate repeated this message: "The postal depository is the *poor man's bank,* and it will carry its blessings into every community in the country."[84]

The proposal reinforced the rhetoric with structural limits on postal savings that would make them unattractive to anyone but the poor. These included account caps and low interest rates. Meyer explicitly indicated that these limits be taken as "evidence of good faith on the part of the Government that it has no desire to enter into competition with existing financial institutions, particularly as the banks in the nearest localities are to be used as depositories and not the United States Treasury."[85]

But the crucial shift that enabled postal banking was the decision that profits would *not* go to the Treasury but would stay under local control. Congressional debates made clear that "the law is carefully safeguarded to protect local communities and local banks against the withdrawal of postal deposits and concentrating them in the United States Treasury or banks in the large cities."[86] Localism was still king, and this federal government bank needed to pay homage to local banking control in order to convince the opposition that postal banking would strengthen rather than compete with local banks. A contemporary economist commented that keeping "the money at home" was "almost a fetish."[87] And there existed widespread anxiety that the money would end up in the hands of the "rich bankers of New York."[88]

To those who worried that during times of crisis, deposits would flow out of banks and into postal bank coffers, Meyer responded that this would actually benefit banks "because the money brought to post-offices would be redeposited at once in the national banks in the localities where it had been temporarily withdrawn."[89] The recent crisis had also emboldened the post office to challenge bankers' arguments about the stability of their industry. Not only would postal banks help banks during a crisis, they would also help prevent future crises. Meyer reminded bankers that the crisis sprung from a contraction in currency due to withdrawals, or in other words, runs on the banks. He claimed that "one of the greatest advantages of the postal savings banks would be their ability to prevent contraction of the currency and to turn back into circulation the money which otherwise would go into the pocket, the tin can, or the stocking." Postal banking would be an antidote to panic, which was what bankers feared most at the time. The problem with the panic was that "hoarding increase[d] as the real need for money [became] more pressing."[90] Postal banks, Meyer argued, would prevent hoarding. Why would people hoard if they knew their money was safe in the postal banks? By offering the scared public a safe haven, this simple government protection would help stop panic in its tracks.

And so, postal banking's popularity increased. Many saw it as a way to respond to the constant banking crises of the time and further, viewed it to be a better alternative than federal deposit insurance because there was less moral hazard involved (insurance protection tends to make banks take more risks). The government would fund *and* oversee postal banks to minimize the chance of moral hazard. And interestingly, it was the Republicans who supported a broad federal banking system rather than a private bank-funded insurance scheme.

During the 1908 presidential election, postal banking became a major issue. Fresh in the wake of a financial crisis, the two candidates, Republican William Howard Taft and Democrat William Jennings Bryan, chose different reform proposals. Destabilizing panics were common because of the inherent instability of unconnected banks across the country that could not lend or borrow from each other in a liquidity crunch. Bryan endorsed federal deposit insurance first and postal banking as a backup. But the Democratic platform made it clear that they would not support postal banking unless the deposits remained in local banks.[91]

Taft backed the more conservative approach: postal banking. He made postal banking a campaign promise, and after winning with a clear majority, he made it the law of the land. Taft was uniquely familiar with the concept of savings banks, having organized one himself in 1906 while serving as governor-general of the Philippines.[92] In his "First Annual Message," Taft endorsed postal banking, stating: "I believe [Postal banks] to be necessary in order to offer a proper inducement to thrift and saving to a great many people of small means who do not now have banking facilities, and to whom such a system would offer an opportunity for the accumulation of capital. They will furnish a satisfactory substitute, based on sound principle and actual successful trial in nearly all the countries of the world, for the system of government guaranty of deposits now being adopted in several western States, which with deference to those who advocate it seems to me to have in it the seeds of demoralization to conservative banking and certain financial disaster."[93]

On January 31, 1910, Senator Thomas Carter, a Republican from Montana, proposed postal banking bill S. 5876, which passed after a month-long debate. In addition to the already mentioned opposition, a major point of debate in Congress was over the constitutionality of the federal government entering into banking services. Senator Carter initially situated the plan under the very broad "general welfare" clause of the Constitution, but Democrats claimed this was too vague.[94] Senator George Sutherland (R-UT), a future Supreme Court justice and one of the "four housemen" who would vigorously fight FDR's New Deal, argued that postal banking was constitutional under Article I, Section 8, which gives Congress the power to coin money and "regulate the value thereof." Sutherland argued that because postal savings would bring money out of hoarding, it would help Congress maintain an adequate currency. He claimed that the Article gave Congress the power to "regulate commerce . . . among the several states," which postal banking would do by increasing the money supply. This clause is referred to as "the commerce clause," and two decades later, Sutherland would interpret the clause narrowly in order to fight most of the New Deal era proposals. He also said that the Constitution gave Congress the power "to establish Post Offices and post roads," and because the post office already issued money orders, the authority could cover savings banks as well.[95] Though the commerce clause was eventually expanded significantly, Democrats fought these arguments at the time as tenuous.[96]

In order to pass the congressional gauntlet and Democratic opposition, the postal banks were required to keep 95 percent of deposits in the community of origin and invested in solvent local banks, with only 5 percent going to the Treasury. The postal banks also carried several features that purposefully made them less attractive than private banks. The interest paid on accounts was set at a low 2 percent—the lowest anywhere in the world. The postal banks also could not pay any interest for deposits held less than a year, making the effective interest rate just over 1 percent—not a great deal for depositors. The main services were passbook savings accounts, with low monthly deposit caps set at $100 and a total savings cap of $500. The savings limit was raised to $2500 in 1918.[97] These concessions to private banks and local control would get the bill passed but would also eventually weaken the institution.

Republicans overcame Democratic opposition, and the bill passed along partisan lines on June 9, 1910, with a vote of 195 to 102.[98] The

Senate approved the House version on June 22, and President Taft signed the bill into law on June 25, 1910.[99] The system of postal banks created by the Taft administration was called the United States Postal Savings System (USPSS).

The banks were immediately successful. At the end of the first year, they received a total of $20 million in deposits, "most of which had been coaxed out of hiding." By the end of 1913, the *New York Times* reported that the postal banks were practically self-sustaining—having received $33 million in deposits within two years—practically all of which came from "stocking banks."[100] The *Times* reported that the banks "have discovered that it has not hurt them in the least" because "[there were] virtually no bank withdrawals." This "astonished the banks, which had supposed that everything deposited with Uncle Sam would mean that much taken from them." Bankers also realized that the system helped them because otherwise-hoarded money was being deposited into local banks for their use and circulation.[101] Still, the *Times* stated with frustration, the inflow of deposits likely represented a fraction of what was available. Due to the deposit caps, many larger deposits were turned away. The *Times* reported that in one western mining town, a miner wanted to deposit $20,000 in coins that were "tarnished and long unused" because they had been saved in canvas sacks. The miner could only deposit $500 of these coins and took "most of his hoard back." The *Times* estimated that "in the aggregate over $30,000,000 had been turned away because of the limit."

But the customer base surprised everyone. In 1913, Theodore Weed, one of the program's administrators, said, "The postal savings system was extremely popular everywhere except where they expected it would be popular." As it turned out, it was not southerners and westerners who most needed the banks (although they eventually came around); it was the recent immigrants in urban areas. The reason, according to congressional testimony in 1913, was that "hundreds of thousands of our newly made citizens distrust banks and will not patronize them. They have absolute confidence in the Government and know what postal savings banks are."[102] Additionally, the postal banking branches offered information to customers in *twenty-four languages,* and local postmasters were provided with phrase books in different languages to allow clerks to handle deposits from non-English speakers.[103] During the

Wilson administration, the post office launched an aggressive promotional campaign using foreign-language presses to advertise the postal savings accounts.[104] By 1915, immigrants comprised 60 percent of the depositors and owned over 75 percent of the postal bank's deposits even though they made up less than 15 percent of the population.[105] (Consider the corollaries today: studies show that many low-income people and undocumented immigrants do not trust banks—and in certain neighborhoods, more payday lenders speak Spanish than do bank tellers.)

Just as Taft had promised, the postal banks would never actually be able to compete with banks. In an attempt to convince private banks and localities that the federal government posed no competition, the postal banks gave away their primary market advantage: the post's nationwide branching network. The post office had more than 8,000 branches across the country. The largest bank network, Bank of America, had 430 branches, but they were all in the state of California.[106] But postal bank customers could not deposit in one location and withdraw from another, and letter carriers were not permitted to handle deposits or withdrawals, a common feature in other nations.[107] In addition, after the first few years, the number of post office locations that could take deposits nationwide was reduced, leading postal banks to withdraw from many rural communities and to abandon the South. They would be the banks of the foreigners—those who hoarded money in stockings. The postal banks were, in effect, designed to appeal "only to those timid persons who are afraid to trust the ordinary banks and who would rather get the 2 per cent or less interest than to place the money in the regular savings banks, where it would draw from 3 to 4 per cent."[108] During the first decade after their formation, their success among immigrants actually stigmatized the banks as being banks for the "provident, ignorant, timid foreigners," in which "no intelligent American will deposit under present restrictions."[109]

At the end of World War I, the United States had significant war debts and needed money. Senators and postmasters proposed that deposits be routed to the Treasury to be used to pay down the war debt, but significant opposition rose up.[110] In his 1921 annual report, Postmaster General William Hays tried to quell banks' fears, without success: "The Government is not in the banking business for profit. The Government is in the banking business to facilitate the increase in national savings and promote economy and thrift. The postal savings has probably not scratched the surface, notwithstanding the magnificent conception of public duty that inspired its founding. The postal savings shall not compete with savings banks. We do not want depositors from savings banks."[111]

THE POSTAL BANKS AS REFUGE

Deposits in postal banks remained stable in the 1920s, but in the 1930s, the postal banks swelled with an influx of depositors running away from banks. In 1930 alone, almost fifty thousand new depositors fled to postal banks with almost $22 million in additional deposits, totaling $191 million in deposits.[112] Those deposits continued to double every year for the next three years.[113] Postal banks' regional focus also shifted dramatically during the Great Depression, from immigrant hubs in the Northeast and West to the Midwest and the South, where bank failures were more prevalent.[114] By 1929, only 39 percent of depositors were foreigners. Not only were fewer immigrants coming to America, but those who had started with postal banking accounts graduated to regular bank accounts.[115] By 1934, postal banks had $1.2 billion in deposits—about 10 percent of the entire commercial banking system. The *Times* reported Postmaster Walter Brown's explanation: "The postal savings system is a logical refuge for the timid, and functions best in areas of financial stress." A historian analyzing the postal banks in 1936 said that this rise in deposits meant that the post office would significantly influence the banking system.[116] This was confirmed by a 2013 economic analysis showing that postal banking actually *reduced* bank runs during the Great Depression by infusing liquidity into local banks and by providing a safe haven for deposits.[117]

In 1933, Congress finally approved the collection of postal bank deposits by the Treasury in order to help pay for mounting government debts.[118] President Roosevelt started selling postal savings bonds and eventually, Treasury bonds, through 1935.[119] But Roosevelt chose to deemphasize the postal banks as a method of banking reform. He had his eyes set on much broader reforms, including creating a federal deposit insurance fund to quell the instability in banks. Once Federal Deposit Insurance Corporation (FDIC) insurance was created, banks became safe enough for even the most timid depositors. Funds flowed out of postal banks and back into mainstream banks almost immediately.

In 1941, the post office began courting patriotic citizens with "Defense Savings Stamps," which were treasury bonds used to fund the war.[120] The post office heavily advertised these bonds in schools, magazines, newspapers, and radio ads.[121] In fact, the majority of these bonds were sold to schoolchildren using a robust advertising campaign and the slogan "Buy war bonds." There was no age minimum for buying the bonds, and the young and the small savers poured in money so that they too could help Uncle Sam. During their first year, the bonds brought in over $100 million.[122] The postmaster general report reveals that war bonds became the post office's most popular service until the end of World War II.

Deposits actually jumped in 1947 to their historic peak of $3.4 billion in deposits and 4 million users. One reason for the boost is that in the 1940s, the USPSS introduced the world to banking by mail. Many servicemen abroad deposited their earnings into postal banks.[123] By the end of World War II, the government had raised about $8 billion in additional war funding through war bonds and Treasury bonds sold through the post office. The post office banks did not lend consumer or mortgage credit, but in wartime, they were successfully retooled to solicit investments in U.S. savings bonds and war stamps.

THE UNRAVELING OF THE SYSTEM

By the 1950s, deposit insurance had become a resounding success, practically halting the tide of bank failures and boosting confidence in the system. With no war to fund, deposits rapidly flowed out of the post office and back into banks at a rate of about a 10 percent loss per year for three years starting in 1950. Although postal banks had enjoyed locational advantages during the previous era, there were now more roads and cars, allowing rural dwellers to reach banks—not to mention the creation of banking by mail, which most banks had by then adopted. By 1950, 68 percent of the nation's towns and cities had both postal savings depositories and banks.[124] And because banks could pay higher interest than the post office and had become just as safe, the USPSS no longer presented an attractive option for depositors. Poverty and immigration were also at a historic low. This was the heyday of banking. During the postwar economic boom, thrifts, credit unions, and commercial banks proliferated into many neighborhoods, and most people could open a bank account if they wanted one. Decades later, however, this would no longer be the case. Banks abandoned poor areas. Post offices remained, but without any banking functions.

By 1952, after two government studies found that the USPSS was no longer justified and that the program's original goals likely no longer applied, bills began being introduced to end the USPSS. The first was proposed in 1952 by first-term senator Wallace F. Bennett (R-UT), the father of Bob Bennett (R-UT) and a member of the Senate banking committee. Eisenhower's postmaster general, Arthur Summerfield, attempted to raise the deposit limit in 1957 to save the system, but both of President Lyndon Johnson's postmaster generals supported legislation to end it.

In 1966, the USPSS was officially abolished as part of Johnson's streamlining of the federal government. There were fewer than one million account holders at the time. Once presidential and postmaster general support was removed, Congress acted quickly to abolish the system. The only opposition came from two unions for postal employees: the United Federation of Postal Clerks and the National Postal Union. Their primary motive was to preserve jobs, but this opposition was ignored and President Johnson signed the bill to abolish the postal savings banks on March 28, 1966.

When the system officially ended on July 1, 1968, about $50 million in the unclaimed deposits of more than 600,000 depositors was turned over to the U.S. Treasury. In 1970, the Treasury Department inactivated the records and postal banking ceased to exist. At this point, $12 million remained in unclaimed deposits.[125] Under the Postal Savings System Statute of Limitations Act of July 13, 1984 (Public Law 98–359), no claims could be brought more than one year after enactment. Thus, no claims made after July 13, 1985, were honored.

The postal-banking system died a quiet death without much discussion about its historic uses. *Time* magazine, one of the few who noted this historic event, focused solely on an aberration in the postal savings system, funding World War II, instead of its purpose and main success: banking the poor. The magazine reproduced the war savings stamp and wrote an obituary full of misinformation: "There was a time when they were as ubiquitous as victory gardens, rationing coupons, or the vats of bacon grease that mothers used to collect as part of the war effort. In World War II, nearly every schoolchild saved his nickels and dimes for Government Defense Savings Stamps to paste in a book toward the day when he could purchase a $25 war bond. In the middle of the war, the nation raised as much as $540 million a year from the stamp program. But for several years, the volume of stamp sales—$18 million in 1969—has barely covered the administrative expense. Many Americans under 30 hardly knew that such stamps existed. Last week the Treasury Department discontinued them."[126]

In fact, the war stamps were discontinued in 1946, not 1970, and the post office phased out the banks, not the Treasury. Savings stamps were sold long after the 1970s.[127] Misstatements aside, the public and the press failed to note the centrality of postal banking in one of the most crucial periods of banking reform in our country. Postal banking almost proved to be the alternative to FDIC insurance and served as such from 1911 until 1933. The system prevented many bank runs during a turbulent time in the nation's banking history—essentially serving as a central bank before the Federal Reserve was up to the task. The deposits that flowed into the postal banks from the poor were centralized in the Treasury, as well as in localities, and then infused back into banks during times of need. Postal banking helped fund World War II and reduced government deficits after the Great Depression.

Most crucially, postal banking was the most successful experiment in financial inclusion in the United States. More effective than any other philanthropic or mutual effort to bank the poor, postal banking brought millions of new immigrants and rural dwellers into the U.S. banking system all at once. One of the central aims of the postal banks was also the most difficult to measure: teaching habits of thrift and saving to the poor.

THE POST OFFICE TODAY

In 1970, as the market-based philosophy swept the banking world, the post office was also transformed. For one, it was spun off the federal government and required to fund itself. It would no longer receive government help to support unprofitable routes. Further, it would have to balance its own budget, even if that meant cutting services. In the last decade, as Internet technology has fundamentally changed the way in which we communicate, the very purpose and necessity of the post office has been called into question. The institution has struggled financially due to technological change as well as competition from private companies like the United Parcel Service and FedEx. But its fiscal woes also have political roots. In 2006, Congress forced the post office to prefund its employee pension plans (something not required of any other government agency)—a political maneuver some claim was designed to hasten the institution's decline. The legislation immediately caused a $5.5 billion shortfall per year, from which the postal service has yet to recover.[128]

The structure of the postal system today is a mix of public and private, but the bottom line is that it is a federal agency that is not funded by the public fisc. After the passage of the Postal Reorganization Act in 1970, which relegated the United States Postal Service (USPS) from a cabinet department into an independent agency, the USPS began operating somewhat like a business. Unlike government-owned corporations such as Amtrak, the USPS is still a federal agency and is governed by an eleven-member board of governors, nine of whom are presidential appointees who serve staggered terms.[129] The Postal Reorganization Act cut the purse strings to the USPS, and it shifted from relying on taxpayer money to cover the cost of operations to generating revenue from postage.[130] The post office has a revolving fund with the Treasury, into which it must deposit all revenues and profits from its products. In other words, the USPS has no shareholders or investors who make money if it becomes profitable. The problem, however, is that the postal service has not been making a profit but has been operating under a deficit since 2006. The Treasury has loaned the postal service a total of $15 billion since the 2006 legislative change, and it reached its debt limit in 2012.[131]

And so, amid financial woes and a decreased demand for physical mail, the U.S. Postal Service has begun to cut costs and services. Without a new revenue source, it will be forced to cut routes and in time, potentially shut down an establishment that helped shape America as an egalitarian democracy. It is within this context that calls for reviving the postal-banking system can be heard.

8

A Public Option in Banking

It is to be considered, that such a Bank is not a mere matter of private property, but a political machine of the greatest importance to the State.

—Alexander Hamilton, Secretary of Treasury, Report on a National Bank (December 13, 1790)

A social contract has existed between banks and the government since the early days of the Republic. The government supports the banks through trust-inducing insurance, bailouts, liquidity protection, and a framework that allows the allocation of credit to the entire economy. Banks, in turn, operate as the central machinery of the economy by providing transaction services, a medium for trade, and individual and business loans that spur economic growth. This entanglement between the state and the banking system must surely mean that banks should not exclude a significant portion of the public from the bounty of government support. This is not just a banking market problem but a threat to our society's democratic principles. When the state becomes so heavily involved in the banking system, that system cannot create or contribute to such a vast inequality.

Many policymakers have inferred this obligation on the part of banks and have attempted to force banks to extend credit beyond their preferred customer base. The banking industry has vigorously opposed these efforts, but the democratization of credit is not an issue that should be left to the banks. The supply of credit has always been a public policy issue, with banks functioning as intermediaries. Insofar as the state enables credit markets, all creditworthy Americans deserve equal access to credit, especially because reasonable and safe credit can provide a smoother path both through and out of poverty. If banks are not providing credit to the poor, the state should provide it directly.

The existing post office framework represents the most promising path toward effectuating such a public option. American banks long ago deserted their most impoverished communities, but post offices, even two centuries later, have remained—still rooted in an egalitarian mission. There have never been barriers to entry at post offices, and their services have been available to all, regardless of income. And so, it is not unreasonable to suggest that as America's oldest instrument of democracy in action, the post office can once again level the playing field, and in the process, save itself from imminent demise. In fact, the post office inspector general's office, a small regulatory branch of the post office, issued a *White Paper* report in January 2014 proposing just such a move. As of this writing, the postmaster general has not publicly supported the proposal and no congressional committee has seriously considered postal banking.[1]

But it is a proposal worthy of serious consideration. Although the purpose of this book has been to lay the theoretical and historical basis for a public option in banking and not the operational blueprint, the basic idea of modern postal banking is a public bank offering a wide range of transaction services, including deposit-taking and small lending. The post offices could offer these services at a much lower cost than banks and the fringe industry because (1) they can use natural economies of scale and scope to lower the costs of the products, (2) their existing infrastructure significantly reduces overhead costs, and (3) they do not have profit-demanding shareholders and would be able to offer products at cost.

Although postal banking could potentially save an institution that predates the Constitution and made our first-rate democracy possible, the most important argument in favor of postal banking is its potential to bank the unbanked. Consider the social and economic benefits of a system that enables the unbanked in the United States to leave the expensive and time-wasting cash economy and pay their bills online, send funds to family, make debit card purchases, and save money without worrying about draconian overdraft fees. And not just the unbanked stand to benefit. An even larger portion of the population do have bank accounts but have been forced to rely on high-cost fringe loans. Postal banking can provide small loans to the creditworthy among the low and middle-income without life-crushing fees and interest.

Critically, by making banking available to those deserted by a government-supported banking system, the state can minimize the threat to democracy posed by the heavily subsidized, exclusionary, and powerful banking sector. The social contract has been breached. Banks enjoy broad government support but do not serve the entire public. Direct government involvement remedies the breach and bridges the gap in services.

Because of the unique institutional capacities of a nationwide post office, its services can significantly underprice any of those on the market. This is not just a hope or an empty promise. The detailed post office White Paper explains how to achieve this by using tools currently available only to the post office. Most of these transaction services are straightforward products that do not require a high level of sophistication. The post office can build on its existing network to meet a significant market demand. Wal-Mart, for example, came to dominate financial services to the poor, practically overnight, without causing a substantial ripple in its core business. The company has been able to use its size and existing infrastructure to offer financial products at a fraction of the price, while making a healthy profit offering them.

Current estimates show that the unbanked spend $89 billion each year on financial fees and services.[2] All of this money goes to alternative financial service providers—payday lenders, check-cashers, and other nonbanks that charge high fees to store and move people's money. Providing these services at much lower costs has a triple advantage of reviving the beleaguered but too-important-to-fail postal service, putting the money back in the pockets of the poor, and providing an alternative to a harmful industry that has proved nearly impossible to regulate away.

Postal banking may seem radical to many in the United States who remain convinced that banking should be a "private market" free from "government intervention," but it is a mundane part of life for the rest of the world. Postal banking abroad is the norm, not an aberration. Postal banking has operated in many Western countries since the 1800s, and currently, fifty-one countries use postal banking as their primary method of financial inclusion—only 6 percent of postal carriers worldwide do not offer banking services. (It is estimated that postal banking has banked over one billion people worldwide.) A variety of models exist worldwide—some focus on the poor and others offer postal banking services to the entire population. In fact, the United States is one of the only developed countries in the world without a postal banking network. However, we do not need to look abroad for a justification or even a model for postal banking when we can refer to our own rich history.[3]

Just as our postal banks did successfully for half a century, their rebirth can lead to increased saving by the broader public. By providing low-barrier savings accounts, the post office can again offer a refuge for the countless small savers in the United States who have been shut out of the banking system because their too-small savings accounts are no match for high bank fees. Increased access to low-cost savings accounts can greatly benefit a population living without any financial cushion. Postal savings accounts could provide a much-needed financial buffer that would even diminish the need for short-term credit. Having just a few hundred dollars stored away can make a significant difference to a moderate-income family facing an emergency. Postal savings accounts can even reinvigorate a culture of saving that has been long lost in the United States but retained in Japan and Germany precisely because of their strong postal banking network.[4] A 2015 survey shows that *over half* the population has savings that they do not deposit in banks and many admit they store their cash in sock drawers, cookie jars, under mattresses, or in their freezers.[5] It is possible that just as in the 1900s, hoarded money from across the country would pour into the postal banks from under mattresses, from prepaid cards, or from funds otherwise wired abroad.

POSTAL LENDING

Historically, only federal government involvement in credit markets has increased lending and lowered the costs of credit. By insuring deposits, providing liquidity through the central bank, creating secondary markets enabled by government-sponsored enterprises (GSEs), and constructing a structure of government support, private banks have been able to lend at unprecedented levels. Postal banks could connect to this existing apparatus and route credit directly to borrowers without having to circulate the money through the bloated banking system.

Postal lending will likely be controversial, but it has the potential to radically advance the lives of the American public while balancing the skewed credit markets. Lending even small loans of less than $500 at a reasonable interest rate can help a significant portion of the American public withstand a short-term credit crunch.[6] Much like central bank liquidity for struggling large banks, the post office would provide liquidity for struggling individuals.

These loans would need to be structured such that they provide borrowers with a reasonable path toward repayment. As "unsecured" loans, or loans without an asset given as a security, these loans can take a few forms. They can be designed as low-cost installment loans, like those created by Arthur Morris. These loans are repaid over time with a set number of scheduled payments for a set term (anywhere from one month to several years). Much like a mortgage, which is a "secured" installment loan, each payment goes toward both principal and interest. Payments can be made in person or electronically deducted from the borrower's bank account, and a cosigner can even be used to guarantee the loan and reduce the risk of default. The post office can also offer a lower-cost short-term loan. The loan would carry a fee or an interest rate for an up-front loan and a term of a few weeks or months. The borrower could pay down the principal without accruing additional fees and if the borrower needed more time to pay, he or she would take out another loan and pay another fee. There would need to be a limit on how many times the loan was "rolled over" so as to avoid accumulating debt.

These funds would come from the same sources from which banks lend: deposits, other business revenues, and central bank lending. However, the scale would be much smaller. Even if the post office were to lend half the American public (about 150 million people) $500 each, that would equal $75 billion, which is just 1 percent of the $7.7 trillion the Federal Reserve pledged to the largest banks in 2009.[7] Just as the federal government has enabled other markets for credit, so too can it enable this one. It would operate as any other bank, with a central-bank cushion and liquidity support. In other words, little to no taxpayer money need be used in postal lending. However, banking is already a heavily subsidized sector, so any required startup or ongoing capital infusion would just bring credit services to the low-income on par with the rest of the population.

Still, all lending is risky. Postal savings accounts and financial transaction products bear little to no risk of loss, but lending money sometimes means losing money, especially when it comes to lending to average people with little financial cushion. Although the case can be made that these households need the credit more than any others, it would be unwise for the post office to lend if it meant losing money.

In order to reduce the risks inherent to lending, the post office would need to create a system of strong collection and underwriting standards. It can mitigate collection risks in the same way as other lenders by requiring a cosigner, securing an interest on future wages, or employing other legal mechanisms. Debt collection costs are one of the primary causes of the high fees attached to small loans. They are also a way in which the post office can use its unique position in the federal government to lower the cost and risk of lending small loans. Though details would need to be hammered out, the post office inspector general's White Paper suggests that the post office can collect debts using a Treasury Department program only available to federal agencies that allows the garnishment of tax refunds. By using a low-cost and effective collection mechanism unavailable to any other lender, the post office can significantly alter the market forces in small lending.

Precautions would need to be taken to maintain the confidentiality of borrowers and provide indebted borrowers with appropriate recourse in the event of error or undue hardship. In this, the government is also uniquely capable. Government agencies can offer much more privacy and process to customers than any fringe lender or bank. The government has developed a set of norms and laws that direct the behavior of its agency actors and ensure that all citizens have the right to contest unfair or arbitrary government action.[8] In contrast, fringe lenders often collect and share customer data and sell defaulting loans to other private buyers—transactions that are often kept secret. Once you have entered into a contract for a loan with one of these lenders, the right to collect on that loan can be sold to any third party. The post office's collection process, on the other hand, would have to be made public and submitted to agency and legislative review, which would offer more transparency than any other current lending and collecting mechanisms. The individuals involved would maintain the same, if not higher, privacy protections granted to all other customers of regulated banks.[9]

A system of strong and accurate underwriting procedures that can adequately separate the insolvent from the merely illiquid will also need developing. Of course, this is easier said than done. Creating a foolproof formula to accomplish such a thing would require the ability to accurately predict the future. There will always be loans that default as long as human beings are responsible for repaying them. Those with low to moderate income are no less responsible or capable of paying back a small low-cost loan than a large corporation is of paying back a large one. Any individual or company, wealthy or poor, can take out too much loan at too high a cost and be crushed by it. Formulas such as credit scores that track an individual's history of previous repayments can eliminate some of the guesswork.

However, when it comes to distinguishing creditworthy borrowers among the low income, credit scores are often too blunt a tool. Innovative private lenders have already realized this and are working to develop fine-tuned underwriting formulas based on publicly available borrower data to predict loan default with better results than credit scores.[10] The "good news is," as the *New York Times* reports, "there are lots of people today working to solve this problem—in government, in the nonprofit sector and increasingly in business."[11] Pioneering peer-to-peer Internet lenders have begun to boast of their success deploying these emerging mathematical models for small lending. The post office can rely on this developed expertise in designing its own underwriting system. The bottom line is that doing any sort of underwriting—even simply using credit scores—would set the post office apart from the payday lending industry, which currently makes no attempt to distinguish between borrowers. The Federal Deposit Insurance Corporation (FDIC) reports that "the prevailing underwriting criteria of most payday lenders require that consumers need proof only of a documented regular income stream, a personal checking account, and valid personal identification to receive a payday loan."[12]

Distinguishing the merely illiquid from the insolvent is no easy task but is at the crux of any successful effort to provide credit to the poor. The credit unions, Morris banks, and savings and loans thrived because they succeeded in doing just that. They used the tools available to them at the time: community ties, close relationships, and character. Relational lending is difficult today, even though postal employees would probably be well suited to the task. After all, in many rural communities across the country, postal workers glean more information about the town's population than any other citizen. However, this is not the case with every community, and it is unclear whether such knowledge could be parlayed into accurate loan underwriting without significant training.

The lesson from history's "banks with a soul" is not to reuse their *tools* but their *philosophy.* Serving the public must be its primary mission. The post office need not rely on relational lending for good underwriting today but must learn to adopt existing modern technology to offer fair, useful, and self-sustaining products to those neglected by mainstream banks. The post office must also account for loan losses through accurate pricing, capital buffers, reserves, and other rules of sound banking so that it does not face a persistent shortfall. However, in the event that it does suffer a liquidity shortage, any government help to restore its balance sheets would only level the lending playing field.

There are several reasons to believe that the post office is uniquely capable of lending responsibly while reducing the costs of small loans. Most importantly, the post office is not an institution motivated by profit-making and therefore, will charge borrowers the actual cost of the loan. This has been the necessary premise behind every successful movement to foster financial inclusion. The savings and loans, the credit unions, and the postal savings banks successfully achieved their goal of financial inclusion as long as they refused to let profits supplant their public duties. The post office is an independent agency connected to the federal government, which means that all excess profits are forfeited to the Treasury. Because the post office has no shareholders demanding a return on investment, it is unlikely to be motivated to take advantage of its customers for private gain. All gains will be public, as will losses. A board of directors, presumably public representatives chosen by a democratically elected president, would be tasked to oversee its activities.

In addition, the post office can naturally reduce the high costs of lending to the poor because of its already large network of existing branches. Compared to payday lenders, the post office can use its present infrastructure and staff, thus saving money otherwise spent on advertising, marketing, personnel, and stores. It can add revenue on day one without the expense of starting from scratch. One of the important lessons of banking history is that large and national banks won out against small unit banks, in part, because of natural efficiencies. The size and reach of the post office can lead to lower costs of credit. This ability to offer more at a lower cost is why large banks now dominate the market. *Economies of scale,* or the control of a large market for a single product, could bring down the costs for financial services and even loans if the post office has enough customers. *Economies of scope,* the costs saved when an institution can sell a variety of products, could result in, for example, lower loan costs because the post office attracts more deposits, cashes more checks, or wires more funds. We know economies of scale and scope work; they are the reason banks conglomerated and rushed to form "banking supermarkets."

Finally, because the post office never left the regions forsaken by the banks and other businesses, it has developed an ongoing relationship of trust with these communities. Many unbanked individuals already buy money orders at their local post office. This means that the post office has access to a customer base that is not comfortable in banks. Surveys of the unbanked show that minority groups are significantly more likely to be unbanked than other groups.[13] This is especially true in certain regions of the country, such as the South for blacks, regardless of income or financial status. Certain groups simply do not patronize banks because they do not trust them. But the cultural and class barriers that keep many people away from mainstream banks do not exist at the local post office.

In many inner-city and rural communities, the post office is the crowded and bustling place where the neighborhood gathers to do its business, helped by clerks who are members of that same community. Even those who never go to their local post office branch are familiar with the mail carrier who visits their home daily. And following history's cue, the postal network can offer information in more languages than do banks and appeal to the large population of immigrants, or even the undocumented, who have money to save, but no access to banks. Many of these workers currently send their money abroad—money that can be induced to stay within America's borders. As it was in the 1900s, this can be a surprising source of revenue for the postal banks.

Trust, especially in banking, consists of more than just a "nice feeling." It is a way to lower costs and reduce barriers of entry. This was the point of government deposit insurance. Banks cannot survive if their customers do not trust them to hold and lend their money. It is hard to predict whether the public will warm to postal banking, but in light of historical and international experience and the significant modern distrust of fringe banks, the public may view the post office as a safer and more trustworthy place to store funds. If this is the case, the post office may even decide to forego the added costs and regulatory burdens of FDIC deposit insurance because the post office's position as a federal agency and its access to the Treasury's deep pockets can fulfill essentially the same function as FDIC insurance. If the goal of federally funded deposit insurance has been to stop bank runs, it would be redundant for a deposit account linked to the federal government to also be insured by it. In fact, in the 1900s postal banking was considered a safer and more complete substitute to quell banking panic than federal deposit insurance.

The public already trusts the U.S. Postal Service and this trust is not undeserved. The post office enjoys a history of service to the American people unrivaled by any other institution or government entity. If our banks with a soul no longer serve the poor, perhaps a government institution with a soul can replace them—an institution that has, at its core, a public-serving function. In a way, the post office serves as a perfect foil for the banking industry. The latter receives hefty federal government support and rejects any public-serving function and the former is currently receiving limited federal government support and yet views public service as its primary mission. Even today, the stated mission of the U.S. Postal Service is "to provide postal services to bind the Nation together through the personal, educational, literary, and business correspondence of the people. It shall provide prompt, reliable, and efficient services to patrons in all areas and shall render postal services to all communities."[14]

OBSTACLES AND CRITICS

Of course, there are challenges to using the postal service or providing a public option in general. Critics will attack the idea on ideological, anticompetitive, and practical grounds. The ideological opposition, much like in the 1800s, will likely revolve around the idea of too much state intervention in markets, a slide toward Socialism, and an overbearing or paternalistic state. If the reader has made it this far in the book, hopefully, that line of reasoning can be dismissed outright. Pitting a public option against a private banking market is a handy rhetorical tool, but it's just smoke and mirrors. The banking system exists on a foundation of heavy state intervention.

Opposition will also come from banks, which for two centuries have reliably and consistently opposed any potential threat to their market share—even before they are certain it will be a threat. When the post office inspector general's office released its White Paper report with the banking proposal, many in the banking industry quickly responded that not only were they already meeting market needs but that it also was a terrible idea—"the worst idea since the Ford Edsel."[15] The credit union lobbyists have also opposed the idea, reasserting that they are meeting these needs.[16] These claims were made a hundred years ago about postal banking, and they were as wrong then as they are now. Banks are no longer interested in small accounts or small loans. Policymakers beholden to payday lenders will also likely oppose the bill by saying that payday lenders do their best to meet the needs of a hard-to-bank public.[17] Although any market share the post office takes would come directly from the payday lending industry, that industry's destruction due to cheaper credit cannot be lamented too greatly. The large and profitable payday industry serves very little public purpose besides meeting the credit demands of the desperate with interest rates only the desperate would pay.

Others will point to the practical difficulties of an inefficient government agency's ability to manage the complexity of offering financial services to a large sector of the population. It is worth noting at this point that the post office manages to deliver mail to every mailbox in the country daily, even to remote U.S. territories that other shippers will not service. Some claim that postal employees, who are trained to sort mail and sell stamps, will not be able to operate financial instruments. However, these critics underestimate postal employees. Unlike many similarly situated companies, the post office still offers its staff a route to the middle class. As such, they are able to recruit many talented and loyal employees.

Not only are postal employees capable individuals, but providing simple financial products does not require years of skilled training. Consider the numerous bank tellers or Wal-Mart and Cash America employees who manage this very thing while earning smaller hourly wages and fewer benefits than postal employees. Can the post office handle the challenges of becoming a quasibanking institution? There is no indication it cannot, especially with the help of specialized banking and industry experts who would almost certainly be enlisted to help with the transition. The post office can even partner with banks or credit unions for their servicing and automated teller machine functions.

Others have pointed to the epic demise of the GSEs Fannie Mae and Freddie Mac during the financial crisis as a reason to avoid government intrusion into credit markets. However, this clearly misunderstands the causes of Fannie Mae's and Freddie Mac's failures. The GSEs, particularly Fannie Mae, successfully brought mortgage lending to the American people. By creating a secondary market for mortgage loans and acting as the central intermediaries for all mortgage lending, they made mortgages accessible to all from the time they were created until they were privatized. The problem with their privatization was that they retained the implicit support of the federal government—the markets treated the GSEs as though they had the federal government's backing when they did not.[18] The private shareholders who controlled these institutions were incentivized to profit in the short term by taking on too much risk, which made them inherently unstable. The government did not share in the corporation's profits during the housing bubble, but when Fannie Mae failed because it had taken on too much mortgage risk, the federal government had to take on its losses and bail it out as the market had assumed it would.

The problem of public losses and privatized gains is inherent to any government-supported bank, but it was magnified with the GSEs due to their size and their ambiguous nature as quasigovernment entities. The same circumstances doomed Freedman's Savings Bank: the façade of government support over a privately run, profit-motivated institution. An institution that operates for the benefit of private shareholders yet advertises that it is a public institution is a dangerous lie. As it is currently structured, the American public is the shareholder of the U.S. Postal Service, and all its losses and profits are public. This structure must remain intact to prevent the distorted and dual mission that primarily caused Fannie Mae and Freddie Mac to fail.

Instead of being a testament to the dangers of government involvement in credit markets, the GSEs' accomplishments reveal that the federal government has a rich and successful history of creating and supporting credit markets to achieve important policy goals. Sallie Mae created and subsidized student loans to facilitate the important policy objective of educating the public. Fannie Mae and Freddie Mac, created to promote homeownership, directly helped create the American middle class. Today, that middle class is struggling, with many families tenuously holding on to its rapidly shrinking borders. Changing times require changes in policy. Enabling low- and middle-income families to cushion their financially tumultuous lives with low-cost credit is no less important a public concern than homeownership or education. Offering good credit to the poor would enable economic mobility, which has lagged significantly in the United States in recent years, and could solve a variety of other public problems linked to entrenched poverty.

Postal banking alone will not cure poverty nor will it reverse the slide of the middle class. But it is clear that when people lack a safe place to save, they will not save. And if they do not have access to a low-cost loan, they will fail faster and harder. When banks are drowning, the government throws them a lifesaver, through cheap credit, so that they can live another day. When the poor are drowning, payday loans are like millstones of crushing debt around their necks. Postal banking could offer to struggling Americans the same type of government credit already given to banks—at a much lower cost and with a much more direct public benefit.

* * *

The United States has just begun an era in the ongoing evolution of the bank-state relationship in which the government's stake in the banks is at its historical apex and the banks' stake in the public's well-being is at an all-time low. Banks and their wealthy customers reap the benefits of unprecedented public support even as the banks no longer service a significant portion of the population. Cheap credit flows from the government to these banks with a vague but unexpressed hope that it will reach the public. After all, this is the function of banks: to serve as credit intermediaries, or middlemen, between the source of credit and the eventual borrower. But the banks feel no compulsion to democratize credit, and our elected leaders make no such demands. This is, of course, the result of a pervasive ideology of the last several decades that has convinced banks and the public alike that nothing could or should be required of the industry besides assuring shareholder profits.

If we hope to democratize credit, it is time to cut out the middlemen.

The central fears motivating banking policy since the foundation of this country, expressed first by Thomas Jefferson but shared by many, was that banking would get too concentrated. All understood that the cause of this concentration was efficiency—money can grow faster as it accumulates. If left alone, banks would grow large and seek the highest profits possible. For two centuries, government forces fought these trends. They finally relented, and the fears of all those years have been realized: banks are large, concentrated, and powerful, and they are motivated solely to make large profits. As such, most of the poor and middle class are of no interest to the banking sector.

For two centuries, local banking provided the solution to equal credit access. But that option has run its course. When confronted with the large void in banking services to the poor and middle class, many immediately assume that the solution must be in some form of community banking. This is why microcredit and the ShoreBank model enjoyed broad support and why credit unions are still believed to be the banks for the poor even though their customers are, in fact, wealthier than bank customers. George Bailey's fight against Henry Potter still rings true for most Americans, and many still hope that small bankers with a heart will beat out the banking oligarchy. But that battle was fought and lost years ago.

Although Henry Potter's vision of banking won, in reality, Potter's bank likely would have been sucked up during the merger wave of the

1980s into a behemoth that may or may not have even kept its branch in Bedford Falls. If Potter's bank had survived the 1980s, by 2005, it would have gotten heavily involved in mortgage lending, failed, been taken over by the FDIC, and been quickly sold to a Too-Big-to-Fail bank flush with a taxpayer bailout.

Due to market forces and policy choices, concentrated banking won the long battle. A member of Obama's National Economic Council said, "We have created [our biggest banks], and we're sort of past that point, and I think that in some sense, the genie's out of the bottle and what we need to do is to manage them and to oversee them, as opposed to hark back to a time that we're unlikely to ever come back to or want to come back to."[19] Larry Summers expressed a similar sentiment: "I don't think you can completely turn back the clock." Even despite the political and economic shifts caused by the federal government bailouts of the banking industry, to insist that money stay put in a community ignores the transformative changes of the last several decades.

Indeed, local banking was a nineteenth-century solution to a nineteenth-century problem, but we cannot solve a twenty-first-century problem with an antique toolkit. The banking sector is large and growing larger, and so is the population it is leaving out. Local banking is a microanswer to a macroproblem. It is time to start discussing a public option in banking. Not because the private markets are broken or too costly but because banking does not operate by pure market principles. Banks not only control "other people's money," making them trustees of the public, but they also are directly and indirectly regulated and supported by a large government-created infrastructure of credit provision, insurance, and regulation.

Recognizing the publicly supported foundation of a private banking system leads, logically, to the demand that this system be available to all. Affordable credit and other financial products not only allow the economy to grow wealth, but also allow individual families to do so. Any difference in access (such as the rich having more access than the poor) undermines the principles of our democracy. Insofar as economic mobility (or at least, prohibiting economic disenfranchisement) is a social good, and credit is the necessary tool to economic advancement, the government must enhance credit availability for certain individuals and communities. Policymakers have understood this but have placed the responsibility on banks and attempted to induce lending through various regulatory carrots and sticks. However, pressing banks into the service of the poor has not produced good outcomes and has only resulted in bitter bankers and destructive products aimed not to help the poor, but to make a profit while trying to appease regulators. A public option cuts out the middleman, allowing the supply of credit to reach the demand without too much skimmed off the top. Providing a public option in banking allows the current stratified banking system to exist without undermining our democracy.

One obvious option for public banking would be to reinvigorate postal banking and use the expansive network of post offices across the country. The postal service, older than the Republic itself, has remained committed to serving every community without differences, but postal banking is not about saving the post office. Providing a public option is about much more than bank accounts or payday lending—it is about equalizing access to credit. Banking policy has always reflected the social goals and the civic principles of each era. A deep-seated problem exists within our stratified banking system: the state is shoring up a powerful banking industry that is, in turn, excluding those Americans most in need. This is corrupting our democracy, and we ignore it at our own peril.

Notes

INTRODUCTION

1. Rakesh Kochhar and Rich Morin, "Despite Recovery, Fewer Americans Identify as Middle Class," *Pew Research Center,* January 27, 2014, accessed March 13, 2015, www.pewresearch.org/fact-tank/2014/01/27/despite-recovery-fewer-americans-identify-as-middle-class.
2. Consumer and Community Development Research Section of the Federal Reserve Board's Division of Consumer and Community Affairs, *Report on the Economic Well-Being of U.S. Households in 2013* (Washington, DC: Board of Governors of the Federal Reserve System, 2014), 3.
3. Michael S. Barr, "Financial Services, Savings and Borrowing among Low- and Moderate-Income Households: Evidence from the Detroit Area Household Financial Services Survey," in *Insufficient Funds: Savings, Assets, Credit, and Banking among Low-Income Households,* ed. Robert M. Blank and Michael S. Barr (2009), 136. Noting interest rates as high as 7000 percent.
4. Emily Bazelon, "How Payday Lenders Prey upon the Poor—and the Courts Don't Help," *New York Times Magazine,* April 18, 2014, accessed March 13, 2015, www.nytimes.com/2014/04/20/magazine/how-payday-lenders-prey-upon-the-poor-and-the-courts-dont-help.html?_r=1.

5. Koran Addo, "Lawmakers Eyeing Limits on Payday Loans," *Advocate,* March 30, 2014, accessed March 13, 2015, www.theadvocate.com/home/8685502-125/lawmakers-eyeing-limits-on-payday.
6. According to the CFPB, over 80 percent of payday loans are followed by another payday loan within fourteen days; half are in a sequence of at least ten loans. And loan sizes go up with each subsequent loan, as do interest rates. Many debtors end up paying more in fees than the original principal amount of the loan, and many are simply unable to reduce the debt over time. Consumer Financial Protection Bureau Office of Research, *CFPB Data Point: Payday Lending* (2014), 4.
7. Major banks provide over $1.5 billion in credit to fund major payday lending companies. These include Wells Fargo, Bank of America, U.S. Bank, JPMorgan, and National City (PNC Financial Services Group). Kevin Connor and Matthew Skomarovsky, *The Predators' Creditors: How the Biggest Banks are Bankrolling the Payday Loan Industry* (National People's Action and Public Accountability Initiative, 2010), 10. Cash America's 2013 public filings reveal that it has a $20 million line of credit from Wells Fargo at 2 percent above prime. Cash America, "2013 Annual Report," 134, accessed September 7, 2014, www.cashamerica.com/InvestorRelations/AnnualReports.aspx. QC Holdings revealed in 2009 that it had a $50 million dollar line of credit from a syndicate of banks at an interest of 2.8 percent. QC Holdings, "2009 Annual Report," 61, accessed September 7, 2014, www.qcholdings.com/investor.aspx?id=6.
8. Banks do pay into the Federal Deposit Insurance Corporation (FDIC) insurance fund through premiums, but most scholars agree that the premiums are underpriced. Furthermore, it is not just the actual funds that are paid out in the event of a failure that is of importance here. It is the fact that bank deposits are backed by the full faith and credit of the federal government, making them a safe repository for their customers' funds. "Until the early 1990s, the FDIC levied flat-rate insurance premiums on banks as a function of deposits, but not the banks' risk. In 1991 the FDICIA required that the FDIC introduce risk-based premiums. However, to date, the range of premiums is much narrower than the range of risk exposures of the FDIC to individual bank failures. Under the Deposit Insurance Funding Act of 1996, when the FDIC reserve fund exceeds 1.25 percent of deposits, the 'safest' of banks pay no deposit insurance premium meaning that recently more than 90 percent of banks holding

over 90 percent of total bank assets paid NO premiums." Joe Peek and James A. Wilcox, "The Fall and Rise of Banking Safety Net Subsides," in *Too Big to Fail: Policies and Practices in Government Bailouts,* ed. Benton E. Gup (Westport, CT: Praeger, 2004), 177–178.

9. Board of Governors of the Federal Reserve System, "Monetary Policy," accessed January 18, 2015, www.federalreserve.gov/monetarypolicy/openmarket.htm.
10. A simple illustration would be a bank having to pay off a depositor before the bank is paid interest on the loan it made with the depositor's money. These banks are "solvent" because their future income will likely cover their debts. But they are not "liquid" because they do not have enough cash on hand to pay off short-term demands.
11. The actual amount of the bailout is difficult to determine because much of it was in guarantees. The special inspector general for the Troubled Asset Relief Program estimated a total potential support package of $23.7 trillion, or over 150 percent of the U.S. gross domestic product. However, many of these guarantees were never used. Simon Johnson and James Kwak, *13 Bankers: The Wall Street Takeover and the Next Financial Meltdown* (New York: Pantheon, 2010), 174.
12. Vikram Pandit, CEO of Citigroup, quoted in David Wessel, *In Fed We Trust: Ben Bernanke's War on the Great Panic* (New York: Crown Business, 2009), 239.
13. George W. Bush, "Address to the Nation," speech given on the State Floor of the White House, Washington, DC, September 24, 2008, accessed November 7, 2014, georgewbush-whitehouse.archives.gov/news/releases/2008/09/20080924-10.html.
14. 110th Cong., 2nd sess., Cong. Rec. 154, S10231 (daily ed. October 1, 2008) (Senator Barack Obama).
15. Ken Lewis, interview by *Frontline*, "Breaking the Bank," directed by Michael Kirk, PBS, April 6, 2009, accessed September 30, 2014, www.pbs.org/wgbh/pages/frontline/breakingthebank/etc/script.html.
16. Gerald C. Fischer, *American Banking Structure* (New York: Columbia University Press, 1968), 27.
17. This logic does not apply to small banks. Over the past few years, hundreds of small banks have failed. See Federal Deposit Insurance Corporation, "Failed Bank List," accessed January 16, 2015, www.fdic.gov/bank/individual/failed/banklist.html.

1. GOVERNMENTS AND BANKS

1. Temples were the central sites of borrowing and lending in early Sumeria, across the Persian Empire, in Jerusalem, and in Egypt. Keith Roberts, *The Origins of Business, Money, and Markets* (New York: Columbia University Press, 2011), 126; "Temple archives demonstrate that the temple held deposits by individuals but did not allow others to access them or in any other way use the negotiable instruments that complete the definition of 'banking.' . . . So temples were not 'banks' in antiquity. Rather, the more precise designation for the role of the temple in antiquity would be 'financial intermediary.' " David Graeber, *Debt: The First 5000 Years* (Brooklyn, NY: Melville House, 2011), 13.
2. Earlier Italian banks formed during the fifteenth century. The Medici Bank and those in the Venetian Republic were family-run institutions that lent to the crown but were not as integrally tied to the state and did not issue government bonds. The Swedish Riksbank of 1668 also predates the Bank of England. Richard S. Grossman, *Unsettled Account: The Evolution of Banking in the Industrialized World since 1800* (Princeton, NJ: Princeton University Press, 2010), 29, 171.
3. Charles W. Calomiris and Stephen H. Haber, *Fragile by Design: The Political Origins of Banking Crises and Scarce Credit* (Princeton, NJ: Princeton University Press, 2014), 60.
4. *Bloomberg* editors described it this way: "Banks get a very big subsidy from taxpayers. This subsidy distorts markets and encourages banks to become a threat to the economy." *Bloomberg* estimated the subsidy at $83 billion. *Bloomberg View,* "Remember That $83 Billion Bank Subsidy? We Weren't Kidding," February 24, 2013, accessed March 13, 2015, www.bloombergview.com/articles/2013-02-24/remember-that-83-billion-bank-subsidy-we-weren-t-kidding.
5. Robin Sidel, "FDIC's Tab for Failed U.S. Banks Nears $9 Billion," *Wall Street Journal,* March 17, 2011, accessed March 13, 2015, www.wsj.com/articles/SB10001424052748704396504576204752754667840.
6. Richard S. Carnell, Jonathan R. Macey, and Geoffrey P. Miller, *The Law of Financial Institutions,* 5th ed. (New York: Aspen, 2013), 13.
7. "Fidelity Fiduciary Bank," lyrics by Richard M. Sherman and Robert B. Sherman from the motion picture *Mary Poppins*, Buena Vista Distribution Co., Inc., Copyright © 1964 Walt Disney Productions.

8. Just as banks use leverage to increase money in the economy, individuals, through credit (i.e., loans), use leverage to increase their own wealth. Each loan mentioned above is a form of personal leverage. This leverage, or the ability to get a large chunk of money up front, allows you to build wealth by buying a home or starting a business. Starting a business, for example, requires a large sum of up-front money, either to buy supplies or real estate, before it can create any profits. Whether the initial loan is to fund a business, an income-producing property, or an education, most of us could not grow wealth without bank credit. Truly, credit is one of the most important ways people can improve their economic situations.
9. Michael McLeay, Amar Radia, and Ryland Thomas, "Money Creation in the Modern Economy," *Quarterly Bulletin* 54 (Bank of England, 2014): 16, accessed November 9, 2014, www.bankofengland.co.uk/publications/Pages/quarterlybulletin/2014/qb14q1.aspx.
10. Standard and Poor's Global Credit Portal, "Repeat after Me: Banks Cannot and Do Not 'Lend Out' Reserves," August 13, 2013, accessed November 9, 2014, www.globalcreditportal.com/ratingsdirect/renderArticle.do?articleId=1177975&SctArtId=176005&from=CM&nsl_code=LIME&sourceObjectId=8163576&sourceRevId=1&fee_ind=N&exp_date=20230814-23:17:33.
11. McLeay, Radia, and Thomas, "Money Creation," 16.
12. "Deposits come from only two places: new bank lending and government deficits. Banks create deposits when they create loans. . . . Governments also create deposits when they run budget deficits because they are putting more money into the public's bank accounts than they are taking out." Standard and Poor's, "Repeat after Me."
13. Bank deposits are just a record of how much the bank itself owes its customers. They are liabilities of the bank, not assets that are lent out. Creating money using this formula seems like an unlimited power, but there are, of course, constraints. James Tobin, "Commercial Banks as Creators of 'Money,' " *Cowles Foundation for Research in Economics, Yale University,* no. 159 (1963): 6–7. Banks need to stay profitable, which means they have to make more from their assets than they pay for their liabilities. The cheapest liabilities are deposits (because the banks do not pay anything for them), so the most profitable loan is one offset by deposits. More important, however, are government policies that limit or expand lending, specifically, the central bank's interest-rate policies. "By influencing the level of interest rates in the economy, the [central bank's] monetary policy affects how much

households and companies want to borrow. This occurs both directly, through influencing the loan rates charged by banks, but also indirectly through the overall effect of monetary policy on economic activity in the economy." McLeay, Radia, and Thomas, "Money Creation," 16.

14. See Peter Conti-Brown, *The Structures of the Federal Reserve Independence* (Princeton, NJ: Princeton University Press, 2015).
15. See Kimberly Amadeo, "What is Quantitative Easing: How the Federal Reserve Created Massive Amounts of Money," *About News*, October 14, 2014, accessed March 13, 2015, useconomy.about.com/od/glossary/g/Quantitative-Easing.htm; "What is Quantitative Easing?," *Economist*, January 14, 2014, accessed March 13, 2015, www.economist.com/blogs/economist-explains/2014/01/economist-explains-7.
16. "No one calculated until now that banks reaped an estimated $13 billion of income by taking advantage of the Fed's below-market rates." Bob Ivry, Bradley Keoun, and Phil Kuntz, "Secret Fed Loans Gave Banks $13 Billion Undisclosed to Congress," *Bloomberg*, November 27, 2011, accessed March 13, 2015, www.bloomberg.com/news/2011-11-28/secret-fed-loans-undisclosed-to-congress-gave-banks-13-billion-in-income.html. For more about which bank received how much from the Federal Reserve from August 2007 through April 2010, see "The Fed's Secret Liquidity Lifelines," *Bloomberg*, accessed March 13, 2015, www.bloomberg.com/data-visualization/federal-reserve-emergency-lending/#/overview/?sort=nomPeakValue&group=none&view=peak&position=0&comparelist=&search=."The Federal Reserve made $9 trillion in overnight loans to major banks and Wall Street firms during the financial crisis, according to newly revealed data released Wednesday. . . . All the loans were backed by collateral and all were paid back with a very low interest rate to the Fed—an annual rate of from 0.5% to 3.5%." See Chris Isidore, "Fed Made $9 Trillion in Emergency Overnight Loans," *CNN Money*, December 1, 2010, accessed March 13, 2015, money.cnn.com/2010/12/01/news/economy/fed_reserve_data_release/.
17. According to 12 U.S.C. 1824, the FDIC is authorized to borrow from the Treasury and the secretary of the Treasury is authorized and directed to make loans to the FDIC on such terms as may be fixed by the corporation and the secretary. Even with this complete assurance of protection, depositors holding more than the insured maximum of $100,000 will still make bank runs. Federal deposit insurance is

capped at $250,000 per depositor per bank; sums above that are uninsured. If the FDIC closes a bank, it also often tries to protect all deposits—insured and uninsured—by selling the deposits to another bank (generally, through a purchase-and-assumption agreement). Finally, in an extraordinary and controversial order, the FDIC temporarily guaranteed business deposits of all sizes in the fall of 2008 (this guarantee eventually came to an end). The FDIC did that to stop large business depositors with uninsured deposits over the insurance caps from making runs on banks (such as Wachovia and Citibank).

18. Sallie Mae ceased being a GSE, and became fully privatized, when Congress terminated its charter on December 29, 2004. At that point, the GSE became SLM Corporation, "a fully private sector corporation." U.S. Department of the Treasury, Office of Sallie Mae Oversight, *Lessons Learned from the Privatization of Sallie Mae,* March 2006, 1, accessed January 18, 2015, www.treasury.gov/about/organizational-structure/offices/Documents/SallieMaePrivatizationReport.pdf. A table on page 3 of the above Treasury report distinguishes the former GSE-Sallie Mae from the fully privatized SLM Corporation. Notable differences include: (1) an act of Congress created the GSE's charter; (2) the president appointed the GSE's board members; (3) the GSE could borrow up to $1 billion from the Treasury, whereas the SLM Corporation cannot borrow from the Treasury; (4) the GSE's debt was eligible for federal open market purchases; (5) the GSE was exempt from SEC registration and financial and other filings with the SEC; and (6) the GSE was exempted from federal, state, and local income taxes.
19. Fannie Mae and Freddie Mac were spun off of the federal government and privatized so that they were run by a board of shareholders. This did not mean that they operated in normal markets. The market still treated them like government entities, meaning that they did not contemplate their failure. When they eventually failed because their managers took excessive risks, the government bailed them out without flinching.
20. A long and rich philosophical discussion exists regarding the social contract between individuals and society. In general, social-contract theory posits that individuals consent to surrender some natural liberties in exchange for protection or other benefits conferred by society. The government and the banks share a similar relationship. Hobbes, Kant, Rousseau, Rawls, and others have taken up the social

contract between individuals and the state. Paul Tucker, "Regimes for Handling Bank Failures—Redrawing the Banking Social Contract," remarks, British Bankers' Association Annual International Banking Conference "Restoring Confidence—Moving Forward," London, June 30, 2009, accessed January 18, 2015, www.bis.org/review/r090708d.pdf.

21. Gary Gorton, "Slapped in the Face by the Invisible Hand: Banking and the Panic of 2007," conference, Federal Reserve Bank of Atlanta's 2009 Financial Markets Conference: Financial Innovation and Crisis, May 9, 2009, accessed March 13, 2015, www.frbatlanta.org/news/conferences/09-financial_markets_agenda.cfm.
22. See "Adding Up the Government's Total Bailout Tab," *New York Times,* July 24, 2011, accessed March 13, 2015, www.nytimes.com/interactive/2009/02/04/business/20090205-bailout-totals-graphic.html?_r=0. As of April 30, 2011, the government had made bail-out commitments of 12.2 trillion dollars. For an extensive overview of the Federal Reserve's role in the 2008 financial crisis, see Cheryl D. Block, "Measuring the True Cost of Government Bailout," *Washington University Law Review* 88 (2010): 174–189.
23. The financial sector is the largest contributor to political campaigns, donating 1.7 billion to political campaigns and spending 3.4 billion on lobby expenses from 1998–2008. Simon Johnson and James Kwak, *13 Bankers: The Wall Street Takeover and the Next Financial Meltdown* (New York: Pantheon, 2010), 90–92.
24. Regulatory "capture" refers to a situation in which the firms that are regulated by an agency actually influence the agency's decisions. These regulated bodies can gather and use their influence in many ways: lobbying, the revolving door, and political pressure through other government bodies.
25. Johnson and Kwak, *13 Bankers,* 154.
26. Timothy F. Geithner, *Stress Test: Reflections on Financial Crises* (New York: Crown, 2014), 8.
27. George W. Bush, "Speech to Nation on the Economic Crisis," September 4, 2008, transcript provided by CQ Transcriptions, accessed January 18, 2015, www.nytimes.com/2008/09/24/business/economy/24text-bush.html?pagewanted=all (emphasis added).
28. 154 Cong. Rec. S10232 (daily ed. October 1, 2008) (statement of Sen. Barack Obama) (emphasis added).
29. *Moral hazard* refers to the dangerous market incentives that insurance and bailouts produce. If firms believe they will be bailed out and their

customers made whole in the event of a failure, they are not incentivized to be prudent.

30. Timothy Geithner, "The Paradox of Financial Crises," *Wall Street Journal,* May 13, 2014, accessed March 13, 2015, www.wsj.com/articles/SB10001424052702304885404579552430842061834?mobile=y.
31. The assumption, of course, was that these Wall Street banks engaged in activities that are useful to the society at large. Here again are various opinions ranging from cynical (Paul Volcker famously derided Wall Street by saying that the only useful financial innovation of the last twenty-five years was the ATM) to those claiming that despite the misfeasance and malfeasance of Wall Street, Wall Street banks remain at the center of many of our secondary markets: they create more money and more credit in the economy, just as banks do.
32. Bush, "Speech to Nation," September 4, 2008.
33. Hank Paulson, "Remarks by Secretary Henry M. Paulson, Jr. on Financial Rescue Package and Economic Update," November 12, 2008, transcript provided by *Financial Times,* accessed March 13, 2015, www.ft.com/intl/cms/s/0/0fe4badc-b0df-11dd-8915-0000779fd18c.html#axzz3DhfqXKhw.
34. 154 Cong. Rec. S10232 (Oct. 1, 2008).
35. Timothy Geithner, "Introducing the Financial Stability Plan," February 10, 2009, accessed March 13, 2015, www.treasury.gov/press-center/press-releases/Pages/tg18.aspx.
36. Mike McIntire, "Bailout Is a Windfall to Banks, if Not to Borrowers," *New York Times,* January 17, 2009, accessed March 13, 2015, www.nytimes.com/2009/01/18/business/18bank.html?pagewanted=all.
37. "This data shows that bank lending to small firms rose from $308 billion in June 1994 to a peak of $659 billion in June 2008 but then plummeted to only $543 billion in June 2011—a decline of $116 billion or almost 18%. Bank lending to all firms rose from $758 billion in 1994 to a peak of $2.14 trillion in June 2008 and then declined by about 9% to $1.96 trillion as of June 2011. Hence, the decline in bank lending was far more severe for small businesses than for larger firms." Rebel A. Cole, "How Did the Financial Crisis Affect Small Business Lending in the United States," *SBA Office of Advocacy,* November 2012, accessed January 18, 2015, www.sba.gov/sites/default/files/files/rs399tot.pdf.
38. Geithner, "Financial Stability Plan," February 10, 2009.
39. Ibid.
40. Geithner, *Stress Test,* 14.

41. Edmund L. Andrews and Stephen Labaton, "Bailout Plan: $2.5 Trillion and a Strong U.S. Hand," *New York Times,* February 10, 2009, accessed March 13, 2015, www.nytimes.com/2009/02/11/business/economy/11 bailout.html?pagewanted=all.
42. "In addition to failing to include terms that would provide incentives to increase lending, Treasury didn't require the banks to report on how they were using TARP funds." Neil Barofsky, *Bailout: An Inside Account of How Washington Abandoned Main Street While Rescuing Wall Street* (New York: Free Press, 2012), 73.
43. Paulson, "Remarks," November 12, 2008.
44. Rebecca Christie and Alison Vekshin, "Paulson, Democrats Clash on Bailout for Homeowners (Update 2)," *Bloomberg,* November 18, 2008, accessed March 13, 2015, www.bloomberg.com/apps/news?pid =newsarchive&sid=ask7NL3CnYq4.
45. Ibid.
46. Ibid.
47. Timothy Geithner, "Remark by Treasury Secretary Timothy Geithner," February 10, 2009.
48. Foreclosures in the United States matched the highest level on record at the end of 2010, according to the Mortgage Bankers Association. "Delinquencies and Loans in Foreclosure Decrease, But Foreclosure Starts to Rise in Latest MBA National Delinquency Survey," MBA press release, November 18, 2010, accessed January 18, 2015, www .mba.org/NewsandMedia/pressCenter/74733.htm.
49. Barofsky, *Bailout,* 157.
50. In his memoir, Geithner explains that all of his actions were meant to restore trust in the banking system, which is the large engine at the center of the economy. Injecting money into banks and returning them to profitability is how governments help the public. Then why did the comment infuriate Warren and Barofsky and why did the bailout elicit such a negative public backlash? Geithner believes it was because of misguided "Populism," a lack of understanding of how markets work, or a desire for "Old Testament justice" to see those responsible punished. Geithner, *Stress Test,* 9.

2. HISTORY OF THE SOCIAL CONTRACT

1. Charles W. Calomiris and Stephen H. Haber, *Fragile by Design: The Political Origins of Banking Crises and Scarce Credit* (Princeton, NJ: Princeton University Press, 2014), 3–4.

2. Ibid., 16.
3. Piergiorgio Alessandri and Andrew G. Haldane, "Banking on the State," November 6, 2009, based on a presentation at the Federal Reserve Bank of Chicago 12th Annual International Banking Conference, *The International Financial Crisis: Have the Rules of Finance Changed?*, September 25, 2009, 1.
4. Richard S. Grossman, *Unsettled Account: The Evolution of Banking in the Industrialized World since 1800* (Princeton, NJ: Princeton University Press, 2010), 29.
5. Ibid., 1. See also C. M. Reinhart and K. Rogoff, *This Time is Different: Eight Centuries of Financial Folly* (Princeton, NJ: Princeton University Press, 2009), 73.
6. Alessandri and Haldane, "Banking on the State," 1.
7. Robert Morris said the bank was "in fact nothing more than a patriotic subscription of continental money . . . for the purpose of purchasing provisions for a starving army." Bray Hammond, *Banks and Politics in America: From the Revolution to the Civil War* (Princeton, NJ: Princeton University Press, 1991), 45.
8. Alexander Hamilton, *The Works of Alexander Hamilton,* vol. I, ed. John C. Hamilton (New York: Charles S. Francis, 1850), 224.
9. Hammond, *Banks and Politics,* 40.
10. The Avalon Project, "Hamilton's Opinion as to the Constitutionality of the Bank of the United States: 1791," accessed March 19, 2015, avalon.law.yale.edu/18th_century/bank-ah.asp, from *The Federalist: A Commentary on the Constitution of the United States by Alexander Hamilton, James Madison, and John Jay,* ed. Paul Leicester Ford (New York: Henry Holt, 1898).
11. Hammond, *Banks and Politics,* 76
12. Alexander Hamilton, *The Works of Alexander Hamilton,* vol. III, ed. John C. Hamilton (New York: Charles S. Francis, 1850), 132.
13. Hammond, *Banks and Politics,* 66. See also Richard S. Grossman, *Unsettled Account*, 261. Noting that prior to 1790, the United States only had four commercial banks.
14. Hammond, *Banks and Politics,* 67.
15. Ibid.
16. Just as the Constitution and the Declaration of Independence reflect a compromise between these two groups, so does the formation of banking. In fact, a compromise about central banking could not be reached for many years. The Constitution specifically omits any reference to central banking and currency, an issue that James

Madison, an advocate for states' rights more aligned with the anti-elite agrarians, vigorously opposed.

17. John Jay Knox, *A History of Banking in the United States* (New York: Bradford Rose, 1900), 35.
18. Thomas Paine wrote: "The principal public use of [the bank] at this time is for the promotion and extension of commerce. The whole community derives benefit from the operation of the bank. It facilitates the commerce of the country. It quickens the means of purchasing and paying for country produce and hastens on the exportation of it. The emolument, therefore, being to the community, it is the office and duty of government to give protection to the bank." Richard Carlile, *The Life of Thomas Paine, Written Purposely to Bind with His Writings* (London: W. T. Sherwin, 1817), 36.
19. *Documentary History of Banking and Currency in the United States* vol. I and II, ed. Herman E. Krooss (New York: Chelsea House, 1969), 264–277.
20. Thomas Jefferson to John Taylor, letter, May 28, 1816, The Thomas Jefferson Papers, Library of Congress, accessed September 30, 2014, memory.loc.gov/cgi-bin/query/r?ammem/mtj:@field%28DOCID+@lit%28tj110172%29%29.
21. John Adams, *The Works of John Adams,* vol. IX, ed. Charles Francis Adams (Boston: Little, Brown, 1854), 638.
22. William M. Gouge, *A Short History of Money and Banking* (New York: Augustus M. Kelly, 1968), 133, accessed March 19, 2015, mises.org/books/shorthistorypapermoney.pdf.
23. Gordon S. Wood, *The Creation of the American Republic 1776–1787* (Chapel Hill: University of North Carolina Press, 1969), 72.
24. Ibid., 375 (quoting David Ramsay, "Oration on Advantages of American Independence," in *Principles and Acts of the Revolution*, ed. William Ogden Niles [Baltimore: William Ogden Niles, 1822], 64).
25. Wood, *Creation,* quoting Thomas Shippen.
26. Hammond, *Banks and Politics, 55.*
27. Ibid., 145–147. See *Documentary History of Banking and Currency in the United States,* vol. I and II, ed. Herman E. Krooss (New York: Chelsea House, 1969).
28. William J. Kambas, "The Development of the U.S. Banking System: From Colonial Convenience to National Necessity," *Rutgers Law Record*, vol. 28 (2004).
29. Ibid.
30. Hammond, Banks and Politics, 19–20.

31. Jackson was well-liked, but his political views were hard to pin down—he was neither a true Progressive nor a conservative by contemporary standards: "As a popular leader he combined the simple agrarian principles of political economy absorbed at his mother's knee with the most up-to-date doctrine of laissez faire." Ibid., 349.
32. The war against the bank was also not a simple matter of Populist versus capitalist. Many capitalist rivals to the national bank joined forces with the Jacksonians to defeat the bank and thereby free state banks from federal credit policies. Ibid., 406.
33. T. F. Gordon, *The War on the Bank of the United States* (Philadelphia: Key and Biddle, 1834), 13.
34. Quoted in Charles Geisst, *Wall Street: A History* (New York: Oxford Press, 1997), 19.
35. Langdon Cheves, *Report on the Condition of the Bank of the United States by the Committee of Inspection and Investigation,* reprinted in *1 Documentary History of Banking and Currency in the United States* (New York: Chelsea House, 1969), 582.
36. Geisst, *Wall Street,* 27.
37. In fact, a legal doctrine began in the 1800s that described this situation perfectly. It described the banking system as a "federal instrumentality." The federal instrumentality doctrine was first introduced in 1819 in *McCulloch v. Maryland,* 17 U.S. 316 (1819). Chief Justice Marshall declared Maryland's tax on the Second Bank of the United States unconstitutional. The court famously said that "the power to tax was the power to destroy," and the federal government would not permit the destruction of an "instrument employed by the government." Ibid., 436–437. The court would thus protect this special relationship between the bank and the federal government from state intrusion. This landmark case reveals the early form of a mutually beneficial partnership.
38. Susan Hoffmann, *Politics and Banking: Ideas, Public Policy, and the Creation of Financial Institutions* (Baltimore: Johns Hopkins University Press, 2001), 72. Charles W. Calomiris, *U.S. Bank Deregulation in Historical Perspective* (New York: Cambridge University Press, 2000), 59.
39. Hoffmann, *Politics and Banking,* 87.
40. *Schaake v. Dolley,* 118 P. 80, 83 (Kan. 1911).
41. The McFadden Act, enacted in 1927, specifically prohibited interstate branching by allowing each national bank to branch only within the

state in which it was situated. McFadden Act, § 3, 44 Stat. 1228 (1927). However, prior to the McFadden Act, most states prohibited interstate branching, and many prohibited branching within the state. Federal Reserve Committee on Branch, Group, and Chain Banking, *Branch Banking in the United States* (Federal Reserve System, 1992), 8, 210. Eighteen states banned branch banking within the state, nine allowed it, and fourteen allowed it with certain restrictions. Ibid., 215–216. A majority of states in 1895 had no mention of branches in their laws. In some states, silence has been taken as permitting and in others, as forbidding branches.

42. Richard S. Carnell, Jonathan R. Macey, and Geoffrey P. Miller, *The Law of Financial Institutions,* 5th ed. (New York: Aspen, 2013), 13.
43. Calomiris and Haber see this as Populist rent-seeking. They claim that because Populists controlled the legislatures, they created a banking system that was fragile by design but that served their needs. Calomiris and Haber, *Fragile by Design,* 459.
44. Starting in the deregulatory era in the United States, some revisionist scholars claimed that the era was not as bad as previously thought, but these claims have been largely rebutted. Lawrence H. White, "Free Banking in History and Theory" (working paper no. 14–07, George Mason University, 2014, 3–4), accessed March 19, 2015, papers.ssrn.com/sol3/papers.cfm?abstract_id=2435536. But see James A. Kahn, "Another Look at Free Banking in the United States," *American Economic Review* 75 (1985): 881, accessed March 19, 2015, www.jstor.org/discover/1821369?sid =21105644997413anduid=2anduid=2134anduid=70anduid =3739256anduid=3739616anduid=4.
45. Some banking observers claim that Scottish banks functioned free of the state, but this is not historically accurate, for they were much tied to the Bank of England. See Walter Bagehot, *Lombard Street: A Description of the Money Market* (London: Henry S. King & Co., 1873), 31, and Charles Hickson and John Turner, "Free Banking and the Stability of Early Joint-Stock Banking," *Cambridge Journal of Economics* 28 (2004): 903–919.
46. Some states that passed free banking legislation (like Georgia, Iowa, Massachusetts, and Pennsylvania) did not actually witness a proliferation in the number of financial institutions. Ranajoy Ray Chaudhuri, *The Changing Face of American Banking: Deregulation, Reregulation and the Global Financial System* (New York: Palgrave Macmillan, 2014), 9.

47. Hammond, *Banks and Politics*, 600.
48. Grossman, *Unsettled Account*, 229–230; Hammond, *Banks and Politics*, 727–728.
49. The Treasury could not buy or sell treasuries from state banks.
50. "To the authorities at Washington it seemed that the resource of loans from the banks was not adequate to the financial necessities of the time. The expenditures were already $1 million a day and very rapidly increasing. . . . These misgivings and apprehensions furnished the motive of the legal tender act of February 23, 1862, by which the government undertook to help itself by the issue of an irredeemable treasury-note currency." William Graham Summer, ed., *A History of Banking in All the Leading Nations,* vol. 1 (New York: Journal of Commerce and Commercial Bulletin, 1896), 413.
51. "'It was under these circumstances that the banks in New York resolved, on the 28th of December, 1861, to suspend specie payment. The suspension of specie payments, therefore, is to be traced primarily to the patriotic efforts of the banks in the great cities to sustain the government.' A conservative bank movement followed the suspension, but after April, 1862, there was a rapid expansion of loans, deposits and circulation, accompanying the premium on gold and silver." Ibid.
52. Knox, "History of Banking." Although President Lincoln "greenbacks" have been portrayed as "Lincoln's money," Lincoln was not a staunch advocate. The Legal Tender Acts were initiated in Congress, and Lincoln recognized the utility of a fiat currency, but he was a reluctant adopter.
53. "The perfection of economy in time, labor and expense would seem to have been attained in a [paper] currency worthy of and honorable to Christian civilization." Bray Hammond, *Sovereignty and an Empty Purse: Banks and Politics in the Civil War* (Princeton, NJ: Princeton University Press, 1970), 97 (quoting Editorial, *New York Tribune,* January 25, 1862) (internal quotation marks omitted).
54. Office of Comptroller of the Currency, *Annual Report* (Washington, DC: Government Printing Office, 1878), 26.
55. When Lincoln accepted the third and final issue of fiat bills, he sent a letter to Congress in which he expressed "sincere regret that it has been found necessary to authorize an additional issue of United States notes." Wesley C. Mitchell, *A History of the Greenbacks* (Chicago: University of Chicago Press, 1903), 109.
56. The United States would return to fiat currency from 1914 to 1925 and then again from 1933 to 1945. When the United States returned

to specie in 1945, it was essentially fiat currency as far as everyone beyond foreign governments was concerned.

57. Lincoln's support for national banking started before he became president. When he ran for state legislature in 1832, he said, "My politics are short and sweet, like the old woman's dance. I am in favor of a national bank . . . in favor of the internal improvements system and a high protective tariff." Abraham Lincoln, *The Works of Abraham Lincoln,* vol. 2, ed. John Herbert Clifford and Francis Bicknell Carpenter (New York: C. S. Hammond, 1907), 1.
58. Edward McPherson, *The Political History of the United States of America, during the Great Rebellion* (Washington, DC: Philp and Solomons, 1864), 138.
59. Many challenged the constitutionality of Treasury secretary Chase's proposal for national banks. Letter from the Secretary of the Treasury, H. R. Exec. Doc. No. 37–25 (1863), 95.
60. Newspapers like the *New York Times* supported a paper currency because it was a symbol of the principles the union stood for. For example, in 1862 the *New York Times* stated that: "All parties who regard the government as anything more than a confederation of States to be broken or weakened at will by secession or rebellion—all who believe the Federal authority a power for the general good of the whole People as well as the symbol of sovereignty and allegiance—will welcome this resumption of one of its most important rights and duties . . . of a National Currency, stamped as a legal tender" (alteration in original). *New York Times,* January 6, 1862.
61. Hammond, *Sovereignty,* 177.
62. Summer, *History of Banking*, 416.
63. National Banking Act of 1864, ch.106, 13 Stat. 99 (1864); "With the exception of the first and second banks of the United States, there has been no interstate branch banking historically in the United States." Charles W. Calomiris, *U.S. Bank Deregulation in Historical Perspective* (New York: Cambridge University Press, 2000), 7; "Full service banking across state lines has been the exception, rather than the rule, in American banking for most of the nation's history. Fear of the concentrated financial power that large banks might acquire and use to the detriment of farmers, ranchers, and other small business interests led state after state in this century to restrict or outlaw the creation of full service branch offices. Some states such as Texas were so set against the spread of branch banking that anti-branching

statutes were made a part of its state constitution . . . the federal government added its own imprimatur to the actions of the states in 1927 and 1933." Peter Rose, *The Interstate Banking Revolution* (New York: Quorum Books, 1989), 4–5.

64. "Official Proceedings of the Democratic National Convention Held in Chicago, Illinois, July 7, 8, 9, 10, and 11, 1896," in *The Annals of America,* vol. 12, *1895–1904: Populism, Imperialism, and Reform* (Chicago: Encyclopedia Britannica, 1968), 100–105.
65. Ibid.
66. Ibid.
67. Ibid.
68. David Graeber, *Debt: The First 5,000 Years* (Brooklyn, NY: Melville House, 2012), 52–53.
69. In fact, Grossman and Calomiris and Haber all remark on just how uniquely unstable this period was. Calomiris and Haber, *Fragile by Design,* 183; Grossman, *Unsettled Accounts,* 68.
70. Political debates during this era, and especially the presidential election of 1908, were focused on banking reform. The Democrat-Populist William Jennings Bryan proposed deposit insurance to stabilize the banking system, and William Taft proposed postal banking, discussed later in the book. This problem manifested itself with catastrophic consequences during the Great Depression.
71. Chaudhuri, *Changing Face,* 49–51.
72. Woodrow Wilson, *The New Freedom* (New York: Doubleday, Page, 1918), 184–185.
73. Louis D. Brandeis, *Other People's Money and How the Bankers Use It* (New York: Frederick A. Stokes, 1914) 18. J. P. Morgan, along with two New York banks, National City and First National, constituted the Money Trust.
74. Ibid., 18–19.
75. Ibid., 49.
76. Ibid., 64.
77. Ibid, 146. Justice Holmes conceded that even if the state did not take on nationalized banking, private banking could compete efficiently in the market if it could focus on people instead of profits, which he termed "democratic banking."
78. Ibid., 66.
79. He even refers to the banking cooperative model in Germany as an example. A model—the credit union—will be discussed at length in Chapter 3.

80. Calomiris and Haber explain that the largest banks opposed deposit insurance, as did Roosevelt, but he capitulated to the political power of the unit banks in order to push the broad reforms.
81. Franklin D. Roosevelt, "First Inaugural Address," Washington, DC, March 4, 1933, National Archives, accessed March 19, 2015, www.archives.gov/education/lessons/fdr-inaugural/images/address-1.gif.
82. Glass-Steagall Act (Banking Act of 1933), Pub. L. No. 73–66, 48 Stat. 162; Grossman, *Unsettled Accounts*, 247–248.
83. Lawrence Chistiano, Roberto Motto, and Massimo Rostagno, "The Great Depression and the Friedman-Schwartz Hypothesis" (working paper series no. 326, European Central Bank, March 2004), accessed March 19, 2015, www.ecb.europa.eu/pub/pdf/scpwps/ecbwp326.pdf (stating that a more accommodative monetary policy could have greatly reduced the severity of the Great Depression); Ben Bernanke, "Non-Monetary Effects of the Financial Crisis in the Propagation of the Great Depression," (NBER working paper series no. 1054, January 1983), accessed March 19, 2015, www.nber.org/papers/w1054.pdf, 2.
84. "I see one-third of a nation ill-housed, ill-clad, ill-nourished. . . . The test of our progress is not whether we add more to the abundance of those who have much; it is whether we provide enough for those who have too little." Franklin D. Roosevelt, "Second Inaugural Address," Washington, DC, January 20, 1937, Franklin D. Roosevelt Presidential Library and Museum, accessed March 19, 2015, www.fdrlibrary.marist.edu/aboutfdr/inaugurations.html.
85. See Federal Home Loan Bank Act, Pub. L. No. 72–304, 47 Stat. 725 (1932).
86. FDIC, "Savings and Loan Crisis and Its Relationship to Banking," in *History of the Eighties*, vol. 1 (1997), 170, accessed March 19, 2015, www.fdic.gov/bank/historical/history/vol1.html.
87. Freddie Mac, "Company Profile," accessed September 30, 2014, www.freddiemac.com/corporate/company_profile/.
88. For a comprehensive discussion of "redlining," see Charles Lewis Nier, III, "The Shadow of Credit: The Historical Origins of Racial Predatory Lending and its Impact upon African American Wealth Accumulation," *University of Pennsylvania Journal of Law and Social Change* (2008).
89. Thomas Piketty, *Capital in the Twenty-First Century* (Cambridge, MA: Harvard University Press: 2014), 80.
90. Martin Luther King Jr., "I Have a Dream," accessed March 19, 2015, www.thekingcenter.org/archive/document/i-have-dream-1.

91. Richard Scott Carnell, Jonathan R. Macey, and Geoffrey P. Miller, *The Law of Banking and Financial Institutions*, 350 (New York: Aspen Publishers, 2009).
92. Jan Blakeslee, "'White Flight' to the Suburbs: A Demographic Approach," University of Wisconsin Institute for Research on Poverty Newsletter Vol. 3, No. 2 (1978–1979), 1.
93. Warren L. Dennis, "The Community Re-investment Act of 1977: Its Legislative History and Its Impact on Applications for Changes in Structure Made by Depository Institutions to the Four Federal Financial Supervisory Agencies" (working paper no. 24, Purdue University, 1978), accessed March 19, 2015, faculty.msb.edu/prog/CRC/pdf/wp24.pdf, 4 (quoting Congressional Record, daily ed. January 24, 1977 at 1202 [internal quotation marks omitted]).
94. Housing and Community Development Act of 1977, Pub. L. No. 95–128, 95th Cong. (October 12, 1977). The language of the bill contains this provision at Section 104 (g)(i)(2).
95. Department of Justice, "Recent Accomplishments of the Housing & Civil Enforcement Section," accessed March 29, 2015, http://www.justice.gov/crt/about/hce/whatnew.php.
96. Consumer Financial Protection Bureau, "CFPB to Pursue Discriminatory Lenders," April 18, 2012, accessed March 19, 2015, www.consumerfinance.gov/newsroom/consumer-financial-protection-bureau-to-pursue-discriminatory-lenders/.
97. Amidst wide criticism that regulators didn't bring any enforcement actions during the crisis, there were several high-profile cases brought by the DOJ and banking regulators based on these anti-discrimination laws. Federal Deposit Insurance Corporation, "What is Economic Inclusion?," accessed March 19, 2015, www.economicinclusion.gov/whatis/.
98. For example, a central tenet of Professor Muhammad Yunus's micro-credit model is that "credit is a fundamental right." See, e.g., Randeep Ramesh, "Credit is a Basic Human Right," *Guardian,* January 5, 2007, accessed March 19, 2015, www.theguardian.com/world/2007/jan/05/outlook.development.
99. Disintermediation describes the elimination of financial intermediaries, such as banks, resulting from high inflation rates and stagnant interest offered by banks (due to regulatory caps). Depositors can get better returns by investing in mutual funds or securities and thus, banks lose customers and revenue.

100. "These agencies are designed with a primary mission to protect the safety and soundness of the banking system. This means protecting banks' profitability." Oren Bar-Gill and Elizabeth Warren, "Making Credit Safer," *University of Pennsylvania Law Review* 157 (2008): 90.
101. For example, Saule Omarova reveals how the Office of the Comptroller, through a series of interpretive letters, allowed banks to engage in highly risky derivatives transactions by examining only their potential profits. However, derivatives, now a robust industry that dwarfs the nation's capital markets and gross domestic product, were laden with risks and have since exposed many banking institutions to heightened vulnerability. Saule T. Omarova, "The Quiet Metamorphosis: How Derivatives Changed the 'Business of Banking,'" 63. *U. Miami L. Rev.* 1041, 1106 (2009).
102. Federal Reserve Bank of Minneapolis, "Are Banks Special?," *Annual Reports 1982*, January 1982, accessed March 19, 2015, www.minneapolisfed.org/publications/annual-reports/ar/annual-report-1982-complete-text.
103. Federal Deposit Insurance Corporation, *Mandate for Change: Restructuring the Banking Industry* (Washington, DC: Federal Deposit Insurance Corporation, 1987), xv.
104. "The public policy implication of this conclusion [systemic risks to the banking industry and potential losses to the deposit insurer will not be increased if activity restrictions and regulatory authority over bank affiliates are abolished] is that both the Bank Holding Company Act and the Glass-Steagall restrictions on the affiliations between commercial and investment firms *should be abolished.*" Ibid., xiv–xv.
105. Actually, zero. The OCC and the OTS announced comprehensive preemption to protect all national banks and thrifts from state consumer protection laws. The rationale was that these public-protecting laws rendered banks less efficient and profitable by limiting the kinds and amounts of loans that these banks could make. Department of the Treasury, *Financial Regulatory Reform: A New Foundation: Rebuilding Financial Supervision and Regulation* (2009), accessed March 19, 2015, www.treasury.gov/initiatives/Documents/FinalReport_web.pdf, 2, 7; Interpretive Letter No. 999, John D. Hawke Jr., comptroller of the currency, to Barney Frank, ranking member, Committee on Financial Services, U.S. House of Representatives, March 9, 2004, accessed March 19, 2015, www.occ.gov/static/interpretations-and-precedents/aug04/int999.pdf.

106. Mehrsa Baradaran, "Banking and the Social Contract," *Notre Dame Law Review* 89 (January 2014): 1283.
107. Elizabeth Warren, "Unsafe at Any Rate," *Democracy Journal* 5 (2007), accessed March 19, 2015, www.democracyjournal.org/pdf/5/Warren.pdf, 14–16 (discussing the inability to pass legislation during this time that would protect consumers and noting that the "main mission" of the OCC and OTS is to "protect the financial stability of banks and other institutions, not to protect consumers").
108. Citizen's Financial Group, 71 Fed.Res.Bull. 473, 475 (F.R.B.), 1985 WL 68579.
109. Greg Smith, "Why I Am Leaving Goldman Sachs," *New York Times,* March 14, 2012, accessed March 19, 2015, www.nytimes.com/2012/03/14/opinion/why-i-am-leaving-goldman-sachs.html?pagewanted=1and_r=2andhp.
110. Jim Wells, "Are Small Banks Big Banks' Pawns in Assault on Dodd-Frank?" *American Banker,* May 11, 2012, accessed March 19, 2015, www.americanbanker.com/bankthink/small-banks-are-big-banks-pawns-in-assault-on-dodd-frank-1049260-1.html.
111. Quoted in Simon Clark and Caroline Binham, "Profit 'Is Not Satanic,' Barclays CEO Varlet Says," *Bloomberg,* November 3, 2009, accessed March 19, 2015, www.bloomberg.com/apps/news?pid=newsarchive&sid=aGR1F_bjSIZw. Also quoted in Johnson and Kwak, *13 Bankers: The Wall Street Takeover and the Next Financial Meltdown* (New York: Vintage Books, 2010), 182.
112. Johnson and Kwak, *13 Bankers,* 182.
113. Ibid., 85.
114. Stephen Gandel, "By Every Measure, the Big Banks are Bigger," *Fortune,* September 13, 2013, accessed March 19, 2015, www.fortune.com/2013/09/13/by-every-measure-the-big-banks-are-bigger/.
115. Trefis Team, "Why Wells Fargo Will Soon Have the Largest Deposit Base among U.S. Banks," *Forbes,* September 15, 2014, accessed March 19, 2015, www.forbes.com/sites/greatspeculations/2014/09/15/why-wells-fargo-will-soon-have-the-largest-deposit-base-among-u-s-banks/.
116. Stephen Gandel, "By Every Measure, the Big Banks are Bigger," *Fortune*, www.fortune.com/2013/09/13/by-every-measure-the-big-banks-are-bigger/.
117. Consumer Education Foundation, "Sold Out: How Wall Street and Washington Betrayed America," March 2009, accessed March 19, 2015, www.wallstreetwatch.org/reports/sold_out.pdf.

118. Johnson and Kwak, *13 Bankers,* 91.
119. Andrew R. Sorkin, *Too Big to Fail: The Inside Story of How Wall Street and Washington Fought to Save the Financial System—and Themselves* (New York: Penguin Books, 2010), 38.
120. Tom Braithwaite and Tracy Alloway, "Wall Street Returns to Era of Big Profits," *Financial Times,* July 19, 2013, accessed March 19, 2015, www.ft.com/intl/cms/s/0/716d6a42-f072-11e2-929c-00144feabdc0.html#axzz3UrnQlAlM.
121. Senator Dick Durbin, interview by Ray Hanania, mp3, April 27, 2009, accessed March 19, 2015, www.progressillinois.com/2009/4/29/durbin-banks-own-the-place.
122. Jordan Malter, "Elizabeth Warren: 'The Game Is Rigged,' " *CNN Money,* accessed January 14, 2015, money.cnn.com/video/news/2014/05/27/elizabeth-warren-new-populism-conference-game-is-rigged.cnnmoney/.
123. Michael McKee and Scott Lanman, "Greenspan Says U.S. Should Consider Breaking Up Large Banks," *Bloomberg,* October 15, 2009, accessed March 19, 2015, www.bloomberg.com/apps/news?pid=newsarchive&sid=aJ8HPmNUfchg.
124. Alessandri and Haldane, "Banking on the State," 7.
125. Johnson and Kwak, *13 Bankers,* 179.
126. Ibid., 192.
127. Ibid.
128. Beim, "2009 08 18 FRBNY Report on Systemic Risk and Bank Supervision Draft," accessed March 19, 2015, www.propublica.org/documents/item/1303305-2009-08-18-frbny-report-on-systemic-risk-and.html.
129. Chicago Public Radio, "Episode 536: The Secret Recordings of Carmen Segarra," *This American Life,* accessed September 30, 2014, www.thisamericanlife.org/radio-archives/episode/536/the-secret-recordings-of-carmen-segarra.
130. Daniel K. Tarullo, "Confronting Too Big to Fail," October 21, 2009, accessed March 19, 2015, www.federalreserve.gov/newsevents/speech/tarullo20091021a.htm.
131. "Glass-Steagall had long separated commercial banks (which lend money) and investment banks (which organize the sale of bonds and equities); I had opposed repeal of Glass-Steagall. The proponents said, in effect, Trust us: we will create Chinese walls to make sure that the problems of the past do not recur. As an economist, I certainly possessed a healthy degree of trust, trust in the power of economic

incentives to bend human behavior toward self-interest—toward short-term self-interest, at any rate, rather than Tocqueville's 'self interest rightly understood.'" Joseph E. Stiglitz, "Capitalist Fools," *Vanity Fair,* January 2009.

132. Michael Bordo et al., "Is the Crisis Problem Growing More Severe?," *Economic Policy* 32 (2001): 53–82.
133. See, e.g., Richard A. Posner, *A Failure of Capitalism: The Crisis of '08 and the Descent into Depression 45–46* (2009); Brian J. M. Quinn, *The Failure of Private Ordering and the Financial Crisis of 2008,* 5 N.Y.U. J.L. and Bus. (2009) 549, 555 (arguing that a root cause of the financial crisis of 2008 was "financial innovation and the corresponding long-term move towards liberalization and self-regulation").
134. Johnson and Kwak, *13 Bankers,* 162.
135. Ibid., 168.
136. Ibid., 164.

3. BANKS WITH A SOUL

1. I refer to these institutions as "banks" even though they are not legally described as banks. They were nonetheless financial intermediaries that gave loans and took deposits. Though they operate much like a bank, they were purposefully not chartered as banks in order to maintain their distinct charters. Thrifts, credit unions, and industrial loan companies retain that technical distinction today.
2. Lee J. Vance, "Banks for the People," *North American Review* 180 (1895): 382–384.
3. J. Carroll Moody and Gilbert Courtland Fite, *The Credit Union Movement: Origins and Development, 1850–1970* (Lincoln: University of Nebraska Press, 1971), 9–11.
4. *New York Times,* April 28, 1869.
5. Moody and Fite, *Credit Union Movement,* 17.
6. Vance, "Banks for the People," 383.
7. "Alphonse Desjardins, II—His Political View," *Ontario Credit Union News,* December 1949, x.
8. Moody and Fite, *Credit Union Movement,* 21–22.
9. Canada, House of Commons, Reports of the Special Committee of the House of Commons, to whom was referred Bill No. 2, An Act Respecting Industrial and Cooperative societies (Ottawa, 1907).
10. "Trip Around the World: Edward A. Filene, 1907," entry February 8, 1907.

11. Moody and Fite, *Credit Union Movement,* 30.
12. Ibid., 34.
13. Ibid., 35.
14. Massachusetts Credit Union Act of 1909, 1909 Mass. Acts 409, sec. 1; The act authorized credit unions to "receive the savings of its members . . . lend to its members at reasonable rates or invest . . . the fund so accumulated; and may undertake such other activities relating to the purpose of the association, as its by-laws may authorize." Ibid., sec. 2.
15. Moody and Fite, *Credit Union Movement,* 37.
16. Ibid., 43.
17. Ibid., 52.
18. Ibid., 75.
19. Bergengren memo, Legislative Activities 1923, Georgia Bankers Associations statement.
20. Edward A. Filene, "Dictation to Edward A. Filene Concerning His Work and Objectives," May 19, 1937, quoted in Moody and Fite, *Credit Union Movement,* 236.
21. Moody and Fite, *Credit Union Movement,* 236.
22. Ibid., 253.
23. Ibid., 93.
24. Ibid., 128–129.
25. Ibid., 94–95.
26. Ibid., 94.
27. Ibid., 220. This legislation was passed in 1936, with the support of President Roosevelt.
28. District of Columbia Credit Unions Act, ch. 272, 47 Stat. 326 (1932); Moody and Fite, *Credit Union Movement,* 135–136.
29. William R. Emmons and Frank A. Schmid, "Credit Unions and the Common Bond," Federal Reserve Bank of St. Louis, 1999, accessed March 12, 2014, research.stlouisfed.org/publications/review/99/09/9909we.pdf; *The Bridge* (June–July, 1929): 6, quoted in Moody and Fite, *Credit Union Movement,* 162.
30. 78 Cong. Rec. 7259–61 (1934) (comments of Senator Sheppard) (noting that credit unions "came through the depression practically without runs or failures"); Federal Credit Union Act, ch. 750, 48 Stat. 1216 (1934).
31. Federal Credit Union Act, ch. 750, 48 Stat. 1216 (1934) §§ 1, 7(6)-(7), 9.
32. Moody and Fite, *Credit Union Movement,* 223.

33. Ibid., 210–211.
34. See Act of Oct. 19, 1970, Pub. L. No. 91–468, § 203(a), 84 Stat. 994, 999–1000 (codified as amended at 12 U.S.C. § 1783 [2006]).
35. 82 Cong. Rec. 358 (1937) (statement of Rep. Steagall).
36. Federal Credit Union Act Amendments, ch. 3, 51 Stat. 4, 4 (1937) (amending section 18 of the Federal Credit Union Act). Studies suggest that traditional banking institutions would need to earn 40 percent more than a credit union to achieve the same level of retained earnings due to the tax exemption. See Donald Novajosky, "From *National Credit Union Administration v. First National Bank and Trust* to the Revised Federal Credit Union Act: The Debate over Membership Requirements in the Credit Union Industry," *New York Law School Law Review* 44 (2000): 221.
37. R. E. Gormley, cochairman of the Bankers Committee for Tax Equality, to *Dear Sir,* June 12, 1956; "Credit Unions, Their Growth Poses Questions," reprint from *American Banker* (May 17, 1956).
38. Federal Credit Union Act, ch. 750, §7, 48 Stat. 1216, 1218 (1934).
39. Ibid.
40. *First National Bank and Trust Co. v. National Credit Union Administration,* 90 F.3d 525, 529–30 (DC Cir. 1996) (quoting *First National Bank and Trust Co. v. National Credit Union Administration,* 988 F.2d 1272, 1276 [DC Cir. 1993]), aff'd, 522 U.S. 479 (1998).
41. Ibid., 530.
42. Moody and Fite, *Credit Union Movement,* appendix.
43. Credit Union National Association, executive committee, minutes from May 1954, 50–51; CUNA directors, minutes 5–7, 47–49, 52, 76–77, 207–215.
44. Moody and Fite, *Credit Union Movement,* 341–342.
45. Ibid., 342. Between 1956 through 1969, credit unions increased by 37 percent while total membership increased by 138 percent.
46. Olin S. Pugh and Franklin J. Ingram, *Credit Unions: A Movement Becomes an Industry,* (Reston, VA: Reston, 1984), 9.
47. The National Credit Union Administration began this process in 1982 by issuing Interpretive Ruling and Policy Statement 82–1, *Membership in Federal Credit Unions,* 47 Fed. Reg. 16,775 (April 20, 1982). It was later replaced by Interpretive Ruling and Policy Statement 82–3, *Membership in Federal Credit Unions,* 47 Fed. Reg. 26,808 (June 22, 1982), which further expanded the common bond requirement.
48. NCUA, *Membership in Federal Credit Unions,* 808.

49. After this expansive interpretation, the membership in credit unions increased by 30 percent from 1982 until 1998. Wendy Cassity, "The Case for a Credit Union Community Reinvestment Act," Columbia Law Review 100, no. 1 (2000): 331. See also Brief for Petitioners, *First National Bank and Trust Co. v. National Credit Union Administration,* 522 U.S. 479 (1998) (nos. 96–843, 96–847), 1997 WL 245673, at *10. The number of credit unions grew fourfold from 1982 until the mid-1990s and combined to control nearly $330 billion in funds from 70 million members. See Dean Foust, "Clipping the Wings of Credit Unions," *Bloomberg Businessweek,* August 25, 1996, accessed March 12, 2014, www.businessweek.com/stories/1996-08-25/clipping-the-wings-of-credit-unions. This growth has been primarily attributed to attracting customers from outside the typical common bond requirement. For example, nearly two-thirds of all the members in the AT&T Family Federal Credit Union do not work for AT&T and are considered to be outside of the company.
50. *First National Bank and Trust Co. v. National Credit Union Administration,* 522 U.S. 479 (1998).
51. *Issues Currently Facing the Credit Union Industry: Hearing before the Subcomm. on Fin. Inst. and Consumer Credit of the H. Comm. on Banking and Fin. Servs.,* 105th Cong. 12, 15–16 (1997) (statement of Norman E. D'Amours, chairman, NCUA).
52. This argument gained traction in Congress partly due to the fact that most credit union members were now middle-class voters, and credit unions had turned into a formidable lobby. "Even before the Supreme Court decision was announced, . . . it was almost inevitable that . . . Congress would amend the FCUA. . . . The typical credit union member—educated, middle-class, mortgage-owning—is also the average voter." Cassity, "Case for a Credit Union," 344 (footnote omitted). See also, *Hearing before the House Committee on Banking and Financial Services: The Supreme Court's February 25, 1998 Decision Regarding the Credit Union Common Bond Requirement,* 105th Cong. 15–16 (1998) (statement of Paul Kanjorski, rep., House Committee on Banking and Financial Services). Bankers still complain about the credit union lobby and its power. See, e.g., Stacy Kaper, "CUs' Deal on Mortgage Bill Irks Bankers," *American Banker,* February 26, 2008, 1.
53. Credit Union Membership Access Act, Pub. L. No. 105–219, 112 Stat. 913 (1998) (codified as amended in scattered sections of 12 U.S.C.); H.R. Rep. No. 105–472, at 1, 18 (1998). See also Cassity, "Case for a

Credit Union," 345, no. 92 (noting that the CUMAA passed 411–8 in the House and 96–2 in the Senate).

54. Credit Union Membership Access Act § 203.
55. George Cleland, "Bank-like Credit Unions Should Face Bank-like Taxes," *ABA Banking Journal,* January 1989, 14, which explains that the origin of the federal credit unions as self-help cooperatives with members sharing a common bond had been rejected for a more inclusive, profitable cooperative; Walter A. Dods Jr., "This Is a Common Bond?," *ABA Banking Journal,* July 1997, 17, which states that "the typical credit union member is more likely to have above-average income and be college-educated and a homeowner—not low-income and underserved by banks."
56. U.S. Government Accountability Office, *Credit Unions: Greater Transparency Needed on Who Credit Unions Serve and on Senior Executive Compensation Arrangements,* 2006, GAO-07–29, 5, 8 (2006); According to a 1996 study by CUNA, credit union members had an average household income of $43,480, whereas nonmembers had an average income of $31,660—a difference of 37 percent. Kelly Culp, "Banks v. Credit Unions: The Turf Struggle for Consumers," *Business Law* 53 (1997): 193, 193–194. And according to the American Banking Association, "Credit union members have more years of education and are more likely to be employed full-time." Ibid., 194, no. 161.
57. Foust, *Clipping the Wings* (quoting Joe G. Howard, senior vice-president at First National Bank and Trust in Asheboro, North Carolina).
58. National Federation of Community Development Credit Unions, "About Us," accessed March 12, 2015, www.cdcu.coop/about-us/.
59. Charles D. Tansey, "Community Development Credit Unions: An Emerging Player in Low Income Communities," *Brookings Institute,* September 2001, accessed March 12, 2015, www.brookings.edu/research/articles/2001/09/metropolitanpolicy-tansey#recent/; Statutory and regulatory efforts have been made to assist these credit unions in fulfilling their mission. Lehn Benjamin et al., "Community Development Financial Institutions: Current Issues and Future Prospects," *Journal of Urban Affairs* 26 (2004): 177, 178–179.
60. They seem to have short life cycles (although this information was based on credit unions up until 1992). In 1966, the Office of Economic Opportunity created over four hundred credit unions. By 1975, only half were still active, and by the 1990s, only 10 percent were left. John

Isbister, *Thin Cats: The Community Development Credit Union Movement in the United States* (Davis, CA: Center for Cooperatives, University of California, 1994) 3, 65.

61. Financial Service Centers of America (FISCA), "Consumer Financial Services Fact Sheet," cited by Christopher S. Fowler, Jane Cover, and Rachel Garshick Kleit, "The Geography of Fringe Banking," *Journal of Regional Science* 54 (2014): 709.
62. National Federation of Community Development Credit Unions, "Member Directory," accessed March 12, 2015, www.cdcu.coop/about-us/member-directory/; Clifford Rosenthal, "Credit Unions, Community Development Finance, and The Great Recession," February 2012:12, 24; Federal Reserve Bank of San Francisco Community Development Investment Center (working paper no. 2012-01, 2012, 25, 33), accessed March 12, 2015, www.frbsf.org/community-development/files/wp2012-011.pdf.
63. See Tansey, "Community Development." Another study of Vermont's Opportunity Credit Union showed that borrowers with little or no credit history were 30 percent less likely to receive auto loans from traditional banks than similarly situated individuals with some credit history. Jessica Holmes et al., "Does Relationship Lending Still Matter in the Consumer Banking Sector? Evidence from the Automobile Loan Market," *Social Science Quarterly* 88 (2007): 585, 595.
64. Marva E. Williams, "The Un-Banks: The Community Development Role of Alternative Depository Institutions," in *Financing Low-Income Communities: Models, Obstacles, and Future Directions,* ed. Julia Sass Rubin (New York: Russell Sage, 2007), 159, 173 (summarizing other studies with similar findings).
65. Garon, *Beyond Our Means: Why America Spends While the World Saves* (Princeton, NJ: Princeton University Press, 2012), 8.
66. Garon, *Beyond Our Means,* 88.
67. Ibid., 31.
68. See generally, James Henry Hamilton, *Savings and Savings Institutions* (New York: Macmillan, 1902), 149–300 (discussing various forms of savings institutions); James H. Manning, *Century of American Savings Banks* (New York: B. F. Buck, 1917), 20–25. Benjamin Franklin, William Defoe, and other civic and religious leaders all espoused the virtue of thrift. Franklin's *Poor Richard's Almanac* was filled with praise for the frugal: "A Man may, if he knows not how to save as he gets, *keep his Nose all his Life to the Grindstone,* and die not worth a *Groat* at last. A *fat Kitchen makes a lean Will . . . If you would be*

wealthy . . . think of Saving as well as Getting." Just as thrift was extolled, the vice of debt was disparaged. Defoe advised against any kind of debt: "If you would know the Value of Money, go and try to borrow some; for he that goes a borrowing goes a sorrowing." Garon, *Beyond Our Means,* 28, 29.

69. Hamilton, *Savings and Savings Institutions,* 161.
70. Donald B. Schewe, "A History of the Postal Savings System in America, 1910–1970," 4–5 (PhD diss., Ohio State University, 1971).
71. Garon, *Beyond Our Means,* 88.
72. Emerson Willard Keyes, *A History of Savings Banks in the United States: From Their Inception in 1816 down to 1874,* vol. 1 (New York: Bradford Rhodes, 1876), 2–4 (emphasis in original).
73. Ibid., 5.
74. Garon, *Beyond Our Means,* 87.
75. Ibid., 90, 91.
76. But ironically, the rise of credit, for example more accessible mortgage loans, increased savings among workers. They now had something to work toward, like a down payment on a home.
77. Keyes, *History of Savings Banks,* 4. In 1820, there were ten savings banks, with a total of 8,635 depositors and an average deposit of $131.86. By 1910, there were 1,759 savings banks with 9,142,908 depositors and an average deposit of $445.20. U.S. Comptroller of the Currency, *Annual Report of the Comptroller of the Currency,* 1910, 47–48.
78. Keyes, *History of Savings Banks,* 49.
79. Garon, *Beyond Our Means,* 95.
80. Massachusetts, General Law 1834, An Act to Regulate Institutions for Savings.
81. Keyes, *History of Savings Banks,* 61.
82. Schewe, "Postal Savings," 7–8.
83. Garon, *Beyond Our Means,* 104.
84. Abram L. Harris, *The Negro as Capitalist: A Study of Banking and Business among American Negroes* (Concord, NH: Rumford Press, 1936), 25.
85. Ibid.
86. Ibid.
87. Frederick Douglass, *Life and Times* (London: Christian Age, 1882), 487.
88. Ibid., 459.
89. Harris, *Negro as Capitalist,* 27.

90. Quoted by Carl R. Osthaus, *Freedmen, Philanthropy, and Fraud: A History of the Freedman's Savings Bank* (Urbana: University of Illinois Press, 1976), 55.
91. Harris, *Negro as Capitalist*, 28.
92. U.S. Senate, 62nd Congress, 2nd Session, Document 759, 4.
93. Douglass, *Life and Times*, 352–353.
94. U.S. Senate, Select Committee on the Freedman's Savings and Trust Co., Report to Accompany bills S.711 and S.1581, S. Rep. No. 46–440, at II (1880).
95. Harris, *Negro as Capitalist*, 31.
96. Specifically, the charter stated that: "Sec. 12. No president, vice-president, trustee, officer or servant of the corporation shall, directly or indirectly, borrow the funds of the corporation or its deposits, or in any manner use the same, or any party thereof, except to pay necessary expenses, under the direction of the board of trustees. . . . Whenever it shall appear that, after the payment of the usual interest to the depositors, there is in the possession of the corporation an excess of profits over the liabilities amounting to ten per centum upon the deposits, such excess shall be invested for the security of the depositors in the corporation; and . . . any surplus . . . [shall] be divided ratably among the depositors in such a manner as the board of trustees shall direct. Sec. 14. The trustees shall not directly or indirectly receive any payment or emolument for their services as such, except the president and vice-president."
97. Report to Accompany Bills S.711 and S.1581, at II.
98. Ibid.
99. For example, section 6 of the charter required the trustees to invest "all sums received by them beyond an available fund not exceeding one third of the total amount of deposits with the corporation, at the discretion of the trustees" in stocks, bonds, Treasury notes, or other U.S. securities. However, the charter did not define "available fund," so it was subject to the trustees' interpretation. Despite this seemingly broad discretion, however, section 3 of the charter only required nine out of fifty trustees to form a quorum, and only "the affirmative vote of at least seven members of the board [was required before] making any order for, or authorizing the investment of any moneys, or the sale or transfer of any stock or securities . . . or the appointment of any officer receiving any salary."
100. Report to Accompany Bills S.711 and S.1581, S. Rep. No. 46–440, Appendix 41; Monique Nelson, "The Freedman's Savings Bank: A

Historical Place in the Financial Empowerment of African Americans," *Department of the Treasury,* February 21, 2014, accessed March 12, 2015, www.treasury.gov/connect/blog/Pages/Freedmans-Savings-Bank .aspx.

101. Nelson, "Freedman's."
102. Douglass, *Life and Times,* 353, 488.
103. U.S. House of Representatives, Select Committee on the Freedman's Bank, H.R. Rep. No. 44–502 (1876), II.
104. Specifically, the amendment stated: "The fifth section of the act entitled 'An act to incorporate the Freedman's Savings and Trust Company' . . . is hereby amended, adding thereto, at the end thereof, the words following: and to the extent of one-half in bonds or notes, secured by mortgage on real estate in double the value of the loan; and the corporation is also authorized hereby to hold and improve the real estate now owned by it in the city of Washington . . . *Provided,* That said corporation shall not use the principal of any deposits made with it for the purpose of such improvement."
105. Harris, *Negro as Capitalist,* 35.
106. U.S. House of Representatives, H.R. Rep. 44–502, VII.
107. Report to Accompany Bills S.711 and S.1581, S. Rep. No. 46–440, III.
108. Douglass, *Life and Times,* 355–356.
109. Ibid., 354.
110. Ibid., 355–356.
111. U.S. House of Representatives, Select Committee on the Freedman's Bank, Freedman's Bank, H.R. Rep. No. 44–502 (1876).
112. W. E. B. Du Bois, *The Souls of Black Folk* (Chicago: A. C. McClurg, 1903), 36.
113. David L. Mason, *From Buildings and Loans to Bail-Outs* (Cambridge: Cambridge University Press, 2004), 16.
114. Hamilton, *Savings and Savings Institutions,* 132–133, 143–144.
115. Joseph Walker and S. K. Cox, *Mutual Benefit Building and Loan Associations: Their History, Principles, and Plan of Operation* (Charleston: Walker and James, 1852), 9.
116. Ibid.
117. Mason, *Buildings and Loans,* 18.
118. Carroll D. Wright, *Ninth Annual Report of the Commissioner of Labor, Building and Loan Associations* (Washington, DC: Government Printing Office, 1894), 280, 316–319, 336. Women made up 25 percent of B&L charter memberships and were specifically sought out because

women were viewed as thrifty and could use their sphere of influence in the home to teach such values to their children.

119. Walker and Cox, *Mutual Benefit Building,* 20–21.

120. Edmund Wrigley, *The Working Man's Way to Wealth* (Philadelphia: J. K. Simon, 1874), 79.

121. J. R. Moorehead, "Are You Selling the Building and Loan Association to the Public?," *Twenty-Eighth Annual Convention of the United States League of Local Building and Loan Associations* (Chicago: American Building Association, 1920), 103–105.

122. Charles K. Clark, "A Review of the Evolution of the Various Premium and Non-Premium Plans," in *The American Savings and Loan Industry: 1831–1935,* vol. 2, ed. David L. Mason 1893, 97.

123. The Knights of Labor, founded in 1869, described themselves as "the great brotherhood" of the working class. It was an inclusive organization that included blacks and women and formed cooperatives allowing the members to increase their financial power in the South. The Knights of Labor would become the Farmers' Alliance, bringing farmers together into cooperatives to gain leverage in negotiations with the railroad and the shipping industries. The group had over three million members by 1890. It was also a Populist political movement that advocated easier access to credit through free coinage of silver. These two groups, along with several other Christian cooperatives, propelled the thrift industry, and because of the grassroots and political nature of these groups, made the B&L a movement with a purpose to improve individual lives and strengthen the democracy. Mason, *Buildings and Loans,* 22–23.

124. Edward L. Rubin, "Communing with Disaster: What We Can Learn from the Jusen and the Savings and Loan Crises," *Law and Policy International Business* 29 (1997): 79, 80–81.

125. Mason, *Buildings and Loans,* 12, 26–28, 40.

126. The National Housing Association (NHA) was created in 1911 to address substandard tenement conditions. Although it did not engage with the B&L at first, it did create cooperative remedial banks that would loan small amounts to the poor with the aim of eventually enabling them to borrow from B&Ls, which lent to the class above the lowest. It saw the B&L as providing an exit from the inner-city slums after the remedial bank attended to the emergency needs of the poor. Mason, *Buildings and Loans,* 42.

127. The inclusion of immigrants into the movement was one of the reasons it advanced so quickly. Immigrants took to the B&Ls because they

formed within a community, allowed membership control and decision-making, and also enabled a soft entry into American life through homeownership and savings. Edward Hartmann, *The Movement to Americanize the Immigrant* (New York: AMS Press, 1967), 8–11.

128. See Mason, *Buildings and Loans,* 78. See also Richard F. Babcock and Fred P. Bosselman, "Suburban Zoning and the Apartment Boom," *University of Pennsylvania Law Review* 111, no. 50 (1963): 1040, 1046; Kenneth A. Stahl, "The Suburb as a Legal Concept: The Problem of Organization and the Fate of Municipalities in American Law," *Cardozo Law Review* 29 (2008): 1193, 1253.
129. Herbert Hoover, commerce secretary, "How to Own Your Own Home" (1923).
130. Stahl, "Suburb as a Legal Concept," 1253; *Miller v. Board of Public Works of L.A.,* 234 P. 381, 387 (Cal. 1925).
131. Mason, *Buildings and Loans,* 107.
132. Ibid., 106–108.
133. Ibid., 78.
134. Herbert Hoover, "Statement about Signing the Federal Home Loan Bank Act," (July 22, 1932).
135. The Home Owners' Loan Act, ch. 64 § 5, 48 Stat. 128 (1933) (current version at 12 U.S.C. § 1467 et seq.); Mason, *Buildings and Loans,* 90–93.
136. The FHLBB was charged with implementing the home loan bank. Its responsibilities included overseeing the federal B&Ls and ensuring that there was enough credit to satisfy the purchasing needs of Americans. Not only did the board have to inject capital into the federal home loan bank system, but as a result of an amendment attached to the Federal Home Loan Bank Act by Senator James Couzens, the FHLBB had to operate a retail mortgage operation. The board struggled with implementing the retail lending service, and in 1933, the Couzens amendment was repealed by the Emergency Mortgage Act of 1933. Mason, *Buildings and Loans,* 86–88, 91–93.
137. The HOLC allowed homeowners to refinance with a lower-interest loan, fixed monthly payments, and long-term amortization. The agency successfully issued more than $3.1 billion in loans, and despite a 20 percent default rate, it eventually turned a profit for the U.S. Treasury.
138. Mason, *Buildings and Loans,* 111–117.
139. Mason, *Buildings and Loans,* 8.
140. Ibid., 16–21, 91.

141. Susan Hoffmann, *Politics and Banking: Ideas, Public Policy, and the Creation of Financial Institutions* (Baltimore: Johns Hopkins University Press, 2001), 43; Mason, *Buildings and Loans,* 12, 17–18.
142. Richard S. Carnell, Jonathan R. Macey, and Geoffrey P. Miller, *The Law of Financial Institutions* (New York: Aspen, 2013), 22.
143. Mason, *Buildings and Loans,* 205.
144. Ibid., 153–154.
145. Garn-St. Germain Depository Institutions Act of 1982, Pub. L. No. 97–320, 96 Stat. 1469 (codified as amended in scattered sections of 12 U.S.C.); Depository Institutions Deregulation and Monetary Control Act of 1980, Pub. L. No. 96–221, 94 Stat. 132 (codified as amended in scattered sections of 12 U.S.C.).
146. Depository Institutions Deregulation and Monetary Control Act §§ 401, 402. See Mason, *Buildings and Loans,* 216.
147. Case note 289 in 12 U.S.C. § 24.
148. Stephen Pizzo, Mary Fricker, and Paul Muolo, *Inside Job: The Looting of America's Savings and Loans* (New York: McGraw-Hill, 1989), 12. See also Depository Institutions Deregulation and Monetary Control Act § 308; Barbara Crutchfield George et al., "The Opaque and Under-Regulated Hedge Fund Industry: Victim or Culprit in the Subprime Mortgage Crisis?," *New York University Journal of Law and Business* 5 (2009): 359, 383.
149. See, generally, Pizzo, Fricker, and Muolo, *Inside Job;* James B. Stewart, *Den of Thieves* (New York: Simon and Schuster, 1991). But see Lawrence J. White, *The S & L Debacle: Public Policy Lessons for Bank and Thrift Regulation* (New York: Oxford University Press, 1991), 117.
150. Implementation of New Powers; Limitation on Loans to One Borrower, 48 Fed. Reg. 23,032, 23,061, 23,070 (May 23, 1983) (codified at 12 C.F. R. §§ 545.33, .75 (1984)); Garn-St. Germain Depository Institutions Act of 1982, Pub. L. No. 97–320, 96 Stat. 1469 (codified at 12 U.S.C. § 226).
151. See Vikas Bajaj, "Mortgage Defaults Reach a New High," *New York Times,* March 6, 2008, accessed March 12, 2015, www.nytimes.com/2008/03/06/business/06cnd-mortgage.html?_r=0; Steve Denning, "Lest We Forget: Why We Had a Financial Crisis," *Forbes,* November 11, 2011, accessed March 12, 2015, www.forbes.com/sites/stevedenning/2011/11/22/5086/.
152. White, *S & L Debacle,* 118–119 (asking, "Where did the money go?").

153. See Competitive Equality Banking Act of 1987, Pub. L. No. 100–86, 101 Stat. 552 (codified as amended in scattered sections of 12 U.S.C.); Arthur E. Wilmarth Jr., "The Expansion of State Bank Powers, the Federal Response, and the Case for Preserving the Dual Banking System," *Fordham Law Review* 58 (1990): 1133, 1245–1247; U.S. Government Accountability Office, *Financial Audit: Resolution Trust Corporation's 1995 and 1994 Financial Statements*, GAO/AIMD-96–123, 9–10 (1996).
154. Daniel Brumbaugh, *Thrifts under Siege* (Cambridge: Ballinger, 1988), 173.
155. Chicago Public Radio, "The Watchmen," *This American Life*, June 5, 2009, accessed September 24, 2014, www.thisamericanlife.org/radio-archives/episode/382/the-watchmen.
156. See Jennifer Taub, *Other People's Houses* (New Haven, CT: Yale University Press, 2014), 277–278. It discusses the Levin-Coburn Report, which "included more than eighty pages focused exclusively on the regulatory failure at . . . the OTS."
157. James Grant, *Money of the Mind: Borrowing and Lending in America from the Civil War to Michael Milken* (New York: Farrar, Straus and Giroux, 1992), 92–95.
158. Ibid., 92.
159. Peter W. Herzog, *The Morris Plan of Industrial Banking* (Chicago: A.W. Shaw Company, 1928), 12–13. Testifying before Congress, Morris repeatedly explained his desire to supply credit to the poor and working classes. *House Committee on Banking and Currency, Control and Regulation of Bank Holding Companies: Hearings on H.R. 2674*, 84th Cong. 585 (1955); *Senate Subcommittee on Banking and Currency, Providing for Control and Regulation of Bank Holding Companies: Hearings on S. 829*, 80th Cong. 98 (1947) (statement of Arthur J. Morris, chairman of the board, Morris Plan Corporation of America); *Joint Subcommittees of the Committees on Banking and Currency, Rural Credits: Joint Hearings before the Subcomms. of the Comms. on Banking and Currency of the S. and of the H.R. Charged with the Investigation of Rural Credits*, 63d Cong. 717 (1914) (statement of Arthur J. Morris).
160. *The Morris Plan of Industrial Loans and Investments* (New York: Industrial Finance, 1915), 10.
161. Grant, *Money of the Mind*, 92.
162. Herzog, *Morris Plan*, 17.

163. O. Emre Ergungor and James B. Thomson, Federal Reserve Bank of Cleveland, *Industrial Loan Companies,* economic comment, October 2006, accessed September 24, 2014, www.clevelandfed.org/research/commentary/2006/1001.pdf.
164. A borrower (with her cosigners) agrees to a loan at a certain interest rate, and rather than repaying the loan directly, the borrower further agrees to deposit equal sums of money into a savings account over the term of the loan (alternatively, the borrower could agree to purchase a certain amount of installment certificates at certain periods over the term of the loan). At the end of the term, the borrower makes a "lump sum" payment by transferring the savings to the Morris Bank or by liquidating the installment certificates. Morris R. Neifeld, *Neifeld's Manual on Consumer Credit* (Easton, PA: Mack Publishing, 1961), 372. Herzog, *Morris Plan,* 42.
165. Neifeld, *Neifeld's Manual,* 371. See also Louis N. Robinson, "The Morris Plan," *American Economic Review* 21 (1931): 222–223; Morris, *Industrial Loans and Investments,* 51.
166. "Inventory of the Papers of Arthur J. Morris: Biographical Sketch," *University of Virginia Law School,* accessed September 30, 2014, www.law.virginia.edu/main/Morris,+Arthur+J.
167. Grant, *Money of the Mind,* 92. See also Ralph N. Larson, "The Future of Installment Banking," *Industrial Banker,* August 1962, 12.
168. Morris, *Industrial Loans and Investments,* 8.
169. Grant, *Money of the Mind,* 94, 95.
170. It is worth noting that the credit life insurance offered by Morris plan banks has evolved into a predatory product with extremely low value. In a Senate hearing available at www.gpo.gov/fdsys/pkg/CHRG-107shrg82969/html/CHRG-107shrg82969.htm, accessed March 12, 2015, Paul Satriano explains his unfortunate experience with credit insurance. After taking out a mortgage on his home and subsequently refinancing it with Beneficial, Satriano was led to believe that he would be able to pay off his $7,000 of credit card debt. The refinanced loan from Beneficial, however, only covered $1,200 of his credit card debt, exceeded the promised interest rate, and cost him $10,000 in fees, including $5,000 in credit insurance. In that same report, Senator Paul Sarbanes describes predatory lending as the targeting of people with substantial consumer and credit card debt who usually are facing a crunch. The lenders underwrite the borrowers' property irrespective of their ability to repay and "make their money by charging extremely high origination fees and by packing other products into the loan,

including upfront premiums for credit life, disability, and unemployment insurance, and others, for which they get significant commissions right at the outset, but for which homeowners continue to pay for years since it is folded into the mortgage." The problem with packing these additional products into the loan amount is that it strips equity and can lead to foreclosure. A report by the Consumers Union and the Center for Economic Justice noted that consumers of credit insurance are overcharged by roughly $2 billion per year.

171. Raymond J. Saulnier, *Industrial Banking Companies and Their Credit Practices* (New York: National Bureau of Economic Research, 1940), 28, 30, 52.
172. Ibid., 1.
173. Ibid., 132, 172. By 1938, Saulnier's study claimed that the sector was lending to clerical or office workers at a higher proportion than wage earners based on the total population. Still, the sector issued proportionally more loans to wage earners than banks. Ibid., 177.
174. Ibid., 161, 167.
175. Ibid., 175. By 1937, industrial banks issued only 1 percent of the market in installment credit.
176. Lendol Calder, *Financing the American Dream: A Cultural History of Consumer Credit* (Princeton, NJ: Princeton University Press, 1999), 361.
177. Neifeld, *Neifeld's Manual,* 380.
178. See *House Committee on Banking and Currency, Control and Regulation of Bank Holding Companies Hearings on H.R. 2674,* 84th Cong. 585, 578 (1955).
179. Morris Plan Bankers Convention, 105 Bankers' Mag. 924, 924 (1922).
180. Though their interest is less than payday lenders, the industry has not attracted much regulatory attention because of its relatively small size and established business in regions like the South. www.propublica.org/article/installment-loans-world-finance, accessed March 12, 2015. "Installment loans can be deceptively expensive. World and its competitors push customers to renew their loans over and over again, transforming what the industry touts as a safe, responsible way to pay down debt into a kind of credit card with sky-high annual rates, sometimes more than 200 percent. And when state laws force the companies to charge lower rates, they often sell borrowers unnecessary insurance products that rarely provide any benefit to the consumer but can effectively double the loan's annual percentage rate. Former World employees say they were instructed not to tell

customers the insurance is voluntary. When borrowers fall behind on payments, calls to the customer's home and workplace, as well as to friends and relatives, are routine. Next come home visits. And as Sutton and many others have discovered, World's threats to sue its customers are often real." Ibid.

181. U.S. Government Accountability Office, *Industrial Loan Corporations: Recent Asset Growth and Commercial Interest Highlight Differences in Regulatory Authority,* GAO-05–621, 17 (2005) (explaining that owning a bank exempt from the BHCA prior to CEBA would allow these banks to escape certain regulations).
182. Pursuant to CEBA, an ILC is not a "bank" for purposes of the BHCA if it meets one of the following conditions: "(1) the institution does not accept demand deposits, (2) the institution's total assets are less than $100,000,000, or (3) control of the institution has not been acquired by any company after August 10, 1987." Mindy West, "The FDIC's Supervision of Industrial Loan Companies: A Historical Perspective," (2004), 5, 9, accessed March 12, 2015, www.fdic.gov/regulations/examinations/supervisory/insights/sisum04/sisum04.pdf. See also Competitive Equality Banking Act of 1987, Pub. L. No. 100–86, § 101, 101 Stat. 552 (1987) (defining banks as institutions insured by the FDIC or that accept demand deposits and make commercial loans).
183. Randall Dodd, Fin. Policy Forum, Special Policy Report 13, "Industrial Loan Banks: Regulatory Loopholes as Big as a Wal-Mart," 2006, 7–8, accessed March 12, 2015, www.financialpolicy.org/fpfspr13.pdf. Commercial firms could also buy qualified credit card banks, trust companies, and a single "unitary" S&L.
184. West, "FDIC's Supervision," 8.
185. Dodd, "Industrial Loan Banks," 3.
186. Kenneth Spong and Eric Robbins, "Industrial Loan Companies: A Growing Industry Sparks a Public Policy Debate," Federal Reserve Bank of Kansas City, accessed March 12, 2014, www.kc.frb.org/publicat/econrev/pdf/4q07spong.pdf, 46. ; U.S. Government Accountability Office, *Industrial Loan Corporations: Recent Asset Growth and Commercial Interest Highlight Differences in Regulatory Authority,* 5; *House Committee on Financial Services, Industrial Bank Holding Company Act of 2007: Hearing on H.R. 698,* 110th Cong. 1 (2007) (statement of Donald L. Kohn, vice chairman, board of governors of the Federal Reserve System), accessed March 12, 2015, archives.financialservices.house.gov/hearing110/htkohn042507.pdf.
187. Dodd, "Industrial Loan Banks," 311.

188. Spong and Robbins, "Industrial Loan Companies," 46; Federal Reserve, "Bulletin Report on the Condition of the U.S. Banking Industry: Third Quarter" 2005, accessed May 15, 2010, www.federalreserve.gov/pubs/bulletin/2006/bank_condition/default.htm.
189. FDIC, "Internet Archive of Wal-Mart Bank Federal Deposit Insurance Application," accessed February 28, 2009, www.fdic.gov/regulations/laws/federal/06notices.html.
190. Moratorium on Certain Industrial Bank Applications and Notices, 72 Fed. Reg. 5290 (February 5, 2007); Parija B. Kavilanz, "Wal-Mart Withdraws Industrial Banking Push," *CNNMoney,* March 16, 2007, accessed March 12, 2015, www.money.cnn.com/2007/03/16/news/companies/walmart/index.htm.
191. See ICBA Letter, "The Perils of Walmart," accessed March 12, 2015, www.icba.org/publications/NewsletterDetailMemberUpdate.cfm?itemnumber=15740&pf=1.
192. Carolyn Whelan, "Wal-Mart Gets Its Bank—In Mexico," *CNNMoney,* January 29, 2008, accessed March 12, 2015, www.money.cnn.com/2008/01/28/news/international/walmart_bank.fortune/index.htm.

4. HOW THE OTHER HALF BORROWS

1. Courts will not enforce contracts that run counter to public policy or are not allowed by law, such as selling babies, organs, cocaine, or human slaves.
2. This is not to say that human civilization was ever free of usury. In fact, predatory lending has been present ever since human societies have existed but has generally operated on the fringe of society within a sphere of corruption, violence, and stigma. David Graeber, *Debt: The First 5000 Years* (Brooklyn, NY: Melville House 2011), 10–11.
3. Ronald W. Del Sesto, "Should Usury Statutes Be Used to Solve the Installment Sales 'Problem?,'" *Boston College Law Review* 5, no. 7 (1964): 389, 390.
4. L. C. Jain, *Indigenous Banking in India* (London: Macmillan, 1929). Vasishtha, a well-known Hindu lawmaker of that time, made a special law that forbade the higher castes of *brahmanas* (priests) and *kshatriyas* (warriors) from being usurers or lenders at interest.
5. Neh. 5:12 NIV.
6. See, generally, Michael Hudson, "The Lost Tradition of Biblical Debt Cancellations" (PhD diss., New York University, 1993), accessed

March 17, 2015, michael-hudson.com/wp-content/uploads/2010/03/HudsonLostTradition.pdf.

7. Yaron Brook, "The Morality of Moneylending: A Short History," *The Objective Standard* 2, no. 3 (2007), accessed March 17, 2015, www.theobjectivestandard.com/issues/2007-fall/morality-of-moneylending/.
8. Ibid.
9. "The Parable of the Unmerciful Servant," Matt. 18:21–35 NIV.
10. Jacques Le Goff, *Your Money or Your Life* (New York: Zone Books, 1988), 23, 26; Brook, "Morality of Moneylending."
11. Judith Civan, *Abraham's Knife: The Mythology of the Deicide in Anti-Semitism* (Bloomington, IN: Xlibris, 2004), 267.
12. Paul M. Johnson, *A History of the Jews* (New York: Harper and Row, 1987), 242.
13. Roger Ruston, "Does It Matter What We Do with Our Money?," *Priests and People,* May 1993, 173–174.
14. Iacopo Scaramuzzi, "Francis: Usury is not Human. It is a Social Evil." January 2014, *Vatican Insider*, http://vaticaninsider.lastampa.it/en/the-vatican/detail/articolo/31630/.
15. Jeremy Rifkin, *The European Dream* (New York: Penguin, 2004), 105.
16. Shaikh Mahmud Ahmad, *Economics of Islam: A Comparative Study* (Lahore: Ashraft, 1958), 25.
17. Jain, *Indigenous Banking,* 110–111.
18. Masudul Alam Choudhury and Uzir Abdul Malik, *The Foundations of Islamic Political Economy* (London: St. Martin's Press, 1992), 51.
19. Humanity lives in time, so our "sin is a debt of punishment we owe to God. But God lives outside time. By definition, he cannot owe anything to anyone." David Graeber, *Debt: The First 5,000 Years* (New York: Melville House, 2011), 286.
20. Ibid., 403 n.25 and accompanying text, pointing out that both "debt" and "sin" are translations of the Aramaic "hoyween" and the Greek "opheilema" used in Biblical sources.
21. Ibid., 407 n.59.
22. J. M. Jadlow, "Adam Smith on Usury Laws," *Journal of Finance* 32 (1977): 1195–1200.
23. John Maynard Keynes, *A General Theory of Employment, Interest and Money* (New York: Harcourt, Brace, 1936), 352.
24. Aristotle, *The Politics of Aristotle,* revised edition, trans. Benjamin Jowett (New York: Colonial Press, 1899), 16.
25. Brook, "Morality of Moneylending."

26. See, e.g., Philip Swagel, "The Financial Crisis: An Inside View" (working paper, Brookings Institute, Spring 2009, 21), accessed March 17, 2015, www.brookings.edu/~/media/Projects/BPEA/Spring-2009/2009a_bpea_swagel.PDF. "Many were unwilling to put public money on the line to prevent additional foreclosures, because any such program would inevitably involve a bailout of some "irresponsible" homeowners. Put more cynically, spending public money on foreclosure avoidance would be asking responsible taxpayers to subsidize people living in McMansions they could not afford, with flat-screen televisions paid for out of their home equity line of credit." Ibid.
27. John Tamny, "The Ongoing and Hideous Lie about 'Victimized' Mortgage Holders," *Forbes*, March 2013, accessed March 17, 2015, www.forbes.com/sites/johntamny/2013/03/05/the-ongoing-and-hideous-lie-about-victimized-mortgage-walkers/.
28. CNBC "Squawk Box," quoted in "Rick Santelli: Tea Party," *Freedom Eden*, February 19, 2009, accessed January 18, 2015, freedomeden.blogspot.com/2009/02/rick-santelli-tea-party.html.
29. Matt Taibbi, "The Great American Bubble Machine," *Rolling Stone*, April 5, 2010, accessed June 4, 2015, www.rollingstone.com/politics/news/the-great-american-bubble-machine-20100405; John Cassidy, "Wall Street Protests: Signs of the Times," *New Yorker*, October 6, 2011, accessed March 17, 2015, www.newyorker.com/news/john-cassidy/wall-street-protests-signs-of-the-times.
30. See, e.g., Jim Puzzanghera, "Timothy Geithner Unapologetic in Memoir of the Financial Crisis," *L.A. Times*, May 15, 2014, accessed March 17, 2015, www.latimes.com/books/jacketcopy/la-et-jc-timothy-geithner-20140515-story.html#page=1.
31. "Many states dismantled their usury laws in the 1980s as a result [of the proliferation of adjustable rate mortgages]." See Charles R. Geisst, *Beggar Thy Neighbor: A History of Usury and Debt* (Philadelphia: University of Pennsylvania Press, 2013), 258.
32. Christopher Peterson, *Taming the Sharks* (Akron, OH: University of Akron Press, 2004), 108. Today, the states with the highest average interest rates are Idaho at 582 percent APR, South Dakota and Wisconsin at 574 percent APR, Nevada at 521 percent APR, Delaware at 517 percent APR, and Utah at 474 percent APR. Center for Responsible Lending, "Effective State and Federal Payday Lending Enforcement: Paving the Way for Broader, Stronger Protections," *CRL Issue Brief*, October 4, 2013, accessed January 18, 2015, www.responsiblelending.org/payday-lending/research-analysis

/State-Enforcement-Issue-Brief-10-4-FINAL-fix.pdf. The five lowest are: Colorado (129 percent), Oregon (156 percent), Washington (192 percent), Maine (217 percent), and Minnesota (252 percent).

33. See Nathalie Martin and Joshua Schwartz, "The Alliance between Payday Lenders and Tribes: Are Both Tribal Sovereignty and Consumer Protection at Risk?," *Washington and Lee Law Review* 69 (2012).
34. Graeber, *Debt,* 376.
35. Federal Reserve Bank of New York, "Total Household Debts," *The Center for Microeconomic Data,* accessed September 29, 2014, www.newyorkfed.org/microeconomics/hhdc.html; Tim Chen, "American Household Credit Card Debt Statistics: 2014," *NerdWallet Finance,* accessed September 29, 2014, www.nerdwallet.com/blog/credit-card-data/average-credit-card-debt-household/; Over 60 percent of small businesses are funded through loans and over 90 percent use credit cards, even though 20 percent of them fail within the first year. Federal Reserve Board of Governors, *Report to the Congress on the Availability of Credit to Small Businesses,* (September 2012), 2, 17, accessed March 17, 2015, www.federalreserve.gov/publications/other-reports/files/sbfreport2012.pdf; The average large commercial firm had $650 billion in debt in 2014. Federal Reserve Board of Governors, *Assets and Liabilities of Commercial Banks in the United States,* accessed January 18, 2015, www.federalreserve.gov/releases/h8/current/default.htm#fn1; In 2008, Lehman brothers buckled under approximately that much debt without anyone accusing these high level bankers of not understanding basic finance. Sam Mamudi, "Lehman Folds with Record $613 Billion Debt," *MarketWatch,* September 15, 2008, accessed March 17, 2015, www.marketwatch.com/story/lehman-folds-with-record-613-billion-debt.
36. I have limited the scope of state control to the banking sphere, where state support is obvious and tangible. Others would extend it further, claiming that the state enables all markets. Anthropologist David Graeber highlights the compelling case that credit and debt markets have always been enabled by states. Graeber, *Debt,* 54–55. And, that there are no markets independent of state control and that debt and credit, therefore, are only possible through state control. This book does not need to go that far to prove its central point.
37. Heather Morton, "NCSL Payday Lending State Statutes," September 12, 2013, accessed March 17, 2015, www.ncsl.org/research/financial-services-and-commerce/payday-lending-state-statutes.aspx; Consumer Federation of America, "Payday Loan Consumer Informa-

tion: Legal Status of Payday Loans by State," accessed September 29, 2014, www.paydayloaninfo.org/state-information.

38. The CFPB sample size was 12 million loans in 2013. "Payday Loans and Deposit Advance Products," *CFPB White Paper,* 23, April 24, 2013, accessed March 17, 2015, files.consumerfinance.gov/f/201304_cfpb_payday-dap-whitepaper.pdf.
39. Kathleen Burke et al., "CFPB Data Point: Payday Lending," March 25, 2014, accessed March 17, 2015, files.consumerfinance.gov/f/201403_cfpb_report_payday-lending.pdf.
40. Ibid., 12.
41. Center for Responsible Lending, "Fast Facts: Payday Loans," accessed September 29, 2014, www.responsiblelending.org/payday-lending/tools-resources/fast-facts.html.
42. Pew Charitable Trusts, "Payday Lending in America: Who Borrows, Where They Borrow, and Why," July 2012, 4, accessed March 17, 2015, www.pewtrusts.org/~/media/legacy/uploadedfiles/pcs_assets/2012/PewPaydayLendingReportpdf.pdf. The CFPB found that the average consumer had over ten transactions over a twelve-month period and paid a total of $574 in fees, which does not include the loan principal.
43. "On average, a payday loan takes 36 percent of a person's pre-tax paycheck, Bourke [project director at Pew] said." "States with Highest, Lowest Payday Loan Rates," *USA Today,* April 20, 2014, accessed March 17, 2015, www.usatoday.com/story/money/personal finance/2014/04/20/id-nv-ut-have-among-highest-payday-loan-rates/7943519/.
44. Richard Cordray, "Remarks at the Payday Field Hearing," March 25, 2014, accessed March 17, 2015, www.consumerfinance.gov/newsroom/director-richard-cordray-remarks-at-the-payday-field-hearing/.
45. CFPB, "Ask CFPB: What Is a Payday Loan?," accessed September 29, 2014, www.consumerfinance.gov/askcfpb/1567/what-payday-loan.html.
46. Ibid.
47. According to a study done by the Center for Responsible Lending, the median loan-to-value ratio among borrowers is 26 percent. In other words, the loan received is worth less than a third of the collateral. Susanna Montezemolo, "The State of Lending in America and its Impact on U.S. Households: Car-Title Lending," *Center for Responsible Lending,* July 2013, 3, accessed March 17, 2015, www.responsiblelending.org/state-of-lending/reports/7-Car-Title-Loans.pdf.

48. Ibid., 16 (explaining the difference between title and payday loans). See also Delvin Davis et al., "Driven to Disaster: Car-Title Lending and Its Impact on Consumers," *Center for Responsible Lending,* February 28, 2013, 2, accessed March 17, 2015, www.responsiblelending.org/other-consumer-loans/car-title-loans/research-analysis/CRL-Car-Title-Report-FINAL.pdf (with similar but not identical figures).
49. Ibid.; States that allow car-title lending include Alabama, Arizona, California, Delaware, Georgia, Kansas, Louisiana, Idaho, Illinois, Mississippi, Missouri, Nevada, New Mexico, South Carolina, South Dakota, Tennessee, Texas, Utah, Virginia, and Wisconsin. Center for Responsible Lending, "Car Title Lending by State," accessed March 17, 2015, www.responsiblelending.org/other-consumer-loans/car-title-loans/tools-resources/car-title-lending-by-state.html.
50. Jim Hawkins, "Credit on Wheels: The Law and Business of Auto-Title Lending," *Washington and Lee Law Review* 69 (2012): 535, 536, accessed March 17, 2015, scholarlycommons.law.wlu.edu/cgi/viewcontent.cgi?article=4272&context=wlulr.
51. Davis et al., "Driven to Disaster," 2.
52. Michael Corkery and Jessica Silver-Greenberg. "Miss a Payment? Good Luck Moving that Car," *New York Times Dealbook,* September 24, 2014, accessed March 17, 2015, dealbook.nytimes.com/2014/09/24/miss-a-payment-good-luck-moving-that-car/.
53. The United States also had charitable pawn institutions: The Provident Loan Society, established in 1894 with $100,000 provided by the richest men in New York City, was a charitable organization that aimed to "relieve distress through enlightened and liberal lending but also, through competition, to force lower margins on profit-making pawnbrokers." By 1919, it was making more loans than any domestic savings bank with a policy "first, to make small and costly loans and, only second, to make large and profitable ones. It made loans of as little as one dollar [that required minimal collateral]." The fund's humanity was in stark contrast to the pawnbrokers at the time, but due to the nature of the bank's loans, "the truly indigent, almost by definition, were excluded, as they had nothing to pawn." James Grant, *Money of the Mind: How the 1980s Got That Way* (New York: Farrar, Straus and Giroux, 1992), 77, 85, 87.
54. David K. Randall, "Taxes: Why 'Rapid Refunds' Are Rip-Offs," *Forbes,* February 9, 2010, accessed March 17, 2015, www.forbes.com/2010/02/09/taxes-rapid-refund-personal-finance-refund-anticipation-loans.html.

55. Consumer Financial Protection Bureau, "Nashville, TN: Field Hearing on Payday Loans," March 2014, accessed March 17, 2015, youtu.be/ZpnXG0UdeoQ; CFPB, "Payday Loans and Deposit Advance Products," April 24, 2013, 15; *CFPB White Paper of Initial Data Findings,* accessed March 17, 2015, files.consumerfinance.gov/f/201304_cfpb_payday-dap-whitepaper.pdf; Susan Urahn et al., "Payday Lending in America: Who Borrows, Where They Borrow, and Why," *Pew Charitable Trust,* 2012, 32, accessed March 17, 2015, www.pewtrusts.org/~/media/legacy/uploadedfiles/pcs_assets/2012/PewPaydayLendingReportpdf.pdf.
56. FDIC, "National Survey of Unbanked and Underbanked Households," *Executive Summary,* September 2012, 5, accessed March 17, 2015, www.fdic.gov/householdsurvey/2012_unbankedreport_execsumm.pdf; Gregory Elliehausen and Edward C. Lawrence, "Payday Advance Credit in America: An Analysis of Consumer Demand," Georgetown University McDonough School of Business Credit Research, monograph no. 35, 2001, 28, 33, accessed March 17, 2015, www.fdic.gov/bank/analytical/cfr/2005/jan/CFRSS_2005_elliehausen.pdf.
57. John P. Caskey, "Payday Lending: New Research and the Big Question" (working paper no. 10-32, Federal Reserve Bank of Philadelphia, October 2010), accessed March 17, 2015, www.philadelphiafed.org/research-and-data/publications/working-papers/2010/wp10-32.pdf; Financial Service Centers of America, "Consumer Financial Services Fact Sheet," cited in Christopher S. Fowler et al., "The Geography of Fringe Banking," *Journal of Regional Science* 54 (2014): 690.
58. Pew Charitable Trusts, "Payday Lending in America, Report 2: How Borrowers Choose and Repay Payday Loans," February 2013, 6, accessed March 17, 2015, www.pewtrusts.org/~/media/Assets/2013/02/20/Pew_Choosing_Borrowing_Payday_Feb2013-(1).pdf.
59. Ibid., 7.
60. The Pew survey found that "sixty-nine percent of first-time payday borrowers used the loan to cover a recurring expense, such as utilities, credit card bills, rent or mortgage payments, or food, while 16 percent dealt with an unexpected expense, such as a car repair or emergency medical expense." Ibid., 8. However, the loan may have gone to pay for basics that would have been met by funds diverted to pay for such unexpected events. Thus, these potentially are not loans that people subsist on.

61. Federal Reserve System, Board of Governors, "Supplemental Appendix to the Report on the Economic Well-Being of U.S. Households in 2013," July 2014, 5, accessed March 17, 2015, www.federalreserve.gov/econresdata/2013-report-economic-well-being-us-households-supplemental-appendix-201407.pdf; A 2011 National Bureau of Economic Research study showed about half of households surveyed reported that they couldn't come up with $2,000 within thirty days in a pinch, even if they turned to relatives for help. Annamaria Lusardi et al., "Financially Fragile Households: Evidence and Implications," (NBER working paper no. 17072, May 2011), accessed March 17, 2015, www.nber.org/papers/w17072; A 2011 FDIC survey put 29.3 percent of households without a savings account. FDIC, "Unbanked and Underbanked Households," 3.
62. Dan Mangan, "Medical Bills Are the Biggest Cause of U.S. Bankruptcies: Study," CNBC, June 25, 2013, accessed March 17, 2015, www.cnbc.com/id/100840148.
63. Federal Reserve Board of Governors, "Report on the Economic Well-Being of U.S. Households in 2013," accessed March 17, 2015, www.federalreserve.gov/econresdata/2013-report-economic-well-being-us-households-201407.pdf; www.nytimes.com/2014/12/04/business/unsteady-incomes-keep-millions-of-workers-behind-on-bills-.html, accessed March 17, 2015.
64. Neil Bhutta, Paige Marta Skiba, and Jeremy Tobacman, "Payday Loan Choices and Consequences," *Journal of Money, Credit, and Banking* (forthcoming), 14, accessed March 17, 2015, http://assets.wharton.upenn.edu/~tobacman/papers/Payday%20Loan%20Choices%20and%20Consequences.pdf.
65. Caskey, "Payday Lending"; Elliehausen "Payday Advance Credit," 45–46.
66. Applied Management and Panning Group, *2007 Department of Corporations Payday Loan Study,* Report Submitted to California Department of Corporations, December 2007, 57.
67. For discussion of the muddled empirical evidence, see Annamaria Lusardi and Olivia S. Mitchell, "The Economic Importance of Financial Literacy: Theory and Evidence," *Journal of Economic Literature* 52 (2014): 5, accessed March 17, 2015, www.umass.edu/preferen/You%20Must%20Read%20This/Financial%20Literacy%20JEP%202014.pdf.

68. For example, see Discover's balance transfer offers, www.discover.com/credit-cards/member-benefits/balance-transfer.html, accessed March 17, 2015.
69. Comments received in response to this request for information are available for review at www.regulations.gov/#!searchResults;rpp=25;po=0;s=cfpb-2012-0009, accessed March 17, 2015.
70. Pew Charitable Trusts, "Payday Lending in America, Report 2: How Borrowers Choose and Repay Loans," February 2013, 9.
71. Dave Ramsey, "A Game You'll Never Win: The Payday Loan Trap," accessed March 17, 2015, www.daveramsey.com/blog/get-out-payday-loan-trap.btxt?atid=davesays.
72. Liz Weston, "Five Stupid 'Solutions' to Money Woes," *MSN Money,* accessed October 26, 2012, money.msn.com/personal-finance/5-stupid-solutions-to-money-woes.
73. Sheyna Steiner, "Seven Brainless Borrowing Behaviors," *Bankrate,* accessed March 17, 2015, www.bankrate.com/finance/financial-literacy/7-brainless-borrowing-behaviors-1.aspx.
74. Rich White, "Don't Fear the 401(k) Loan," *Forbes,* September 2, 2008, accessed March 17, 2015, www.forbes.com/2008/09/02/401k-loan-borrowing-pf-education-in_rw_0902investopedia_inl.html; Amy Fontinelle, "Four Smart Moves for Using Home Equity," *Interest.com,* November 7, 2014, accessed March 17, 2015, www.interest.com/home-equity/news/4-smart-moves-for-using-home-equity; Rande Spiegelman, "Borrow Smart: How to Use Debt Wisely," March 20, 2014, accessed March 17, 2015, www.schwab.com/public/schwab/nn/articles/Borrow-Smart-How-to-Use-Debt-Wisely; During the housing bubble, many people "flipped houses" by putting up very little down payment, waiting for the price to increase, and selling the house at high profits. There were even TV shows like "Flip This House" that encouraged the middle class to make easy money by using debt. A&E, "Flip This House," 2005–2009, accessed March 17, 2015, www.aetv.com/flip-this-house/video.
75. Investopedia, "Leveraged Buyout—LBO: Definition," accessed March 17, 2015, www.investopedia.com/terms/l/leveragedbuyout.asp.
76. Lloyd B. Thomas, *The Financial Crisis and Federal Reserve Policy* (New York: Palgrave Macmillan, 2011), 87.
77. See Anat R. Admati, "We're All Still Hostages to the Big Banks," *New York Times,* August 25, 2013, accessed March 17, 2015, www.nytimes.com/2013/08/26/opinion/were-all-still-hostages-to-the-big-banks.html

?pagewanted=all&_r=1& (highlighting lobbyists' success in preventing substantial reforms in the U.S. and Germany); Anat Admati and Martin Hellwig, *The Banker's New Clothes: What's Wrong with Banking and What to Do about It* (Princeton, NJ: Princeton University Press, 2013), 15.

78. *Bearden v. Georgia,* 461 U.S. 660, 103 S. Ct. 2064 (1983).
79. Joseph Shapiro, "Supreme Court Ruling Not Enough to Prevent Debtors Prisons," *NPR: Morning Edition,* May 21, 2014, accessed March 17, 2015, www.npr.org/2014/05/21/313118629/supreme-court-ruling-not-enough-to-prevent-debtors-prisons.
80. Katie McDonough, "Woman Dies in Jail While Serving Sentence for Her Kids' Unpaid School Fines," *Salon,* June 12, 2014, accessed March 17, 2015, www.salon.com/2014/06/12/woman_dies_in_jail_while_serving_sentence_for_her_kids_unpaid_school_fines.
81. Matt Taibbi, "Why Isn't Wall Street in Jail?," *Rolling Stone,* February 16, 2011, accessed March 17, 2015, www.rollingstone.com/politics/news/why-isnt-wall-street-in-jail-20110216; Kareem Serageldin, a former Credit Suisse executive, was sent to jail for embezzling "hundreds of millions in losses in Credit Suisse's mortgage-backed securities portfolio" and sentenced to jail time in a minimum security prison. A *New York Times* article called Serageldin the "only Wall Street executive sent to jail for his part in the financial crisis," but his crime was run-of-the mill fraud and his conviction happened eight years after the crisis. Jesse Eisinger, "Why Only One Top Banker Went to Jail for the Financial Crisis," *New York Times Magazine,* April 30, 2014, accessed March 17, 2015, www.nytimes.com/2014/05/04/magazine/only-one-top-banker-jail-financial-crisis.html?_r=0.
82. Sheldon Garon, *Beyond Our Means: Why Americans Spend While the World Saves* (Princeton, NJ: Princeton University Press, 2012), 1–15.
83. Andrew J. Bacevich, "He Told Us to Go Shopping. Now the Bill Is Due," *Washington Post,* October 5, 2008, accessed March 17, 2015, www.washingtonpost.com/wp-dyn/content/article/2008/10/03/AR2008100301977.html.
84. Peterson, *Taming the Sharks,* 24; Ronald J. Mann and Jim Hawkins, "Just Until Payday," *UCLA Law Review* 54 (2007): 855, 857.
85. Caskey, "Fringe Banking," 6; Elliehausen and Lawrence, "Payday Advance Credit," 2.
86. Joe Mahon, "Tracking 'Fringe Banking': The Location of Alternative Financial Services in the District Shows That They Serve a Distinct

Need," *Federal Gazette,* September 2008, 18, accessed March 17, 2015, www.minneapolisfed.org/publications_papers/pub_display.cfm?id=4030.

87. Caskey, "Fringe Banking," 3.
88. Alex Kaufman, "Payday Lending Regulation," *Finance and Economic Discussion Series,* August 15, 2013, 4, accessed March 17, 2015, www.federalreserve.gov/pubs/feds/2013/201362/201362pap.pdf; Richard Brooks, "Credit Past Due," *Columbia Law Review* 106 (2006): 994, 996.
89. "About 18% of unbanked respondents to surveys reported that they were not 'comfortable' dealing with banks." Michael S. Barr, "Banking the Poor," *Yale Journal on Regulation* 21, no. 282 (2004): 121, 180.
90. Ibid., 180 no. 282; Arthur Kennickell et al., "Recent Changes in U.S. Family Finances: Evidence from the 2011 and 2004 Survey of Consumer Finances," *Federal Reserve Bulletin* (2006): 9–11.
91. Regina Austin, "Of Predatory Lending and the Democratization of Credit: Preserving the Social Safety Net of Informality in Small-Loan Transactions," 53 AM. U. L. REV. 1217, 1227 (2004). "Focus groups of low-income and ethnic consumers . . . identified five ways in which check cashers were superior to banks: (a) easier to access for immediate cash; (b) more accessible locations; (c) better service in the form of shorter lines, more tellers, more targeted product mix in a single location, convenient operating hours, and Spanish-speaking tellers; (d) more respectful, courteous treatment of customers; and (e) greater trustworthiness." See Michael A. Stegman and Robert Faris, "Payday Lending: A Business Model that Encourages Chronic Borrowing," *Economic Development Quarterly* 17 (2003): 8, 13.
92. "One summary measure suggests a common pecuniary mistake: two-thirds of the matched sample has at least $1000 of credit card liquidity on the day they take their first payday loans, much more than the typical $300 payday loan. For a two-week payday loan with a finance charge of 18 percent, using credit card liquidity first would save these households $300 . . . if the credit card APR is 18 percent." Sumit Agarwal, Paige M. Skiba, and Jeremy Tobacman, "Payday Loans and Credit Cards: New Liquidity and Credit Scoring Puzzles?," NBER working paper no. 14659, January 2009, accessed March 17, 2015, www.nber.org/papers/w14659.
93. "For example, in 718 payday lender inspections conducted over a three-year period, North Carolina Banking officials found 8,911

violations of simple state consumer-protection rules." Peterson, *Taming the Sharks,* 16.

94. Brett Williams, "What's Debt Got to Do with It?," in *New Poverty Studies: The Ethnography of Power, Politics, and Impoverished People in the United States,* eds. Judith Goode and Jeff Maskovsky (New York: New York University Press, 2001), 87.
95. Cathy Lesser Mansfield, "Predatory Mortgage Lending: Summary of Legislative and Regulatory Activity, Including Testimony on Subprime Mortgage Lending before the House Banking Committee, in Consumer Financial Services Litigation," *PLI Corporate Law and Practice* (2001), 40.
96. "These results suggest that the effect of restricting access to payday loans on overall short-term, expensive borrowing is muted by the continued availability of overdrafts and late bill payment; i.e., that overdrafts and late bill payment are imperfect substitutes for payday loans." Jonathan Zinman, "Restricting Consumer Credit Access: Household Survey Evidence on Effects around the Oregon Rate Cap," *Journal of Banking and Finance* 34 (2010): 546, 551.
97. See, e.g., Adam Mayle, "NOTE, Usury on the Reservation: Regulation of Tribal-Affiliated Payday Lenders," *Review of Banking and Financial Law* 31 (2011–2012): 1053, 1057–58 (describing the issue).
98. Kevin Wack, "Abuses in Online Payday Lending Are Widespread, Report Finds," *American Banker,* October 2, 2014, accessed March 17, 2015, www.americanbanker.com/issues/179_191/abuses-in-online-payday-lending-are-widespread-report-finds-1070347-1.html?zkPrintable=1&nopagination=1.
99. New York State Department of Financial Services, "Press Release: Governor Cuomo Announces Department of Financial Services Notifies Debt Collectors not to Seek Collection on Illegal Payday Loans," February 22, 2013, accessed March 17, 2015, www.dfs.ny.gov/about/press2013/pr1302221.htm.
100. See, e.g., Benjamin M. Lawsky, "Letter to Governor and Legislature," June 15, 2014, 7, accessed March 17, 2015, www.dfs.ny.gov/reportpub/annual/dfs_annualrpt_2013.pdf (describing the practice); Jessica Silver-Greenberg, "Major Banks Aid in Payday Loans Banned by States," *New York Times,* February 23, 2013, accessed March 17, 2015, www.nytimes.com/2013/02/24/business/major-banks-aid-in-payday-loans-banned-by-states.html?pagewanted=all&_r=0.
101. Caskey, "Payday Lending," 4.

102. 10 U.S.C. §987.
103. "CFPB Report Finds Loopholes in Military Lending Act Rules Rack Up Costs for Servicemembers," December 29, 2014, accessed March 17, 2015, www.consumerfinance.gov/newsroom/cfpb-report-finds-loopholes-in-military-lending-act-rules-rack-up-costs-for-servicemembers/.
104. Brady Dennis, "Holly Petraeus Will Lead Consumer Financial Protection Bureau's Office for Service Member Affairs," *Washington Post*, January 4, 2011, accessed March 17, 2015, www.washingtonpost.com/wp-dyn/content/article/2011/01/04/AR2011010405627.html; Holly Petraeus, "Hollister K. Petraeus before the U.S. Senate Committee on Commerce, Science and Transportation," November 20, 2013, accessed March 17, 2015, www.consumerfinance.gov/newsroom/hollister-k-petraeus-before-the-u-s-senate-committee-on-commerce-science-transportation.
105. Michael D. Shear and Jessica Silver-Greenberg, "Consumer Protection Agency Proposes Rules on Payday Loans," *New York Times*, March 26, 2015, accessed March 29, 2015, www.nytimes.com/2015/03/27/business/dealbook/consumer-protection-agency-proposes-rules-on-payday-loans.html?_r=0.
106. Letter from Darrell Issa and the House Committee on Oversight and Government Reform to Attorney General Eric Holder, 2, January 8, 2014, accessed March 18, 2015, oversight.house.gov/wp-content/uploads/2014/05/Appendix-2-of-2.pdf, 307.
107. Ibid.
108. Michael Blume and [redacted], "Enforcement Strategies and Cases," 1, 3, accessed March 18, 2015, oversight.house.gov/wp-content/uploads/2014/05/Appendix-1-of-2.pdf, 460, 462.
109. Benjamin M. Lawsky, "Letter to Banks," accessed September 30, 2014, www.dfs.ny.gov/about/press2013/pr130806-link1.pdf.
110. U.S. House of Representatives Committee on Oversight and Government Reform, "The Department of Justice's 'Operation Choke Point': Illegally Choking Off Legitimate Businesses?," *Staff Report*, 2, May 29, 2014, accessed March 18, 2015, oversight.house.gov/wp-content/uploads/2014/05/Staff-Report-Operation-Choke-Point1.pdf.
111. Four Oaks Fincorp, "Four Oaks Fincorp, Inc. and Four Oaks Bank and Trust Company Agree to Settlement Terms with the United States Department of Justice," *Yahoo! Finance*, January 9, 2014, accessed March 18, 2015, finance.yahoo.com/news/four-oaks-fincorp-inc-four-212100217.html.

112. U.S. House of Representatives Committee on Oversight and Government Reform, "Operation Choke Point."
113. Ibid.
114. See *CFPB v. CashCall* complaint.
115. Peterson, *Taming the Sharks.*
116. "Predatory Lending," Last Week Tonight with John Oliver, HBO, August 10, 2014, accessed March 18, 2015, www.youtube.com/watch?v=PDylgzybWAw.
117. Ibid.
118. Paige M. Skiba, "Regulation of Payday Loans: Misguided?," *Washington and Lee Law Review* 69 (2012): 1023, 1038.
119. Pew Charitable Trusts, "Payday Lending in America: Who Borrows, Where They Borrow, and Why," July 2012, 5, accessed March 18, 2015, www.pewtrusts.org/~/media/legacy/uploadedfiles/pcs_assets/2012/PewPaydayLendingReportpdf.pdf.
120. Caskey, "Payday Lending," 25.
121. Brian Melzer, "The Real Costs of Credit Access: Evidence from the Payday Lending Market," *Quarterly Journal of Economics* 126, 1 (2011): 517–555.
122. Paige Marta Skiba and Jeremy Tobacman, "Do Payday Loans Cause Bankruptcy?," Vanderbilt Law and Economics Research Paper No. 11–13, 1, 4, 14 (2009), accessed September 29, 2014, papers.ssrn.com/sol3/papers.cfm?abstract_id=1266215; Morgan and Strain also made a similar finding. Don Morgan and Michael Strain, "Payday Credit Access and Household Financial Outcomes," (unpublished manuscript: October 2009).
123. Jonathan Zinman, "Restricting Consumer Credit Access: Household Survey Evidence on Effects around the Oregon Rate Cap," *Journal of Banking and Finance* 34 (2010): 546–556.
124. Caskey, "Payday Lending," 26.
125. Cathy Lesser Mansfield, "Predatory Mortgage Lending: Summary of Legislative and Regulatory Activity, including Testimony on Subprime Mortgage Lending before the House Banking Committee," *Practical Law Institute* 1242 (2001): 9, 40 (describing testimony during the House banking committee).
126. Robert DeYoung and Ronnie J. Phillips, "Payday Loan Pricing," (working paper 09-07, Federal Reserve Bank of Kansas City, February 2009), accessed March 18, 2015, kansascityfed.org/PUBLICAT/RESWKPAP/PDF/rwp09-07.pdf.
127. Ibid., 27.

128. Christopher R. Knittel and Victor Stango, "Price Ceilings as Focal Points for Tacit Collusion: Evidence from Credit Cards," *American Economic Review* 93, 5 (December 2003): 1703, accessed March 18, 2015, web.mit.edu/knittel/www/papers/Focal_AER.pdf.
129. Knittel, "Price Ceilings as Focal Points," 28.
130. For example, Check 'n Go, Check into Cash, and Cash America have very similar fee schedules for the state of Tennessee based on a fourteen-day lending period. CashNetUSA's fee schedule for Tennessee was less, as the company charges fifteen dollars for every one hundred dollars borrowed. The reduced cost may be attributed to CashNet-USA's solely online product offering, while the other companies offer both "brick and mortar" and online options. Check 'n Go, "Payday Loan Rates and Terms," accessed September 29, 2014, www.checkngo.com/.rates; Check into Cash, "Payday Loan Information by State," accessed September 29, 2014, checkintocash.com/payday-loan-information-by-state/; CashNetUSA, "Rates and Terms," accessed September 29, 2014, www.cashnetusa.com/rates-and-terms.html; Cash America, "Cash Advance Rates/Fees," accessed September 29, 2014, www.cashamerica.com/LoanOptions/CashAdvances/RatesandFees.aspx.
131. Mark Flannery and Katherine Samolyk, "Payday Lending: Do the Costs Justify the Price?" (working paper no. 2005-09, FDIC Center for Financial Research, 2005, 10), accessed March 18, 2015, www.fdic.gov/bank/analytical/cfr/2005/wp2005/cfrwp_2005-09_flannery_samolyk.pdf.
132. Ibid., 4.
133. Ibid.
134. Robert B. Avery, "Payday Loans versus Pawnshops: The Effects of Loan Fee Limits on Household Use," *Board of Governors of the Federal Reserve System,* May 13, 2011, accessed March 18, 2015, www.frbsf.org/community-development/files/2-avery-paper.pdf.
135. Ibid. See also Aaron Gold, "Payday Lending: Grounding the Policy Debate through Economic Analysis" (thesis, NYU Stern School of Business, 2009), 12–15, accessed March 18, 2015, www.stern.nyu.edu/sites/default/files/assets/documents/con_043130.pdf.
136. Ben S. Bernanke, "Nonmonetary Effects of the Financial Crisis in the Propagation of the Great Depression," *American Economic Review* 73, no. 3 (1983): 263, accessed March 18, 2015, www.jstor.org/stable/1808111.

5. UNBANKED AND UNWANTED

1. Stephen Wexler, "Practicing Law for Poor People," *Yale Law Journal* 79 (1970): 1049, 1053.
2. Michael S. Barr, "An Inclusive, Progressive National Savings and Financial Services Policy," *Harvard Law and Policy Review* 1 (2007): 164, 164.
3. Michael S. Barr, *No Slack: The Financial Lives of Low-Income Americans* (Washington, DC: Brookings Institution, 2012), 3.
4. USPS, Office of the Inspector General, "Providing Non-Bank Financial Services for the Underserved," White Paper Report Number: RARC-WP-14-007 January 27, 2014, accessed March 17, 2015, www.uspsoig.gov/sites/default/files/document-library-files/2014/rarc-wp-14-007.pdf. Based on 34 million households earning an average of $25,500 per year, spending a total of $82 billion in 2011; KPMG, "Serving the Underserved Market, 2011," 1, accessed September 29, 2014, www.kpmg.com/US/en/IssuesAndInsights/ArticlesPublications/Documents/serving-underserved-market.pdf; Center for Financial Services Innovation (CFSI), "2012 Financially Underserved Market Size Study," December 2013, 1, www.cfsinnovation.com/content/2012-financially-underserved-market-sizing-study.
5. CFSI, "2012 Financially Underserved Market Size Study," 1.
6. Ibid.
7. Derek Thompson, "When You're Poor, Money is Expensive," *Atlantic,* July 14, 2014, accessed March 17, 2015, m.theatlantic.com/business/archive/2014/07/its-expensive-to-be-poor-money/374361/.
8. Barr, *No Slack,* 120.
9. FDIC, "2013 FDIC National Survey of Unbanked and Underbanked Households," October 2014, accessed March 17, 2015, www.fdic.gov/householdsurvey/2013report.pdf; University Neighborhood Housing Program, "Banking in the Bronx: Assessing Options in a Historically Redlined and Underbanked Borough," April 2012, accessed March 17, 2015, www.unhp.org/pdf/BankingInTheBronx.pdf.
10. "In fact, the ABA says, the annual cost of a checking account is actually $250 to $300." The American Bankers Association (ABA) claims that the cost of opening an account runs between $150 and $200, and the annual cost of maintaining an account runs between $250 and $300. The American Bankers Association catalogs the costs of maintaining an account: "These costs reflect the expense of processing transactions, providing monthly statements, investing

in payment system technology and software, paying the cost of tellers, ATMs, and online banking, staffing call centers, complying with countless regulations, ensuring privacy and data protection, and preventing fraud and covering fraud losses." Marcie Geffner, "Bank Account Costs $250," *Bankrate*, July 26, 2010, accessed March 17, 2015, www.bankrate.com/financing/banking/bank-account-costs-250/.

11. Mark Maremont and Tom McGinty, "Why Banks at Wal-Mart Are among America's Top Fee Collectors," *Wall Street Journal*, May 11, 2014, accessed March 17, 2015, www.wsj.com/news/articles/SB10001424052702304734304579515730198367754?KEYWORDS=maremont&mg=reno64-wsj.
12. Anna Bernasek, "In Checking Accounts, the Less You Have, the More You Pay," *New York Times*, September 20, 2014, accessed March 17, 2015, www.nytimes.com/2014/09/21/your-money/in-checking-accounts-the-less-you-have-the-more-you-pay.html.
13. www.youtube.com/watch?v=J0rSXjVuJVg. Accessed March 17, 2015.
14. Annamaria Andriotis, "Overdraft Fees at Banks Hit a High, Despite Curbs," *Wall Street Journal*, April 1, 2014, accessed March 17, 2015, www.wsj.com/news/articles/SB100014240527023041572045794755736 02576630.
15. Justin Lutz, "Overdrawn and Underwhelmed: A College Student's Tale of Bank of America," *Roosevelt Institute*, accessed March 17, 2015, www.rooseveltinstitute.org/new-roosevelt/overdrawn-and-underwhelmed-college-student-s-tale-bank-america.
16. FDIC, *FDIC Study of Bank Overdraft Programs*, November 2008, 79, accessed March 17, 2015, www.fdic.gov/bank/analytical/overdraft/FDIC138_Report_Final_v508.pdf. Banks collected 32 billion in overdraft fees in 2012. Maremont and McGinty, "Why Banks at Wal-Mart."
17. The Federal Reserve has issued regulation on requirements for overdraft services for electronic funds transfers like ATM transactions (12 CFR 205.17). Generally speaking, the financial institution needs to provide consumers notice of the fees, and the consumer must opt-in. The Consumer Financial Protection Bureau's regulations on overdraft services can be found in 12 CFR 1030.11. This regulation requires financial institutions to disclose, in each periodic statement, the total amount of overdraft fees and the total amount of fees for returning unpaid items. 12 CFR 1030.11(a)(1). Additionally, advertisements promoting overdraft fee services must clearly, and in a conspicuous manner, state the fees charged for each overdraft, the

types of transactions covered by the overdraft fee, the time period over which a consumer needs to repay or cover the overdraft, and the circumstances under which the institution will not pay the overdraft. 12 CFR 1030.11(b)(1).

18. In re: Checking Account Overdraft Litigation, Third Amended Consolidated Class Action Complaint, Case No. 1:09-MD-02036-JLK (S.D. FL.), accessed March 17, 2015, bofaoverdraftsettlement.com/LinkClick.aspx?fileticket=pSsSlbBGB6s%3D&tabid=67&mid=415.
19. Ibid.
20. In re: Checking Account Overdraft Litigation, Third Amended Consolidated Class Action Complaint, Case No. 1:09-MD-02036-JLK (S.D. FL.), accessed March 16, 2015, www.bofaoverdraftsettlement.com/LinkClick.aspx?fileticket=912Y0QkAV2E%3d&tabid=67&mid=415&forcedownload=true.
21. Basically, this Bank of America customer "borrowed" $87.04 and had to pay back $262.04. Matt Levine, "New York Prosecutors Go after Tennessee Loan Sharks," *BloombergView,* August 12, 2014, accessed March 17, 2015, www.bloombergview.com/articles/2014-08-12/new-york-prosecutors-go-after-tennessee-loan-sharks.
22. Ibid.
23. See also Martha C. White, "Want to Get Bank Fees Waived? Complain!," *Time,* August 23, 2013, accessed March 17, 2015, business.time.com/2013/08/23/want-to-get-bank-fees-waived-complain/.
24. Jillian Berman, "Having a Bank Account Really is Getting More Expensive," *Huffington Post,* August 29, 2014, accessed March 17, 2015, www.huffingtonpost.com/2014/08/29/free-checking-accounts-down_n_5730166.html?1409312196.
25. FDIC, "Addendum to the 2011 FDIC National Survey of Unbanked and Underbanked Households: Use of Alternative Financial Services," June 2013, accessed March 17, 2015, www.fdic.gov/householdsurvey/2013_afsaddendum_web.pdf. Michael Barr's survey results from his book *No Slack* shows that when the unbanked are asked what changes to bank accounts would induce them to open an account, 29 percent of respondents said lower fees, 20 percent convenience, 10 percent get money faster, 14 percent lower minimum balance, 16 percent less confusing fees, and 11 percent nothing. Barr, *No Slack,* 32.
26. The majority of banks, 87 percent, require a third-party screen before they will open checking accounts, and 81 percent of banks require third-party screens to open savings accounts. FDIC, "Banks' Efforts to Serve the Unbanked and Underbanked," December 2008, 11, accessed

March 17, 2015, www.fdic.gov/unbankedsurveys/2008survey/index.html.

27. Ibid., 193. The number of individuals currently on record is unknown since the 2007 acquisition of ChexSystems by Fidelity National Information Services.
28. Jessica Silver-Greenberg, "Over a Million Are Denied Bank Accounts for Past Errors," *New York Times Deal Book,* July 30, 2013, accessed March 17, 2015, dealbook.nytimes.com/2013/07/30/over-a-million-are-denied-bank-accounts-for-past-errors/.
29. Dennis Campbell, Asis Martinez Jerez, and Peter Tufano, "Bouncing out of the Banking: System: An Empirical Analysis of Involuntary Bank Account Closures," *Boston Federal Reserve,* June 6, 2008 (draft) 6, accessed March 17, 2015, www.bostonfed.org/economic/cprc/conferences/2008/payment-choice/papers/campbell_jerez_tufano.pdf.
30. James Perez, "Blacklisted: The Unwarranted Divestment of Access to Bank Accounts," *New York University Law Review* 80 (2005): 1586; ChexSystems' website states that "each report submitted to ChexSystems remains on our files for five years, unless the source of the information requests its removal or ChexSystems becomes obligated to remove it under applicable law." ChexSystems, Consumer Assistance, "Frequently Asked Questions," accessed September 30, 2014, www.consumerdebit.com/consumerinfo/us/en/chexsystems/faqs.htm#FAQ_01. In 2006, the database had a record of 22 million "closed for cause accounts" at 8,900 institutions. An account is considered closed-for-cause when, for example, a consumer refuses to pay the account fee and the bank closes the account. Ibid.
31. Silver-Greenberg, "Over a Million."
32. Ibid.
33. The McFadden Act, Pub. L. No. 69–639, 44 Stat. 1224 (1927).
34. For example, there were 14,000 banking institutions in 1934 and there are only around 5,000 today. The number of savings institutions decreased from around 3,500 in 1984 to 930 today. A 1962 Federal Reserve study shows that "about two-thirds of all liquid asset holdings were in savings accounts, with the remainder divided about equally between checking accounts and U.S. savings bonds. FDIC, "Historical Statistics on Banking," accessed September 30, 2014, www2.fdic.gov/hsob/HSOBRpt.asp; Dorothy S. Projector and Gertrude S. Weiss, "Survey of Financial Characteristics of Consumers" (Federal Reserve Technical Papers: 1966), 13, accessed March 17, 2015, www.federalreserve.gov/econresdata/scf/files/6263_sfcc62book.pdf.

35. There were those who were left out, of course, but it was the same group that was left out of everything during the time: African Americans. Before the civil-rights-era laws forbidding discrimination in banking were passed, many blacks were left out of the mainstream banking institutions. Many blacks had to form their own institutions—black-owned banks. The story of black banking is too rich to be summarized in this text but will be the topic of the author's future research and study.
36. Regulation Q, 12 CFR §217.
37. Thomas Picketty, *Capital in the Twenty-First Century* (Cambridge, MA: Harvard University Press, 2014).
38. Connecticut Department of Banking, "ABCs of Banking," accessed March 17, 2015, www.ct.gov/dob/cwp/view.asp?a=2235&q=297892.
39. "The relaxation of restrictions on intrastate branching and interstate banking that took place in the 1980s and early 1990s facilitated both mergers and consolidations. While only sixteen states permitted unrestricted intrastate branching in 1984, by 1994 the number had risen to forty. Similarly, while forty-two states restricted interstate combinations of banking charters in 1984, by 1994 only Hawaii retained this restriction. The Interstate Banking and Branching Efficiency (or Riegle-Neal) Act of 1994 allowed full interstate branching, which made possible the interstate consolidation of charters within banking companies." FDIC, "Community Banking Study," December 2012, 2, accessed March 17, 2015, www.fdic.gov/regulations/resources/cbi/report/cbi-full.pdf.
40. Noncommunity banks reported a Return on Investment (ROI) that averaged thirty-five basis points higher than community banks. Ibid.
41. FDIC, "Community Banking Study," 2–7.
42. Dan Fitzpatrick and Michael Rapoport, "Profits Show Biggest Banks Are Back from the Brink," *Wall Street Journal,* January 18, 2014, accessed March 17, 2015, www.wsj.com/news/articles/SB10001424052702304419104579327043941676608.
43. Frank Bass and Dakin Campbell, "Predator Targets Hit as Banks Shut Branches amid Profits," *Bloomberg,* May 2, 2013, accessed March 17, 2015, www.bloomberg.com/news/2013-05-02/post-crash-branch-closings-hit-hardest-in-poor-u-s-areas.html.
44. Stephen Greer and Bob Meara, "Branch Boom Gone Bust: Predicting a Steep Decline in US Branch Density, *CELENT,* April 30, 2013, accessed March 17, 2015, www.celent.com/reports/branch-boom-gone-bust-predicting-steep-decline-us-branch-density.

45. "In low-income areas, where the median household income was below $25,000, and in moderate-income areas, where the medium household income was between $25,000 and $50,000, the number of branches declined by 396 between 2008 and 2010. In neighborhoods where household income was above $100,000, by contrast, 82 branches were added during the same period." Bass and Campbell, "Predator Targets." See also Nelson D. Schwartz, "Bank Closings Tilt toward Poor Areas," *New York Times,* February 22, 2011, accessed March 17, 2015, www.nytimes.com/2011/02/23/business/23banks.html?pagewanted=all&_r=0.
46. "The Future of Superbanks," PBS *Frontline*, accessed September 30, 2014, www.pbs.org/wgbh/pages/frontline/breakingthebank/themes/future.html.
47. Tanya D. Marsh and Joseph W. Norman, Federal Reserve Bank of St. Louis, "Reforming the Regulation of Community Banks after Dodd-Frank," 1–2, accessed March 17, 2015, www.stlouisfed.org/banking/community-banking-conference/PDF/Marsh_Norman_Reforming_Regulation.pdf. See also Hester Peirce, Testimony before the House Committee on Oversight and Government Reform, "Regulatory Burdens: The Impact of Dodd-Frank on Community Banking," July 18, 2013, accessed March 17, 2015, mercatus.org/publication/regulatory-burdens-impact-dodd-frank-community-banking. Regulatory costs "tend to be proportionately heavier for small banks."
48. Charles Dugan also describes the risk inherent in the large banking consolidation: "But the superbanks also revealed themselves to just be vulnerable to this crisis so quickly. . . . It's kind of like the cheetah. . . . It can run faster than anything else; it just so happens that because there are so few cheetahs and they've become such genetically undiverse creatures that anytime a disease moves through the community, it infects all the cheetahs immediately, and they all start dying off. What we found out about the superbank concept is, the superbank concept works exactly how it's supposed to. But because there are so few banks, because they're so undiversified, because they all do business with each other, once the financial virus enters the system, it infects everyone immediately." PBS *Frontline*, "The Future of Superbanks," accessed March 17, 2015, www.pbs.org/wgbh/pages/frontline/breakingthebank/themes/future.html.
49. Allen N. Berger, Astrid A. Dick, Lawrence G. Goldberg, and Lawrence J. White, "The Effects of Competition from Large, Multimarket Firms on the Performance of Small, Single-Market Firms: Evidence

from the Banking Industry," *Federal Reserve Board,* February 2005, accessed March 17, 2015, www.federalreserve.gov/pubs/feds/2005/200515/200515pap.pdf.

50. Banks also have loans on their books that they initially sold off but had to take back under a recourse clause. See HUD, "The Secondary Market in Residential Mortgages," accessed March 17, 2015, www.huduser.org/Publications/pdf/HUD-11648.pdf.
51. Michael Barr states, "As currently structured, the financial services system does not work for [Lower Middle Income] households. Many of these households find that checking accounts are ill suited to their needs, and many financial institutions find low-balance checking accounts unprofitable." Michael Barr, *No Slack,* 25.
52. U.S. Government Accountability Office, Report to Congressional Committees, "Banking: Government Check-Cashing Issues," GAO/GGD-89–12, October 1988, accessed March 17, 2015, www.gao.gov/assets/150/147069.pdf.
53. In ten years, the number of households without bank accounts rose from about 6.5 million in 1977 to about 11.5 million in 1989 but with large variations depending on class. Caskey, *Fringe Banking: Check-Cashing Outlets, Pawnshops, and the Poor,* 87; March 1, 1996; Robert B. Avery et al., "Survey of Consumer Finances, 1983," *Federal Reserve Bulletin,* September 1984, 685, accessed March 17, 2015, www.federalreserve.gov/econresdata/scf/files/1983_bull0984.pdf.
54. FDIC, "2013 FDIC National Survey of Unbanked and Underbanked Households: Executive Summary," Oct. 2014, 3, accessed March 17, 2015, www.fdic.gov/householdsurvey/2013execsumm.pdf.
55. See, e.g., David Malmquist et al., "The Economics of Low-Income Mortgage Lending," *Journal of Financial Services Research* 11 (1997): 169, 181–182; Bruce G. Posner, "Behind the Boom in Microloans," *Inc.,* April 1994, 114.
56. Ivan Light and Michelle Pham, "Beyond Creditworthy: Microcredit and Informal Credit in the United States," *Journal of Developmental Entrepreneurship* 3 (1998): 35, 39.
57. Most of these policy efforts have focused on lending. As historian Sheldon Garon has noted in *Beyond Our Means,* U.S. policymaking has not focused on savings accounts in the last century. This focus is out of sync with the rest of the world. Sheldon Garon, *Beyond Our Means: Why America Spends While the World Saves* (Princeton, NJ: Princeton University Press, 2012).

58. FDIC, "Small-Dollar Loan Pilot Program," accessed September 30, 2014, www.fdic.gov/smalldollarloans/.
59. Ibid.
60. *House Subcommittee on Financial Institutions and Consumer Credit, An Examination of the Availability of Credit for Consumers,* 112th Cong. 141, 2011 (Washington, DC: Government Printing Office, 2012), 9–10, 16–17, accessed March 17, 2015, www.gpo.gov/fdsys/pkg/CHRG-112hhrg72606/html/CHRG-112hhrg72606.htm.
61. Many of the banks volunteered for the program because they were told that they would be fulfilling their CRA requirements. See ibid., 44–45 (statement of Michael A. Grant, president, National Bankers Association).
62. Ibid. (statement of Robert W. Mooney, deputy director, Consumer Protection and Affairs).
63. Ibid., 19, 24, 30 (statement of Mr. Renaci centered on banks being against these small loans: "And I have talked to some of the banks. I have had meetings for the last 6 weeks with small banks and community banks, and they are not going toward these programs. They don't feel they are profitable"). See also ibid. (comments of Representative Luetkemeyer, Representative Pearce, and Representative Scott); ibid., 44–45 (statement of Michael A. Grant, president, National Bankers Association).
64. Michael V. Berry, "Historical Perspectives on the Community Reinvestment Act of 1977," *Federal Reserve Bank of Chicago,* accessed October 5, 2014, www.chicagofed.org/webpages/publications/profitwise_news_and_views/2013/pnv_dec2013.cfm.
65. Carolina Reid and Elizabeth Laderman, "Constructive Credit: Revisiting the Performance of Community Reinvestment Act Lending during the Subprime Crisis," 2010, accessed March 17, 2015, fdic.gov/bank/analytical/cfr/mortgage_Future_house_finance/papers/Reid.PDF.
66. Ibid; Anthony D. Taibi, "Banking, Finance, and Community Economic Empowerment: Structural Economic Theory, Procedural Civil Rights, and Substantive Racial Justice," *Harvard Law Review* 107 (1994): 1463, 1485–1489.
67. Warren L. Dennis, *The Community Re-Investment Act of 1977: Its Legislative History and Its Impact on Applications for Changes in Structure Made by Depository Institutions to the Four Federal Financial Supervisory Agencies* (Lafayette, IN: Credit Research Center, Krannert Graduate School of Management, Purdue University, 1978).

68. "Civil Rights Chief Faults CRA as Toothless Legislation," May 21, 1992, accessed March 17, 2015, www.americanbanker.com/issues/157_4/-12102-1.html "Regulators are not enforcing the law aggressively." Ibid.
69. Jeffrey Marshall, "Lenders Cry Foul over Fair Lending Prosecutions," *American Banker,* October 1, 1994, accessed March 17, 2015, www.americanbanker.com/issues/159_115/-47003-1.html.
70. See Richard S. Carnell, Jonathan R. Macey, and Geoffrey P. Miller, *The Law of Financial Institutions,* 5th ed. (New York: Aspen, 2013), 328; "CRA's broad standards and 'enforcement' mechanisms . . . have long been derided by both proponents and detractors of CRA. Community advocates urge stricter rules and harsher consequences of failure. Bankers lament the lack of clear rules or safe harbors and the intrusive role of the public." Michael S. Barr, "Banking the Poor," *Yale Journal on Regulation* 21 (2004): 121, 603; Charles W. Calomiris et al., "Housing-Finance Intervention and Private Incentives: Helping Minorities and the Poor," *Journal of Money, Credit and Banking* 26 (1994): 634, 673 (stating that "the vagueness of the CRA has led to arbitrary enforcement"); Keith N. Hylton, "Banks and Inner Cities: Market and Regulatory Obstacles to Development Lending," *Yale Journal on Regulation* 17 (2000): 191, 203 (explaining that enforcement of the CRA has been uneven and unpredictable).
71. FDIC, "Community Reinvestment Act (CRA) Performance Ratings," accessed September 30, 2014, www.fdic.gov/crapes/crafaq_v4.asp.
72. Carnell et al, *Law of Financial Institutions,* 385; Calomiris et al., "Housing-Finance."
73. Drew Dahl et al., "Community Reinvestment Act Enforcement and Targeted Mortgage Lending," (working paper, Department of Economics and Finance, Utah State University, January 1, 2009), accessed March 17, 2015, EconPapers.repec.org/RePEc:uth:wpaper:200806.
74. David Min, "Faulty Conclusions Built on Shoddy Foundations," February 8, 2011, accessed March 17, 2015, papers.ssrn.com/sol3/papers.cfm?abstract_id=2103379.
75. In fact, before the financial crisis, Wallison himself complained that the CRA and the GSEs were getting in the way of subprime lending. He argued in 2000 at the Cato institute that "study after study has shown that Fannie Mae and Freddie Mac are failing to do even as much as banks and S&Ls in providing financing for affordable housing, including minority and low income housing." Mike Konczal, "No, Marco Rubio, Government Did Not Cause the Housing Crisis,"

Washington Post: Wonkblog, February 13, 2003, accessed March 17, 2015, www.washingtonpost.com/blogs/wonkblog/wp/2013/02/13/no-marco-rubio-government-did-not-cause-the-housing-crisis/.

76. Elizabeth Laderman and Carolina Reid, "CRA Lending during the Subprime Meltdown," *Federal Reserve Bank of San Francisco,* February 2009, 115, accessed March 17, 2015, www.frbsf.org/community-development/files/cra_lending_during_subprime_meltdown.pdf.
77. Timothy F. Geithner, *Stress Test: Reflections on a Financial Crisis* (New York: Crown, 2014) 391–392. See also Press release, Senator Robert Menendez, "Fed Chairman Bernanke Confirms To Menendez That Community Reinvestment Act Is Not To Blame For Foreclosure Crisis," December 2, 2008, accessed March 17, 2015, www.menendez.senate.gov/newsroom/press/fed-chairman-bernanke-confirms-to-menendez-that-community-reinvestment-act-is-not-to-blame-for-foreclosure-crisis; Jared Ruiz Bybee, "In Defense of Low Income Homeownership," *Alabama Civil Rights and Civil Liberties Law Review* 5 (2013): 116.
78. Neil Bhutta and Glenn B. Canner, "Did the CRA Cause the Mortgage Meltdown?" *Community Dividend,* March 1, 2009, accessed March 17, 2015, www.minneapolisfed.org/publications_papers/pub_display.cfm?id=4136&. See also Governor Randall S. Kroszner, "Speech at the Confronting Concentrated Poverty Forum," December 3, 2008, accessed March 17, 2015, www.federalreserve.gov/newsevents/speech/kroszner20081203a.htm#f3.
79. Konczal, "Marco Rubio."
80. www.gao.gov/products/GAO-09-782 (GAO, Fannie Mae and Freddie Mac, Analysis of Options for Revising the Housing Enterprises' Long-term Structures). See also Harvard Joint Center for Housing Studies, Financial Crisis Inquiry Commission, accessed March 17, 2015, fcicstatic.law.stanford.edu/cdn_media/fcicreports/fcic_final_report_conclusions.pdf; Glaeser et al., Federal Housing Agency Report, *Harvard Economics,* accessed March 17, 2015, research.stlouisfed.org/conferences/gse/Van_Order.pdf, research.stlouisfed.org/wp/2012/2012–005.pdf.
81. Konczal, "Marco Rubio."
82. See Simon Johnson and James Kwak, *13 Bankers: The Wall Street Takeover and the Next Financial Meltdown* (New York: Pantheon, 2010), 129, citing JPMorgan Chase marketing flyer.
83. Ibid., 144.
84. Ibid., 142.

85. Yield spread premiums (YSPs) given to brokers correlated with the interest the customer paid on the loan. Thus, the higher the interest on the loan, the more money the broker or originator of the loan made.
86. Wells Fargo settled the case with the DOJ for $175 million and did not admit wrongdoing. The DOJ complaint relied on disparate impact to show illegal lending/steering; discriminatory intent is immaterial. Charlie Savage, "Wells Fargo Will Settle Mortgage Bias Charges," *New York Times,* July 12, 2012, accessed March 17, 2015, www.nytimes.com/2012/07/13/business/wells-fargo-to-settle-mortgage-discrimination-charges.html?_r=0. This DOJ press release further discusses the settlement with Wells Fargo and the nature of the investigation into the illegal lending practices: Department of Justice, press release, "Justice Department Reaches Settlement with Wells Fargo Resulting in More than $175 Million in Relief for Homeowners to Resolve Fair Lending Claims," July 12, 2012, accessed March 17, 2015, www.justice.gov/opa/pr/justice-department-reaches-settlement-wells-fargo-resulting-more-175-million-relief. The extent of Wells Fargo's steering is set out in the DOJ's complaint, available here: *United States v. Wells Fargo Bank,* Complaint, Case No: 1:12-cv-01150, accessed March 17, 2015, www.justice.gov/iso/opa/resources/9512012712113719995136.pdf. The DOJ settled the case against Bank of America in 2011 for $355 million, to benefit the 200,000 African American and Hispanic borrowers that Countrywide had allegedly discriminated against. A DOJ press release discussing the settlement in detail is available here: The United States Attorney's Office, Central District of California, press release, accessed March 17, 2015, www.justice.gov/usao/cac/countrywide.html. The complaint can be found here: *United States v. Countrywide Financial Corporation;* Countrywide Home Loans, Countrywide Bank, Complaint, Case No. CV 11 10540-PSG (AJWN), accessed March 17, 2015, www.justice.gov/crt/about/hce/documents/countrywidecomp.pdf.
87. Michael Powell and Janet Roberts, "Minorities Affected Most as New York Foreclosures Rise," *New York Times,* May 15, 2009, accessed March 17, 2015, www.nytimes.com/2009/05/16/nyregion/16foreclose.html?pagewanted=all.
88. See Barr, "Banking the Poor," 517, 561–566, 623. Some early proponents of the CRA counter these claims by showing that the act has indeed increased lending to low-income communities and led to more branch openings in these underserved areas.

6. CHANGING THE WORLD WITHOUT CHANGING THE RULES

Epigraph source: www.ibiblio.org/pub/academic/political-science/speeches/clinton.dir/c23.txt.

1. Sharon Stangenes, "South Shore Bank Thrust into Spotlight," *Chicago Tribune,* November 15, 1992, sec. 7, 1; Richard Douthwaite, "How a Bank Can Transform a Neighborhood," *Short Circuit: Strengthening Local Economies for Security in an Unstable World,* 1996, accessed March 15, 2015, www.feasta.org/documents/shortcircuit/index.html?sc4/shorebank.html.
2. James Post and Fiona Wilson, "Too Good to Fail," *Stanford Social Innovation Review,* Fall 2010, accessed March 15, 2015, www.ssireview.org/articles/entry/too_good_to_fail.
3. David Moberg, "The Left Bank," *Chicago Reader,* May 26, 1994, accessed March 15, 2015, www.chicagoreader.com/chicago/the-left-bank/Content?oid=884620.
4. Ibid; Maf Smith et al. *Greening the Built Environment,* 188 (New York: EarthScan, 1998); Central Illinois 9/12 Project, "Shorebank's Evolution from Community-Based Banking to the Microfinancing Arena," *Breitbart,* March 5, 2010, accessed March 15, 2015, www.breitbart.com/Big-Government/2010/03/05/ShoreBanks-Evolution-from-Community-Based-Banking-to-the-Microfinancing-Arena.
5. Robert A. Solomon, "The Fall (and Rise?) of Community Banking: The Continued Importance of Local Institutions," *University of California, Irvine Law Review* 2 (2012): 955, accessed March 15, 2015, papers.ssrn.com/sol3/papers.cfm?abstract_id=2201901.
6. Post and Wilson, "Too Good to Fail."
7. Ibid.
8. Ibid.
9. Ibid.
10. In every market they entered, they took up a range of issues, including environmental sustainability, community development lending, and consulting local organizations. The bank's reach extended globally as well—along with direct investments in developing banks internationally, it founded the National Community Investment Fund, the largest investor in CDFIs in the country, and the Center for Financial Innovation, whose mission was to help the unbanked.
11. Ibid.
12. "Shorebank presents a success story in the community development banking world. As of May 1991, its total loan portfolio was $125

million, with a delinquency rate of 1–2%, a bit lower than the national average of 3–5%. In 1992, it had $244 million in assets and a net income of $1.60 million. Shorebank demonstrates that deliberate investment in disinvested communities can revive a local economy, rekindle the imagination of its people, and restore market forces to health and interdependency." See, e.g., Rochelle E. Lento, "Community Development Banking Strategy for Revitalizing Our Communities," *University of Michigan Journal on Legal Reform* 27 (1994): 790 (footnotes omitted); "In Chicago, a group of activists purchased South Shore Bank, a declining [institution] in a deteriorating neighborhood, to demonstrate that a financial institution offering development services could stop the blight and decay infecting this 95 percent black inner-city community." See Patricia Hanrahan and Katharine Rankin, "Ignoring the Homeless: An American Pastime," *Human Rights* 17 (1990): 37.

13. See Nick Carey, "Regulators Close Well-Connected ShoreBank," *Reuters,* August 20, 2010, accessed March 15, 2015, www.reuters.com/article/2010/08/20/us-shorebank-failure-idUSTRE67J5AE20100820.
14. "When the economic crisis hit in 2008, Chicago's South Shore was economically devastated. Unemployment exceeded 30% and may have been as high as 40%. A 2009 analysis of census data reported that the South Side had an unemployment rate of at least 23.2% (and probably higher), second only to neighborhoods in Detroit. ShoreBank had expanded into Arkansas in 1987 and later into Cleveland and Detroit, as well as the West Side of Chicago, all of which proved to be difficult markets." Solomon, "The Fall (and Rise?)," 956.
15. Tim Fernholz, "Too Small to Save," *American Prospect,* January/February 2011, accessed March 15, 2015, prospect.org/article/too-small-save-0.
16. Becky Yerak, "ShoreBank's Financial Hole Deepens," *Chicago Tribune: Breaking Business,* August 2, 2010, accessed March 15, 2015, archive.chicagobreakingbusiness.com/2010/08/shorebanks-financial-hole-deepens.html.
17. Solomon, "The Fall (and Rise?)," 956.
18. Ludwig's reason for applying for the rescue was that "this is an institution that's recognized by world figures all over the world, and for it to have failed would have been, I think, a blow not just to the Midwest, and not just to the people at ShoreBank, but to U.S. prestige and leadership in this important area of global development." Jeremy Hobson, "Big Banks to ShoreBank's Rescue," *American Public Media,*

May 18, 2010, accessed March 15, 2015, www.marketplace.org/topics/world/big-banks-shorebanks-rescue.

19. Solomon, "The Fall (and Rise?)," 957 (referring to Glenn Beck, "Shorebank's Tangled Web," *Fox News,* May 20, 2010, accessed March 15, 2015, www.foxnews.com/story/0,2933,593343,00.html).
20. The irony, of course, is that Barack Obama was bailing out his favorite Wall Street banks, but it was this bank's potential bailout that drew the ire of many conspiracy theorists.
21. John D. McKinnon and Elizabeth Williamson, "GOP Lawmakers Probe Chicago Bank Bailout," *Wall Street Journal,* updated May 10, 2010, accessed March 15, 2015, www.wsj.com/news/articles/SB10001424052748704691304575254812737842880.
22. David Greising, "Recession Played a Part, But ShoreBank Wounded Itself, Too," *New York Times,* May 22, 2010, A25A, accessed March 15, 2015, www.nytimes.com/2010/05/23/business/23cncshorebank.html?pagewanted=all.
23. David Roeder, "Urban Partnership Bank Pledges to Pick Up ShoreBank's Local Mission," *Chicago Sun-Times,* August 4, 2011, accessed March 15, 2015, www.suntimes.com/business/3603025-420/shorebank-vitale-bank-partnership-urban.html#.VHJVKIvF_Kg.
24. Solomon, "The Fall (and Rise?)," 960.
25. Post and Wilson, "Too Good to Fail."
26. "[The CDFI Fund of $382 million proposed by Clinton is] significantly less ambitious than Mr. Clinton's campaign proposal to use $850 million of federal money to establish 100 community development banks around the country modeled after Chicago's successful South Shore Bank." "Banking on the Inner City," *Washington Post,* July 19, 1993.
27. House Subcommittees on Policy Research and Insurance and on Economic Stabilization, *Traditional and Non-Traditional Lenders' Role in Economic Development,* July 22, 1992, 21.
28. House Subcommittee on Consumer Credit and Insurance of the Committee on Banking, Finance and Urban Affairs, *New Hope for Old Victims,* January 27, 1993, 8.
29. Ibid., 1.
30. Ibid., 4–5 (emphasis added).
31. Riegle Community Development and Regulatory Improvement Act of 1994, Pub. L. No. 103–325, 108 Stat. 2160 (codified as amended in scattered sections of 12 U.S.C.).
32. 12 U.S.C. § 4701(b) (2006).

33. 12 U.S.C. §§ 4702(5) (A) (i)–(iii) (2006).
34. Donald A. Lash, "The Community Development Banking Act and the Evolution of Credit Allocation Policies," *Journal of Affordable Housing and Community Developmental Law* 7 (1998): 397–398. The fund was also brought within the purview of the Treasury Department in 1996 and has been mentioned as one of the accomplishments of the Clinton administration. Ibid., 398.
35. "Funding for the CDFI Fund, the primary mechanism of public support for CDFIs, has been cut by almost half during the Bush Administration." See Sarah Molseed, "An Ownership Society for All: Community Development Financial Institutions as the Bridge between Wealth Inequality and Asset-Building Policies," *Georgetown Journal on Poverty Law and Policy* 13 (2006): 509; Katie Kuehner-Hebert, "CDFI Fund Appropriation Could Increase to $100M," *American Banker,* June 13, 2007, 4 (indicating that the Bush administration sharply reduced funding from its peak in 2001, however, it requested an increase for fiscal year 2008); David Morrison, "Bush Administration Lowballs CDFI Fund Once Again," *Credit Union Times,* February 4, 2008, 2 (stating that the proposed budget under the Bush administration was an almost 70 percent cut to the CDFI fund).
36. Community Development Financial Institutions Fund, "CDFI Snapshot Analysis: Fiscal Year 2012," March 6, 2014, 2, accessed March 15, 2015, www.cdfifund.gov/docs/2014/CDFI/CDFI_Institute_Final_2014.pdf. In 2012, there were 808 certified CDFIs. See also Community Development Financial Institutions Fund, "CDFI Fund Releases Most Comprehensive CIIS Data on CDFI Program Awardee Reporting to Date," April 28, 2014, accessed March 15, 2015, www.cdfifund.gov/news_events/CDFI-2014-12-CDFI_Fund_Releases_Most_Comprehensive_CIIS_Data_on_CDFI_Program_Awardee_Reporting_to_Date.asp; "At the time of the recertification announcement [2013 directive from Treasury that CDFIs get reevaluated every three years to ensure at least 60% of their services are to low- and middle-income (LMI) communities], there were roughly 1,000 certified CDFIs. . . . As of February 28, 2014, the Treasury recognized 806." Federal Reserve Bank of Minneapolis, "Mass CDFI Recertification Push Winnows List, Ensures Compliance," *Community Dividend,* April 1, 2014, accessed March 15, 2015, www.minneapolisfed.org/publications_papers/pub_display.cfm?id=5289.
37. FIELD at the Aspen Institute, "Surviving the Recession: How Microlenders Are Coping with Changing Demand, Risk and Funding," *Field*

Trendlines Series, issue 1 (July 2010), accessed March 15, 2015, www.fieldus.org/publications/TrendlinesMicrofinance.pdf; Robert Barba, "Deal Shows ShoreBank Was Savvy to the End," *American Banker,* August 24, 2010, 1; Lehn Benjamin et al., "Community Development Financial Institutions: Current Issues and Future Prospects," *Journal of Urban Affairs* 26 (2004): 189.

38. Post and Wilson, "Too Good to Fail."
39. "The theory seems to be that supporting CDFIs will ultimately bring investment from conventional financial institutions after the CDFIs have shown how to lend profitably in distressed communities." Lash, "Community Development Banking," 399.
40. Lawrence H. Summers, U.S. Secretary of Treasury, *Building Emerging Markets in America's Inner Cities,* Remarks to the National Council for Urban Economic Development, March 2, 1998, accessed March 15, 2015, www.treasury.gov/press-center/press-releases/Pages/rr2262.aspx.
41. Ibid.
42. Lash, "Community Development Banking," 401.
43. PBS Enterprising Ideas, Stories, "Q&A with Muhammad Yunus," accessed March 15, 2015, www.pbs.org/now/enterprisingideas/Muhammad-Yunus.html.
44. Rashmi Dyal-Chand, "Reflection in a Distant Mirror: Why the West Has Misperceived the Grameen Bank's Vision of Microcredit," *Stanford Journal of International Law* 41 (2005): 225.
45. Grameen Bank, "16 Decisions," updated July 15, 2014, "The 16 Decisions of Grameen Bank," *Global Development Research Center,* accessed March 15, 2015, www.gdrc.org/icm/grameen-16.html.
46. Grameen Bank's reported repayment rate was 98 percent. The U.S. banking sector rate of repayment is 96 percent. Actual repayment rate of Grameen Bank was 92 percent, with overall creditors in Bangladesh at 75 percent. Michal Kowalik and David Martinez-Miera, "The Creditworthiness of the Poor: A Model of the Grameen Bank," *The Federal Reserve Bank of Kansas City Economic Research Department,* 2010, 1, accessed March 15, 2015, www.kansascityfed.org/PUBLICAT/RESWKPAP/PDF/rwp10-11.pdf.
47. Tom Gallagher, "Microcredit Lending: An Alternative to Payday Loans for the Working Poor," *National Catholic Reporter,* August 21, 2009, 27.
48. As late as 2008, this bipartisan support was evident. That year, thirty senators (including eleven Republicans) and forty-three members of

the House signed a letter urging the World Bank president to invest more heavily in microfinance. "Members of Congress Call on World Bank to Support Microfinance for the Very Poor," accessed March 15, 2015. Results available at www.results.org/newsroom/members_of_congress_call_on_world_bank_to_support_microfinance_for_the_very/; "The reason behind this unquestioned support of World Bank for microfinance lies in that fact that from the beginning it has been in accordance with the market led poverty resolutions including financial liberalization, commercialization and self-help." See Ayten Davutoglu, "Two Different Poverty Reduction Approaches: Neoliberal Market Based Microfinance versus Social Rights Defender Basic Income," *International Journal of Social Inquiry* 6 (2013): 41.

49. "Informal banking institutions have existed for centuries, including such industries as susus of Ghana, chit funds in India, and tandas in Mexico. . . . 18th century author Jonathan Swift donated part of his wealth for [interest-free loans] to poor tradesmen. . . . The Irish Reproductive Loan Fund Institution was founded post-famine in 1822. . . . Group microlending was documented as early as the nineteenth century in Germany." Jesse Fishman, "Microfinance: Is There a Solution? A Survey on the Use of MFIs to Alleviate Poverty in India," *Denver Journal of International Law and Policy* 40 (2012): 592.

50. "Unfortunately, however, the image of Grameen Bank that the U.S. public has imported is at best incomplete and at times quite disputable." Dyal-Chand, "Distant Mirror," 24. In 1997, Microcredit Summit was held with the goal of eliminating poverty worldwide by the year 2025. Ibid., 235; "The empirical evidence on the impact of microcredit on poverty, carried out for Bangladesh as well as for a number of other countries in Asia, Africa and Latin America is very mixed." M. Jahangir Alam Chowdhury et al., "The Impact of Micro-Credit on Poverty: Evidence from Bangladesh," *Progress Developmental Studies* 5 (2005): 299; "Despite its overwhelming success in reaching the poor, induced benefits of microfinance . . . are debated." Shahidur R. Khandker and Hussain A. Samad, "Dynamic Effects of Microcredit in Bangladesh," World Bank Development Research Group Agriculture and Rural Development Team (2014), 2.

51. Fishman, "Microfinance," 603.

52. Dyal-Chand, "Distant Mirror," 242, no. 116. Grameen interest rates in 1994–95 were 20 percent, 8–10 percent above commercial rates in Bangladesh. Ibid.; "Interest rates . . . can vary greatly," with some

sources saying they're 24–30 percent and others saying they start around 15 percent but can rise to 40–100 percent. Fishman, "Microfinance," 602; Barbara Kiviat, "Can Microfinance Make It in America?," *Time,* January 11, 2009, accessed March 15, 2015, content.time.com/time/magazine/article/0,9171,1950949,00.html. Overseas, even Grameen charges interest rates "as high as 60% to 70%," which is necessary to compensate for risk but by U.S. standards seem usurious.

53. Neil MacFarquhar, "Banks Making Big Profits from Tiny Loans," *New York Times,* April 14, 2010, accessed March 15, 2015, www.nytimes.com/2010/04/14/world/14microfinance.html?pagewanted=all&_r=1&.
54. For a tool to explore microcredit entities in the United States, see FIELD at the Aspen Institute, "microTracker," microtracker.org/explore; "10 Top Microfinance Companies," *CNN Money,* updated July 15, 2011, accessed March 15, 2015, money.cnn.com/galleries/2011/smallbusiness/1107/gallery.top_microfinance_companies/index.html; Courtney L. Gould, "Grameencredit: One Solution for Poverty, But Maybe Not in Every Country, *Pacific Basin Law Journal* 28 (2010): 1.
55. James Barron, "Newly in Business, and Finding a Lifeline," *New York Times,* April 1, 2012, accessed March 15, 2015, www.nytimes.com/2012/04/02/nyregion/microlender-accion-extends-a-lifeline-to-small-businesses.html; Sarah Todd, "An Alternative Lender Whose Credit Reviews Are Academic," *American Banker,* July 8, 2014, accessed March 15, 2015, www.americanbanker.com/issues/179_130/an-alternative-lender-whose-credit-reviews-are-academic-1068506-1.html; Sarah Todd, "Online Lender Kabbage Closes on $270 Million Credit Facility," *American Banker,* April 9, 2014, accessed March 15, 2015, www.americanbanker.com/issues/179_69/-lender-kabbage-closes-on-270-million-credit-facility-1066787-1.html; John Adams, "Square Begins Lending to Small Businesses," *American Banker,* May 28, 2014, accessed March 15, 2015, www.americanbanker.com/issues/179_102/square-begins-lending-to-small-businesses-1067728-1.html; PayPal, "Take Your Business Further with PayPal Working Capital," accessed September 30, 2014, www.paypal.com/webapps/workingcapital/.
56. Lan Cao, "Looking at Communities and Markets," *Notre Dame Law Review* 74 (1999): 887.
57. See ibid., 878–879. "These associations are entirely self-sustaining and their capital base comes solely from their members' own contributions.

In that sense, they promote independence from rather than dependence on outside funding." Ibid. See also Carlos G. Vélez-Ibañez, *Bonds of Mutual Trust: Cultural Systems of Rotating Credit Associations among Urban Mexicans and Chicanos* (New Brunswick, NJ: Rutgers University Press, 1983), 38–40 (describing the basic structure of Chicano rotating credit associations).

58. Cao, "Looking at Communities," 881.
59. Ibid., 863 (emphasis omitted).
60. Ibid., 877–878.
61. One way to remedy some of the shortcomings outlined above is to formalize these lending circles. One example of such an arrangement was initiated by the Mission Asset Fund in San Francisco, which has linked a lending circle called a "cesta" (which means "basket" in Spanish) with Citibank. See Alexa Vaughn, "Mission District Lending Circle Helps Low-Income Earners Pursue Dreams," *SFGate,* June 6, 2011, accessed March 15, 2015, www.sfgate.com/cgi-bin/blogs/kalw/detail?entry_id=90450. See Jen Haley, "The Mission Asset Fund: A Bridge between Informal and Formal Banking," Dowser, February 17, 2011, http://dowser.org/the-mission-asset-fund-a-bridge-between-informal-and-formal-banking/.
62. This particular venture capitalist interviewed by Bloomberg explains that those who have wanted to meet the demands of the unbanked fit into "two buckets: the missionary camp or the mercenary camp." He says that they are the "visionary camp." Bloomberg TV, "Unbanked: Making Financial Services Available to All," October 2, 2014, accessed March 15, 2015, www.bloomberg.com/video/unbanked-making-financial-services-available-to-all-cTgDHvp2TOO5pXJAudnZdg.html.
63. Consumer Financial Protection Bureau, "Is the Money on My Prepaid Debit Card FDIC-insured?," May 22, 2013, accessed March 15, 2015, www.consumerfinance.gov/askcfpb/529/money-my-prepaid-debit-card-fdic-insured.html.
64. Stephanie M. Wilshusen et al., "Consumer's Use of Prepaid Cards: A Transaction-Based Analysis," (discussion paper, Payment Cards Center, Federal Reserve Bank of Philadelphia), accessed March 15, 2015, www.philadelphiafed.org/consumer-credit-and-payments/payment-cards-center/publications/discussion-papers/2012/D-2012-August-Prepaid.pdf; Federal Reserve Board of Governors, "Consumers and Mobile Financial Services," March 8, 2014, accessed

March 15, 2015, www.federalreserve.gov/econresdata/consumers-and-mobile-financial-services-report-201403.pdf.

65. Anisha Sekar, "NerdWallet Study: Average Prepaid Debit Card Can Cost over $300 a Year," *NerdWallet,* January 25, 2012, accessed March 15, 2015, www.nerdwallet.com/blog/pre-approved-credit-cards/nerdwallet-study-average-prepaid-debit-card-cost-300-year/; Thomas Olson, "Prepaid Card Fees Can Ouch," *TribLIVE,* July 12, 2013, accessed March 15, 2015, triblive.com/business/headlines/4344488-74/cards-prepaid-card#axzz3K92NdOek.
66. "What You Need to Know about Prepaid Cards," *ConsumerReports,* July 2013, accessed March 15, 2015, www.consumerreports.org/cro/2013/07/prepaid-cards-fees/index.htm#26cards.
67. Cardhub claims that the amount of money loaded onto these cards tripled from 2008 to 2012 to $77 billion. Alina Comoreanu, "Prepaid Cards Report—2014," *CardHub,* accessed March 15, 2015, www.cardhub.com/edu/prepaid-cards-report/.
68. Deirdre Fernandes, "More Relying on Walmart for Financial Services," *Boston Globe,* July 10, 2014, accessed March 15, 2015, www.bostonglobe.com/business/2014/07/09/walmart-isn-bank-but-consumers-are-choosing-its-financial-services/0oJtrqVKl8OXTuQ3SBtrSI/story.html.
69. Katie Lobosco, "Walmart Offers Less Costly Money Wire Service," *CNN Money,* April 17, 2014, accessed March 15, 2015, money.cnn.com/2014/04/17/news/companies/walmart-money-transfers/.
70. Adams, "Wal-Mart's GoBank Deal."
71. Andy Peters, "Wal-Mart Move Further Tests Banks' Defenses against Disruption," *American Banker,* September 24, 2014, accessed March 15, 2015, www.americanbanker.com/issues/179_185/wal-mart-move-further-tests-banks-defenses-against-disruption-1070205-1.html.
72. See George White, "Wal-Mart Guilty of Predatory Price Cutting," *Los Angeles Times,* October 13, 1993, accessed March 15, 2015, articles.latimes.com/1993-10-13/business/fi-45290_1_predatory-pricing.
73. The banks Wal-Mart is partnering with: Fort Sill National Bank, City National Bank and Trust, Woodforest National Bank, First Convenience Bank, and Sunbank NA. Mark Maremont and Tom McGinty, "Why Banks at Wal-Mart are Among America's Top Fee Collectors," *Wall Street Journal,* May 11, 2014, accessed March 15, 2015, www.wsj.com/news/articles/SB10001424052702304734304579515730198367754?KEYWORDS=maremont&mg=reno64-wsj.

74. Keith Epstein and Geri Smith, "The Ugly Side of Microlending," *Bloomberg Businessweek,* December 12, 2007, accessed March 15, 2015, www.businessweek.com/stories/2007-12-12/the-ugly-side-of-microlending.
75. Steven Weisman, "Scam of The Day—September 8, 2014—Green Dot Phasing Out MoneyPak Debit Card," *Scamicide,* September 8, 2014, accessed March 15, 2015, scamicide.com/2014/09/08/scam-of-the-day-september-8-2014-green-dot-phasing-out-moneypak-debit-card/.
76. A recent study found that 72 percent of people ages eighteen to thirty-four would bank with companies like Wal-Mart, Google, or T-Mobile if they offered services. Undoubtedly, as the generations of people accustomed to using the Internet as their interface with the world begin to use banking services, they will also want to bank on the Internet. It is also probable that they will trust companies like Google, Amazon, and PayPal even more than the likes of Bank of America or Wells Fargo, whether this trust is warranted or not. Danielle Douglas-Gabriel, "How Wal-Mart and Google Could Steal Young Customers from Traditional Banks," *Washington Post,* May 27, 2014, accessed March 15, 2015, www.washingtonpost.com/blogs/wonkblog/wp/2014/05/27/how-wal-mart-and-google-could-steal-young-customers-from-traditional-banks/.
77. "Why Does Kenya Lead the World in Mobile Money?," *Economist,* May 27, 2013, accessed March 15, 2015, www.economist.com/blogs/economist-explains/2013/05/economist-explains-18.
78. "[Sixty-nine] percent of the unbanked . . . [and] 88 percent of the underbanked have access to a mobile phone . . . 39 percent of underbanked consumers have used mobile banking in the past 12 months." Federal Reserve Board of Governors, "Consumers and Mobile Financial Services 2014," March 2014: 2, accessed March 15, 2015, www.federalreserve.gov/econresdata/consumers-and-mobile-financial-services-report-201403.pdf.
79. Wizzit, "Vision," accessed October 5, 2014, www.wizzit.co.za/?q=node/65.
80. Carmen Nobel, "Mobile Banking for the Unbanked," *Working Knowledge,* June 13, 2011 (quoting case author V. Kasturi Rangan).
81. Kevin Wack, "Boost Mobile Makes a Play for the Unbanked," *American Banker,* June 23, 2014, accessed March 15, 2015, www.americanbanker.com/issues/179_120/boost-mobile-makes-a-play-for-the-unbanked-1068254-1.html.

82. "About Lending Club," *Lending Club,* accessed January 15, 2015, www.lendingclub.com/public/about-us.action.
83. "Both the number of loans and the average dollar amount of loans disbursed through Lending Club has grown tremendously since Lending Club's inception in 2007. Table 3 shows the volume of lending from mid-2007 through 2012. Total loans funded for small businesses grew from just under $700,000 in 2008 to over $22 million in 2012. Loans for other purposes grew from just over $8 million in 2008 to nearly $700 million in 2012. The average loan size has also grown for both groups, from $5,400 to $16,200 for small business loans, and from $3,600 to $13,400 for non-business loans. The interest rate is similar across small business loans and loans for other purposes." Traci L. Mach et al., "Peer-to-Peer Lending to Small Businesses," Federal Reserve Board of Governors, March 2013, 4, accessed March 15, 2015, www.frbatlanta.org/documents/news/conferences /13resilience_rebuilding_paper_Mach.pdf. Bonnie McGeer and Glen Fest, "P2P Lending: 2B or Not 2B?," *American Banker,* February 25, 2014, accessed March 15, 2015, www.americanbanker.com/magazine /124_02/p2p-lending-2b-or-not-2b-1065594-1.html?pg=4.
84. Kiva Zip, "What is Kiva Zip?" accessed September 30, 2014, zip.kiva .org/learn.
85. Jim Marous, "Traditional Banks at Risk Due to Digital Disruption," *The Financial Brand,* November 13, 2013, accessed March 15, 2015, thefinancialbrand.com/37334/insight-retail-banking-research-digital -mobile-channel-disruption-accenture/.

7. POSTAL BANKING

1. Francis Lieber, *Encyclopaedia Americana,* vol. 10 (Philadelphia: Carey and Lea, 1832), 289.
2. Richard R. John, *Spreading the News: The American Postal System from Franklin to Morse* (Cambridge, MA: Harvard University Press, 1995), 8.
3. Eli Bowen, *The United States Post-office Guide* (New York: D. Appleton, 1851), 5–6.
4. John, *Spreading the News,* 24, 53.
5. Alexis de Tocqueville, *Democracy in America,* 1831, (New York: Modern Library, 1981), 283; J. P. Mayer, ed. *Journey to America,* trans. George Lawrence (Garden City, NY: Doubleday, 1971), 283.
6. John, *Spreading the News*, 53.

7. Ibid., 53–54.
8. Ibid., 86.
9. Ibid., 143.
10. Ibid., 25.
11. Ibid., 52.
12. Ibid., 39.
13. Ibid., 34–36, 41.
14. Benjamin Rush, "Address to the People of the United States," January 1787, accessed September 30, 2014, teachingamericanhistory.org /library/document/address-to-the-people-of-the-united-states/.
15. James Madison, "Notes on Debates, December 6, 1782," in *Papers of James Madison,* vol. 5, ed. William T. Hutchinson et al. (Chicago: University of Chicago Press; 1962), 372.
16. John, *Spreading the News,* 37.
17. Ibid., 52.
18. Ibid., 63.
19. Ibid., 57.
20. Ibid., 47.
21. Thomas Sowell, *Basic Economics: A Common Sense Guide to the Economy* (New York: Basic Books, 2011), 102.
22. Sheldon Garon, *Beyond Our Means: Why America Spends While the World Saves* (Princeton, NJ: Princeton University Press, 2012), 58.
23. British postal banks publish deposit interest rates on their website. See "Interest Rates," *The Post Office, Your Finances,* accessed October 4, 2014, www.postoffice.co.uk/savings-accounts/interest-rates#current _rates.
24. Then to Singapore in 1877, India in 1882, the Cape of Good Hope in 1884, and Ceylon in 1885.
25. Garon, *Beyond Our Means,* 66.
26. Ibid., 74–75.
27. United States Post Office, *Annual Report of the Postmaster General on the Operations of the Department* (Washington, DC: Government Printing Office, 1871), 106.
28. The 1871 postmaster general report said, "The Post Office Department is now prepared to undertake the organization and management of the telegraph in connection with its other duties. Indeed, I believe that the Department itself can aid materially in raising the money needed for the purchase through post-office savings banks, if Congress will authorize their establishment." Ibid.

29. United States Post Office, *Annual Report of the Postmaster General on the Operations of the Department,* (Washington, DC: Government Printing Office, 1873), xxv–xxvi.
30. Transcript available at www.thisnation.com/library/sotu/1873ug.html, accessed March 12, 2015; James D. Richardson, *A Compilation of the Messages and Papers of the Presidents,* vol. 6 (Bureau of National Literature and Art; 1897), 4200–4204.
31. Garon, *Beyond Our Means,* 106.
32. Ibid., 61. In fact, they wanted to compete with savings banks. A *Times* writer hoped that "these 531 fallible Savings banks will all cease to exist."
33. Donald B. Schewe, "A History of the Postal Savings System in America, 1910–1970," (PhD diss., Ohio State University, 1971), 23.
34. Kirk H. Porter and Donald B. Johnson, *National Party Platform, 1840–1964* (Urbana: University of Illinois, 1966), 91.
35. Chester McArthur Destler, *American Radicalism, 1865–1901* (New London, CT: Connecticut College, 1946), 186; Norman Pollack, ed., *The Populist Mind,* (New York: Bobbs-Merrill, 1967) 64.
36. Pollack, *Populist Mind,* 9. Speech of Lorenzo D. Lewelling, made July 28, 1894.
37. *Annual Report of the Postmaster General, 1873,* xxvi.
38. *Lafayette* (IN) *Courier,* February 21, 1891.
39. Ibid.
40. *Annual Report of the Postmaster General, 1873,* xxiv.
41. United States Office of the Comptroller of the Currency, *Annual Report of the Comptroller of the Currency to the Third Session of the Sixty-first Congress of the United States, 1910* (Washington, DC: Government Printing Office, 1911), 72, 238–239. See Ibid., 51, for state banks.
42. In 1871, Creswell recommended that the profits would help start the telegraph system. *Annual Report of the Postmaster General, 1873,* xxvi.
43. *Annual Report of the Postmaster General, 1873,* xxviii (emphasis added).
44. The first bill in Congress came in 1873 from Representative Horace Maynard (R-TN). H.R. 797 was proposed "to establish and maintain a national savings depository as a branch of the Post-Office Department." Senate Committee on Post-Offices and Post-Roads, Postal Savings Depositories, S. Doc. No. 125-61. 2nd sess., 63.

45. Charles Hall Davis, "The Postal Savings Certificates," *Albany Law Journal,* 70 (1908–1909): 340. See also 45 Cong. Rec. 7676 (June 9, 1910) (testimony of Ebenezer J. Hill). "Our postmasters for nearly forty years have recommended the establishment of postal savings banks, and at this late date it seems very strange that nothing has heretofore been done in the interest of thrift and economy of the masses and wage-earners and those to whom banks were not accessible." Ibid.
46. Postal Savings Depositories, 63–66. See appendix A for a comprehensive listing of postal savings bank legislation introduced into Congress.
47. Garon, *Beyond Our Means,* 110.
48. Schewe, "Postal Savings System," 29–30.
49. Herbert Adams Gibbons, *John Wanamaker,* vol. 1 (New York: Harper and Brothers, 1926), 284–286.
50. United States Post Office, *Annual Report of the Postmaster General, 1892,* 44–47, 104–124.
51. Schewe, "Postal Savings System," 33.
52. *Philadelphia Record,* November 30, 1891.
53. *New York Sun,* February 7, 1891.
54. *Philadelphia Herald,* December 12, 1891.
55. *New York Sun,* December 2, 1891.
56. *Galveston Daily News,* January 18, 1891.
57. George V. L. Meyer, "The Need of Postal Savings-Banks," *The American Review of Reviews* 39, January to June 1909, 47.
58. *Manufacturer's Record,* February 14, 1891.
59. 31 Cong. Rec. (December 13, 1897), 110–114.
60. Ibid., 111.
61. Ibid.
62. Garon, *Beyond Our Means,* 111.
63. *Minneapolis Journal,* December 4, 1891.
64. *Omaha Herald,* November 26, 1891.
65. *Boston Globe,* November 26, 1891.
66. *Omaha Herald,* December 28, 1891; "Postal savings banks are objectionable because they bring the Government into competition with individual enterprise on unequal terms." *Philadelphia Herald,* November 25, 1891.
67. Senate Committee on Post Offices and Post Roads, *Postal Savings Banks, An Argument in Their Favor by the Post Master General* (Washington, DC: Government Printing Office, 1891), 7, 61.

68. Charles Burwell, "Should the Government Establish Postal Savings Banks?," *The Chautauquan,* October, 1897–March 1898, 410.
69. "The benefits to be derived from the system are largely more than the money that can be saved. . . . The inculcation of the habit of saving is the important thing. . . . It is the foundation of all fortunes." *Troy* (PA) *Register,* January 3, 1891.
70. *Aurora* (IL) *Democrat,* January 16, 1891.
71. Frank L. Stocking, "Postal Savings Banks," Tacoma, 53.
72. 33 Cong. Rec. 2251 (February 26, 1900).
73. *Annual Report of the Postmaster General, 1897,* 27–28.
74. 55th Cong. sess., 113 U.S. Senate. 60th Congress, 1st Session. *Senate Reports (Public)* (Washington, DC: Government Printing Office, 1908) (Serial Set 5219), 51.
75. Stocking, "Postal Savings Banks," 53–54; *The Rand McNally Bankers' Monthly,* vol. 35 (Chicago: Rand McNally, 1907), 395.
76. "At times paper money received for deposit is rusty, rough and badly stained, the denominations being almost indistinguishable. . . . [It is] wadded up in balls or made up in rolls; . . . its emitting musty odors, and of its being frequently in the form of old gold certificates. The receipt of gold coin is common, which is sometimes so old and moldy that the dates are undecipherable. Funds brought to post offices are often bulky and come in such receptacles as bags, cigar boxes, shoe boxes, socks, baskets, and jars." "Postal Savings Fund Total $191,865,798," *New York Times,* December 2, 1930.
77. 45 Cong. Rec. (July 6, 1910).
78. U.S. Senate. 60th Congress, 1st Session. *Senate Reports (Public)* (Washington, DC: Government Printing Office, 1908) (Serial Set 5219), 45; Or, Senate Report No. 1504, 55th Congress, 3rd Session.
79. Senate Committee, *Postal Savings Banks,* 11.
80. Theodore Roosevelt, "Seventh Annual Message, December 3, 1907," accessed March 12, 2015, www.presidency.ucsb.edu/ws/index.php?pid=29548&st=postal+savings&st1.
81. Theodore Roosevelt, "Special Message to Congress on Labor, March 25, 1908," accessed March 12, 2015, www.presidency.ucsb.edu/ws/?pid=69676.
82. American Bankers Association, "Proceedings of the Thirty-Third Annual Convention of the American Bankers Association," (1907), 287–304. E. W. Kemmerer, "The United States Postal Savings Bank," *Political Science Quarterly*, Vol. 26, No. 3 (Sep. 1911), 474.
83. Meyer, "Need of Postal Savings-Banks," 48.

84. 45 Cong. Rec. 8482 (June 18, 1910) (testimony of Mr. Crumpacker).
85. "It should be remembered that the deposits that bear interest will be limited to $500 for each individual and that not more than $100 can be deposited in any one month. The rate of interest will be 2 per cent. Per annum." Meyer, "Need of Postal Savings-Banks," 48.
86. 45 Cong. Rec. 8482 (June 18, 1910).
87. Garon, *Beyond Our Means,* 112.
88. Ibid.
89. Meyer, "Need of Postal Savings-Banks," 48.
90. Ibid.
91. "We favor a postal savings bank if the guaranteed bank cannot be secured and that it be constituted so as to keep the deposited money in the communities where it is established. But we condemn the policy of the Republican Party in providing postal savings banks under a plan of conduct by which they will aggregate the deposits of rural communities and redeposit the same while under Government charge in the banks of Wall Street, thus depleting the circulating medium of the producing regions and unjustly favoring the speculative markets." Porter and Johnson, *National Party Platforms,* 147.
92. Garon, *Beyond Our Means,* 112.
93. William Howard Taft, "First Annual Message, December 7, 1909," accessed September 30, 2014, www.presidency.ucsb.edu/ws/index.php?pid=29550&st=postal+savings&st1.
94. The "general welfare" clause is contained within the "tax and spending" clause, which states that: "The Congress shall have Power to lay and collect Taxes, Duties, Imposts and Excises, to pay the Debts and provide for the common Defence and general Welfare of the United States; but all Duties, Imposts and Excises shall be uniform throughout the United States."
95. Cong. Rec. 61st Cong., 2nd sess., XLV, part 3, 2652–2655, *Political Science Quarterly,* vol. 26, 487. They cite that quote as coming from Senator Sutherland, Congressional Record, March 2, 1910, 2652–2655.
96. Reed Smoot (R-UT) proposed an amendment to the bill that quieted some of this opposition. He allowed the government to borrow from the postal banks in times of war or need, which made the bill fit more neatly into the commerce clause. This was still not adequate for many Democrats.
97. As the postal banks succeeded and gained support, the limits on deposits were slowly raised. The American Bankers Association

(ABA) still opposed any increase in deposit limits, but most bankers had realized that the postal banks were helping and not threatening them. American Bankers Association, *Proceedings of the Thirty-Ninth Annual Convention of the American Bankers Association* (New York: American Bankers Association, 1913), 495; "Postal savings deposits were reinvested by local postmasters in local banks, and by 1913, 7,226 banks were qualified as postal savings depositories. These included, 3,786 national banks, 2,405 state banks, 377 savings banks, 609 trust companies, and 49 private banks." *Annual Report of the Postmaster General, 1913,* 27 (listing various ways the post office was a boon to banks and savings banks, including by keeping money that would have been sent abroad in circulation); In 1916, the limit on deposits was raised to $1,000. In 1918, the limit was raised to $2,500 with very little opposition because the government needed the deposits to aid in the war effort. Cong. Rec. 65th Cong., 2nd sess., 1918, LVI, part 4, 4102, 4104 (alternate citation: 56 Cong. Rec. 4102, 4104 [March 26, 1918]); Each of the bills that increased limits was proposed by initial opponents of the postal banks. Representative Moon, who had spoken against the banks in 1910, introduced amendments in 1914, 1916, and 1918 to raise the limits on deposits. Schewe, "Postal Savings System," 113.

98. Cong. Rec. 61st Cong., 2nd sess., XLV, part 7, 7766–7768. See appendix B for the roll call vote results; 45 Cong. Rec. 7766–7768 (June 9, 1910).
99. Cong. Rec. 61st Cong., 2nd sess., XLV, part 8, 7926–7928, 892, 8632–8634, 8740–8741, 9078.
100. "Postal Savings System Practically Self Sustaining," *New York Times,* May 25, 1913. Much of the growth and success of the postal banks was a direct result of the hard work and advocacy of the first director of the postal savings system, Carter B. Keene, ironically a Democratic appointee, who served from 1913 to 1921; *Annual Report of the Postmaster General, 1911,* 6; *Annual Report of the Postmaster General, 1912,* 6–7; *Annual Report of the Postmaster General, 1913,* 302–303, appendix D. The *Times* reports a figure of 28 million, but by the end of the year, the *Post Office Annual Report* stated that deposits totaled $33 million.
101. *New York Times,* "Practically Self Sustaining."
102. American Bankers Association, *Proceedings of the Thirty-Ninth Annual Convention,* 481.

103. United States Post Office, *Annual Report of the Postmaster General, 1921* (Washington, DC: Government Printing Office, 1921), 86. President Harding's postmaster General William Hays also made reforms to the postal savings banks, including printing leaflets in twenty-four languages and passing them out to immigrants as they disembarked at the ports of entry into the United States.
104. American Bankers Association, *Proceedings of the Forty-Second Annual Convention of the American Bankers Association* (New York: American Bankers Association, 1916), 403.
105. Ibid., 47.
106. Louise Sissman, "Development of the Postal Savings System," *Journal of the American Statistical Association,* 31, no. 196 (December 1936): 710.
107. Garon, *Beyond Our Means,* 114.
108. Ibid., 113.
109. Ibid.
110. One of the suggestions to increase the flow of money to the federal government came from Eugene Meyer, a New York banker and adviser to the Senate Committee on Reconstruction and Production, who suggested that the postal banks could accomplish this if they were allowed to offer more deposits and send the deposits to the Treasury instead of retaining them at local banks. Eugene Meyer Jr., "The Importance of Being Earnest in Saving," *Current Opinion* 70 (January 1921): 110. The proposal was immediately opposed by the American Bankers Association (ABA), but did get the support of Herbert Hoover, who suggested much more modest amendments to the system. Hoover said that the postal banks could be made to be more attractive to depositors without raising interest rates and competing with banks, for example, by paying out interest quarterly instead of annually. "What the Postal Savings-bank Might be, But is Not," *Literary Digest,* January 29, 1921, 74–76.
111. *Annual Report of the Postmaster General, 1921,* 84–85.
112. United States Post Office, *Annual Report of the Postmaster General, 1930* (Washington, DC: Government Printing Office, 1930), 47. See *New York Times,* "Postal Savings Funds Total $191,865,798."
113. In 1930, there were a total of 466,401 depositors, and by 1933, there were 2,342,133. See *Annual Report of the Postmaster General, 1930,* 93; United States Post Office, *Annual Report of the Postmaster General, 1931* (Washington, DC: Government Printing Office,

1931), 92; United States Post Office, *Annual Report of the Postmaster General, 1932* (Washington, DC: Government Printing Office, 1932), 92; United States Post Office, *Annual Report of the Postmaster General, 1933* (Washington, DC: Government Printing Office, 1933), 78.

114. Sissman, "Development of the Postal," 712; "Going from east to west, Postal Savings became of more importance in the community the further west one traveled." Ibid. The same trend held for large cities. In 1923, large cities had 67 percent of the deposits; this declined to 31 percent by 1932. In 1915, foreign-born depositors held 72 percent of all deposits, and out of 14 million immigrants, 9 million of those lived in large cities. Ibid., 713–714. From 1921 to 1929, there was "an average of 20 closed banks for every 100 banks active in 1920." Ibid., 715. Even though total deposits didn't rise during this time, most of the bank failures happened in those midregions, where the deposits did rise the most. When more banks started to fail nationwide, postal savings increased correspondingly.
115. Ibid., 718.
116. Ibid., 710.
117. David Hu, "The Influence of the U.S. Postal Savings System on Bank Runs," *Yale Journal of Economics* 2, iss. 1 (2013), accessed March 12, 2015, econjournal.sites.yale.edu/articles/2/influence-us-postal-savings-system-bank-runs.
118. Sissman, "Development of the Postal," 710.
119. United States Post Office, *Annual Report of the Postmaster General, 1935* (Washington, DC: Government Printing Office, 1935), 28.
120. United States Post Office, *Annual Report of the Postmaster General, 1941* (Washington, DC: Government Printing Office, 1941), 35.
121. United States Post Office, *Annual Report of the Postmaster General, 1942* (Washington, DC: Government Printing Office, 1942); United States Post Office, *Annual Report of the Postmaster General, 1943* (Washington, DC: Government Printing Office, 1943); United States Post Office, *Annual Report of the Postmaster General, 1944* (Washington, DC: Government Printing Office, 1944); United States Post Office, *Annual Report of the Postmaster General, 1945* (Washington, DC: Government Printing Office, 1945); Schewe, "Postal Savings System," 163–164.
122. *Annual Report of the Postmaster General, 1935*, 98.
123. *Annual Report of the Postmaster General, 1942*, 18; *Annual Report of the Postmaster General, 1945*, 13–14. Even after the war, the postal

system continued to grow with a 17 percent increase in 1946 to more than $3 billion in deposits.

124. Cong. Rec. 89th Cong., 2nd sess., 1966, CXII, part 5, 5595; 112 Cong. Rec. 5595 (March 14, 1966).
125. House Committee on Post Office and Civil Service, *Hearings on Unclaimed Postal Savings Deposits,* 92nd Cong., 1st sess. (1971), 1–2.
126. "Nation: Stamps Out," *Time,* July 13, 1970, 13.
127. Schewe, "Postal Savings System," 185.
128. United States Postal Service, "Retiree Health Benefits Prefunding," *United States Postal Service Annual Report 2010,* accessed March 12, 2015, about.usps.com/who-we-are/financials/annual-reports/fy2010/ar2010_4_002.htm; See Lori Ann LaRocco, "Fixing the US Postal Service's Finances," CNBC, October 28, 2011, accessed March 12, 2015, www.cnbc.com/id/45049636#.
129. These nine governors are authorized to appoint, remove, and set the term of a postmaster general. The postmaster general is also a governor, as is the deputy postmaster general. In turn, these ten governors have the power to appoint and remove for cause the inspector general of the post office, who typically serves a seven-year term. 39 USC § 202 (a)–(b).
130. This is subject to certain exceptions (e.g., mailing voter materials to people with disabilities and people overseas). See Brianna Lee, "The U.S. Postal Service," *Need to Know,* PBS, September 13, 2011, accessed March 12, 2015, www.pbs.org/wnet/need-to-know/five-things/the-u-s-postal-service/11433/.
131. 39 USC § 2003 sets up the Postal Service Fund with the Treasury, which is a revolving fund available to the USPS, without a fiscal-year limitation, to carry out its functions and purposes authorized by Title 39 (39 USC § § 101–5605), except for purposes, functions, or powers, for which the Competitive Products Fund (CPF) is available. The Competitive Products Fund is a revolving fund of the Treasury, which is available to the USPS without fiscal year limitations, for the payment of: (1) costs attributable to competitive product; and (2) all other costs incurred by USPS, to the extent that they're allocable to competitive products. The USPS must deposit into the CPF, subject to withdrawal by it: (1) revenue from competitive products; (2) receipts from obligations issued under § 2011(e), which permits the USPS to borrow money and issue and sell such obligations as it deems necessary to provide for competitive products and deposit such amounts in the

CPF; (3) interest and dividends earned on investments of CPF; and (4) other USPS receipts (including the sale of assets) to the extent allocable to competitive products. If the USPS determines that the fund has more money than current needs, it can request to invest the money by the secretary of the Treasury in obligations of/obligations secured by the U.S. government, and other appropriate obligations or securities if the secretary approves. With the secretary's approval, the USPS may deposit fund money in any Federal Reserve bank, depository for public funds, or in other mutually agreeable places. 39 USC § 2005 authorizes the USPS to borrow money and issue and sell such obligations as it determines necessary to carry out any of the purposes of the title, except for Competitive Products/CPF. 39 USC § 2401—Appropriations: this section appropriates to USPS all of its revenues. 39 USC § 2002 (a) defines USPS's "capital." money.cnn.com/2012/10/17/news/usps-debt-limit/, accessed March 12, 2015.

8. A PUBLIC OPTION IN BANKING

1. USPS, Office of Inspector General, "Providing Non-Bank Financial Services for the Underserved," White Paper Report No. RARC-WP-14-007, January 27, 2014, accessed April 1, 2015, www.uspsoig.gov/sites/default/files/document-library-files/2014/rarc-wp-14-007.pdf, i.
2. Ibid., 16.
3. Alexandre Berthaud and Gisela Davico, "Global Panorama on Postal Financial Inclusion," *Universal Postal Union,* March 2013, accessed April 1, 2015, www.uniglobalunion.org/sites/default/files/pictures/post/globalpanoramafinancial_inclusion_-upu_-en.pdf.
4. Sheldon Garon, *Beyond Our Means: Why America Spends While the World Saves* (Princeton, NJ: Princeton University Press, 2012).
5. Kelli B. Grant, "Under a Mattress, in the Freezer: Why So Many are Hiding Cash," *CNBC,* January 29, 2015, accessed April 7, 2015, www.cnbc.com/id/102377632.
6. The post office *White Paper* suggests that they can offer loans with a 28 percent APR, a rate sustainable for the post office and its customers. USPS, "Providing Non-Bank Financial Services," 13.
7. Mark Pittman and Bob Ivry, "U.S. Pledges Top $7.7 Trillion to Ease Frozen Credit (Update2)," *Bloomberg,* November 24, 2008, accessed April 7, 2015, www.bloomberg.com/apps/news?sid=an3k2rZMNgDw&pid=newsarchive.

8. This process has been used to administer and adjudicate government actions in the realms of veterans affairs, social security, immigration, patents, and all other areas in which citizens are involved with the government. A large body of case law, constitutional law, and administrative law sets the standards and rules that agency officials must follow in their interactions with citizens. For example, the U.S. Supreme Court decided in *Mathews v. Eldridge* 424 U.S. 319 (1976) that citizens have a right to due process when their welfare benefits are taken away. The Administrative Procedure Act (APA) also gives citizens a right to a trial in front of an administrative law judge for most agency decisions affecting their rights. If a citizen wished recourse against the federal government for garnishment of tax returns, such a process would likely be granted.
9. These privacy protections are contained in Title V of the Gramm-Leach-Bliley Act.
10. Sarah Todd, "An Alternative Lender Whose Credit Reviews are Academic," July 8, 2014, *American Banker*, accessed April 7, 2016, www.americanbanker.com/issues/179_130/an-alternative-lender-whose-credit-reviews-are-academic-1068506-1.html; Brian Browdie, "Can Alternative Data Determine a Borrower's Ability to Repay?," February 24, 2015, *American Banker,* accessed April 7, 2015, www.americanbanker.com/news/consumer-finance/can-alternative-data-determine-a-borrowers-ability-to-repay-1072785-1.html.
11. David Bornstein, "'Invisible' Credit? (Read This Now!)," *New York Times*, October 2, 2014, accessed April 7, 2015, http://opinionator.blogs.nytimes.com/2014/10/02/invisible-credit-read-this-now/?_r=1.
12. FDIC, "An Update on Emerging Issues in Banking" (Jan 2003), accessed April 7, 2015, www.fdic.gov/bank/analytical/fyi/2003/012903fyi.html.
13. FDIC, "National Survey of Unbanked and Underbanked Households," Executive Summary (September 2012), 4. Available at www.fdic.gov/householdsurvey/2012_unbankedreport_execsumm.pdf.
14. The United States Postal Service is an independent establishment of the executive branch of the government of the United States and operates in a business-like manner. Its mission statement can be found in Section 101(a) of Title 39 of the U.S. Code, also known as the Postal Reorganization Act. 39 U.S. Code § 101(a).
15. Rachel Witkowski and Kevin Wack, "Post Office Offering Loans is 'Worst Idea Since the Edsel': Banks," *American Banker,* January 27, 2014, accessed April 7, 2015, www.americanbanker.com/issues/179

_18/post-office-offering-loans-is-worst-idea-since-the-edsel-banks-1065231-1.html.

16. David Morrison, "Experts Debate USPS Financial Services," *Credit Union Times,* July 16, 2014, accessed April 1, 2015, www.cutimes.com/2014/07/16/experts-debate-usps-financial-services.
17. Pew Charitable Trusts, "Keynote: Representative Darrell Issa," video file, July 16, 2014, accessed April 1, 2015, www.pewtrusts.org/en/multimedia/video/2014/congressman-darrell-issa-ca-discusses-proposal-for-financial-services-at-the-post-office.
18. Federal Housing Finance Agency, Office of Inspector General, "A Brief History of the Housing Government-Sponsored Enterprises," 3, accessed April 1, 2015, fhfaoig.gov/Content/Files/History%20of%20the%20Government%20Sponsored%20Enterprises.pdf.
19. Simon Johnson and James Kwak, *13 Bankers: The Wall Street Takeover and the Next Financial Meltdown* (New York: Pantheon, 2010), 209.

Acknowledgments

Thank you, Jared Bybee, for reminding me to start with an outline; Cyra, for being proud of me; Lucia, for offering to do the cover illustrations; and Ramona, for writing your own "book." Thank you, Baba and Madar, for your love and support, even though it's "a boring book." And thank you, Shima, Hediyeh, and Darius, for acting interested in my research. Thank you, Rebecca Smylie, for reading this entire book and for your brilliant editing.

Special thanks to Senator Elizabeth Warren and her staff, especially Bharat Ramamurti. Thank you to David C. Williams, Christopher Backley and Bryan Switzky at the post office inspector general; Lisa Donner at Americans for Financial Reform; and Susan Weinstock at the PEW Charitable Trust.

Thank you, Joyce Seltzer, for believing in this project, and thank you to Harvard University Press. Thank you, Brian Distelberg, for shepherding me through this process. Thank you to Dean Bo Rutledge and Dean Rebecca White at the University of Georgia. Also, many of my colleagues spent time reading early versions of this book and making invaluable comments. I want to especially thank Patricia McCoy, Christopher Peterson, Sheldon Garon, Sally Barringer Gordon, Peter Conti-Brown, Oren Bar-Gill, Simon Johnson, Jessica Lustig, Dahlia Lithwick, David Dayen, Frank Partnoy, Orly Lobel, Daria Roithmayr, Kent Barnett, Logan Sawyer, Dan Coenen, Usha Rodrigues, and Andrea Dennis for their encouragement, time, comments, and insights.

T. J. Striepe expertly selected and sorted all of the books and articles that went into making this one. My enthusiastic and hardworking research assistants never ceased to amaze me with their thorough research, organizational skills, and tireless efforts to find the right answers. Thank you, Ricardo Lopez, Hannah Jarrells, Amble Johnson, Kelsie Willett, Michelle Tang, Maria Rivera-Diaz, Alex Russo, and Ryan Sullivan.

Index